LINUx
ANNOYANCES
for Geeks

Other Linux resources from O'Reilly

Related titles   Knoppix Hacks™   Linux Network
Linux Cookbook™   Administrator's Guide
Linux Desktop Hacks™   Linux Server Hacks™
Linux in a Nutshell   Running Linux
Linux Multimedia
Hacks™

Linux Books   *linux.oreilly.com* is a complete catalog of O'Reilly's
Resource Center   books on Linux and Unix and related technologies, including sample chapters and code examples.

ONLamp.com is the premier site for the open source
web platform: Linux, Apache, MySQL and either Perl,
Python, or PHP.

Conferences   O'Reilly brings diverse innovators together to nurture
the ideas that spark revolutionary industries. We specialize in documenting the latest tools and systems,
translating the innovator's knowledge into useful skills
for those in the trenches. Visit *conferences.oreilly.com*
for our upcoming events.

Safari Bookshelf (*safari.oreilly.com*) is the premier
online reference library for programmers and IT professionals. Conduct searches across more than 1,000
books. Subscribers can zero in on answers to time-critical questions in a matter of seconds. Read the
books on your Bookshelf from cover to cover or simply flip to the page you need. Try it today for free.

LINUX
ANNOYANCES
for Geeks

Michael Jang

O'REILLY®

Beijing · Cambridge · Farnham · Köln · Paris · Sebastopol · Taipei · Tokyo

Linux Annoyances for Geeks
by Michael Jang

Published by O'Reilly Media, Inc., 1005 Gravenstein Highway North, Sebastopol, CA 95472.

O'Reilly books may be purchased for educational, business, or sales promotional use. Online editions are also available for most titles (*safari.oreilly.com*). For more information, contact our corporate/institutional sales department: (800) 998-9938 or *corporate@oreilly.com*.

Editor: Andy Oram
Production Editor: Sanders Kleinfeld
Copyeditor: Chris Downey
Proofreader: Sanders Kleinfeld

Indexer: John Bickelhaupt
Cover Designer: Karen Montgomery
Interior Designer: David Futato
Illustrators: Robert Romano, Jessamyn Read, and Lesley Borash

Printing History:

April 2006:   First Edition.

RepKover This book uses RepKover™, a durable and flexible lay-flat binding.

0-596-00801-5
[C]

I thank the amazing woman who is now my wife, Donna, and I thank my fellow younger widowed from the Hampton Roads area for helping me through this journey. That group includes Cindy, Wendy, Linda, Rick, Mary, Ed, Cliff, Gail, Betty (x2), Karen, Marsha, Deb, Debe, Phil, Nikki, Joyce, Adrienne, Irene, Lee, Marie, Lisa, Jane, Stevie, Mike, and Joanne (and a couple of dozen more people). Finally, thank you and rest in peace, Michael Anderson.

Nancy, thank you for loving me so well. Randy, thank you for loving Donna so wonderfully. And thank you both for bringing us together from the hereafter.

And Bub, thank you for being this man's best friend.

Table of Contents

Preface

To most of the world, all Linux users are geeks. But there are users who don't even realize that they're using Linux at work, and users who have recently installed Linux for the first time. On the other hand, there are users to whom everyone turns when they have a problem. We target this book to that group of experts to help them solve the annoyances they face on the job: finding the right hardware, configuring servers, supporting less experienced users, and more.

Linux Annoyances for Geeks provides a guide to many of the more common complaints faced by the experienced Linux user. Sometimes the annoyance comes directly from Linux, and sometimes from the adaptations required to support a regular user. The solutions are designed for three of the more prominent Linux distributions: Fedora Core, SUSE, and Debian. As Fedora Core serves as the test bed for Red Hat Enterprise Linux, many of the annoyances (and solutions) have also been tested for that distribution.

There are many other excellent Linux distributions. I wish I could have covered more. In writing this book, perhaps the biggest annoyance was the subtle differences in how things work (and how annoyances are solved) among distributions. As each distribution evolves, annoyances change. And too many details pertaining to different distributions would not be fair to those among us who are focused on a single distribution.

This book is an outgrowth of a long conversation with Andy Oram at the O'Reilly Open Source Convention. He was looking for a Linux equivalent to *Windows XP Annoyances for Geeks*, and I had the experience with the distributions on which he wanted a focus. He has been instrumental in shepherding this book from start to finish.

My own background includes administering, tinkering with, testing, and writing about a wide variety of Linux distributions. While studying for my

MCSE, I started working with SUSE Linux, and I've been sold on open source ever since. While my RHCE certification has focused me on Red Hat distributions, I actually use Debian, and now Ubuntu Linux, as my primary home distributions.

Conventions Used in This Book

The following typographical conventions are used in this book:

Italic
> Indicates new terms, URLs, email addresses, filenames, file extensions, and Linux utilities.

`Constant width`
> Indicates the contents of files and the output from commands.

`Constant width bold`
> Shows commands or other text that should be typed literally by the user. Also used to highlight portions of code

`Constant width italic`
> Shows text that should be replaced with user-supplied values.

 This icon signifies a tip, suggestion, or general note.

 This icon indicates a warning or caution.

Organization of This Book

Linux Annoyances for Geeks is divided into three sections. Chapters 1 through 4 are focused on the desktop, with tips for the geek who needs to help regular users adapt to Linux. Chapters 5 through 8 examine issues associated with hardware and system configuration. The final three chapters, 9 through 11, examine administrative annoyances related to servers, users, and more:

Chapter 1, *Configuring a Desktop Environment*
> Provides solutions for some of these everyday annoyances.

Chapter 2, *Configuring User Workstations*
> Gives some basic tips for less experienced users.

Chapter 3, *Optimizing Internet Applications*
Helps the geek make Internet access as convenient and simple as possible for regular users.

Chapter 4, *Setting Up Local Applications*
Provides solutions for the geek who needs to set up regular users with access to popular tools, such as PDF files, MP3 players, and Windows-based applications.

Chapter 5, *Installation Annoyances*
Helps the geek make choices in hardware, distributions, and systems that are appropriate for his or her users.

Chapter 6, *Basic Start Configuration*
Helps the geek optimize Linux, solve some annoying boot issues, and address some basic security concerns.

Chapter 7, *Kernel Itches and Other Configuration Annoyances*
Focuses primarily on those kernel-related tasks that make most Linux users look to the geek for help.

Chapter 8, *System Maintenance*
Focuses on a variety of annoyances related to keeping your systems running smoothly and up-to-date.

Chapter 9, *Servicing Servers*
Helps you select and configure servers to solve a variety of problems, with a higher degree of security.

Chapter 10, *User Management*
Focuses on annoyances created by and associated with the presence of different kinds of users in an organization.

Chapter 11, *Administration Tips*
Provides solutions for a wide variety of other annoyances related to system administration.

Using Code Examples

This book is here to help you get your job done. In general, you may use the examples in this book in your own scripts and documentation. You do not need to contact us for permission unless you're reproducing a significant portion of the examples. For example, writing a program that uses several chunks of code from this book does not require permission. Selling or distributing a CD-ROM of examples from O'Reilly books *does* require permission. Answering a question by citing this book and quoting examples does not require permission. Incorporating a significant amount of examples from this book into your product's documentation *does* require permission.

We appreciate, but do not require, attribution. An attribution usually includes the title, author, publisher, and ISBN; for example: *"Linux Annoyances for Geeks* by Michael Jang. Copyright 2006 O'Reilly Media, Inc., 0-596-00801-5."

If you feel your use of examples falls outside fair use or the permission given above, feel free to contact us at *permissions@oreilly.com*.

Safari® Enabled

 When you see a Safari® Enabled icon on the cover of your favorite technology book, that means the book is available online through the O'Reilly Network Safari Bookshelf.

Safari offers a solution that's better than e-books. It's a virtual library that lets you easily search thousands of top tech books, cut and paste code samples, download chapters, and find quick answers when you need the most accurate, current information. Try it for free at *http://safari.oreilly.com*.

How to Contact Us

Please address comments and questions concerning this book to the publisher:

> O'Reilly Media, Inc.
> 1005 Gravenstein Highway North
> Sebastopol, CA 95472
> 800-998-9938 (in the United States or Canada)
> 707-829-0515 (international or local)
> 707-829-0104 (fax)

We have a web page for this book, where we list errata, examples, and any additional information. You can access this page at:

> *http://www.oreilly.com/catalog/linuxannoygks*

To comment or ask technical questions about this book, send email to:

> *bookquestions@oreilly.com*

For more information about our books, conferences, Resource Centers, and the O'Reilly Network, see our web site at:

> *http://www.oreilly.com*

Acknowledgments

Every technical book is a team effort. Andy Oram spent many long hours with me, making sure that every little bit of information is as relevant as possible for the Linux geek. Great thanks to Elizabeth Zinkann, technical editor for this book, for making sure I stayed on track during the long hours it took to complete this book. Many thanks to the technical reviewers who brought their experience and insights to make this book useful for as many Linux geeks as possible: Michael Boerner, Keith Burgess, Phil Hughes, Chris Lawrence, Rick Rezinas, and Kevin Shockey.

## CHAPTER 1

Configuring a Desktop Environment

I start the list of annoyances at the desktop, as that's where most new users learn to work with Linux. While most geeks believe in the command-line interface, new users demand an intuitive GUI configured with the applications they need. To add to configuration demands, many organizations demand a standard desktop environment, with a common set of applications, icons, login managers, and so on. Cleaning up every last detail can be annoying for the geek.

In this chapter, I illustrate some of the annoyances related to configuring the desktop environment.

I Want the Advantages of Both KDE and GNOME

The major question for a Linux user or site administrator, after the selection of a distribution, is which graphical desktop environment to use. While this annoyance focuses on the two major desktops (GNOME and KDE), there are over a dozen other options you can install on the major Linux distributions.

Whatever your choice, you can still take advantage of applications associated with either desktop and other applications that use the X Window System or display their output on a terminal. In this annoyance I show you several ways to integrate KDE applications into a GNOME environment and vice versa.

Each distribution has its preferred desktop. Ubuntu originally went to an extreme, shipping with just GNOME; later the developers created the Kubuntu project to include KDE support. If you choose something other than the preferred desktop in any distribution, expect to do more administration and fix some glitches. Another criterion that can affect your choice is the background of the new user coming to Linux from another operating system. As shown in this annoyance, KDE more closely resembles Microsoft Windows, and GNOME more closely resembles the Apple Macintosh.

While most Linux administrators prefer to configure using the command-line interface, I use GUI tools where possible in this annoyance. This is because when you're configuring a GUI, it's important to be in the GUI to confirm that your changes match your intent.

Basics of GNOME

GNOME is short for the GNU Network Object Model Environment. The current version of the GNOME Desktop (2.12) has a look and feel similar to the Apple Macintosh GUI. The default settings include menus, dates, and system information applets on a top taskbar and a list of currently open applications in a bottom taskbar, as shown in Figure 1-1.

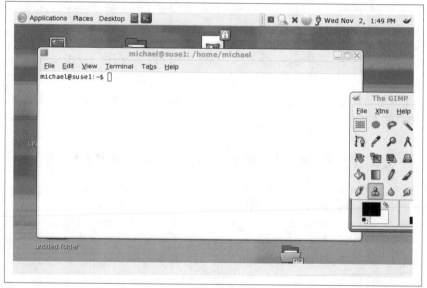

Figure 1-1. A typical GNOME desktop

GNOME is the default desktop environment associated with the most popular Linux distribution, Red Hat/Fedora Linux. It provides GUI-based configuration tools through a variety of icons under the Control Center submenu.

Basics of KDE

KDE is short for the K Desktop Environment. The current version of the KDE desktop (3.5) has a look and feel similar to the Microsoft Windows GUI. The default settings include menus, dates, and system information applets on a bottom taskbar (see Figure 1-2). The K Menu button in the lower-left corner works in a fashion similar to the Microsoft Windows Start button.

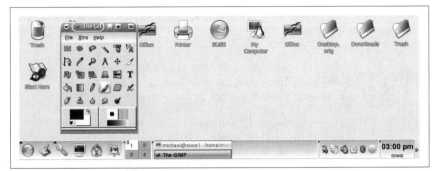

Figure 1-2. A typical KDE desktop

KDE is the default desktop environment associated with most Linux distributions, including SUSE Linux. KDE centralizes GUI-based configuration tools within its Control Center.

Configuring KDE Applications on a GNOME Menu

Some distributions preconfigure applications in the appropriate GNOME menu. For example, when I install the Synaptic Package Manager on a GNOME Debian Linux desktop, it automatically includes a link from the System → System Settings submenu. But while it is less friendly to KDE applications, you can still include them in the GNOME menu. I'll show you how you can configure them on a single computer using the GUI, and then how to tweak a configuration file, a solution you can automate through a script and therefore share with a large number of users on your network.

As this section shows, it's easy to change menus by editing the configuration files for each user. But this flexibility contains its own annoyance for site administrators, because it means all users can edit their own GUI menus. That may be a problem for managers who want a standard GUI desktop. If you want to freeze your users' menu configurations, see the "My Users Mess Up Their Desktops" annoyance later in this chapter.

Customizing the GNOME menu

If possible, I recommend that you use the Simple Menu Editor for GNOME (SMEG). It is easy to use. But as of this writing, none of the distributions that we examine in this book use SMEG. (However, it is available as part of the *alacarte* RPM in the Fedora Extras repository.)

Alternatively, you can start the Nautilus File Browser and then open a window that specifies the applications in the main menu. For the purposes of this example, I'll add the KOffice Write application under the Office submenu. To do so, take the following steps, which apply to older versions of GNOME (=< 2.8) associated with active distributions such as Red Hat Enterprise Linux 3 and 4:

 To find the applications listed in your GUI menus, run the *gnome-menu-spec-test* command, available from the *gnome-menus-devel* RPM in Fedora or the *gnome-menus* RPM in SUSE. You'll have to edit the *.desktop* files shown by the tool. Whenever you delete a file from this directory, the associated application is immediately removed from the GUI menus. Alternatively, you can use these files as a template for adding menu items; as they are text files, they are readily editable for new menu items. Once you've made your changes, you can share them with other systems on your network, and they'll apply to all users.

1. In a command line in a GUI desktop, run the *nautilus* command. This opens the Nautilus browser.
2. Press Ctrl-L. In the Location text box, navigate to *applications:///*. This opens the Applications window. Compare the entries to what you see in your Applications menu. They should be nearly identical. My version is shown in Figure 1-3.

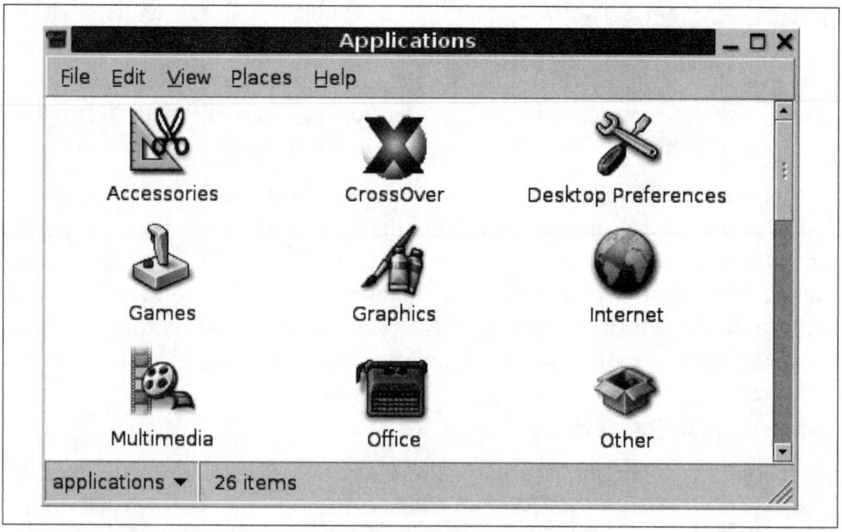

![Applications window screenshot showing icons for Accessories, CrossOver, Desktop Preferences, Games, Graphics, Internet, Multimedia, Office, and Other. Menu bar: File Edit View Places Help. Status bar: applications ▾ 26 items]

Figure 1-3. Editing the GNOME Applications menu

3. Use the Office icon to open a window that shows the current items in the Office submenu. Right-click in the menu and select Create Launcher from the pop-up menu.

4. In the Create Launcher window, enter the information associated with the application. In this example, to add the KOffice Word application, in the Name text box, enter KOffice Word, which is what gets shown in the Applications submenu.

5. In the Comment text box, enter a name that will be shown when the user hovers the pointer over the menu item.

6. In the Command text box, enter the complete path, /usr/bin/kword.

    If you can't find the complete path to your desired application, the *locate* command can help. For more information, see the "I Don't Remember Where That File Is" annoyance in Chapter 2. If you know the name of the file, the *dpkg -S packagename* or *rpm -ql packagename* commands list all files installed from the package.

7. Click Icon to see options for icons you can link to this entry. Alternatively, click Browse to find the icon you prefer.

8. When you click OK to exit from the Create Launcher window, the item is added to the menu and is ready for use.

Sharing the custom GNOME menu

Now you can share your changes with other systems configured to use GNOME. All you need to do is share the files in the *~/.gnome2/vfolders/* and *~/.gnome/apps/* subdirectories, to make them a part of the home directory of each user. The activities in this section do not actually install KOffice Write, of course; you must do that separately.

To make sure these changes are part of the home directories of new users, add these files and subdirectories to the */etc/skel* directory. They're then automatically added to the home directory of every new user you create.

To make sure they're part of the home directories of existing users, you need to adapt your solution to the particular distribution you're using. You could copy the subdirectories directly to each user's home directory, but you also have to assign ownership and read permissions to each user. Default permissions vary slightly by distribution.

Alternatively, you could edit the base configuration files directly; they're located in the */etc/gnome-vfs-2.0/vfolders* directory and are in XML format. If you choose to edit these files, back them up first! Once you've edited them and tested them to make sure they aren't corrupt, you can copy them to the other systems on your network.

Configuring GNOME Applications on a KDE Menu

While Linux distributions preconfigure many GNOME applications under the appropriate KDE menus, you'll need to do more to complete the job. Not all applications are picked up by the KDE desktop. KDE may even miss some that are not GNOME-specific applications.

 One option that goes beyond GNOME to other X Window System applications (also known as "legacy applications") is the KAppfinder tool, which scans your executable directories for applications you can add to your KDE menu. Start this tool with the *kappfinder* command.

Customizing the KDE menu

For this example, I decided to include the XWhois application under the KDE Internet submenu. To do so, take the following steps:

1. As a regular user, run the *kmenuedit* command. This opens the KDE Menu Editor shown in Figure 1-4.

   If you encounter an error message, such as failed to create /home/michael/.config/menus/, you may already have a *.config* file in your home directory. You'll have to move it. If you see an error message such as kmenuedit: WARNING: Could not read /home/michael/.config/menus/applications-kmenuedit.menu, which tends to appear the first time someone uses the KDE Menu Editor on a given desktop, ignore the message.

2. Note how the lefthand pane matches what you see when you click the K Menu button in the lower-left corner of your desktop.

3. Highlight the submenu of your choice—in this case, the Internet menu.

4. Click File → New Item. This opens the New Item window, where you can enter the name you want to see in the K Menu. Here, I use XWhois. Click OK.

5. Back in the Menu Editor, you'll see the Internet submenu open, with the new entry. You can now add a Description and Comment of your choice in the respective text boxes.

6. In the Command text box, enter the path to the application. In this case, on Debian Linux, it's */usr/bin/xwhois*.

7. If you want an icon for this application, click on the icon to the right of the Name and Description text boxes. This opens a list of icons in

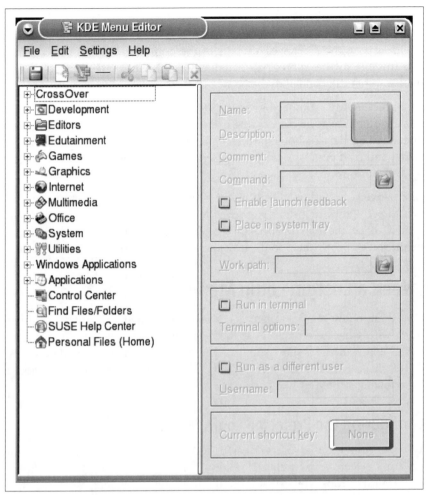

Figure 1-4. The KDE Menu Editor

the */usr/share/icons* subdirectory. (The actual icon files may be deep in this sudirectory.) I've used an icon that came with the *xwhois* package.

8. When you're done, click File → Save and then File → Quit. KDE saves the changes to the *applications-kmenuedit.menu* file associated with the error message described in step 1.

Sharing the custom KDE menu

Now you can share your changes with other systems configured to use KDE. All you need to do is share the *applications-kmenuedit.menu* file in the

~/.config/menus/ subdirectory, to make it a part of the home directory of each user you've configured with KDE.

To make sure these changes are part of the home directories of new users, add this file to the appropriate subdirectory of the */etc/skel* directory. It's then automatically added to the home directory of every new user you create.

As with GNOME, you need to adapt to each distribution in adding changes to the home directories of existing users. You could copy the subdirectories directly to each user's home directory, but then you also have to assign ownership and read permissions to each user, and these permissions vary slightly by distribution.

Alternatively, as with GNOME, you can edit the generic KDE configuration files directly; they're located in the */etc/xdg/menus* directory and are in XML format. Back the files up first in case you make a mistake. After editing them, you can copy them to the other systems on your network.

I Need a Custom Login Menu

One thing many managers like is consistency. In many organizations, that starts with what everyone sees at the beginning of the day, the login menu. In this annoyance, I'll show you how you can customize and standardize the GNOME and KDE login menus. But first, you need to select a standard login manager for your workstations.

Configuring the Preferred Login Menu

Whether you want to use GNOME, KDE, or another GUI desktop, you need to select your preferred login manager. Even if you're running GNOME desktops, you can still use the KDE login manager, and visa versa. Each of the book's preferred distributions allows you to select the preferred login manager in a configuration file specific to that distribution, as described in Table 1-1.

Table 1-1. General tab of the GDM Login Screen

Distribution	File	Description
Debian	*/etc/X11/default-display-manager*	Use the full path to the login manager of your choice, such as */usr/bin/kdm* or */usr/bin/gdm*.
Red Hat/Fedora	*/etc/X11/prefdm*	Set the preferred variable to the display manager of your choice, such as *gdm* or *kdm*. (While you could use */etc/sysconfig/desktop*, that also sets the default desktop environment.)

Table 1-1. General tab of the GDM Login Screen (continued)

Distribution	File	Description
SUSE	*/etc/sysconfig/displaymanager*	Set the DISPLAYMANAGER variable to the display manager of your choice in quotes, such as "gdm" or "kdm".

There are other login managers available. Some people prefer the X Login Manager, also known as *xdm*. Its simple interface does not include menu options for other desktops, languages, or shutdown/reboot commands. If you've installed the X Login Manager, you can substitute *xdm* for *gdm* or *kdm* in Table 1-1.

As you review what each login manager can do in this annoyance, you may change your mind on what's best. You can always return to this section and configure a different preferred login manager for your systems. If you're configuring a standard across many users' computers, you'll have to copy the appropriate file to the other systems that you administer.

Customizing the GNOME Login Menu

Before you start editing the GNOME Login Menu, back up the defaults in the GNOME configuration directory. The location of this directory varies by distribution. As of this writing, it is:

- */etc/X11/gdm* on Red Hat/Fedora
- */etc/opt/gnome/gdm* on SUSE
- */etc/gdm* on Debian

As distributions evolve, these directories may change. To find the directory on your distribution, run one of the following commands:

```
rpm -ql gdm | grep gdm.conf
dpkg -L gdm | grep gdm.conf
```

If you get no output, either you haven't installed the GNOME Login Menu package or the name of the directory has changed.

The standard tool to edit the GNOME Login Menu is the Login Screen Setup tool, which you can start with the *gdmsetup* command. This opens the Login Screen Setup window shown in Figure 1-5. I'll examine each of the tabs in turn.

Login Screen Setup

| General | Standard greeter | Graphical greeter | Security | Accessibility | XDMCP |

Greeter

Local: Standard greeter ▽

Remote: Standard greeter ▽

☐ Always use 24 hour clock format

Welcome string: Welcome

Remote welcome string: Welcome to %n

Automatic Login

☐ Login a user automatically on first bootup

Automatic login username: ▼

Timed Login

☐ Login a user automatically after a specified number of seconds

Timed login username: ▼

Seconds before login: 30

◉ Help   ✗ Close

Figure 1-5. The GNOME Login Screen Setup window

If you want to do some arcane customization that you can't find in the Login Screen Setup window on the GNOME display manager, you can try directly editing the associated *gdm.conf* configuration file. It includes a wide variety of options that go beyond the scope of what I can cover in this annoyance. For more information, run the *yelp* command to open the GNOME help documentation and navigate to Desktop → GNOME Display Manager Reference Manual. The version associated with Fedora Core 5 includes two additional tabs: "XServer settings for remote servers" and Users, where you can specify the visible users in the GDM login screen.

General

The General tab defines the basic settings associated with the GNOME Display Manager login screen and allows you to configure several options, which are described in Table 1-2. Be aware that SUSE Linux Professional enables automatic logins by default. This is all right for a system dedicated to a single user in an environment, such as laptop or home office, where intruders are not expected to meddle with it. It also is a good choice for a locked-down public terminal offering a guest account. It should be disabled otherwise.

Table 1-2. GDM Login Screen General tab

Setting	Description
Local Greeter	Standard or Graphical greeter for local logins (the Standard greeter provides a default login screen; the Graphical greeter is more customizable with pictures or other graphics; for details, see the following subsections).
Remote Greeter	Standard or Graphical greeter for remote logins.
Always use 24 hour clock format	If checked, time is shown in a 24-hour instead of a standard U.S. A.M./P.M. format.
Welcome string	Greeting for a successful login.
Remote welcome string	Greeting for a successful remote login.
Login a user automatically	Supports automatic logins to a standard account; a reasonable option for public terminals or some single-user systems.
Automatic login username	Default login account.
Login a user automatically after a specified time	Suitable for a guest account.
Timed login username	Default account if there is no login; suitable for a guest account.
Seconds before login	Wait time before login to a timed login account.

Standard greeter

Under the "Standard greeter" tab, you can configure the look and feel of the Standard Greeter for local and remote users. You can configure a logo and an image (or enable "choosable" images so each user can configure her image to her taste), as well as a background image and color. The Standard Greeter is known as the GTK+ Greeter in Fedora Core.

Graphical greeter

Under the "Graphical greeter" tab, you can configure the look and feel of the Graphical Greeter for local and remote users. Linux distributions include several optional themes, and you can configure your own. In fact, this is one way to create a customized look and feel for your organization. The Graphical Greeter is known as the Themed Greeter in Fedora Core.

You can use the current themes as a model for your own. With a little trial and error, you can replace the *.png* files in the appropriate *themes/* subdirectory with the images of your choice.

The location of the *themes/* subdirectory varies. While the default is */usr/ share/gdm/themes*, SUSE stores Graphical Greeter themes in */opt/gnome/ share/gdm/themes*. Alternatively, you can download your own themes; one source is *http://themes.freshmeat.net/browse/991/*, where most of the themes are available under the GNU General Public License (GPL).

If I had to create a custom theme for my organization, I'd use one of the themes available as a template and substitute the appropriate image files. Of course, you can create your own, using one of the many models available.

Security

The Security tab includes several options, described in Table 1-3.

Table 1-3. GDM Login Screen Security tab

Setting	Description / recommendation
Allow root to log in with GDM	I recommend you disable this setting to discourage administrators from logging in with the root account.
Allow root to log in remotely with GDM	I strongly recommend disabling this setting, as it would transmit the root password over the network, without encryption.
Allow remote timed logins	Associated with the timed login setting under the General tab.
Show actions menu	Displays the Actions menu in the login screen.
Secure actions menu	Supports options that require the root password, such as reboot and shutdown.
Allow configuration from the login screen	Supports access to the GDM Login Screen Setup Tool from the login screen; disable unless you're experimenting with the login screen.
Allow running XDMCP chooser from the login screen	Enables logins to remote GUI systems.
Always disallow TCP connections to X server	Disables GUI logins from remote systems.
Retry delay (seconds)	Specifies the delay after a failed login attempt.

Accessibility

Accessibility modules support users who need assistive technologies, particularly those who are unable to use keyboards or pointing devices in a "standard" fashion. For more information, see Appendix A of the GNOME Desktop Accessibility Guide; a version for GNOME 2.10 is available from *http://www.gnome.org/learn/access-guide/2.10/*. (The GNOME 2.12 Desktop Accessibility Guide was not available as of this writing.)

XDMCP

The X Display Manager Control Protocol (XDMCP) supports logins to remote GUI systems. As you can see from the XDMCP tab, there are several ways you can configure this protocol if you want to allow remote users to log in to your system using the GNOME Display Manager, as described in Table 1-4.

 XDMCP is inherently insecure. A potentially more secure option for remote access to your GUI applications is the Secure Shell protocol. I describe its use for GUI applications in Chapter 11.

Table 1-4. XDMCP Configuration options

Option	Description
Enable XDMCP	Enable if you want to allow remote GUI access.
Honour Indirect Requests	Supports access even if GDM is not available on the remote system (note the British spelling of "Honour").
Listen on UDP port	Specifies the TCP/IP port for XDMCP communication; the default is 177.
Maximum pending requests	Sets the maximum number of requests from remote displays; can vary from maximum remote sessions.
Max pending indirect requests	Sets the maximum number of requests from remote displays that do not have a display manager.
Maximum remote sessions	Limits the number of actual (not pending) remote sessions.
Maximum wait time	Limits the time a request can wait; may help if the network is slow.
Maximum indirect wait time	Limits the time a request from a system without a display manager can wait; may help if the network is slow.
Displays per host	Limits the number of displays allowed to a particular remote system.
Ping interval (seconds)	Checks connections with remote systems periodically, as defined here.

Replicating login configuration to multiple systems

Once you're satisfied with the changes on one system, you'll want to transmit those changes to other systems on your network. As the GNOME Login Manager is system-wide instead of specific to each user, associated settings depend on standard configuration files in the distribution-dependent directories defined earlier. Just copy the files in the noted directories from system to system to implement the changes on the desired computers.

Customizing the KDE Login Manager

Before you start editing the KDE Login Manager, back up the defaults in the KDE configuration directory. The location of this directory varies by distribution. As of this writing, it is:

- */etc/kde/kdm* on Red Hat/Fedora and Debian (Red Hat links to a number of files in the */etc/X11/xdm* directory)
- */opt/kde3/share/config/kdm* on SUSE

In any case, the key file is *kdmrc*, which you can edit directly.

Alternatively, you can start the KDE Login Manager editing tool from the KDE Control Center. Navigate to System Administration → Login Manager. You can also run the *kcmshell kdm* command. Either action opens the Login Screen Setup window shown in Figure 1-6. I'll examine each of the tabs in turn.

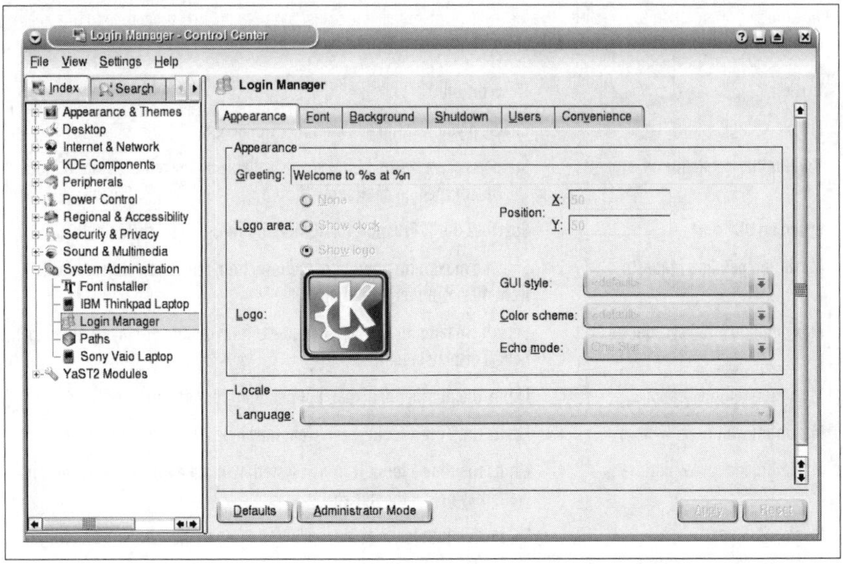

Figure 1-6. The KDM Login Manager configuration tool

> As with the GNOME display manager, you can edit the associated *kdmrc* configuration file directly to change KDE. It includes a wide variety of options that go beyond the scope of what I can cover in this annoyance. For more information, run the *khelpcenter* command to open the KDE help documentation and navigate to Control Center Modules → Login Manager.

Appearance

The options under the Appearance tab allow you to customize the overall look and feel of the KDE Login Manager, as described in Table 1-5.

Table 1-5. KDM Appearance tab

Setting	Description /recommendation
Greeting	Provides a standard greeting; the default is `Welcome to %s at %n`, where `%s` is the operating system (Linux) and `%n` is the hostname; for more options, see the `GreetString` directive in the KDE Login Manager help documentation.
Logo area	Determines what is displayed in the lefthand part of the main screen; if you select "Show logo," you can use the logo of your choice (such as your corporate image).
Position	Defines the location of the upper-left corner of the main screen, relative to the upper-left corner of the display.
GUI style	Allows you to select from available themes, in */usr/share/apps/kstyle/themes* or */opt/kde3/share/apps/kstyle/themes*; if you create your own, add them to the *themes/* subdirectory appropriate to your distribution.
Color scheme	Allows you to select from available color schemes, available in */usr/share/apps/ kdisplay/color-schemes* or */opt/kde3/share/apps/kdisplay/color-schemes*; if you create your own, add them to the *color-schemes/* subdirectory appropriate to your distribution.
Echo mode	Defines the number of asterisks displayed for each keystroke when typing in your password.
Locale	Selects from available languages.

Font

The options under the Font tab allow you to customize the fonts you see in the KDE Login Manager. There are three categories and one other option, as described in Table 1-6.

Table 1-6. KDM Fonts tab

Setting	Description
General	Default font for most of the KDE Login Manager
Failures	Font for error messages and failed login attempts
Greeting	Font for the Greeting, as defined in Table 1-5
Use anti-aliasing for fonts	Supports the use of smoothing for fonts; don't use unless necessary, as this may slow your system

Background

The options under the Background tab allow you to customize the display behind the main part of the KDE Login Manager. While details go beyond the level of annoyances, the impact is that you can add the picture or slideshow of your choice. You may use this tab to customize the login screen with a corporate or organizational seal.

Shutdown

The Shutdown tab defines who can shut down or reboot a computer from the KDE Login Manager window. By default, all users are allowed to shut down or reboot the local computer using the KDE Login Manager. I recommend that you disable this option for most systems (with the possible exception of single-user workstations) because no password is required.

Users

The Users tab defines the users listed in the KDE Login Manager. By default, all regular and nonstandard users as defined in */etc/passwd* within a certain UID range are listed. I believe this is a bad default. Even if you've disabled users such as *ftp* with a home directory such as */sbin/nologin*, this is a clue that a cracker might be able to use to break into your system.

I recommend that you disable this setting by deselecting the Show List option. If you're focused on user convenience, see the next tab.

Convenience

Sometimes it's OK to configure a workstation with an automatic login. In fact, it's the default for SUSE Linux Professional Workstation. If you need to choose "Enable auto-login," I recommend that you do so for a specific user, selected under the Preselect User area, with relatively minimal permissions. If you're comfortable with the relative security of that account, you may also want to choose "Enable password-less logins."

I Can't Configure a Standard Background

I define a standard desktop as one with a consistent look and feel after login. It's consistent for all users, at least before individual users customize their desktop environments.

In general, desktop settings are the sum of their parts. Both KDE and GNOME have standard desktop environments, defined in specific directories, such as */etc/kde3* or */opt/gnome/share*, as well as hidden directories associated with specific users, such as *~/.kde/share*.

If you want a standard desktop, you need consistency with respect to the following:

- Installed packages
- Desktop resolution
- Program menu
- Menu bar
- Uniform group of icons
- Login screen
- Background

I address some of the other components of a standard desktop (desktop resolution, a consistent program menu, a standard menu bar, a custom login screen, and a uniform group of icons) in different annoyances. In this annoyance, I show you how to configure a consistent background and screensaver for a KDE and a GNOME desktop environment.

One benchmark in a consistent organizational image is what people see when they walk through your offices. Everyone has different items on their desks, such as family photos, personal souvenirs, etc. However, almost everyone has a computer with a monitor.

Personally, I think people should be able to put what they want (with the possible exception of obscene words and pictures) on their monitor desktops and screensavers at work. But your manager and/or company may think differently. They might tell you that what visitors (and his bosses) see on everyone's GUI desktop background and screensaver should look and feel professional, as it affects their opinion of your organization.

A Consistent Background

The foundation of a consistent look and feel on the desktop is a consistent background. Assuming you use one of the two standard Linux desktop environments, you can configure it through the KDE Control Center or the GNOME desktop background applet.

KDE backgrounds

If you want to customize the background on a KDE desktop, run the *kcmshell background* command to open the Configure - Background window. This applet is surprisingly versatile; it allows you to configure the image or even a slideshow of images. If you want to set up your corporate logo as the background on your KDE desktops, you could add the image to the */usr/share/wallpapers* directory and then configure it as the picture for your background.

To make this background the standard for your users, copy the *kdesktoprc*, *kcmshellrc*, and *kdeglobals* files from your *~/.kde/share/config* directory to the home directories of the other KDE users on your network.

GNOME backgrounds

If you want to customize the background on a GNOME desktop, run the *gnome-background-properties* command to open the Desktop Background Preferences window. This applet is simple; it allows you to select the image of your choice for a desktop background.

If you want to add a standard image for a background, put it into the */usr/share/images/desktop-base* directory (*/usr/share/backgrounds/images* on Red Hat/Fedora and */usr/share/wallpapers* on SUSE). You can then copy this directory to the other GNOME desktop systems on your network.

Any changes are saved to the *backgrounds.xml* file in the individual user's *~/.gnome2/* directory. To make this the standard background for your GNOME systems, you'll have to copy this file to each user's home directory.

If you want to keep users from changing their backgrounds, you can disable regular user access to the *gnome-background-properties* applet. What I do is limit executable access to the root user with the following command:

```
chmod 700 /usr/bin/gnome-background-properties
```

A Secure Screensaver

In a secure environment, you may not want customers or visiting rivals (or anyone who might be considered a security risk) to see what your users are doing. When your users leave their workstations temporarily, they often don't shut down their computers. With password protection on their screensavers, you can help protect any critical or confidential information.

In addition, screensavers are one more opportunity to set up a consistent look and feel in your office environment.

GNOME screensavers

The GNOME desktop environment takes advantage of a group of standard screensavers available to all Linux systems, part of the *xscreensaver* package. The configuration tool is *xscreensaver-demo*, which is in either */usr/bin* (SUSE, Fedora, and Debian) or */usr/X11R6/bin* (Red Hat Enterprise Linux). This opens the Screensaver Preferences window.

There are a substantial number of things you can configure in the Screensaver Preferences window. I'll focus on only those two items critical to your system security:

Blank after _ _ minutes

Specifies the amount of time before a screensaver activates. If you want to keep your systems secure after a user walks away, you should keep this to a minimum; I suggest one minute.

Lock Screen after _ _ minutes

Sets the amount of time, after the screensaver starts, after which a password is required to dismiss the screensaver and start work again. This should also be kept to a reasonable minimum; zero minutes is probably too short, as it would make users enter a password each time they turn away from the computer for a few seconds.

Once you select a screensaver and close the utility, the configuration is saved in the *~/.xscreensaver* configuration file, which you can copy to each of your users' home directories.

Before any changes take effect, you'll need to restart the *xscreensaver* daemon (it's not a standard daemon, as it doesn't have a start script in the */etc/init.d* directory). The easiest way to restart it is from the *xscreensaver-demo* utility; click File → Restart Daemon. Alternatively, you can restart the daemon from the command line. First, find the Process Identifier (PID) associated with the *xscreensaver* daemon with the following command:

```
ps aux | grep xscreensaver
```

The PID is the number in the second column. For example, if the PID is 1111, you can restart the daemon with the following command:

```
kill -hup 1111
```

KDE screensavers

There is little difference in the workings of the GNOME and KDE screensaver tools; both use the *xscreensaver* package described earlier. To start the KDE screensaver tool, run the *kcmshell screensaver* command. This opens the Configure - Screen Saver (which may be named Configure KDE Control Module) window. If available, select the XScreensaver and then click Setup. You'll see the same Screensaver preferences window described earlier.

Alternatively, if you want to use one of the KDE screensavers, the menu is straightforward. For system security, two settings are critical:

Start automatically after _ _

Specifies the amount of time before a screensaver activates. If you want to keep your systems secure after a user walks away, you should keep this to a minimum; I suggest one minute.

Require password to stop after _ _
> Sets the time, after the screensaver starts, after which a password is required. This should also be kept to a reasonable minimum; don't make it too short, or your users will be highly annoyed at entering a password every time they turn away from their computers.

Once you select a screensaver and close the utility, the configuration is saved in the *~/.kde/share/config/kdesktoprc* configuration file, which you can copy to each of your users' home directories.

Going Further

There are lots of things you can do to customize each desktop environment. If you want to keep a standard environment for your users, take away the tools that they can use to change their environment. Remove or limit permissions to use key configuration tools. For example, you could limit use of the KDE Control Center to the root administrative user with the following command:

```
chmod 700 /usr/bin/kcmshell
```

(In SUSE Linux, *kcmshell* is in the */opt/kde3/bin* directory.) Naturally, you should change the permissions of each GNOME Control Center utility that you don't want your users to take advantage of.

I'd Like Desktop Icons for My Applications

Creating and locking GUI desktop icons is a straightforward process and is one more thing that you can do to configure a consistent look and feel for the GUI desktops in your office. In general, the easiest way to lock the icons on the desktop is by assigning appropriate ownership on the *~/Desktop* directory. What you do may vary slightly if you're using the KDE Desktop Environment or SUSE Linux Professional.

KDE Desktop Icons

You can easily configure a standard set of desktop icons for the KDE Desktop Environment either within the GUI or from the command line. To use the GUI, right-click on the desktop and select Create New → File → Link to Application. You can then create the desktop icon that you need from the properties menu that appears.

To create a desktop icon from the command-line interface, use a procedure such as the following. Essentially, you will use an existing text file that configures a desktop application as the model for one customized for your new application. For this example, I added a desktop icon for the Open-Office.org Writer as follows:

1. KDE icons are stored in each user's *Desktop/* subdirectory. I have an existing Clock icon file, which I've copied with the following commands:

   ```
   cd /home/michael
   cp Desktop/Clock.desktop Desktop/OpenOffice\ Writer.desktop
   ```

2. I opened the newly created *OpenOffice Writer.desktop* file in a text editor. The minimum directives I needed to change to make the file work for a new application were:

   Name

   What you see on the desktop, which I set to OpenOffice.org Writer.

   Exec

   The full path to the application—in this case, */usr/bin/oowriter*.

   Icon

   The file containing the icon to be displayed. Unless you know the default directory (which varies by distribution), it's best to specify the full path to the icon of your choice. In my case on SUSE Linux, I used */usr/share/pixmaps/ooo-writer.png*.

   For more detailed information on the KDE Desktop, see the KDE User Guide, available from *http://people.fruitsalad.org/phil/kde/userguide-tng/*.

3. I saved my changes. You may need to log out and log back in to KDE to see the changes. Test your new icon.

4. For future users, I copied the contents of my personal *Desktop/* subdirectory to */etc/skel*, so all new users get the same subdirectory.

   ```
   cp -a /home/michael/Desktop /etc/skel/
   ```

5. I ran the *chown* command on the *Desktop/* subdirectory to assign ownership to *root*, so the icons can't be changed by new users.

Once you're satisfied with your icons, add the following to the *kdesktoprc* configuration file:

```
[KDE Action Restrictions][$i]
editable_desktop_icons=false
```

The location of *kdesktoprc* varies by distribution. On Red Hat/Fedora, it's in */usr/share/config*; on SUSE, it's in */opt/kde3/share/config*; on Debian, it's in */etc/kde3*. Once configured, all you need to do is copy this file to other servers that contain your user's home directories. Alternatively, you can use the individual configuration directory for each user, which happens to be consistent for all three distributions: *~/.kde/share/config/kdesktoprc*.

Whatever your selection, check the result. The next time you start the KDE Desktop, right-click on the screen. Notice how the pop-up menu has changed. Right-click on an icon. See how that pop-up menu has changed. If you made the change of ownership recommended in the procedure, you won't be able to use the Create New option. Generally, all you can do once you've made this change is click on the icon to open the associated application, directory, or linked file.

For more information on restricting actions on KDE, see the "My Users Mess Up Their Desktops" annoyance.

GNOME Desktop Icons

As with KDE, you can configure a standard set of desktop icons for the GNOME desktop environment through its GUI. For example, I added a desktop icon for OpenOffice.org Writer with the following steps:

1. In the GNOME desktop environment, I right-clicked on the desktop. In the pop-up menu that appeared, I clicked Create Launcher to open the Create Launcher window.

2. In the Name text box, I entered OpenOffice.org Writer, which is the name I want to see on the desktop.

3. In the Comment text box, I added a simple description—in this case, The OpenOffice.org Word Processor.

4. In the Command text box, I added the full path to the command that starts the OpenOffice.org Writer—in this case, /usr/bin/oowriter.

5. I didn't change the type, as this word processor is an application. However, I could have set the type to a directory, a link, or a filesystem device (FSDevice) for directories mounted on specific devices. The other options in this drop-down box are not used.

6. Now it was time to configure this launcher with an icon to be shown on the desktop. I know that there's an *ooo_writer.png* icon available from the *openoffice.org* package. So I clicked on the icon and navigated to the associated location. When successful, the icon is shown in the Create Launcher window.

7. If I were configuring a command-line application such as the *vim* editor, I'd want to run it in a terminal. However, that's not appropriate for a GUI application such as OpenOffice.org Writer.

8. I clicked OK and saw the OpenOffice.org Writer icon appear on my desktop. I can click on this icon to open the word processor.

9. I continued creating any more icons that I need.

10. Once complete, I froze the configuration. I changed the permissions on the files in the ~/*Desktop/* directory with the following command (my home directory is /*home/michael*):

```
chmod 400 /home/michael/Desktop/*
```

And then I changed ownership on the ~/*Desktop/* directory. The following command takes ownership, and the ability to change any files contained within, from any regular user.

```
chown root.root /home/michael/Desktop
```

Now, if I try deleting any icon, I get an error message. While users can still right-click to change permissions, this helps preserve a standard desktop. Other issues are discussed in the following section.

11. Then I wanted to add the same icons to other users' desktops on this server. I could do so with a command similar to:

```
find /home/*/Desktop -maxdepth 0 -exec cp /home/michael/Desktop/* '{}' ';'
```

This command copies all files, but no directories, from /*home/michael/ Desktop* to every user's *Desktop/* subdirectory.

12. I also needed to change the ownership and permissions of each user's *Desktop/* subdirectory, as I did with my own. Fortunately, that command is simpler; all I needed was the proper wildcard to make sure ownership and permissions were changed on the ~/*Desktop* directory of all users (the -*R* ensures that the changes are made recursively through *Desktop/* subdirectories):

```
chown -R root.root /home/*/Desktop
chmod -R 770 /home/*/Desktop
```

13. For future users, I copied the contents of my personal *Desktop/* subdirectory to /*etc/skel*, so all new users get the same subdirectory.

```
cp -a /home/michael/Desktop /etc/skel/
```

14. Finally, I applied the *chown* command to the *Desktop/* subdirectory to make sure icons aren't changed by new users.

Special Problem: Customizing SUSE Desktop Icons

SUSE presents special problems for custom desktop icons. When you customize the SUSE Desktop as described earlier, it works on KDE. However, changing ownership of each user's *Desktop/* subdirectory to *root* renders the icons unusable on GNOME.

The solution is to change the permissions on SUSE Desktop icons without changing ownership to *root*. You can then keep users from changing the permissions on their icons, courtesy of the immutable flag.

Specifically, to add the immutable flag to the files in my *Desktop/* subdirectory, I ran the following command:

```
chattr +i /home/michael/Desktop/*
```

Extend this to all users with the following command:

```
chattr +i /home/*/Desktop/*
```

 The Linux kernel has recently included support for *chattr* on SUSE's default filesystem, ReiserFS.

The Desktop Is Too Big for My Monitor

I'm nearsighted, so I don't fully appreciate the focus on higher dot pitches on the latest monitors. Yes, more dots do mean a higher level of resolution, which is important in many applications. If you're working on something with a lot of detail, such as an airplane drawing, you need to see those little details, such as those parts that might interfere with one other.

However, as I type this chapter, I much prefer bigger letters. I use a resolution of 800×600 on my 15" laptop screen. While I could increase font sizes on a higher-resolution screen, that means additional work to customize applications, desktop icons, and more.

You can configure the resolution directly in the associated X configuration file. But even most Linux geeks use tools to help. In this annoyance, I'll show you how you can use the standard X Window tool, as well as the graphical tools from Red Hat/Fedora, SUSE, and Debian. I'll also show you how to use the GNOME and KDE display tools, which allow individuals to modify the display resolution on their workstations.

With the exception of the GNOME and KDE display tools, all the tools in this annoyance require *root* account privileges. While you can disable the GNOME and KDE display tools, I recommend against it. After all, people work more efficiently with screens set to the resolution that is most comfortable for their eyes. However, if you do want to disable those tools for individual users, use the techniques described in the "My Users Mess Up Their Desktops" annoyance in this chapter.

X Window Configuration

You can configure your GUI from the command-line interface. While it can be difficult, a Linux expert like yourself should know the basics, at least to know if the tool that you've used has caused problems with your configuration. If you aren't confident in your distribution's graphical tool, you can invoke the command-line tool with the *xf86config* command.

Because of licensing issues, most Linux distributions have recently converted from the XFree86 to the X.org GUI server. Others, such as SUSE, use the standard X.org configuration filename */etc/X11/xorg.conf*. This also affects the associated utilities; for example, the *xf86config* and *xf86cfg* utilities may be known by new names, such as *xorgconfig* and *xorgcfg*. While Red Hat Enterprise Linux 4 still uses *XF86Config*, in the */etc/X11* directory, Fedora and Debian have recently made the switch as well.

If you're more familiar with the XFree86 configuration files, don't worry. Whatever configuration file you see in the */etc/X11/* directory, the format of the file remains the same.

 Some distributions store their X configuration file in the */usr/X11R6/etc/X11* directory.

Before you change any configuration file, you should back it up in a secure location such as your home directory. Many tools do back up the X configuration file. So if you make a mistake, you may be able to restore your original configuration from a file with a name such as */etc/X11/XF86Config-4.bak*. However, if you make a mistake and then use the same tool again, you'll overwrite the automatic backup. So it's best to keep a working backup of the X configuration file in your home directory; then you won't be out of luck.

The X configuration file

The X configuration file is split into several sections. If you prefer to configure your X configuration files directly, you need to know at least how these sections interact. If you need to know how each directive in your X configuration file works, refer to the online documentation for that server, either XFree86 or X.org.

xorgconfig/xf86config

As described earlier, *xf86config* and *xorgconfig* are two names for the same utility, and the name depends on whether you're using the XFree86 or X.org servers. (The GUI versions of this utility are *xf86cfg* and *xorgcfg*, respectively.) If this utility is not available on your distribution, you should be able to install the RPM or DEB package of the same or similar name. On Debian Linux, the associated package is *xbase-clients*; on SUSE Linux, the package is *xorg-x11*.

Red Hat discourages the use of the generic *xorgconfig* or *xf86config* tools; they're not included in either the Red Hat Enterprise Linux or Fedora Core distributions. If you prefer, you can install these tools from third-party sources; alternatively, you can use Red Hat's Display Management tool, which you can start with the *system-config-display* command.

When you start the *xorgconfig* or *xf86config* utility, you'll see a warning that you need to know your video card, the amount of video memory, and the associated chipset. If you don't have this information (or if you have a problem with any of the other queries), you can press Ctrl-C to abort the utility before writing a new X configuration file. Otherwise, to run this utility, use the following steps:

1. Run the *xorgconfig* (or for XFree86 servers, the *xf86config*) command. Read the associated warning. Assuming you know your video card, memory, and associated chipset, continue to the next step.

2. Specify the protocol most appropriate for your mouse or pointing device. The latest versions of this utility support auto-detection. Accept auto-detection (option 1 when auto-detection is available) or enter the number associated with the protocol.

3. If you specified a mouse-related protocol and have a two-button mouse, you can now support emulation of a third button (pressing the left and right buttons simultaneously produces the same effect as pressing the middle button on a three-button mouse). As described in "My Mouse Doesn't Do What I Want," later in this chapter, the third mouse button lets you do more in some GUI desktop environments.

```
Option      "Emulate3Buttons"      "true"
```

4. Now, specify the device associated with the mouse. The default, */dev/mouse*, is sufficient if it is already linked to the actual mouse device. To confirm, go to another text console and run the *ls -l /dev/mouse* command. If you don't see a link, you should either specify the right device for your mouse in this step or accept the default and create a symbolic link to the right device yourself.

5. Next, select the keyboard most closely related to what you have. If you don't see your keyboard at first, press Enter without making a selection. The utility scrolls through the available options.

6. In the following step, you can specify a language associated with your keyboard. As before, if you press Enter without making a selection, the utility scrolls through the available options.

7. Now enter the name of your choice. The name becomes associated with the XkbVariant directive in the configuration file.

   There are additional keyboard options available in the next step; some are language-dependent.

8. Read carefully when you see the note about monitor specifications. If you don't know the specs for your monitor, check your documentation. If it isn't readily available, you may see reference to a monitor database file, which can help. Incorrect settings can damage the monitor.

9. Enter the horizontal sync range and allowable resolution of your monitor. Several preconfigured selections are available. Whatever you select here and in the next step must be within the limits specified in your monitor documentation.

10. Enter the vertical refresh rate of the monitor.

11. At the note associated with video card specifications, type y and hit Enter to check out the available database of graphical cards. If you can't find yours among the 500+ available in the database, you may select an option such as "Generic VESA compatible," which is also known as Super VGA.

12. Select the amount of video memory available for your card.

13. Enter a name of your choice. The name becomes associated with the Identifer of your video card in the configuration file.

   Based on the video card, monitor, and memory, the utility now calculates possible video modes, also known as resolutions. Review them and make any changes if needed.

14. Specify the default color depth. Generally, 24 or 32 bits is best, unless you have a limited amount of video memory—less than 8 MB—or a monitor that can handle only the simplest color modes.

15. Finally, specify the name for your configuration file. By default, the utility overwrites the current X Window configuration file; however, if you're just experimenting with options, you can specify the filename of your choice.

Graphical X Configuration Tools

Linux offers additional graphical X Configuration tools. As it's one way distributions distinguish themselves, you may find different GUI tools available on each distribution that you try.

As each of these tools is elementary for the geek, I'll just briefly describe the tools available for the major distributions covered in this book.

SUSE's SAX

The tool associated with SUSE Linux is known as SaX2, the SUSE advanced X11 configuration tool, version 2. If you're already in the GUI and just want to tweak your configuration, you can start SaX2 with the */usr/X11R6/bin/sax2* command. If you haven't yet configured a GUI, you may be able to start SaX2 from the command-line interface with the */usr/X11R6/bin/sax2-vesa* command.

In Figure 1-7, I've started SaX2 from a remote computer using the *sax2-vesa* command. It's helpful to be able to configure the GUI on remote workstations.

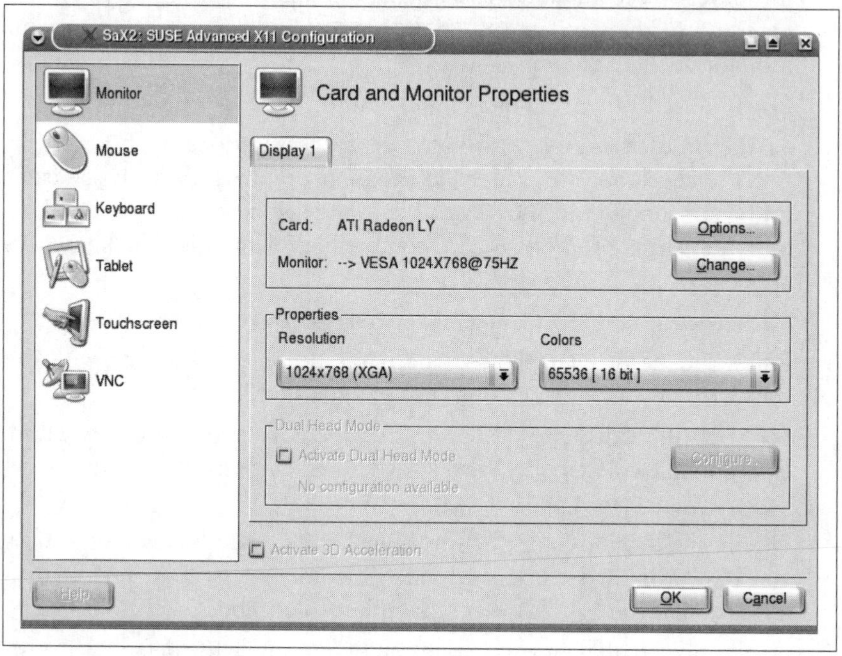

Figure 1-7. SaX2 (from SUSE Linux Professional Workstation 9.3)

As you can see, SaX2 is quite capable. It can help you configure your GUI over and above the generic *xorgconfig/xf86config* tool, including (but not limited to):

- The 3-D acceleration option, which includes a database of video cards that support this capability
- Multihead mode, which supports multiple monitors
- VNC configuration, which allows you to control how the GUI is seen using the remote access service of the same name

Fedora/Red Hat Display settings tool

The current X configuration tool associated with Red Hat distributions is known as "Display settings," which you can start with the *system-config-display* command. In Figure 1-8, I've started the Red Hat GUI tool from a remote computer.

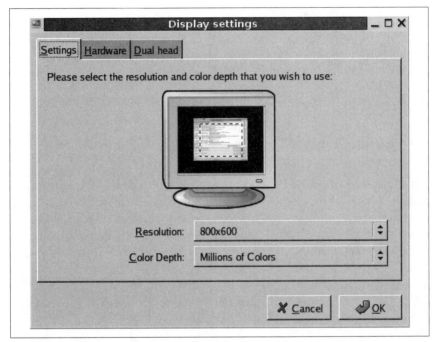

Figure 1-8. Display settings tool (from Red Hat Enterprise Linux 4)

This is just the latest in the evolution of Red Hat tools. Much older versions of Red Hat used the Xconfigurator, as well as the now-ancient XF86Setup tool. Prior to Fedora Core 1 and Red Hat Enterprise Linux 4, you could start the "Display settings" tool with the *redhat-config-display* command. As you can see, the "Display settings" tool is quite capable. It can help you configure your GUI over and above the generic *xorgconfig/xf86config* tool, including the ability to configure two monitors for this workstation.

Debian's X configuration tool

Debian's X configuration tool is surprisingly straightforward. It's a frontend to the *xorgconfig/xf86config* tool, which you can start with the following command:

```
dpkg-reconfigure xserver-xfree86
```

This command walks you through the different steps associated with the text-based tool, as described earlier. One weakness is that you can't easily exit from this tool, because Ctrl-C does not stop the utility. Run the *ps aux | grep dpkg* command to find the associated process and then use the standard *kill* command to stop the process.

GNOME's X configuration tool

GNOME includes a very simple tool, Screen Resolution Preferences, that can help you reconfigure the resolution and refresh rate applied to your display. It works within the limits configured by the previously mentioned X configuration tools.

Start the Screen Resolution Preferences tool with the *gnome-display-properties* command. This command can be invoked by regular users on each of the distributions discussed in this book. The settings are limited to what was previously configured for the monitor and video card.

Both the GNOME and KDE X configuration tools use the X resize, rotate, and reflection (Xrandr) extension, which is designed to help individual users customize the resolution of their GUI desktops. Changes are reflected in the user's home directory, in the *~/.gconf/%gconf-tree.xml* configuration file. For more information, see *http://www.xfree86.org/4.4.0/Xrandr.3.html*.

 As of this writing, the Screen Resolution Preferences tool does not work in Red Hat Enterprise Linux 4. For more information, see bug ID 163385 at *bugzilla.redhat.com*.

KDE's X configuration tool

KDE includes a similar tool, which also uses the Xrandr extensions to help individual users customize the resolutions on their desktops. You can start it as a regular user with the *kcmshell display* command. It starts the Configure - Display tool, associated with the KDE Control Center.

This command can be invoked by regular users on each of the distributions discussed in this book. The settings are limited to what was previously configured for the monitor and video card. Changes are saved to each user's home directory, in the *~/.kde/share/config/kcmrandrrc* configuration file.

My Mouse Doesn't Do What I Want

The mouse (or pointing device, such as a touchpad) is important to users on any graphical desktop environment. Each button has its function. Left-handed users often find it helpful to switch the functionality of the left and right buttons. All users may want to customize the size of the cursor, as well as the speed of motion. Many users may have problems with the scroll wheel.

The middle mouse button is important for some users. It activates a pop-up menu in the KDE desktop environment, and it pastes recently highlighted text into editors and the command-line interface.

But most PC-based pointing devices, including mice, have only two buttons—or it might just seem that way. In many cases, you can configure a middle mouse button using the appropriate X Window configuration tool; I've described several in the previous annoyance and won't describe their uses here.

 If you have a two-button mouse and a scroll wheel in the middle, you may really have a three-button mouse. Press down on the scroll wheel. If it clicks, it can function as a middle mouse button and is often detected as such by Linux X Window System configuration tools.

You may be able to configure what you need with the GNOME Mouse Preferences tool or the KDE Configure - Mouse tool. If you need to do more, such as configure a scroll wheel or touchpad, you may need to modify your X Window configuration file directly. I illustrate how to help you meet both needs in this annoyance.

GNOME Mouse Preferences

Any user can start the GNOME Mouse Preferences tool with the *gnome-mouse-properties* command. In each of the distributions discussed in this book, it includes three tabs:

Buttons
> Under the Buttons tab, you can configure a "left-handed" mouse, which switches the left and right buttons on a standard mouse. This is often preferred by left-handed users. The double-click timeout specifies the amount of time that can pass between clicks when double-clicking on an item. Users who have problems with double-click speed may want to experiment with this setting.

Cursors
> Under the Cursors tab, you can specify the size of the cursor. The default size may be too small, especially for nearsighted users who have configured a high dot-pitch resolution (such as 1600 × 1200).

Motion

Under the Motion tab, you can specify the speed (Acceleration) with which you can move the pointer, the Sensitivity of your pointer to motion, and the Threshold associated with drag-and-drop actions.

If you're running Debian or SUSE Linux, changes are saved to the individual user's home directory, in the *~/.gconf/%gconf-tree.xml* configuration file. If you're running Red Hat/Fedora Linux, changes are saved to the *%gconf.xml* file in the *~/.gconf/desktop/gnome/peripherals/mouse* directory (which you won't see if you use default settings).

KDE Mouse Preferences

Any user can start the KDE Configure Mouse tool with the *kcmshell mouse* command. In each of the distributions discussed in this book, it includes four tabs:

General

Under the General tab, you can configure a "left-handed" mouse, which switches the left and right buttons on a standard mouse. You can even reverse the effect of a scroll wheel. You can also modify the behavior of single- and double-clicks with respect to opening files and folders.

Cursor Theme

You can select the cursor theme of your choice. Some themes may be easier to see in your GUI than others.

Advanced and Mouse Navigation (two tabs)

You can customize the way the mouse moves on your screen, as well as the drag-and-drop behavior of the mouse, using the options available under both of these tabs. Users with problems working with their pointing devices may want to experiment with some of these settings.

Changes are written to several KDE configuration files in each individual user's *~/.kde/share/config* directory. The actual files vary by distribution. If you need to know what they are, after you make changes, log in as the target user and run the following command:

```
ls -ltr ~/.kde/share/config
```

The Scroll Wheel

When you're in an application with a long array of data, such as a 30-page document or a big web page, you can often use the scroll wheel to move up and down the document. The scroll wheel is usually a wheel in the center of a mouse. Virtual scroll wheels are also offered by some touchpads. In many cases, if you move your finger up and down the right quarter of the touch-pad, the effect is the same as that of a scroll wheel.

Linux may have already configured your scroll wheel when it detected your mouse. If so, you should have no problems using your scroll wheel.

However, the configuration of a virtual scroll wheel on a touchpad is a more difficult exercise. I illustrate the necessary changes to the *xorg.conf* file here using the working configuration from my SUSE workstation on a Sony lap-top. The same settings work well on my Debian workstation on an HP lap-top, with a couple of modifications:

```
Section "InputDevice"
    Driver      "synaptics"
    Identifier  "Mouse[2]"
    Option      "Device" "/dev/input/mice"
    Option      "Emulate3Buttons" "on"
    Option      "InputFashion" "Mouse"
    Option      "Name" "Synaptics;Touchpad"
    Option      "Protocol" "explorerps/2"
    Option      "SHMConfig" "on"
    Option      "Vendor" "Sysp"
    Option      "ZAxisMapping" "4 5"
EndSection
```

These directives may not work for your touchpad. If you have a touchpad on a laptop computer, you may be able to benefit from the experience of others. Search for the name of your laptop computer online. Alternatively, search for your laptop on a web site such as *http://www.linux-laptop.net*.

Now, I'll explain each of these directives in Table 1-7. The first and last directives are straightforward; they bracket the stanza. All mice, touchpads, other pointing devices, and even keyboards are known as the `InputDevice` directive.

Table 1-7. Directives for a touchpad

Directive	Description
Section "Input Device"	Start of the stanza.
Driver "synaptics"	Points to the Synaptics driver; may work for touchpads of other brands.
Identifier "Mouse[2]"	Identifies this Input Device as the second mouse.
Option "Device" "/dev/input/mice"	Specifies the device associated with the touchpad; may also be */dev/psaux*.
Option "Emulate3Buttons" "on"	Supports middle-mouse-button emulation; the features of the middle button can be invoked by clicking the left and right mouse buttons simultaneously.

Table 1-7. Directives for a touchpad (continued)

Directive	Description
Option "InputFashion" "Mouse"	Allows input from the touchpad as if it were a regular mouse.
Option "Name" "Synaptics;Touchpad"	Specifies an appropriate name for the InputDevice.
Option "Protocol" "explorerps/2"	Most touchpads work as a PS2 device; if you're not sure of yours, you may be able to substitute "auto-dev".
Option "SHMConfig" "on"	Allows sharing of the touchpad space between the main area for navigation and the right-hand quarter for scrolling.
Option "ZAxisMapping" "4 5"	Configures scrolling up and down.
Option "RTCornerButton" "0"	Disables a middle click when you tap on the upper-right corner of the tap area, which provides more control on desktops with middle-mouse-button functionality, such as KDE.
Option "RBCornerButton" "0"	Disables a right click when you tap on the upper-right corner of the tap area, which requires you to use the touchpad button for right clicks.
EndSection	End of the stanza.

> You may note that the Option "Vendor" "Sysp" directive is missing from the table; it's a label. RTCornerButton and RBCornerButton are directives you might consider if you have a touchpad.

Configuration data for other types of pointing devices is available in the *README.mouse* file, typically available in the */usr/X11R6/lib/X11/doc* directory. It includes configuration information for an alternative touchpad, the Alps GlidePoint.

If this configuration doesn't work for you, make sure you've inserted the names of the appropriate drivers into a file such as */etc/modprobe.conf*, */etc/modules.conf*, or */etc/modprobe.d/mouse*.

You may want to customize your touchpad further. While there is no dedicated HOWTO or FAQ that explains the directives that you can use, there is hard-won experience available from other Linux users on web sites such as *http://tuxmobil.org*. They include directives such as LeftEdge, RightEdge, TopEdge, BottomEdge, FingerLow, FingerHigh, MaxTapTime, MaxTapMove, VertScrollDelta, MinSpeed, MaxSpeed, EdgeMotionSpeed, and AccelFactor.

Some trial and error may be required, so remember to back up your X Window configuration file before you start editing!

My Users Mess Up Their Desktops

Once you've made all of these changes, you may want to keep your users from messing them up. While I personally prefer allowing every user to customize his system, your managers may not agree.

There are two basic approaches to this process. First, you can disable access to the key tools. Second, you can change ownership and permissions on associated configuration files to prevent changes by regular users.

 If you're interested in more detailed information, there's an excellent discussion on configuring a standard KDE desktop environment at *http://enterprise.kde.org/articles/kiosk-lp.php*. An excellent guide to configuring a standard GNOME desktop environment is available in a Gentoo wiki at *http://gentoo-wiki.com/HOWTO_Gnome_Desktop_Admin_Guide*, and you can also refer to the Red Hat Desktop Deployment Guide available at *http://www.redhat.com/docs/manuals/enterprise/RHEL-4-Manual/desktop-guide/*.

You can also make your changes a part of the */etc/skel* directory, which causes them to be copied into the home directories of all users created subsequently. For example, the following command creates the new user *nancy*; the *-m* option (not required on Red Hat/Fedora) creates Nancy's home directory in */home/nancy*, and activates the defaults in */etc/default/useradd*, copying the files from */etc/skel*,with appropriate ownership and permissions, into Nancy's home directory:

```
useradd -m nancy
```

Disabling Changes on KDE

The KDE desktop configuration is driven by both default and individual configuration files. Naturally, what you do depends on what you want to customize; do you want a standard desktop for just a few users or for every user on your network?

The default configuration files depend on the distribution, as shown in Table 1-8.

Table 1-8. KDE default configuration directory

Distribution	KDE default configuration directory
Red Hat/Fedora	*/usr/share/config*
SUSE	*/opt/kde3/share/config*
Debian	*/etc/kde3*

Individual configuration files are stored in each user's home directory in the *~/.kde/share/config* directory. If you haven't yet configured custom settings for a specific user, the user-specific configuration file probably does not yet exist.

Once you make desired changes to one individual's *~/.kde/* directory, you can copy it to the home directory of other users. You can also copy it to the */etc/skel* directory. As described earlier, this directory is often used to populate the home directories of new users with standard configuration files.

The key to preventing changes by pesky users is the immutable flag. In KDE configuration files, you can specify it through [$i]. For example, to lock the standard configuration, I've added this flag to the beginning of each stanza—for example:

```
[Desktop0][$i]
```

In any case, changes aren't displayed until the next time you log in to the KDE desktop environment.

Restricting Actions on KDE

The KDE desktop environment includes a number of options suitable for kiosks, which are common locations for public terminals. If you administer a public terminal, you'll probably want to freeze the desktop configuration of that terminal. What you do for workstations in an office may also incorporate some of the same limitations.

In the previous section, I've covered some of the things you can do to disable configuration changes. You can also restrict such actions as starting a command-line interface, running as the *root* user, or changing the background. Open a *kdeglobals* configuration file and start a stanza with the following title:

```
[KDE Action Restrictions][$i]
```

On a workstation, you may want to keep certain users away from the command-line interface. You can do so in this stanza with the following directive:

```
shell_access=false
```

By default, users can also start applications from the Run Application window, invoked through Alt-F2. If you want to disable access to this window, add the following directive:

```
run_command=false
```

You can keep users from using any KDE utilities that require the *root* account with a directive such as:

```
user/root=false
```

But users don't need the *root* account to customize many things on the KDE desktop. You can further limit access to different modules in the KDE Control Center, in a different stanza, starting with:

```
[KDE Control Module Restrictions][$i]
```

Here, you can limit access to the modules of your choice. For example, if you want to keep users from changing their own KDE desktop backgrounds, add the following directive to this stanza:

```
kde-background.desktop=false
```

To keep your users from changing their screensavers, include the following directive:

```
kde-screensaver.desktop=false
```

If you want to limit access to another module, you simply need to know the name, as defined in the output from the following command:

```
kcmshell --list
```

Then, to limit access to the module of your choice, just substitute the name of that module in the following directive:

```
kde-module name.desktop=false
```

Disabling Changes on GNOME

The key to a standard GNOME desktop environment is the GConf system. Readers familiar with Microsoft Windows might notice parallels to the Registry Editor. You can start the GConf editor with the *gconf-editor* command (normally, it's in the */usr/bin* directory; on SUSE, it's in the */opt/gnome/bin* directory). There are three types of GNOME settings. What each user sees is an amalgamation of these:

Mandatory
> Mandatory settings can't be changed by regular users, unless they have access to the GConf system or the associated configuration files in the */etc/gconf/gconf.xml.mandatory* directory. (For SUSE, it's the */etc/opt/gnome/gconf/gconf.xml.mandatory* directory.) Mandatory settings supersede default settings.

Default
> Default and mandatory settings, taken together, define the standard desktop environment seen by regular users; however, default settings can be changed. The associated configuration files are in the */etc/gconf/gconf.xml.default* directory. (For SUSE, it's the */etc/opt/gnome/gconf/gconf.xml.default* directory.)

User

User-specific and customizable settings are stored in each user's home directory, in *~/.gconf*.

Configuring system-wide GNOME desktop settings

To configure system-wide settings on the GNOME Desktop Environment, open the GConf editor as the *root* user. In some distributions, this is possible only with the *sudo* command; for example, on Debian Linux, I can open GConf while logged in to the K Desktop Environment with the following command:

```
sudo gconf-editor
```

 Some distributions return an error message if you try to open GConf as *root*. In that case, use the *sudo gconf-editor* command as a regular user. Access to the *sudo* command for a regular user requires that user be configured as part of the */etc/sudoers* file, which you can configure with the *visudo* command.

Disabling Menu Items on GNOME

Sometimes the easiest way to keep users from changing their standard desktop environments is to disable the GUI menu items. In other words, if the user doesn't see the administrative tool, he's less likely to want to try to use it.

 You can disable KDE menu items with the KDE Menu Editor described in the first annoyance in this chapter, "I Want the Advantages of Both KDE and GNOME."

Default GNOME main-menu files are located in the */usr/share/applications* directory. User-specific menu files are located in each user's home directory, in *~/.config/menus*. Managing the GNOME menu items is a straightforward process; for example, if your SUSE Linux computers are configured with the GNOME Desktop Environment, and you want to disable GNOME menu-based access to the YaST configuration tool, move (don't delete) the *YaST.desktop* file from the */usr/share/applications* directory. (I move it to my home directory, in case I ever want to restore the menu option.)

If you're already in the GNOME Desktop Environment, check your menu. The changes are shown immediately on the Red Hat/Fedora and Debian distributions. The changes aren't shown on SUSE Linux until the next time you start GNOME.

Now you can implement these changes to the other desktop systems on your network. Remember, if you're removing items from the GNOME desktop menus, you'll have to remove the corresponding items from the *usr/share/applications* directory on each of your target systems.

My CD/DVD Is Locked

When you press the eject button on your CD or DVD drive, you'd think that the drive should open. Unfortunately, it doesn't always happen. Anything that is using a file or reading a directory on that CD/DVD can keep your system from opening that drive. This could be something as simple as a user whose current directory lies on the CD/DVD drive.

If you're running Linux as a server, you probably need to accept the locking of the CD/DVD drive. Other users may be installing Linux from a shared DVD on your system and may need access to the data on the drive. While you may have good reasons as an administrator to unlock a drive, be aware that you may be interrupting some task being run by one or more of your users (or fellow administrators).

On the other hand, if you're working with a single-user Linux workstation, users won't understand why their CD/DVD is locked. They'll just complain, and you'll be annoyed, as they won't be interested in learning "simple" commands such as *umount*. All they'll tell you is that the CD is broken.

In this annoyance, I'll show you how I believe servers and workstations should be configured with respect to the CD/DVD drive. The defaults vary depending on your distribution. Based on those defaults, if you still have problems, there are a series of common steps that you can follow.

Recommended /etc/fstab Defaults for a CD/DVD on a Server

When you configure a server, you'll want full control over any CD/DVD drives on your system. Generally, you'll want to limit privileges to administrative users. Take the following default entry from my *etc/fstab* on Red Hat Enterprise Linux 4, with a regular CD/DVD drive:

```
/dev/hdc /media/cdrecorder  auto  pamconsole,exec,noauto,managed 0 0
```

The applicable entry from my SUSE Linux workstation is:

```
/dev/cdrecorder /media/cdrecorder  subfs  noauto,users,gid=users 0 0
```

Finally, the associated directive from my Debian system is:

```
/dev/hdc /media/cdrecorder  auto  ro,users,noauto,unhide,exec 0 0
```

As you should already know, the first column is the CD/DVD drive device file, and the second column is the default directory where the drive is mounted. The third column specifies the filesystem, such as *ext3* or *reiserfs*. auto auto-detects the filesystem. subfs represents the Linux removable-media-handling system and is most closely associated with SUSE. The fourth column specifies the mount options, and that's the focus for this annoyance. (For more information on the fifth and sixth columns, which are rarely changed these days, see the *fstab* manpage.) Examine the options described in Table 1-9. This table is not comprehensive, but is limited to options that may contribute to problems unmounting a CD/DVD drive.

Table 1-9. Some /etc/fstab mount options

Option	Description
auto / noauto	Generally, noauto is best for removable media; otherwise, Linux will try to mount the CD/DVD even if there's nothing in that drive.
user / nouser	Many distributions permit mounting and unmounting by all users with the user directive; the nouser directive limits mount privileges to the *root* user.
pamconsole	A Red Hat innovation that supports mounting by all users. It works only for explicit mounting at the console. However, this does not prevent regular users from mounting automatically in the GUI, thanks to other options.
userid=*xxxx*	Limits mount access to a specific user.
gid=*xxxx*	Limits mount access to a specific group.
exec / noexec	exec allows binary commands to be run from the CD/DVD.
managed	Any directive with this parameter is rewritten by the *fstab-sync* command when you reboot.
nosuid	Prevents execution of SUID or SGID scripts on the CD/DVD.
unhide	Supports reading of some hidden partitions, such as DVDs.

With these options in mind, I recommend that you change the directives associated with the CD/DVD drive in your */etc/fstab* to disallow mounts by regular users. I'd change the SUSE Linux 9.3 directive to delete users access by user and group:

```
/dev/cdrecorder  /media/cdrecorder  subfs  noauto 0 0
```

I'd change the Debian Sarge directive to delete regular user access by removing the users and uid options.

```
/dev/hdc  /media/cdrecorder  auto  ro,noauto,unhide,exec 0 0
```

The situation with Red Hat Enterprise Linux 4/Fedora Core is different. The directive associated with the CD/DVD drive is governed by the relatively new Hardware Abstraction Layer daemon, using the *storage-policy.fdi* configuration file. On Fedora Core, this file is located in the *usr/share/hal/fdi/90systempolicy/* subdirectory; on Red Hat Enterprise Linux 4, it's located in the *usr/share/hal/fdi/90defaultpolicy/* directory.

By default, the user who owns the device file associated with the CD/DVD drive can also mount and unmount that drive. In other words, based on the following, the user *michael*, and no other regular user, is allowed to mount the CD/DVD drive associated with */dev/hdd*:

```
$ ls -l /dev/hdd
brw------- 1 michael disk 22, 64 Jul 22 02:35 /dev/hdd
```

If the specified user is your regular account as an administrator, that's generally good enough for a server.

As an alternative to changing *fstab*, you can remove the following line from the noted *storage-policy.fdi* configuration file:

```
<merge key="storage.policy.default.mount_option.pamconsole" type="bool">
true</merge>
```

When you restart the HAL daemon with the */etc/init.d/haldaemon restart* command, not even the regular owner of the CD/DVD device file is allowed to mount that drive. Access is limited to the root user, and that's appropriate on a server.

Recommended Defaults for a CD/DVD on a Workstation

Workstations should be configured differently from servers. One difference is in the way they handle removable media. Regular users expect CDs and DVDs to be automatically mounted when placed in their drives.

It's important that the applicable directives in */etc/fstab* support access by normal users. Based on the directives from the previous section, I'd make sure at least the user option is included in the appropriate directive; the following example works on my SUSE Professional workstation:

```
/dev/cdrecorder  /media/cdrecorder  subfs  noauto,users,gid=users 0 0
```

The following works well on a Debian Sarge workstation:

```
/dev/hdc  /media/cdrecorder  auto  ro,users,noauto,unhide,exec 0 0
```

The situation is a bit different with Red Hat/Fedora workstations. The directive is acceptable as is; all you need to do is make sure the owner of the CD/DVD device file, such as */dev/hdc* or */dev/hdd*, is the primary user of the workstation.

Modifying the GUI device-management tool

GNOME provides removable device-management tools that are not affected by the options in */etc/fstab*. For example, in the GNOME Desktop Environment, run the *gnome-volume-properties* command. This starts the Drives and Media Preferences tool, which allows you to control how GNOME reacts when you insert a CD/DVD into the drive. On a server, I recommend that you disable all automatic mounting.

There is no corresponding stable utility available on the KDE Desktop Environment; the last information I can find on the Kautorun software is from 2000. However, you can take advantage of the *.kde/Autostart* directory to create your own Autorun system on KDE. The Autorun system is available only on Red Hat distributions. The associated RPM doesn't work on SUSE Linux, so if you want Autorun on KDE for SUSE or Debian Linux, you'll have to compile it from the source code. To do so, take the following steps:

1. Download the latest source package from the Autorun project web site at *http://sourceforge.net/projects/autorun/*.

2. Unpack the package. For this example, I've downloaded it to my */home/ michael* directory, so I've run the following commands (substitute the version number for *versionnum*):

   ```
   cd /home/michael
   tar xzvf autorun-versionnum.tar.gz
   ```

3. Navigate to the directory that's created; it's the *autorun-versionnum* subdirectory:

   ```
   cd autorun-versionnum
   ```

4. Configure the source code; the local configure file is already set up as a script for this purpose:

   ```
   ./configure
   ```

   Address any errors that may arise during the configuration process. I did not find any errors when I ran this command on my SUSE and Debian Linux workstations.

5. Run the following command as the *root* user (to make sure you have permissions and PATH access to appropriate directories) to compile the code:

   ```
   make
   ```

   You may get errors at this point because of other packages that you may need to install. Some educated guesses may be required. For example, on my Debian workstation, I installed the *libxml-parser-perl* package because of the following error message:

   ```
   checking for XML::Parser... configure: error: XML::Parser perl module is
   required for intltool
   ```

Some error messages are simpler; the following from my SUSE worksta-tion led me to install the *xmlto* RPM (and several dependencies):

```
make[2]: xmlto: Command not found
```

6. Run the following command to install the compiled packages in appro-priate locations:

```
make install
```

Pay attention to the final messages, which list the location of the *Autorun.desktop* script.

7. Copy the *Autorun.desktop* script to an appropriate location on desired users' home directories, and, if necessary, make sure ownership is appropriate:

```
cp /usr/local/share/autorun/Autorun.desktop /home/michael/.kde/Autostart/
chown michael.users /home/michael/.kde/Autostart/Autorun.desktop
```

8. Update the *Autorun.desktop* script to point to the actual location of the *autorun* command; when I compiled from source, it was copied to the */usr/local/bin* directory. The next time you start KDE, it will automati-cally look for and mount any drive in your CD/DVD drive.

Remember to tell your users how they can unmount their drives—at least how they can right-click on the CD/DVD icon in their GUI desktops to bring up a menu that lets them unmount the drive. I describe this and other options in the next section.

Getting the CD/DVD Out

As problems with a CD/DVD drive can vary, I provide a simple checklist of steps you can take. The first steps may seem elementary for geeks but are shown because we all forget the obvious sometimes:

1. If you're in the GUI, you may see an icon related to the CD/DVD drive. Right-click on it; on the menu that appears, you'll probably have an option such as "eject" or "umount." Click on the available option (if both are available, try "eject" first).

   You may get an error message to the effect that the mounted volume is not in */etc/fstab* (especially if you're not the *root* user). In that case, pro-ceed to the next step.

2. Check to see if your CD/DVD drive is mounted. You can do so with the *mount* command (by itself). If you're not sure how your CD/DVD drive is mounted, check your */etc/fstab* and */etc/auto.misc* configuration files for clues.

It's certainly possible for another administrator to mount your CD/DVD drive on a different directory, which should show up in the output to the *mount* command.

You can get a more complete list of mounted devices from the */proc/mounts* file.

 If your system has mounted the CD through your */etc/auto.misc* file, see "Regular Users Can't Mount the CD/DVD Drive" in Chapter 7.

3. If your drive is mounted on a directory defined by */etc/fstab* (or another directory shown in the output from *mount*), try ejecting it. For example, if it's mounted on */media/cdrecorder*, try the following command:

```
eject /media/cdrecorder
```

If your drive is automounted as configured in */etc/auto.misc*, the *eject* command may not work. But after there's been no activity for a timeout defined in */etc/auto.master*, the automounter automatically unmounts the drive.

If you get an error message such as:

```
umount: /media/cdrecorder: device is busy
```

you know that some process, local or remote, is trying to read the device. Before you unmount the CD/DVD, you'll need to somehow stop the process. Proceed to the next step.

4. Try unmounting the drive in question with a command such as the following. Remember, the *umount* command is spelled differently from the English-language word:

```
umount /media/cdrecorder
```

You can substitute the device to be unmounted. You may get an error message such as that described in the previous step. Otherwise, try pressing the button on your drive to see whether you can manually eject the disk.

5. If you're still having problems unmounting the drive, you should now try to identify the process that's reading the drive. That's where the list-open-files (*lsof*) command can help. It even shows files shared via Samba; for example, the following output from the *lsof +D /media/cdrecorder* command points to a remote user accessing your CD via Samba (the *+D* switch is key; without it, the command doesn't know where to start looking):

```
COMMAND PID    USER   FD   TYPE DEVICE SIZE NODE NAME
smbd    4812 michael  cwd   DIR  22,64 2048 1856 /media/cdrecorder
```

The limitation of the *lsof* command is that it can't help you with files opened via a shared NFS directory.

6. If you've shared your CD/DVD via Samba, you can check if anyone has accessed any of your Samba shares with the *smbstatus* command.

7. If you've shared your CD/DVD via NFS, checking access is more problematic. The *showmount -a* command, in concert with the shares defined in */etc/exports*, can only help you define the workstations that have accessed shares from your NFS server.

8. If there are current users on other workstations using your CD/DVD, warn them. You may need to use other means, such as Instant Messaging, to warn them that you're about to cut off all processes that access the CD/DVD. Then issue the following command as *root*:

```
fuser -km /media/cdrecorder
```

Ejecting CDs and DVDs Used by Games

One problem with some game installations can be solved (in advance) by exporting the following environment variable:

```
export SETUP_CDROM=/media/dvd
```

You can then run the installation program for the game. You should be able to eject the CD when prompted and insert the next CD in the installation sequence.

I Can't Get to the GUI

Sometimes the GUI just won't start. You've configured your */etc/inittab* to boot Linux in a runlevel associated with the GUI. You may see a command-line login prompt for a very few seconds. You may get to a GUI Login Manager and enter the correct username and password, and the GUI Login Manager just reappears.

There are several possible causes of this failure:

• The key packages associated with the GUI desktop environment aren't installed.

• The configuration files aren't set to automatically start the GUI.

• The X font server is not running.

• Key directories are either full or missing.

In this annoyance, I limit coverage to the most popular desktop environments, KDE and GNOME.

Packages Associated with the GUI

If you can't start the GUI, you might have forgotten to install the associated packages. You could navigate to the package-management tool of your choice, but for Red Hat and Fedora's *system-config-packages* or *pirut*, that requires the GUI. If all you're familiar with on Debian is the Synaptic package manager, that requires the GUI. SUSE's YaST won't work if the */tmp* directory is completely deleted. I'll describe what you can do in each of these cases.

Fedora Core

Fedora Core Linux comes with an excellent command-line update system, known as the *Yellowdog Updater, Modified*, or *yum* for short. I'm assuming that the repositories specified in your */etc/yum.repos.d* directory are up-to-date, as described in "Find the Right Update Repository" in Chapter 8.

There are two approaches that you can take with *yum*. One approach is to focus on a key package and make sure it's installed or up-to-date. Either of the following commands upgrades the noted package if it's already installed:

```
yum install gnome-desktop
yum install kdebase
```

Alternatively, you can focus on the package group. For example, if you want to install the KDE Desktop Environment on your system, the following command installs the default and mandatory packages from the associated package group, as defined in the *comps.xml* file in the */usr/share/comps/i386/* directory (if your architecture is different, substitute accordingly for i386):

```
yum groupinstall KDE
```

If you want to see a list of package groups, run the following command; you may want to pipe it to a pager such as *more* or *less*:

```
yum grouplist
```

Red Hat Enterprise Linux

If you're running Red Hat Enterprise Linux and need to install a GUI, you don't have the option of *yum* for updates from the Red Hat Network. You'll need to install the appropriate packages via the Red Hat Network. As the *up2date* utility also installs any dependent packages, the following commands will install the packages required for the GNOME and KDE Desktop Environments:

```
up2date -u gnome*
up2date -u kde*
```

Debian Linux

If you need to install the GNOME or KDE desktop environments on Debian Linux, first make sure your *apt* databases are up-to-date with the following command. You may need to run it more than once if you get an error message, as the packages in some repositories may depend on others:

```
apt-get update
```

While there are no appropriately configured package groups for Debian Linux, you can take advantage of dependencies. Install critical packages with commands such as:

```
apt-get install gnome-desktop-environment
apt-get install kdebase
```

If you need to list packages associated with a desktop environment, you can use a command such as the following to get a full list:

```
apt-cache search kde
```

The associated list is long; you may want to pipe the output to a pager such as *less* or *more*. For more information on the *apt* commands, see "Avoid Dependency Hell with apt" in Chapter 8.

SUSE Linux

Generally, SUSE's YaST works even in command-line consoles. However, it won't start if the */tmp* directory is missing. No special files are required. Just add the directory, and you can take advantage of YaST to install the GNOME or KDE desktop environment.

Making Configuration Files Point to the GUI

When you configure a desktop for ordinary users, you'll generally want to let them log directly in to the GUI. The "I Need a Custom Login Menu" annoyance, earlier in this chapter, illustrates how you can create a custom GUI login menu. You'll also need to make sure the boot system, as defined in */etc/inittab*, starts you in a runlevel appropriate for the GUI.

Assuming you've installed the appropriate GUI login manager, open the */etc/ inittab* file in a text editor. Inspect the line with the id directive. If you're running Debian Linux, make sure this directive reads as follows:

```
id:2:initdefault
```

If you're running SUSE, Fedora Core, or Red Hat Enterprise Linux, make sure the id directive reads as follows:

```
id:5:initdefault
```

The X Font Server Is Not Running

The X Font Server is important to the GUI only on Red Hat/Fedora distributions. If it isn't running, the X Window System won't start. If your system is configured to start in GUI runlevel 5, the screen will just flash for a while. If you try navigating to another console with the Alt-Ctrl-F2 keys, you'll see the console login prompt for a second or two.

After a couple of minutes, you'll see a blue screen with the following message:

```
I cannot start the X server (your graphical interface). It is likely that it
is not set up correctly. Would you like to view the X server output to
diagnose the problem?
```

If you see the message, you're offered the opportunity to review the logfiles, and then a chance to start the Red Hat display tool. If the X Font Server is not running, the display tool won't start. If you refuse to restart X, Red Hat/Fedora disables the GUI and returns you to the command-line console.

If you can't get back to the command-line console, you'll have to reboot the computer and make sure to restart in a different runlevel. Generally, you can do so at the bootloader with the following steps:

1. Restart the computer. If necessary, use the power button.
2. At the bootloader, use the up or down arrow keys to stop the timer.
3. If a password is required, press p and enter your GRUB bootloader password when prompted.
4. Press a to display the kernel command line. At the end of the line, enter the runlevel of your choice. For Red Hat/Fedora, this should be runlevel 3, which corresponds to full multiuser mode without the GUI.

Now you can start diagnosing problems with the X Font Server:

1. Make sure it's configured to run in runlevel 5 with the following commands:

   ```
   chkconfig xfs on
   chkconfig --list xfs
   ```

2. Make sure the X Font Server runs with the following command:

   ```
   /etc/init.d/xfs restart
   ```

   As the GUI depends on the X Font Server, this command won't work from the GUI.

3. If there are other problems with the X Font Server, do an Internet search based on the error messages.

Key Directories Are Full or Missing

As described in the next annoyance, the GUI depends on files stored in the */tmp* directory. You'll see that the cron jobs that clear temporary files on a regular basis take care to exclude directories and files required to start the GUI.

If for some reason someone deletes the */tmp* directory, users won't be able to start the GNOME or KDE desktops. The quickest solution is to re-create the directory with appropriate permissions:

```
mkdir /tmp
chmod 1777 /tmp
init 5
```

As you've seen throughout this chapter, key configuration files are stored in each user's home directory. If the partition with */home* is full, the GUI won't be able to update those files, and it can't start. In that case, you may see an error message such as:

```
Fatal server error:
could not open default font 'fixed'
```

It's true that Linux could not start the X window because it couldn't open the default font. However, the problem is not related to the X Font Server just described; it's just a symptom of the lack of space on the aforementioned directories. The *df* command can tell you whether one or more critical partitions are full. What you do to make more space is up to you.

User Downloads Are Overloading Workstations

As with all annoyances in this book, there is more than one method available to solve problems. In this case, I'll show you how you can keep downloads to a minimum on our selected Linux distributions.

The basic premise is that, as an administrator, you've limited downloads to the */tmp* directory. You can further limit user downloads with appropriate quotas as described in "Some User Is Taking Too Much Disk Space" in Chapter 10.

Alternatively, you can extend the scripts shown in this annoyance to the applicable subdirectories for each user.

You can configure the default download directories associated with Internet-related applications such as Firefox. I'll describe the options briefly in Chapter 3. For more information on customizing Firefox for consistent settings, see *Firefox Hacks* by Nigel McFarlane (O'Reilly).

 There may be security vulnerabilities associated with the Linux tools that maintain */tmp*. While I believe they've been addressed by the major distributions, the article on this subject is worth reading; it's available from: *http://www.bindview.com/Services/Razor/Papers/2002/mkstemp.cfm*.

Red Hat/Fedora

The Red Hat/Fedora distributions configure the */usr/sbin/tmpwatch* command to check various temporary directories and remove old files as part of a daily cron job in the */etc/cron.daily* directory. *tmpwatch* is a script of three commands that look more complex than they are.

With the *-x* option, the first command excludes from consideration a number of directories essential to starting the GUI. Then it specifies that files older than 240 hours in the */tmp* directory (other than those already excluded) will be deleted.

```
/usr/sbin/tmpwatch -x /tmp/.X11-unix -x /tmp/.XIM-unix -x /tmp/.font-unix -x
/tmp/.ICE-unix -x /tmp/.Test-unix 240 /tmp
```

The next command in the script deletes files older than 720 hours from the */var/tmp* directory. This directory usually holds temporary configuration files associated with the KDE desktop environment.

```
/usr/sbin/tmpwatch 720 /var/tmp
```

The final command searches through caches of manpages. As a geek, you know that manpages are organized into nine different categories. When a manpage is loaded, it is stored in cache for easier retrieval. If you haven't accessed that manpage in 10 days (720 hours), the cache is purged by the following loop:

```
for d in /var/{cache/man,catman}/{cat?,X11R6/cat?,local/cat?}; do
    if [ -d "$d" ]; then
        /usr/sbin/tmpwatch -f 720 $d
    fi
done
```

Remember that the ? represents a wildcard for a single character, so the `for` directive shown covers the */var/cache/man/cat1* through */var/cache/man/cat9* directories.

SUSE

SUSE Linux manages temporary files through a daily cron job in the */etc/cron.daily* directory, known as *suse.de-clean-tmp*. It's a substantial script that depends on directives set in the */etc/sysconfig/cron* configuration file. Generally, you won't need to change anything in the cron job; just modify the */etc/sysconfig/cron* as needed. This configuration file includes the directives defined in Table 1-10.

Table 1-10. SUSE tmp management directives

Directive	Description
MAX_DAYS_IN_TMP	By default, SUSE sets this to 0, which retains all files in */tmp* directories; this directive is associated with the TMP_DIRS_TO_CLEAR directive.
MAX_DAYS_IN_LONG_TMP	By default, SUSE sets this to 0, which retains all files in the directory defined by the LONG_TMP_DIRS_TO_CLEAR directive.
TMP_DIRS_TO_CLEAR	Normally set to */tmp*.
LONG_TMP_DIRS_TO_CLEAR	Set to the directory of your choice; commonly used for */var/tmp*.
OWNER_TO_KEEP_IN_TMP	Specifies the owner for files to be retained; commonly assigned to *root*, which retains the files in */tmp* required for the GUI.
CLEAR_TMP_DIRS_AT_BOOTUP	Normally set to no; if set to yes, deletes all files from the */tmp* directories (including those owned by the *root* user). Don't change unless you're not using a GUI.
REINIT_MANDB	Configures re-creation of the manpage database; normally set to yes.
DELETE_OLD_CATMAN	Deletes preformatted manpages, as stored in */var/catman* directory; normally set to yes.
CATMAN_ATIME	Specifies a time after which preformatted manpages are deleted.
DELETE_OLD_CORE	Deletes older databases of files created with the *updatedb* command; don't change unless you have installed the *findutils-locate* RPM.
MAX_DAYS_FOR_CORE	Specifies a maximum age for file databases, in days.

 The *tmpwatch* RPM is no longer available for SUSE Linux. As of SUSE 9.2, the appropriate script is now part of the SUSE *aaa_base* RPM.

Debian

Debian Linux configures the */usr/sbin/tmpreaper* command as part of a daily cron job in the */etc/cron.daily* directory. It depends on settings that you can configure in */etc/tmpreaper.conf* and */etc/default/rcS*. I'll examine both the configuration files and the script.

The *etc/default/rcS* file is key to a number of configuration files associated with the boot process. The default version of this file includes one related directive:

```
TMPTIME=0
```

This specifies the time that files are stored in */tmp* in days. The default of 0 specifies that files in */tmp* are stored per the TMPREAPER_TIME directive in */etc/tmpreaper.conf*.

Now examine the */etc/tmpreaper.conf* configuration file, as that is where you can set the directives used in the */etc/cron.daily/tmpreaper* cron job. This configuration file includes directives as defined in Table 1-11.

Table 1-11. Debian /etc/tmpreaper.conf management directives

Directive	Description
SHOWWARNING	Related to the *README.security.gz* warning in the */usr/share/doc/tmpreaper* directory.
TMPREAPER_TIME	If TMPTIME is not set in */etc/default/rcS*, this directive determines how long files are stored in */tmp*.
TMPREAPER_PROTECT_EXTRA	Lets you specify file patterns to protect from deletion; some are already protected in the default *tmpreaper* cron job.
TMPREAPER_DIRS	Specifies the directories to apply the *tmpreaper* cron job.
TMPREAPER_ADDITIONALOPTIONS	Sets additional options to pass to the *tmpreaper* command.

These directives are applied to the *tmpreaper* cron job in the first few lines of the script. First, this stanza makes sure that the *tmpreaper* command exists:

```
if ! [ -x /usr/sbin/tmpreaper ]; then
    exit 0
fi
```

The next stanza checks for and then uses the */etc/tmpreaper.conf* configuration file:

```
if [ -s /etc/tmpreaper.conf ]; then
    . /etc/tmpreaper.conf
fi
```

The script then checks key directives; the default TMPREAPER_TIME is seven days, and the default TMPREAPER_DIRS is */tmp*.

```
TMPREAPER_TIME=${TMPREAPER_TIME:-7d}
TMPREAPER_PROTECT_EXTRA=${TMPREAPER_PROTECT_EXTRA:-''}
TMPREAPER_DIRS=${TMPREAPER_DIRS:-'/tmp/.'}
```

Finally, the script is run, with a lowered priority (courtesy of *nice -n10*) to help prevent this job from interfering with other running processes. It avoids deleting directories critical to the running of the Linux GUI.

I Need to Manage Sound Events

In this annoyance, I describe the elementary utilities available to our major distributions for configuring sound cards. I then describe the utilities that can help you manage sound events. As this chapter is focused on the desktop, I focus on sound events associated with the GNOME and KDE desktop environments. I also focus on the Advanced Linux Sound Architecture (ALSA), which was incorporated into the current Linux kernel (2.6). If you need detailed information on support for your sound card, refer to ALSA's web site at *http://www.alsa-project.org*.

When your distribution detects a sound card, it may include commands for the appropriate modules in a file such as */etc/modprobe.conf*, */etc/modules.conf*, or */etc/modprobe.d/sound*.

I've broken this annoyance into distribution-specific sections, followed by the tools associated with the GNOME and KDE desktop environments. You can control the sound environment for all users with the distribution-specific tools. Your users can control their individual sound settings with the GNOME and KDE-based tools.

All three distributions include the *alsaconf* utility. As you can run it from the console, it's not associated with any particular desktop environment. For more information, see the description of the utility later in this annoyance.

Red Hat/Fedora

Immediately after the installation process, Red Hat/Fedora distributions normally test the sound card as part of the *firstboot* process. This process calls the *system-config-soundcard* utility. If it finds an ALSA-compliant sound card, it installs the card for you and allows you to check the result with a standard set of musical notes.

For more details on how you can configure ALSA-compliant sound cards, refer to the commands associated with the *alsa-utils* RPM. This package includes a number of utilities that can even help you configure and coordinate multiple sound cards.

SUSE

As with most systems, SUSE encourages hardware configuration of sound cards with YaST. Sound configuration options are available when you start YaST, under the Hardware section.

If SUSE detects a sound card, it's listed in the YaST Sound Configuration menu. Alternatively, if the card wasn't properly detected, you may be able to configure it from the available database. In the YaST Sound Configuration menu, select the Add Sound Card option. You'll be able to select from a wide variety of sound-card vendors and associated hardware models.

YaST configures your sound card and adds the result to the */etc/modprobe.d/ sound* configuration file. Other important SUSE sound configuration files include */etc/modprobe.conf** and */etc/sysconfig/sound*.

Debian and alsaconf

Debian includes the generic ALSA configuration tool, */usr/sbin/alsaconf*. While available for the distributions covered in this book, it's the primary tool for Debian—part of the *alsa-utils* package. Install it, and it can help you configure just about any ALSA-compatible sound card. While you're at the installation process, make sure to download and install the *alsa-source*, *alsa-base*, and the *libasound2* packages. As the database of ALSA drivers, the *alsa-source* package is especially important if you have a slightly obscure sound card.

> The *alsaconf* tool is available as part of the *alsa* RPM in SUSE Linux; for Red Hat/Fedora, it's been superseded by *system-config-soundcard*.

When you start the ALSA configuration tool, take the following steps:

1. Stop all currently running applications that require sound, such as Real Player.

2. Start the ALSA configuration tool with the */usr/sbin/alsaconf* command. When you click OK, it unloads any currently running ALSA kernel modules and loads the ALSA sound-card database.

3. The tool should find any ALSA-compatible cards. If you're not satisfied with the results, refer to the documentation and mailing lists at *http://www.alsa-project.org/*.

4. If you have a legacy sound card, select the legacy option. The steps that follow allow you to probe, using the drivers, for several different fairly generic sound cards.

Any special sound-card settings are saved to the */etc/modprobe.d/alsa-base* file.

If you want to make sure any changes to sound settings are saved and reapplied the next time you boot Debian Linux, take the following steps:

1. Stop the ALSA service with the following command:

```
/etc/init.d/alsa stop
```

2. Use the *dpkg-reconfigure* command to reset the ALSA base parameters:

```
dpkg-reconfigure alsa-base
```

3. You'll be able to select from three options: to always autosave, to autosave once at next shutdown, or to never autosave.

4. If you select always autosave, Debian Linux always saves your sound settings when it shuts down. The setting is saved as the alsactl_store_ on_shutdown directive in the */etc/default/alsa* configuration file.

Now, you can adjust the default sound settings for your system. To do so, run the *alsamixer* command, which opens a console-based volume tool, as shown in Figure 1-9.

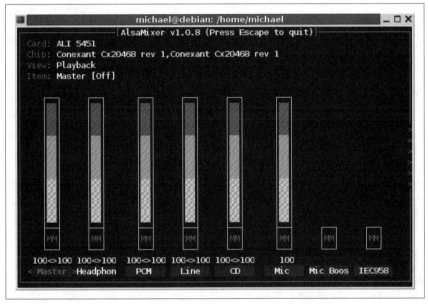

Figure 1-9. AlsaMixer

You can navigate among the options with the left and right arrow keys, and change volume levels with the up and down arrow keys. As shown in the figure, you can exit the utility with the Esc key.

Once you make changes, you'll need to run the following command to store the current sound level in */var/lib/alsa/asound.state*:

```
alsactl store
```

GNOME Sound Preferences

GNOME sound events are managed through the Sound Preferences tool, which you can start with the *gnome-sound-properties* command. It's part of the *capplets* package in Debian, the *control-center* RPM on Red Hat/Fedora, and the *control-center2* RPM on SUSE.

When you start this utility, you'll immediately see its value. As shown on the first tab, it determines whether the sound server is started when you log in to the GNOME Desktop Environment. It also allows you to activate Sounds For Events, as defined under the Sound Events tab. Many of these events require the *gnome-audio* RPM or DEB package.

The System Bell tab allows you to activate a sound for events such as errors. One standard is to activate the Sound An Audible Bell option. For hearing-impaired users, you can also activate visual feedback, which leads to a flash on the screen for sound events.

Sound-event settings are saved in gconf (GNOME Configuration) settings, described in the "Disabling Changes on GNOME" annoyance earlier in this chapter.

KDE Sound Management

There are three tools associated with sound management on the KDE desktop, at least if you're looking for tools functionally equivalent to the GNOME Sound Preferences tool. They include the following:

Sound System Configuration
> You can start the KDE Sound System Configuration tool with the *kcmshell arts* command. It includes two tabs. The General tab allows you to enable the sound system and manage its relative priority. The Hardware tab allows you select and configure the audio and MIDI devices.

System Bell Configuration
> You can start the KDE System Bell Configuration tool with the *kcmshell bell* command. If you activate the system bell, it supersedes settings in the System Notifications Configuration tool.

System Notifications Configuration
> If you haven't activated the KDE system bell in the System Bell Configuration tool, you can customize sounds for different events. You can start the KDE System Notifications Configuration tool with the *kcmshell kcmnotify* command. It allows you to configure and customize sounds in several categories.

These tools are straightforward; they directly configure the sound settings on a per-user basis. Changes are written to several files in each user's *~/.kde/ share/config* directory.

CHAPTER 2

Configuring User Workstations

This chapter is somewhat unlike the others in this book, as it is more focused on the regular desktop user. Linux geeks are normally happy to talk about the advantages of open source software. However, describing those advantages to a non-geeky user who is just converting from Microsoft Windows can be difficult—and to the extent that Linux requires extra steps or does things differently, the need to describe them becomes an annoyance all its own. Regular users have a different level of expectations. Very few regular users work from the command line; most expect a fully configured GUI.

Even with the advances in Linux GUI-based tools, command-line utilities almost always have more features. However, if the GUI tools are good enough, it will be easier to explain how to use them, and the results will be more likely to satisfy your users.

In several cases, the tools described in this chapter are beyond the capabilities of the ordinary desktop user. Here, you'll have to take charge as a Linux geek and assure your users that you'll do the tasks yourself, based in part on the annoyances in this chapter. For those tools, I describe solutions appropriate to you, the Linux geek.

I'm Afraid of Losing Data

Backups are fundamental in the life of any Linux geek. You need to know at least how to back up the files on your home directory. And if you administer systems, you need to know how to keep the data on those systems backed up. In many cases, you'll need real-time backups, as discussed in the next annoyance.

There are a wide variety of excellent backup tools, many of which require (and have) dedicated books covering their use. Some of them work in the

GUI, including the Archive Manager described in the last annoyance in this chapter.

But despite the concern for the end user shown in the introduction to this chapter, backups are primarily a function for administrators—in other words, you as the Linux geek. Therefore, I focus on command-line tools in this annoyance.

 If your users are interested in backing up their own home directories, instructions for creating a zipped archive are available in the last annoyance in this chapter.

Specifically, I focus on a couple of the simpler tools for backups: the *rsync* command, which can synchronize data with remote locations, and the Secure Shell (*ssh*) command, which can encrypt data that travels over networks.

I assume that some of you may not be completely familiar with *rsync* and *ssh*. Therefore, I start by describing the basics of each of these utilities and then show how you can use these commands together to securely back up your home directory—on a remote system. Next, I'll demonstrate how to configure SSH connections without passwords, and finally I'll explain how to configure the backup as a cron job. These details may be basic for some Linux geeks, but *rsync* is so important that I'll take some time to describe the features we'll find useful in this annoyance.

The rsync Command

The *rsync* command has a lot of powerful and advanced features, some under the hood. When you use the command to synchronize files and/or directories, it might be a bit slow to begin with. But the next time you synchronize, all it needs to do is transfer the bits that have changed in each directory or file since last time. In other words, if you've updated a large database file, *rsync* transfers just the differences between the old and new versions. For all of our distributions, the associated package is also named *rsync*.

This command also supports archive mode, which allows you to preserve just about everything associated with each of your files and directories, including:

- User and group ownership, file times, and permissions
- Symbolic links
- Device files
- Recursive synchronization through all subdirectories

It also supports synchronization through remote connection tools, including the Secure Shell. Some of *rsync*'s key options are described in Table 2-1.

Table 2-1. rsync command options

Option	Description
-a	Archive mode, functionally equivalent to -rlptgoD
-D	Preserves device files
-e	Supports transfer over a remote shell command such as ssh
-g	Preserves group ownership
-H	Copies hard-linked files
-l	Copies symlinks, also known as soft-linked files
-o	Preserves user ownership
-p	Retains permissions
-r	Runs recursively into subdirectories
-v	Verbose mode; -vv is extra verbose mode
-z	Compresses data
--rsh=/path	Specifies full path to the remote shell command of your choice; similar to -e

If you prefer to use the Secure Shell (*ssh*) to *rsync* data remotely, you can use the *-e ssh* option, or you can change the default *rsync* behavior to use the Secure Shell. To do so, set the RSYNC_RSH environment variable with the following command:

```
env RSH_RSYNC=ssh
```

You can set this variable as the default for all users by adding it to */etc/profile* (or for SUSE, to */etc/profile.local*); alternatively, you can add it to an individual user's *~/.bashrc* or *~/.bash_profile*, assuming that you use the default bash shell.

The *-a* option combines the functionality of many other useful options, so your *rsync* command does not have to be complex. For example, the following command copies my home directory to */tmp/michael*:

```
rsync -aHvz /home/michael /tmp/
```

If you're not familiar with *rsync*, try a similar command on your own system. Examine the results in the target directory. In this case, I find the files from my home directory in */tmp/michael*. If the command were slightly different, with the trailing forward slash, I'd find my files in the */tmp* directory:

```
rsync -aHvz /home/michael/ /tmp/
```

Naturally, backups aren't very useful unless you can copy data to a different hard drive. A backup to a remote computer—in this case, via the Secure Shell—is one preferred method.

The Secure Shell Command

The basic use of the Secure Shell command, *ssh*, is simple and suffices for most uses with *rsync*. I address only those essentials of *ssh* required to facilitate rsync backups here; for more information, see the "Configure SSH" annoyance in Chapter 11. Once the service is installed and started (and any current firewalls are properly configured), it's easy to log in to a Secure Shell server. From any client, just run the following command:

```
ssh username@remotepc
```

The *username* must be valid on the remote PC; substitute the host, FQDN, or IP address for *remotepc*.

Backing Up Your Home Directory

Now, I'll show you how you can combine the *ssh* and *rsync* commands to back up your home directory from a remote computer. For example, on my Red Hat Enterprise Linux (RHEL) 4 computer, I've backed up my wife's home directory from our SUSE workstation with the following command:

```
rsync -aHvz -e ssh donna@suse1:/home/donna /home/michael/
```

This command prompts you for the user's password. If it's the first time you've connected with SSH, you're prompted to confirm the connection. If you get an error message related to the *known_hosts* list, edit or delete the local *.ssh/known_hosts* file.

Once the transfer is complete, I can find a mirror image of the files from Donna's home directory on the local */home/michael/donna* directory.

In this case, I don't want to use the trailing slash when referring to Donna's home directory. If I use a trailing slash (i.e., */home/donna/*), the individual contents of her directory are transferred instead of the directory as a unit. This means her default shell, browser, profile, KDE, GNOME settings, and more will overwrite those on my home directory! The trailing slash makes an enormous difference, which you can understand by running some experiments with and without it.

Configuring SSH Without Passwords

While you can back up home directories with passwords, that's not enough if you want to automate the process. If you want to configure a cron job for daily backups, a naive solution would be to store passwords in clear text in a cron job in the *etc/cron.daily* directory, but that's generally a bad idea. The better alternative is to configure SSH to connect between computers without passwords using public-key exchange.

For more information on how this is done, see "My Other Computer Has No Monitor" in Chapter 11. When done properly, password-free access is limited to specific computers or a specific command such as *rsync*. For the purpose of this annoyance, I assume that you've created and configured the keys that you need to log in without a password.

Creating a cron Job for Your Backups

Now you can create a cron job for your backups. Assuming you want a daily backup, you'll need to create an appropriate script in the *etc/cron.daily/* directory; each script there runs regularly, thanks to the background cron process. Individual users can create their own cron jobs with the *crontab -e* command. If you need a model for cron jobs, see your *etc/crontab* configuration file, and sample cron jobs in the *etc/cron.daily* directory.

Generally, cron jobs collect commands run in a regular shell. So start by opening the filename of your choice under *etc/cron.daily/* with a text editor and add the following directive, which tells Linux to expect regular bash shell commands:

```
#!/bin/sh
```

While not absolutely necessary, it is good practice to start every script by declaring the shell associated with your scripts. As there is normally no Bourne shell installed, the Linux distributions I know actually link */bin/sh* to the default */bin/bash* (The Bourne Again Shell) shell.

To minimize security risks, cron jobs do not inherit the PATH from any user. You can either define a PATH explicitly before your shell commands, or just specify the full path to each command.

Now we can insert the command shown previously, which backed up Donna's home directory.

```
/usr/bin/rsync -aHvz -e /usr/bin/ssh donna@suse1:/home/donna /home/michael/
```

If you've already set the RSYNC_RSH=ssh environmental variable, the required command is simpler:

```
/usr/bin/rsync -aHvz donna@suse1:/home/donna /home/michael/
```

Naturally, you may want to expand this backup method to cover all files on a workstation. To do so, you'll need *root* permissions and therefore will need to create public and private authentication keys in the workstation and server's */root/.ssh/* directories. You can then create a cron job to back up all files on the workstation, using the techniques described in this section.

My Boss Insists on Real-Time Backups

There are two key reasons to do backups: data redundancy in case of local hardware failure and data availability in case of disaster. Appropriate RAID arrays can ensure the availability of your data in case of hardware failure. Careful network backups can help keep your data available in case of natural or man-made disaster. Naturally, this is an administrative function beyond the capabilities of regular users.

High-speed network backups saved the data from a number of financial firms after the tragedies of September 11, 2001. Without those backups, a lot more financial data would have been lost, and I suspect the subsequent economic declines might have been much worse.

Many standard books and documents tell you how to back up your system while it's down and unavailable to users. But Linux is increasingly being used as a server in environments where downtime is considered a sin. When used with removable hard drives, RAID does not require downtime. And the removable hard drives can be sent to safe locations.

Unfortunately, hardware RAID solutions are more expensive compared to software RAID. And they go beyond the packages that are included with most Linux distributions. There are other high-capacity/high-availability commercial solutions, such as Red Hat Cluster Manager and SUSE Heartbeat. But if you're stuck and need to configure a real-time backup using just the software available with a Linux distribution, consider software RAID, as described in this annoyance.

RAID Basics

As software RAID in Linux has limits, it's useful to review some basic characteristics of RAID. Linux supports four different levels of software RAID:

RAID 0
> RAID 0 doesn't offer data redundancy, but it does support faster data transfer. It allows you to combine the space from two or more approximately equal-sized disks or partitions into one volume. Once created, you can mount a single directory such as / or */usr* onto that volume. To take full advantage of RAID 0, you should combine partitions from separate drives on separate controllers; performance is enhanced because data can be transferred through both controllers simultaneously.

However, if any disk in the array fails, the information from all RAID 0 disks in the volume is lost.

RAID 1

RAID 1 mirrors data onto two disks or partitions of appropriately equal size. When you write a file to a RAID 1 mirror, you're writing to both drives. Writes are therefore slower than to a standard hard disk. However, if one disk fails, a complete backup of the data is available on the other disk. You can replace either of the disks, if one fails or if you just want to move a backup to a remote location. Once a disk is replaced, the data from the other disk in the array is copied to the new disk. In short, RAID 1 supports robustness through redundancy.

RAID 4 and RAID 5

RAID 4 and RAID 5 allow you to configure three or more disks together in an array. Data is striped across multiple disks. Parity information supports recovery if a disk fails. On RAID 4, the parity information is stored on a single disk. On RAID 5, the parity information is distributed among all disks in the array. Recovery uses the parity data. Both forms support robustness, as with RAID 1, using less space.

There are other levels of RAID supported by Linux. For example, there is partial support for RAID 6, which includes a second level of striping compared to RAID 5 (and therefore can tolerate failures of two disks in the array). RAID 10 is a combination of RAID 0 and RAID 1, a striped volume built on two RAID 1 arrays.

Until the development of Serial ATA (SATA) and multidisk Parallel ATA (PATA) IDE hard disks (and controllers), effective use of RAID was limited to SCSI drives.

Naturally, if you want a real-time backup, you're looking for some implementation of a RAID 1 array. While hardware RAID is not dependent on the operating system, there is an excellent introduction to how to use it with Linux in the DPT Hardware RAID HOWTO at *http://www.ram.org/computing/linux/ dpt_raid.html*.

RAID supports the use of spare disks. For example, if you have a spare disk on a RAID 1 array, you can remove one of the disks in the array and configure authentic mirroring in the spare.

Tools for Software RAID

Software RAID is configured through the operating system. Unlike hardware RAID, there is no dedicated hardware controller for the disk array. You can control a software RAID array with commands and configuration files.

While Software RAID takes more work than hardware RAID, it can be surprisingly efficient because there is no potential bottleneck at the non-RAID hardware controller. But when you configure a software RAID array, be careful. Make sure to configure partitions on different physical drives. Otherwise, you can't get the benefit of fast access through different controllers. Furthermore, if you've configured more than one RAID 1 or 4/5 partition on a single physical drive and it fails, you'll lose all data in that array.

Before you can use software RAID, your system must meet two requirements:

- The *mdadm* or *raidtools* package must be installed (*raidtools* is obsolete on some distributions).
- The RAID multidevice (md) module must be supported by the kernel. This is easy to verify: just check kernel settings in the associated *config-`uname -r`* file in the */boot* directory, or check for the availability of */proc/mdstat*.

A couple other packages may be useful:

- SUSE's *scsirastools* package is designed to administer and monitor SCSI disks in a RAID 1 array. For other distributions, the source code is available from *http://scsirastools.sourceforge.net*.
- Starting with Fedora Core 3, Red Hat includes the *dmraid* package, which can detect and help you manage software RAID arrays. The *dmraid* package is also available in the Debian Etch (testing) distribution.

Typical RAID 1 Configuration

A Linux software RAID 1 array keeps an exact copy of the files from one partition, such as */dev/hda5*, on a second partition, such as */dev/hdc5*. It's important to place each partition in a RAID 1 array on separate hard disks. While details vary, this is essentially how to set up the */home* directory on a RAID 1 array:

1. Back up the information on */home*.

2. Configure the partitions on the two or more hard disks that you're planning to use for the RAID 1 array.

3. If you're going to use the existing partition with the */home* directory as one of the partitions in the RAID array, unmount it.

4. Make sure you have a backup of your */home* directory, as you're about to destroy the data on the production partition.

5. Run *fdisk* to reconfigure the target partitions with the Linux RAID *autodetect* file type.

6. Edit the */etc/raidtab* configuration file. The default SUSE *raidtools* package includes sample configuration files that you can use in the */usr/share/doc/packages/raidtools* directory. As you may have a different distribution, I show here a sample configuration file, which assumes that you have two IDE hard drives:

```
# Sample raid-1 configuration
raiddev             /dev/md0
raid-level          1
nr-raid-disks       2
nr-spare-disks      0
chunk-size          4

device              /dev/hda5
raid-disk           0

device              /dev/hdc5
raid-disk           1
```

7. Once you've configured */etc/raidtab*, you can initialize the array with the *mkraid /dev/md0* command.

8. Alternatively, if you use the *mdadm* package, you can create the same array with the following command, which creates RAID device */dev/md0*, at RAID level 1, with the two RAID partition devices shown:

```
mdadm --create --verbose /dev/md0 --level=1 --raid-devices=2/dev/hda5 \
/dev/hdc5
```

9. Format the device with the appropriate command, such as *mke2fs* for *ext2* or *ext3* formatted filesystems.

10. To test the result, mount the RAID device on an empty directory. Check the result in your */etc/mtab* file and with the *df* command.

11. Now you can configure the RAID device, in this case, */dev/md0*, in */etc/fstab*, with the directory of your choice.

Networking RAID 1

You can set up one of the mirrors in a RAID array in a remote location. Naturally, this requires a dedicated high-speed connection. Details would take up another full book. There are several techniques for real-time networked RAID mirrors, based on the Enhanced Network Block Device (ENBD). With an ENBD, you can configure a remote partition from a RAID array so that it appears local on your computer. It's an academic research project funded in part by Realm Software; the home page is *http://www.it.uc3m.es/ptb/enbd*.

I Lost Data When I Removed My Floppy/Memory Stick

With older computers, floppy disks were sometimes a challenge for Linux. When you wrote a file to a floppy, the actual data might not get written to the disk for several minutes or more. If you ejected a disk before the write, you would lose the data that you thought you saved.

This is now an even bigger problem. Common options include USB keys or flash drives, as well as external hard drives that plug into a USB or IEEE 1394 (FireWire) port. When you copy data to one of these devices, Linux may not actually write the data to the media for minutes.

Thus, if you eject a floppy disk from its drive, disconnect an external hard drive, or remove a flash drive from its port before its time, you may lose data that you thought you saved.

To minimize this risk, you should change associated settings in your */etc/fstab* and automounter (*/etc/auto.**) configuration files. This annoyance provides just the briefest overview of how you can configure each of these files. For more information on the automounter, see "Regular Users Can't Mount the CD/DVD Drive" in Chapter 7.

In the next section, I'll show you how you can make it easier for regular users to manage floppy disks and USB keys, while minimizing the risks of data loss.

Modifying /etc/fstab for Removable Media

The default */etc/fstab* configuration for removable media leaves something to be desired. Unless otherwise specified, reads and writes to all filesystems are done asynchronously. That's acceptable when the media is local, and permanently attached. But it's a problem for removable media.

 If your */etc/fstab* starts with a reference to *fstab-sync*, do not directly edit your */etc/fstab* file. In the next section, I'll explain which files you should edit to make sure *fstab-sync* places appropriate entries in your */etc/fstab*.

It's also a problem for network media. You may lose data that you think you've saved to a network drive if the network fails. That is why Red Hat recommends the use of the *sync* directive for all mounted NFS drives, as network problems can interrupt file writes at any time.

Naturally, users are unpredictable. Accidents happen even to the most experienced administrators. USB keys may be knocked out of their slots. FireWire connections may come loose. One option is to make sure your */etc/fstab* synchronizes data as quickly as possible. For this purpose, I've changed the defaults on several of my systems to include the sync option, including:

Floppy drive
> This example comes from a Red Hat Enterprise Linux 3 AS system:
>
> ```
> /dev/fd0  /mnt/floppy  auto  noauto,owner,kudzu,sync  0 0
> ```

Network-mounted SCSI disk
> This example comes from a Red Hat Enterprise Linux 4 WS system:
>
> ```
> /dev/sda1  /media/usbdisk  ext3
> pamconsole,noatime,sync,exec,noauto,managed 0 0
> ```

The managed directive is associated with automated updates, as driven by HAL through the *fstab-sync* command.

However, synchronous reads and writes can affect performance. Most flash drives have limits in the number of writes they can handle. While a typical flash drive is supposed to be able to handle several million write cycles, I wouldn't keep a flash drive plugged in all day. Nevertheless, the HAL system associated with SUSE Linux mounts USB drives with the sync option.

Automatic Mounts

As Linux moves forward, distributions are integrating the Hardware Abstraction Layer (HAL) daemon, which automatically detects and configures new hardware components. For example, when some distributions detect new drives such as cameras and USB keys, they add an appropriate directive to your */etc/fstab* configuration file. As HAL is fairly new in many Linux distributions, it may not work with all of your hardware. Here, I show you how you can customize HAL. If you still have problems, I also illustrate how you can disable HAL.

One useful tool to see what HAL has detected is the HAL Device Manager, which is part of the Debian *hal-device-manager* package and the Red Hat/Fedora and SUSE *hal-gnome* packages. When you start the tool with the *hal-device-manager* command, you'll see a graphical overview of your hardware, similar to Figure 2-1.

This section applies primarily to Red Hat/Fedora and Debian Linux; if you have a SUSE system, read the next section, "Other Hotplug Update Methods."

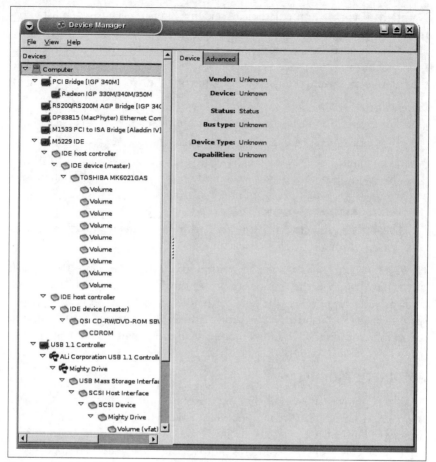

Figure 2-1. The Hardware Device Manager

Customizing HAL

If you just want HAL to add the *sync* directive when it synchronizes detected hardware, you'll want to add a file, with an *.fdi* extension, to the */usr/share/hal/fdi/95userpolicy* directory. For example, I've added the *sync.fdi* file, with the following entries, in the same XML format associated with other *.fdi* files:

```
<deviceinfo version="0.2">
  <!-- Default policies merged onto computer root object -->   <device>
    <match key="info.udi" string="/org/freedesktop/Hal/devices/computer">
      <merge key="storage.policy.default.mount_option.sync" type="bool">
true</merge>
    </match>
  </device>
</deviceinfo>
```

To create *sync.fdi*, I've taken the pattern of XML directives from the *storage-policy.fdi* file in the */usr/share/hal/fdi/90defaultpolicy* directory.

The deviceinfo directive specifies the default policies associated with detected removable drives. The second line, which starts with <!, is a comment. The third line, associated with the info.udi key, defines detected removable devices. The next line is key because it adds sync to the mount options in */etc/fstab* for detected removable devices.

The next time you boot Linux, or the next time you restart the HAL daemon, you should see the sync directive in the mount options for the devices you chose to add it to in your */etc/fstab*.

 In Red Hat/Fedora, HAL uses the *fstab-sync* command to incorporate newly detected hardware in */etc/fstab*. Other methods are described in the next section.

Disabling HAL on Red Hat/Fedora

After you tinker with HAL, it may not work as desired on your particular configuration. If you're running Red Hat/Fedora, you can disable HAL's effect on */etc/fstab* by running the following commands. You can then edit */etc/fstab* to meet your needs:

```
rm /etc/hal/device.d/50-fstab-sync.hal
ln -s /bin/false /etc/hal/device.d/50-fstab-sync.hal
```

If you want to restore HAL's effect on */etc/fstab*, just run the following commands:

```
rm /etc/hal/device.d/50-fstab-sync.hal
ln -s /usr/sbin/fstab-sync /etc/hal/device.d/50-fstab-sync.hal
```

 If you've had to disable HAL, it's helpful if you report your trouble to the developers. For more information, a list of existing bugs, and reporting tools, see *http://hal.freedesktop.org/wiki/Software/hal*.

Other Hotplug Update Methods

SUSE and Debian Linux take different approaches with HAL, as they do not update */etc/fstab* when HAL detects newly connected hardware.

On my SUSE system, I did not have to change the hotplug defaults for my external FireWire hard drive. These defaults are stored in the *hotplug.subfs.functions* file, in the */etc/hotplug* directory, and this file is already configured to mount detected hotplugged drives with the sync directive.

SUSE automatically mounts removable hard drive partitions once they're connected to and detected by your system. However, unlike with Red Hat/Fedora, it does not update the */etc/fstab* configuration file.

Debian Sarge does not configure HAL to automatically mount newly attached drives. In this case, you'll need to mount those drives yourself. For example, after I plug a USB key drive into my Debian system, I make it recognizable to the system with the following command:

```
mount -o sync /dev/sda1 /mnt/usbkey
```

You can also verify through *mount* that the sync directive is in effect. When I run the *mount* command by itself, I find the following entry for my USB key drive:

```
/dev/sda1 on /mnt/usbkey type ext3 (rw,sync)
```

When you run the *mount* command on any of your Linux systems, you should be able to confirm that the sync directive is in effect for any mounted removable media.

Configuring the Automounter for Removable Media

The Automounter supports temporary mounts of removable media, by issuing the proper mount commands when the devices start up and unmounting the devices if they are idle for a while. For detailed information on configuring the Automounter, see Chapter 7. Briefly, all you need to do is configure any mount points in your automounter configuration files, */etc/auto.master* and */etc/auto.misc*, and include the sync directive in the associated options. The *automounter* package also includes the */misc* directory for mounts defined in */etc/auto.misc*. For example, the following directive in my Red Hat Enterprise Linux 4 */etc/auto.misc* configuration file supports synchronous read/write access:

```
floppy  -fstype=auto,rw,sync    :/dev/fd0
```

I've added the rw and sync directives to the floppy command line; after I restart the automounter daemon and run the *ls /misc/floppy* command, I see the following output from the *mount* command:

```
/dev/fd0 on /misc/floppy type vfat (rw,sync)
```

If you've enabled rw (read/write) access but see ro (read-only) mounting, your media may not support read/write access. Check your media. The tab on the floppy may be disabled, or the DVD drive may not support write access.

That Command Doesn't Write to My DVD

The variety of DVD writers available today can be confusing. The command that you use to write to the DVD may vary with the type of DVD writer on your system. There are several commands available, and the switches associated with each command can also be confusing. But remember that, in this chapter, we're making the Linux desktop as user-friendly as possible, so our focus in this annoyance is on GUI tools, specifically Nautilus and K3b.

Regular users want to be able to write to DVDs: when they copy their home movies, when they back up their home directories, and more. Therefore, in this annoyance, I show you how you can use Nautilus and K3b to write to DVDs, so you can show regular users how these tools work. While command-line tools can do more, regular users will lose interest if you go beyond the simplest commands. The issues associated with this annoyance also apply to CDs.

 A wide variety of excellent tools can write to DVDs. It's unfortunate that I cannot cover them all in this book. They include *gnomebaker*, *xcdroast*, *dvd::rip*, and more.

DVD Standards and Packages

If you're discussing DVD writing with regular users, you need to make sure you're conversant with the lingo. As DVD recording is not a core skill, Linux geeks may not be up to speed on the wide variety of standards associated with DVD recorders. It's important to keep the definitions straight, as described in Table 2-2.

Table 2-2. DVD definitions

Acronym	Definition
DVD	Digital Versatile (formerly Video) Disc
DVD-Video	The standard associated with movie DVDs
DVD+R DVD-R	DVD Recordable (the difference between DVD+R and DVD-R may not be relevant with the latest hardware)
DVD+RW DVD-RW	DVD Rewritable (the difference between DVD+RW and DVD-RW may not be relevant with the latest hardware)
DVD-RAM	DVD Random Access Memory
DVD-5	Standard single-sided single-layer DVDs, which contain up to 4.7 GB of data; insufficient for standard movies
DVD-9	Standard single-sided double-layer DVDs, which contain up to 8.5 GB of data; often known as DVD DL

Table 2-2. DVD definitions (continued)

Acronym	Definition
DVD-10	Standard double-sided single-layer DVDs, which contain up to 9.4 GB of data
DVD-18	Standard double-sided double-layer DVDs, which contain up to 17.1 GB of data
El Torito	Bootable DVD format
UDF	Universal Disk Format, which supports reads and writes to a DVD as if it were a conventional computer hard disk
ISO-9660	The older DVD mount format, which supports only 8.3 filenames
Rock Ridge	Extensions to ISO-9660, which support long filenames

I've listed just a few of the DVD "standards." Yes, there are more. For more information, see *http://www.dvdforum.org*. The difference between DVD+ and DVD- formats does still matter in a few current PCs. Check your hardware documentation if you're not sure.

With these standards in mind, you need to at least be aware of the free space on your partitions. If you're copying a DVD-18 disc, you need to make sure that you have a bit more than 18 GB of space available on the receiving partition.

The packages you need vary somewhat by distribution. In most cases, you'll need the *dvd+rw-tools* package.

If you're writing to a DVD+-R, you'll need the *dvdrecord*, *cdrecord*, or *cdrecord-dvd* commands, most commonly associated with the *cdrecord* package. If you're writing to a DVD+-RW, you'll want the *dvd+rw-tools* package. Some DVD+RW drives require the associated *dvd+rw-format* command to format a disc, before you use *growisofs* to record to that disc. For any DVD format, *growisofs* is important for writing from ISO files.

If you're backing up an existing DVD, you'll probably be interested in the *dvdbackup* command. You can create an ISO and then follow up with the *growisofs* to record to the disc.

 With modern Linux distributions, associated with kernel 2.6, you do not need SCSI emulation, associated with directives such as hdc=ide-scsi, in the bootloader. Modern Linux distributions work fine with IDE DVD writers.

As the focus in this annoyance is on the regular user, I'll go back to discussing the GUI tools available for Linux.

The KDE DVD Writer

If you don't see the KDE DVD writer on your system, you'll need to install the *k3b* package. The steps required to start it from the KDE Desktop vary slightly by distribution:

In Debian Linux
  Click on the K menu button → Multimedia → CD & DVD Burning.

In SUSE Linux
  Click on the K menu button → Multimedia → CD & DVD Burning → K3b.

In Red Hat / Fedora Linux
  Click on the K menu button → Sound and Video → K3b.

Once started, the KDE DVD Writer works in same way on all these distributions. In brief, you'll create a project, add files to it, and then write to the DVD. Alternatively, if you already have a DVD ISO image, you can burn it directly to the DVD.

For the purpose of this annoyance, I'll illustrate how I used K3b to copy a DVD movie, specifically one of my wedding. The procedure I've followed allows me to work with a PC that has only one DVD drive and to make multiple copies of my wedding. If you're using DVD+/-RW discs, you'll have to format them first, taking the following steps:

1. Insert the DVD+/-RW disc that you want to use.

2. Open the KDE "CD Kreator" program, K3b. Click on the K menu button → Multimedia → CD & DVD Burning (K3b).

   The menu steps required to access K3b vary by distribution; complete the steps appropriately for your users.

3. Once K3b - The CD Kreator opens, click Tools → DVD → Format DVD-RW/DVD+RW. This opens the DVD Formatting - K3b window.

4. If you have more than one DVD or CD drive, verify the Burning Device. You want to make sure that you're formatting the right disc! Auto speed is the default and should be good for most DVD writers. If you have problems, use a low speed (relative to the capability of the drive) to minimize the risk of errors.

5. Activate the Quick Format option. This should be sufficient. If you have problems, return to this window and try activating the Force option as well.

6. When you're satisfied with the settings, click Start.

Once the process is complete, you're ready to write to this DVD+/-RW disc.

 The command that K3b performed here is *dvd+rw-format -gui -force /dev/hdc*.

Now to copy a DVD movie, take the following steps:

1. Insert the DVD movie that you want to copy.
2. Open the KDE "CD Kreator" program, K3b. Click on the K Menu button → Multimedia → CD & DVD Burning (K3b).

   The menu steps required to access K3b vary by distribution; complete the steps appropriately for your users.
3. Once K3b - The CD Kreator opens, click File → New Project → New Video DVD Project. You'll see a new project in the bottom of the screen, as shown in Figure 2-2.

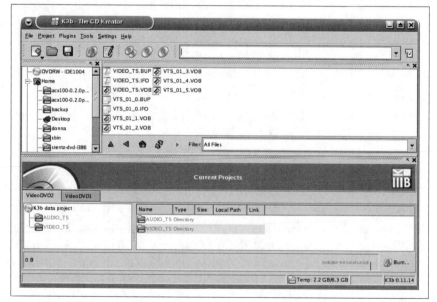

Figure 2-2. The KDE K3b CD Kreator

 If appropriate, tell your users that the DVD copy functionality in K3b doesn't work for commercial movies, as copying does not encode the DVD in the format required by DVD players.

4. Click on the icon associated with your DVD player. Highlight all folders in this directory, and click and drag them to the DVD title associated with the current K3b project. You may need to complete this process one folder at a time.

5. Once you've copied all folders from the DVD to the project, click the Burn button in the lower-right corner. This opens the VideoDVD Project window. Click the Volume Desc tab.

   Naturally, I did not want my wedding DVD labeled with K3b default settings, so I made some changes. You can assign a name for the volume, the publisher, the preparer, the system, and finally the application. These all become part of the label assigned to the DVD.

   If you're making more than one copy of the DVD, you may want to click Save User Defaults, so you don't have to re-enter these settings.

6. Click the Writing tab. Activate the Only Create Image option. As shown in the Temporary File area, this creates an image in the */tmp/kde-$USER/* directory by default (where *$USER* is your username; if no filename is already in the text box, you'll also want to assign an *.iso* file, such as *wedding.iso*). You can change the directory and filename.

   Pay attention to the numbers in the Temporary File area. It lists the free space in the temporary directory, as well as the size of the project. If the project size is greater than the space available, you'll need to find a partition mounted on a different directory with sufficient space.

   If you want to keep the *.iso* file for future use, don't save it in the */tmp* directory. If you do, K3b deletes it after you close the application. A simple alternative is to save the *.iso* file in your home directory, such as */home/michael/wedding.iso*.

7. When you're satisfied with the settings, click Burn. K3b proceeds to write the data from your DVD to the image file assigned. Naturally, with the many gigabytes of data associated with DVDs, this process can take several minutes. Be patient!

   Once complete, if you're a Linux power user, you may be interested in what was done. If you are, click Show Debugging Output. At the end of the output, you'll see the command that was run. In my case, it was:

   ```
   /usr/bin/mkisofs -gui -graft-points -volid Donna and Mike's Wedding -
   volset  -appid K3b -publisher Michael Jang -preparer Michael Jang -sysid
   LINUX -volset-size 1 -volset-seqno 1 -sort /tmp/kde-michael/k3bUgE9Ca.
   tmp -rational-rock -hide-list /tmp/kde-michael/k3bfPYE2a.tmp -full-
   iso9660-filenames -follow-links -iso-level 2 -path-list /tmp/kde-
   michael/k3b6DAEea.tmp -dvd-video /tmp/kde-michael/k3bVideoDvd0 /home/
   michael/.kde/share/apps/k3b/temp/dummydir0/
   ```

   (Don't include this in your instructions—it will overwhelm your users!)

8. Press Close to return to the main K3b - The CD Creator screen.

9. Now you can write this temporary file to a new DVD. Insert a DVD-R into an appropriate drive.

10. Click Tools → DVD → Burn DVD ISO Image. This opens the Burn ISO-9660 Image - K3b window.

11. In the Image To Burn text box, enter the *.iso* file for the image you just created. In my case, it's */tmp/kde-michael/wedding.iso*. You can navigate to the appropriate directory on your system; click the folder to the right of the Image To Burn text box.

12. If you have more than one DVD or CD drive, verify the Burning Device.

13. Verify the speed. Make sure it doesn't exceed the capabilities of your drive, or there will likely be errors in writing the video. Auto is normally the best option for most DVD writers.

14. Verify the Writing Mode; options include DAO (Disk-at-once, which fixes the DVD after the information is written), Overwrite (which may be appropriate for DVD+/-RW discs), and Incremental (which can allow you to add more data to the DVD disc at a later time). If you're unfamiliar with these terms, select Auto.

15. Select an appropriate number of copies. When you're satisfied with the settings, click Start. The writing proceeds.

16. Once writing is complete, you'll see a Show Debugging Output button. If you're interested, you can click this button and see the command that Linux ran in the bottom of the output.

    ```
    /usr/bin/growisofs -Z /dev/hdd=/tmp/kde-michael/wedding.iso -use-the-
    force-luke=notray -use-the-force-luke=tty -speed=4
    ```

17. If you've chosen to write to more than one DVD, you'll be prompted to enter another disc. When you do, the prompt should disappear.

Nautilus Also Writes to DVDs

If you don't see the Nautilus File Browser on your system, you'll need to install the *nautilus* package. To burn images to a DVD (or CD), you may also need the *nautilus-cd-burner* package. The steps required to start Nautilus from the GNOME Desktop may vary slightly by distribution and version.

To start Nautilus, click Applications → File Manager, or Places → Home Directory. Once Nautilus opens, click Places → CD Creator, or Go → CD/DVD Creator. (The steps have changed with recent versions of GNOME.) You'll now show your users how they can write their home directories to a DVD.

If you want to write the contents of your home directory to a DVD, take the following steps:

1. Log in to the GNOME Desktop Environment. Open Nautilus. Depending on your distribution, you may be able to do so by clicking a File Cabinet on the top taskbar, clicking Applications → File Browser, or clicking Places → Home Directory. This opens Nautilus, displaying your home directory.

   As an administrator, you'll want to narrow things down for your users. If they're on a SUSE workstation, for instance, they're not interested in instructions associated with a Red Hat desktop. The instructions also vary if your user has downloaded an ISO file; a simple description follows these steps.

2. Click Places → CD Creator. You'll see a second window labeled CD/DVD Creator.

3. In the first Nautilus window, highlight the files you want to back up. It's easy to display files in different folders just by clicking on them. If you want to back up all files in the folder currently displayed, press Ctrl-A, and then click and drag all of your files to the CD/DVD Creator window.

4. Once the icons are copied to the CD/DVD Creator window, click File → Write to Disc. This opens the Write to Disc window.

5. Verify the options in the Write to Disc window. If you have more than one DVD or CD drive, you'll want to make sure you're writing to the right drive. You can and should use the name of your choice. Unless you have problems, set the Write Speed to Maximum Possible. If you do have problems, make sure to set a speed below the rated capability of the DVD writer.

6. Once you're satisfied with the options, place a DVD in the drive, and click Write.

   If this is a new DVD+/-RW disc, the process may take longer, as Nautilus fixates the disc before starting the write process.

If you're trying to write the *contents* of an *.iso* file to a DVD, right-click on the file. In the pop-up menu, select Write to Disk. This opens the Write to Disk window, which by default writes the contents of the *.iso* file to the writable media in your DVD drive.

I Don't Remember Where That File Is

With the thousands of files available on a Linux computer, people need help finding files now and then. For geeks, the two basic tools are *find* and *locate*.

For regular users, there are KDE and GNOME search tools that are front-ends to the *find* and *locate* commands.

The first part of this annoyance is a review of these commands for geeks. The second part covers the KDE and GNOME tools that your users will demand on their workstations. The key difference between these tools is that by default, the GNOME Search for Files tool uses *locate*, and the KDE Find Files tool uses *find*. As you should already know as a Linux geek, while *locate* works more quickly, it is less reliable than *find*.

The find Command

The *find* command is rich and complex. While I cannot cover everything that you can do with *find*, this book would not be complete without a discussion of it. If you need more information, refer to a book such as *Unix Power Tools* by Shelley Powers et al. (O'Reilly). The basic format of the *find* command is as follows:

```
find path operators
```

When you run this command, the *path* is the directory in which *find* should start looking. In other words, if you set the *path* to */home/michael*, *find* looks in that directory and its subdirectories. It does not move up the directory tree. With the right *operators*, you can specify limitations, such as the file owner.

With the following examples, I describe some of the ways you can use the *find* command. In current Linux distributions, results are automatically sent to the screen; on older distributions, or some versions of Unix, you may need to add the *-print* option.

```
find .
```
Lists all files and subdirectories in the current directory, recursively.

```
find Desktop
```
Displays all files in the directory named *Desktop* right under the current directory.

```
find /home -name Downloads
```
Shows the location of every file or directory with the name *Downloads* that is somewhere in the */home* directory tree.

```
find . -perm 777
```
Finds the location of all files under the current directory with read, write, and execute permissions for all users.

```
find /etc -type l
```
Lists all files in the */etc* directory tree that are links (*l*) to other files; other types include *d* for a directory or *b* for a block file, which is characteristic of some devices. For the full list, see the manpage for *find*.

```
find /tmp -user michael
```
Shows all files in the */tmp* directory that belong to user *michael*; you can substitute a user ID number.

```
find /tmp -group users
```
Shows all files in the */tmp* directory that belong to the group *users*; you can substitute a group ID number.

```
find / -size +20000
```
Displays all files on your system with more than 20,000 blocks; as each block is 512 bytes, this specifies all files larger than approximately 10 MB. If you don't have enough space on your system, this can help you find huge files that you may have forgotten, such as DVD ISOs.

```
find /home/michael -atime -1
```
Finds all files last accessed in the past day (within the past 24 hours).

```
find /home/michael -ctime -2
```
Finds all files last changed in the past two days (within the past 48 hours).

```
find . -mtime +30 -type f -exec rm {} \;
```
Finds and deletes all files modified more than 30 days ago.

Any combination of these options can be specified to narrow the search further. For instance, if you specify both the *-user* and *-perm* options, files must match both the user and the permissions in order to be displayed.

You can configure search terms with multiple words or wildcards, as long as they're in single or double quotes. For example, if you mounted a Microsoft partition on */mnt/dos*, you could find the path to the *My Documents* directory with the following command:

```
find /mnt/dos -name "My Documents"
```

You can configure wildcards in the search in quotes as well. Alternatively, you can "escape" the meaning of a wildcard. For example, if you need to find files whose names contain a quote mark, you might run a search command such as:

```
find / -name \"Documents
```

The locate Command

The *locate* command works more quickly than *find*. It works from a database of files, normally updated as a daily cron job. It works as a *grep*-based compressed database; in other words, wildcards such as the asterisk are not required. Normally, the database is configured to exclude files and directories mounted from network and temporary drives. The database is not updated if your computer is not running when the cron job is scheduled. In other words, if you turn your computers off at night, you may want to reschedule daily cron jobs to make sure this database is up-to-date.

Each of our major distributions configures the *locate* command and associated databases slightly differently:

Red Hat/Fedora
Red Hat/Fedora distributions install by default a secure version of *locate*, known as *slocate* (now *mlocate*, as of Fedora Core 5). It's configured through the */etc/updatedb.conf* file, where you can enable daily updates of the database, and exclude appropriate directories such as */tmp* and network filesystems such as NFS.

SUSE
If you want to take advantage of the *locate* utility on SUSE Linux, you'll have to install the *findutils-locate* RPM. If you do, you can configure its operation in the */etc/sysconfig/locate* configuration file, where you can enable daily updates of the database, and exclude unwanted directories such as */tmp* and network filesystems such as NFS.

Debian
Debian includes the *find* and *locate* utilities in the *findutils* DEB package. In a fashion similar to Red Hat/Fedora, you can configure how the *locate* database is kept up-to-date in the */etc/updatedb.conf* file. When you configure that file, you can exclude unwanted directories such as */tmp* and network filesystems such as NFS.

GNOME File Search Tool

You certainly don't expect ordinary Linux users to manage with the *find* and *locate* commands. Even many Linux geeks have trouble remembering all the associated options. This is one area where GUI tools can help. For example, the GNOME Search for Files tool serves as a frontend to the *find*, *locate*, and *grep* commands, used together. You can open this tool with the *gnome-search-tool* command.

The default settings for the Search for Files tool use the database associated with the *locate* command. If the database hasn't been updated in eight days, the user will see a warning message. When properly configured, the database is updated nightly as a cron job, as described earlier in this annoyance.

This is a very straightforward tool, as shown in Figure 2-3. As you can see, I've activated the "Show more options" settings, which allow you to modify the search by date, size, ownership, links, and more.

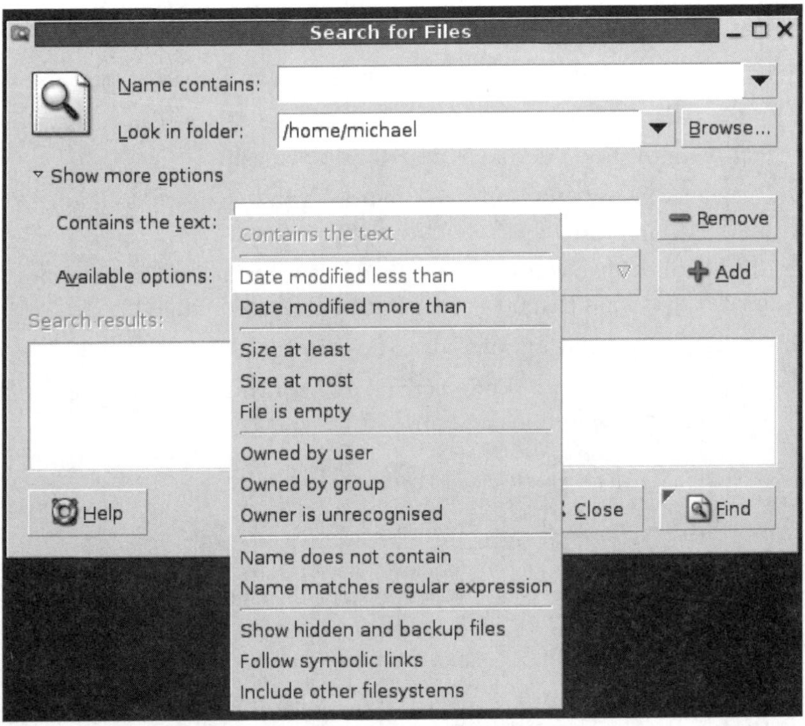

Figure 2-3. The GNOME Search for Files tool

This tool is closely related to the *grep* command. For more information on *grep*, see the next annoyance. For instructions that can help your users, you might adapt the following steps (if necessary, include screenshots with every step to help your users visualize the process):

1. To start searching for files, click Places → Search for Files. This opens the Search for Files window. If you're running an older version of GNOME, such as that associated with Red Hat Enterprise Linux 4 (GNOME 2.8), click Actions → Search for Files.

2. Enter the name of the file that you're looking for in the "Name contains" text box. Partial names are acceptable.

3. By default, the Search for Files tool starts the search in your home directory. If you have permission, you may be able to look for files in other users' home directories. To do so, substitute */home* in the "Look in folder" text box. If your administrator has configured downloads in the */tmp* directory, you may want to search that as well in order to find files left around by your programs.

4. Click Find once you're satisfied with the search parameters. If the search takes too long, you can click Stop during the process.

If you want to limit the search to files with specific characteristics, use the following steps:

1. Start with the first three steps described previously.

2. Click the "Show more options" button. You'll see two additional settings: "Contains the text" and "Available options."

   I'll describe what you can do with the first option in the next annoyance. You'll want to modify your instructions accordingly.

3. Click the "Available options" drop-down menu.

   You'll see a number of options that can help you limit your file search. They include the options described in Table 2-3.

Table 2-3. Search for Files available options

Option	Description
Date modified less than	Searches for relatively new files; specifies how many days (maximum) are allowed to have passed since the file was last modified.
Date modified more than	Searches for relatively old files; specifies how many days must have passed (at minimum) since the file was last modified.
Size at least	Searches for files of at least a certain size, in kilobytes.
Size at most	Searches for files of less than a certain size, in kilobytes.
File is empty	Limits the search to files with 0 kilobytes.
Owned by user	Limits the search to files owned by the user of your choice.
Owned by group	Limits the search to files owned by the group of your choice.
Name does not contain	Limits the search to files whose names do not contain a specified search term.
Name matches regular expression	Searches for files whose names match the specified regular expression; allows you to specify a second search term.
Show hidden and backup files	Adds hidden and backup files to the search.
Follow symbolic links	Searches outside the directory path via symbolic links (see your administrator if you're interested in an explanation).
Include other filesystems	Allows you to search on other filesystems, such as remote directories mounted via Samba.

Select the option of your choice, and click Add. If appropriate, another text box will appear, where you can add information such as the user, file size, or age.

4. Repeat step 3 as desired.

5. Once you've specified your file search parameters, click Find. If the search takes too long, you can click Stop during the process.

You should customize these instructions for your users. For example, if your users are primarily accountants, you could set up a specific example on how they could search through spreadsheet files such as *client1.xls* through *client199.xls* with a specific filename pattern, such as *client1*.xls*.

KDE File Search Tool

KDE has a file search tool similar to GNOME's. While configured differently, it is still a frontend to the *find* and *grep* commands, used together. You can open this tool with the *kfind* command.

The KDE search tool is also straightforward. While it divides search settings into three different tabs—Name/Location, Contents, and Properties—the overall capabilities are almost identical to the GNOME Search for Files tool.

For more information on the workings of the *grep* command, see the next annoyance. For instructions that can help your users, you might adapt the following steps (if necessary, include screenshots with every step to help your users visualize the process):

1. To start searching for files, click the K menu → Find Files. This opens the Find Files window.

   In some cases, the menu entry may be Find Files/Folders.

2. Enter the name of the file that you're looking for in the Named text box. By default, you'll need the full name of the file or directory that you need.

   If you don't know the full name of the file/directory you need, activate the "Use files index" option. This points the Find Files tool at the *locate* database described earlier.

   If you see an error message saying that the database is too old, consult your administrator for help on updating it for your newest files.

3. By default, the Find Files tool starts the search in your home directory. If you have permission, you may be able to look for files in other users' home directories. To do so, substitute */home* in the "Look in" text box. If your administrator has configured downloads in the */tmp* directory, you may want to search that as well.

4. If you're satisfied with the search parameters, skip to step 6. If you want to limit the search to a specific file type, click the Contents tab.

5. Under the Contents tab, click the "File type" drop-down menu. Select one of the available file types, as described in Table 2-4.

Table 2-4. Find Files Contents tab file-type options

Option	Description
All Files and Folders	Searches through and returns all matching entries in files and folders.
Files	Limits the search to files, not folders (directories).
Folders	Limits the search to folders.
Symbolic Links	Limits the search to files that are linked to others (see your administrator if you're interested in an explanation).
Special Files	Searches for nonstandard files, such as devices; this should not concern regular users.
Executable Files	Limits the search to files that you can run as programs.
SUID Executable Files	Limits the search to special files (normally owned by the administrative user) that you can run as programs.
All Images	Limits the search to all image files as defined by your administrator; may not include all image types.
All Video	Limits the search to all video files as defined by your administrator; may not include all video/movie file types.
All Sounds	Limits the search to all sound files as defined by your administrator; may not include all categories of sound files.
Additional settings	Allows you to select from a wide variety of file formats.

If you want to limit the search to a specific file creation time, size, or owner, click the Properties tab.

You can specify a file creation/modification date range, file size minimum or maximum, and the user or group that owns the file.

6. Click Find once you're satisfied with the search parameters. If the search takes too long, you can click Stop during the process.

You should customize these instructions for your users. For example, if your users are primarily design engineers who use a computer-aided design (CAD) system, you could set up a specific example on how they could search for CAD drawing files with a specific filename pattern, such as *project1*.cad*.

I Need to Search Within a Bunch of Files

The *grep* commands work well in Linux because most Linux files are text files. That means *grep* can read through most Linux files of your choice and display the lines with patterns that match the search terms of your choice.

Naturally, the *grep* command, by itself, is suitable only for advanced users. However, the GNOME and KDE file search tools can serve as GUI "front-ends" to the *grep* command for regular users.

The grep Command

There are several related commands that are simply subsets of *grep*. For example, *egrep* is the same as *grep -e*, *fgrep* is the same as *grep -f*, and *rgrep* is the same as *grep -r*.

The GUI tools described in the previous annoyance are also, in part, front-ends to the *grep* command. You can use them to search through the files in the directories you need with the search term of your choice.

This section does not really address an annoyance but provides a detailed description of the *grep* commands. Understanding *grep* is an important skill to addressing other annoyances.

The simplest version of the *grep* command searches within the current directory. For example, the following command searches for all instances of the word "Linux" within the current directory:

```
grep Linux *
```

Unfortunately, this command may do less than you expect. It does not search in hidden files, nor through files in subdirectories. But the output does at least identify the file that contains the search term; for example, the output from this command in my home directory starts with:

```
acroread: Linux)
```

which tells me that the search term Linux exists in the *acroread* file. If you want to search hidden files in the current directory, use the expression and wildcard associated with hidden files. In this case, it would be:

```
grep Linux .*
```

If you want to search in subdirectories, you can search recursively. That's the function of the *rgrep* command, which you can also run as *grep -r*:

```
grep -r Linux .
```

Note that I use the dot to represent the current directory; this command starts in the current directory and then searches files in subdirectories.

 The *rgrep* command is available only for current versions of Debian Linux.

Naturally, you can use multiple words in the search term; all you need are quotes. For example, I can find all instances of "Red Hat" in my directories with the following command (I add the -s switch to suppress error messages;

otherwise, you'll see a bunch when *grep* tries to search inside a directory as if it were a file):

```
grep -rs 'Red Hat' .
```

Many other searches are possible; for more information, see the manpages associated with the *grep* command. For some of the more important *grep* switches, see Table 2-5.

Table 2-5. Some important grep switches

Switch	Description
-a	Includes binary files in the *grep* search.
-c	Substitutes the number of lines in each file that match the search term for regular *grep* output.
-e	Equivalent to the *egrep* command; one good option if you're using a search pattern that starts with a dot.
-i	Ignores the case in the search term.
-n	Includes the line number where the search term is found in the noted files.
-o	Does not display the part of the line other than the search term.
-r	Searches recursively in subdirectories.
-s	Skips error messages.

Searching Within Files in GNOME

The GNOME Search for Files tool can help you find text within files. For more information on this tool, see the previous annoyance. Briefly, if you want to help your users run this tool to search within files, modify and distribute the following instructions.

It's important to emphasize to your users that searches for text within files do not work with binary files such as Adobe PDF or OpenOffice.org documents. This warning is necessary in part because Microsoft Office (for Windows and Macintosh) search tools are built to open and read the binary formats of files known to the system. However, you can emphasize that searches work well with text files such as IM transcripts.

The following steps are one example of what you can give to your users to help them search through files in their home directories:

1. To start searching for files, click Places → Search for Files. This opens the Search for Files window.

   If you're running an older version of GNOME, such as that associated with Red Hat Enterprise Linux 4 (GNOME 2.8), click Actions → Search for Files.

2. In the "Name contains" text box, while not required, you can enter the name of the file or the directory with files that you want to search.

3. Click "Show more options." In the "Contains the text" text box, enter the term you want for your search, and click Find.

   When complete, you'll see a list of files that match your search term. If the search takes too long, you can click Stop at any time.

You should modify these instructions to reflect a real search appropriate to your organization. For example, if you've configured your IM tool to save communication logs as *.im files, you could use that as a search term in the "Name contains" text box.

Searching Within Files in KDE

The KDE Find Files tool can also help you find text within files. For more information on this tool, see the previous annoyance. It's more capable than the GNOME tool, as it allows you to search within binary OpenOffice.org documents, spreadsheets, and presentation files.

Whether you configure the GNOME or KDE tool, it's important to emphasize to your users that tools that search for text within files do not work with binary files such as Adobe PDF documents because the tools don't understand these formats.

Briefly, if you want to help your users run this tool to search within files, modify the following instructions:

1. To start searching for files, click the K menu → Find Files. This opens the Find Files window.

   In some cases, the menu entry may be Find Files/Folders.

2. If available, enter the name of the file or wildcards associated with the files that you're looking through in the Named text box. For example, if you want to search through your OpenOffice.org Writer files, enter *.sxw or *.odt.

   If you don't know the full name of the file/directory you need, activate the "Use files index" option. This points the Find Files tool at the file database described earlier.

3. Select the Contents tab. Enter the desired search term in the box associated with "Containing text," and click Find.

   When complete, you'll see a list of files that match your search term. If the search takes too long, you can click Stop at any time.

You should modify these instructions to reflect a real search appropriate to your organization. For example, if you've configured your IM tool to save communication logs as *.im files, you could use that as a search term under the Contents tab in the "Containing text" box.

I Can't Copy from the Command Line

Long commands can be annoying. It's easy to forget the full directory path to desired commands. It's easy to forget which switches you used, and the sequence of switches and other arguments you need to use.

I address this annoyance in three ways. First, I show how you can use the history of previous commands to help you run a long command. Second, I show you how you can add a directory to your PATH, which can minimize the length of more common commands. Finally, I show you how you can configure a long command in a dedicated script that's easier to run from the command line. It helps if you add these scripts to directories in your PATH.

 As this annoyance is related to the command-line interface, the annoyance is described only from the point of view of a Linux administrator. Any Linux user who is comfortable with the command-line interface can also use the lessons from this annoyance.

Using Your History

When you run a long command for the first time, it takes work. You may have read through the associated manpages to find the right arguments. You may have searched through your system to find the directory with the command you need.

You may not run a command like the following very often:

```
/home/michael/Desktop/scripts/dbmanage -opcg /home/michael/Desktop/process/
logwriter
```

If you have to rerun the command again, you may not remember the function of the -o, -p, -c, and -g switches. You might not remember the directory with the hypothetical *dbmanage* command or the *logwriter* file.

If you've run a command before, the easiest way to run it again is to use your history of previous commands. By default, the last 1,000 commands are available in the ~/.bash_history file. The number of commands in this file is associated with the HISTSIZE directive in /etc/profile.

You can scroll through the list of previous commands with the up and down arrows on the keyboard. With the Page Up and Page Down keys, you can move to the top and bottom of the history. Once you find the command you need, just press Enter.

If you've run the desired command on another system, you can use the middle mouse button to copy the command (see the next section).

But scrolling through 1,000 commands can be a drag. As with any other Linux command, you can use *grep* to search through the output. For example, to find the *find* commands in your history, use the following command:

```
history | grep find
```

As a Linux geek, you probably use the *find* command often, so you may see a number of lines such as:

```
387  find | xargs grep -3 -s 'bashrc' | more
526  find . -atime +7 -name users -print | exec grep -1 linux {}
```

Notice how each command is associated with a number, which represents the sequence in your command history. For example, if you want to run command number 387 again on the local computer, you don't have to retype the command; just "bang" out the number:

```
!387
```

The "bang" in Linux is an exclamation point. In this case, it allows you to specify the command number from your history that you want to run. (Within many commands, it allows you to specify "anything but" the term you use.) In other words, you can tell your friends that "bang" is actually an important technical term.

If you don't remember the number, bang out the first few letters. For example, if you've run a complex *iptables* command recently and need to run it again, enter the following at your shell prompt:

```
!iptables
```

But be careful; if there is more than one *iptables* command in your history, you may need more information, as *!iptables* runs the most recent *iptables* command in your history.

Copying with the Middle Mouse Button

It's often not enough to search through the history of previous commands. You may want to apply the command of your choice on different computers. If you create an encrypted password at the command line, you may want to transfer it to a configuration file. These situations are when the middle mouse button can be most helpful.

If you already have a middle mouse button, great! If you see only two buttons, you should still be able to access the middle button's functionality. If you have a scroll wheel, press on it. If it clicks, it may already be configured as a middle mouse button. If your mouse has only two buttons, and no scroll wheel, click on both together. Linux often configures this action as the click of a middle mouse button.

 If your middle mouse button doesn't work using the instructions described here, see "My Mouse Doesn't Do What I Want" in Chapter 1.

Now to see if the middle mouse button works for copying commands, take the following steps:

1. Open a command-line console in the GUI or from a command-line interface.

   If your mouse is properly enabled, you should be able to left-click, drag, and highlight the text of your choice in the console. If you're in the text console and your mouse doesn't work, try it in a GUI-based console, such as konsole, gnome-terminal, or xterm.

2. Run a command, or find one in the output of the *history* command.

3. Highlight the command.

4. With the text still highlighted, open another text console.

5. Click the middle mouse button, or use one of the related techniques described earlier in this section. If your middle mouse button is properly enabled, the command you highlighted in the first console will be pasted into the second.

The middle mouse button is also good for other purposes, such as transferring encrypted passwords. For example, to add a password to the GRUB configuration file, the best course is to use GRUB's own command for creating an encrypted password, *grub-md5-crypt*, and then to paste it into the GRUB configuration file in a text editor.

For example, if you want to add an encrypted password to the */boot/grub/menu.lst* configuration file, take the following steps:

1. Run the *grub-md5-crypt* command. Its location varies depending on your distribution.
2. When prompted, enter the password of your choice and confirm.
3. You'll see an encrypted password in the output, such as:

   ```
   $1$AGpe11$/8PRQuTCbVTxMMHoRbTmB/
   ```

   You certainly wouldn't want to have to retype this password. Any error in retyping the 32 characters in this encrypted password would change the password.
4. Highlight the encrypted password.
5. Open another console, and open the */boot/grub/menu.lst* configuration file in a text editor.
6. Insert the following command before the stanzas associated with individual boot options:

   ```
   password --md5
   ```
7. Stay in insert mode. Add a space after the command. Click the middle mouse button. This action should insert the encrypted password into the GRUB configuration file.
8. Save and close the GRUB configuration file. The next time you boot using GRUB, you'll notice that a password is required before you can modify GRUB, such as if you want to boot into Single User Mode.

Adding a Directory to Your Path

If you haven't run a complex command before, you can still create a short-cut by taking advantage of your PATH. While the command completion feature associated with the bash shell can help you complete long paths to a specific command, it's still easier if you add directories with key scripts and commands to your PATH—or modify your PATH to reflect the scripts you need.

Defining your current PATH

But first, you need to figure out the directories in your current PATH. Then you can see what directories you need to add. To find the directories in your PATH, run the following command:

```
echo $PATH
```

The output includes the directories in your PATH. Linux distributions define different values for PATH. If you work with different distributions, the variations can be annoying. For example, my systems have the following values for PATH:

Debian
/usr/local/bin:/usr/bin:/bin:/usr/X11R6/bin:/usr/games

SUSE
/home/michael/bin:/usr/local/bin:/usr/bin:/usr/X11R6/bin:/bin:/usr/games:/opt/gnome/bin:/opt/kde3/bin:/usr/lib/jvm/jre/bin:/usr/lib/mit/bin:/usr/lib/mit/sbin:/usr/lib/mit/bin:/home/michael/sbin

Red Hat Enterprise Linux
/usr/kerberos/bin:/home/michael/sbin:/usr/local/bin:/bin:/usr/bin:/usr/X11R6/bin:/home/michael/bin

Fedora Linux
/usr/kerberos/bin:/usr/local/bin:/bin:/usr/bin:/usr/X11R6/bin:/home/michael/bin

If you've installed software from source code on downloaded tarballs, key files may get unpacked to the same directory on all distributions. You may want to make sure that directory is copied to your PATH on your systems.

When you run a command, your shell searches files in your PATH from left to right. In other words, if there were an *ls* command in the */usr/local/bin* directory, Linux would run that command instead of the standard */bin/ls*.

In fact, the PATH is one way a cracker can wreck havoc. For example, if a cracker found a way to modify the *su* command to send the root password to another computer, he could break right into your system with administrative privileges. All he would need to do is copy this command to a higher-level directory in your PATH, such as */usr/local/bin*.

Adding to your PATH

If you're going to run a number of commands from a directory not in your PATH, you should add it. If you want to add it for all users, modify your */etc/profile*. The best way to modify this file varies by distribution.

Some distributions, including SUSE Linux, suggest that you use another file, such as */etc/profile.local*, for edits you make from the command-line interface. Otherwise, be sure to back up any key configuration file before editing it.

SUSE and Debian specify the directories associated with the PATH directive separately for the *root* and for other users. In their versions of */etc/profile*, the *root* user's PATH is associated with User ID 0. For example, in SUSE Linux, the following directive in */etc/profile* specifies directories for User ID 0:

```
test "$UID" = 0 && PATH=/sbin:/usr/sbin:/usr/local/sbin:$PATH
```

But the objective here is to add the *~/sbin* directory to the PATH for regular users. If you're running SUSE Linux, add the following directive to the */etc/profile.local* configuration file:

```
PATH=$PATH:$HOME/sbin
```

If you're running Debian Linux, edit the following stanza in */etc/profile*:

```
if [ "`id -u`" -eq 0 ]; then
  PATH="/usr/local/sbin:/usr/local/bin:/usr/sbin:/usr/bin:/sbin:/bin:/usr/
bin/X11"
else
  PATH="/usr/local/bin:/usr/bin:/bin:/usr/bin/X11:/usr/games"
fi
```

The conditional specifies a PATH for the *root* user; to modify the PATH for all regular users, you would modify the directive associated with ELSE. Therefore, to add the *~/sbin* directory to the path for all regular users, you would modify this directive to read:

```
PATH="/usr/local/bin:$HOME/sbin:/usr/bin:/bin:/usr/bin/X11:/usr/games"
```

Red Hat and Fedora Linux configure a pathmunge directive in their versions of */etc/profile*, which adds the noted directories one by one to the default PATH for the *root* user, in the following stanza:

```
if [ `id -u` = 0 ]; then
        pathmunge /sbin
        pathmunge /usr/sbin
        pathmunge /usr/local/sbin
  fi
```

You can add the directories of your choice to this stanza. For example, if you want to add the *$HOME/sbin* directory for regular users, add the following directives in that stanza:

```
                 else
        pathmunge $HOME/sbin
```

The next time you log in to one of these distributions as a regular user, run the *echo $PATH* command again. You'll see the desired directory in your PATH.

How Do I Deal with Spaces and Odd Characters in Filenames?

Sometimes, the defaults associated with Linux shells are annoying. For example, the spaces associated with many Microsoft directories, such as *My Directory*, can adversely affect a Linux command. Yes, you can use quotes, but if you have a variable or command inside the quotes, the wrong quote character can have unintended consequences. The asterisk (*) is a common character in many files, but it's also a wildcard. Therefore, if you want to search for an asterisk, you'll need to escape the meaning of the character.

You can manage the effect of spaces, special characters, commands, and variables with appropriate use of backslashes (\), single quotes ('), double quotes ("), and back quotes (`).

Single Quotes

Single quotes can help you manage spaces. For example, if you want to mount a shared "My Documents" directory from a Microsoft computer, you might try mounting it locally on the *test/* directory with the following command:

```
smbmount //allaccess/My Documents test
```

This assumes, of course, that you've shared the *My Documents* directory from the computer named *allaccess*.

Unfortunately, this command would lead to an error message relating to how Linux is unable to resolve the mount point Documents. In other words, it thinks you're trying to mount a directory, shared under the name "My," in the local Documents directory. The simplest solution is to use single quotes. In other words:

```
smbmount '//allaccess/My Documents' test
```

But if you're working with an expression where you want to process a variable such as $NAME or a command such as *date*, single quotes won't work. For example, you might find the following directive in a script:

```
echo 'Welcome to America, $USER'
```

And the output is:

```
Welcome to America, $USER
```

because single quotes prevent the shell from interpreting the *$USER* variable. Other options can process this variable, as I'm about to illustrate.

Double Quotes

Double quotes can help if you have variables in your expressions. For example, if you have the following directive in a script, the double quotes allow Linux to interpret the variable. Thus, the following directive:

```
echo "Welcome to America, $USER"
```

is interpreted on my user account as:

```
Welcome to America, michael
```

Back Quotes

The back quote (`` ` ``) key is commonly the lowercase character on the key above Tab on a U.S. keyboard. It is on the same key as the ~, which represents users' home directories. Sometimes known as a backtick, it allows you to process commands and scripts within quotes. For example, you might find the following directive in a welcome script:

```
echo "Welcome to America, $USER, it is now `/bin/date`"
```

This is interpreted on my user account as:

```
Welcome to America, michael; it is Wed Dec 10 16:05:13 PDT 2005
```

Escaping a Character

There are characters that can make life a bit more interesting on Linux. As described earlier, the space between "My" and "Documents" can make Linux think there's another expression in your command. If you're looking for an asterisk in the files of your home directory, the following command won't do what you want:

```
grep * *
```

While you might think this command searches for the asterisk (*) in all files in the local directory, you have to remember that the asterisk is itself a wildcard, a type of metacharacter. The shell doesn't use the asterisk as a search term. The shell interprets the asterisk before it is ever seen by the *grep* command, so the command uses the first file in your directory as a search term.

To make Linux use the asterisk as the search term, you have to "escape" the meaning of the character. To do so, you can use the backslash. In other works, the following command actually looks for the asterisk in all commands in the current directory:

```
grep \* *
```

But wait, the asterisk is actually a metacharacter in two ways—within the bash shell and as a *grep* search term. So while this command works, technically it needs to be escaped twice:

```
grep \\* *
```

The backslash is useful in other ways. For example, if you're constructing a long command in a script, a backslash can help you make the command more readable for others who review that script.

Users Are Complaining There's No ZIP

Users who are converting from Microsoft Windows depend on the various ZIP utilities that collect files together in an archive and compress them for easier transmission, such as by email.

You could teach your users about the switches associated with the *tar* command, but you have to remember the annoyances involved for users who already have problems with Linux.

For regular users, you'll need to create a step-by-step procedure. Your choices are either to create a procedure for using the *zip* command, for using the Archive Manager (sometimes known as the File Roller), or for connecting to the Archive Manager via the Nautilus File Browser. I provide one example of each in this annoyance.

One more element in this annoyance is how Microsoft uses *zip* compression, which is different from the *bzip* and *gzip* compression formats often popular in Linux archives. Not all Linux distributions install the *zip* package by default. (Remember to install it for the sake of your users!)

Installing the Components

If you don't install the right components, your users won't find all the features described in this annoyance, and they might believe that you're full of hogwash. (No offense intended to hogs....) For example, if you've forgotten to install the *file-roller* package, you won't be able to create an archive from the Nautilus utility. To ensure that the techniques in this annoyance work, make sure the following packages are installed:

- *tar*
- *file-roller*
- *zip*
- *nautilus*

KDE advocates might notice that I've left out Konqueror and the KDE archive utility, known as *ark*. As of this writing, these tools don't interact in the same way as the *file-roller* and Nautilus packages. As you'll see, Nautilus and *file-roller* work together in a fashion more familiar to Microsoft Windows users. And one key to overcoming the annoyances of regular users is to provide tools they find more familiar. Once installed, Nautilus and *file-roller* work the same way on the KDE Desktop.

While this discussion may annoy KDE users, my focus is on the best way to get Microsoft Windows users to convert to Linux. Your experience with your Microsoft users may vary. Both desktop environments provide excellent options for those converting from Microsoft Windows.

Helping Regular Users Zip Up

Most Linux geeks prefer to work at the command-line interface, because it includes more capabilities. The process of creating an archive is no exception. But if you want regular users to use command-line tools, you'll have to provide precise explanations. And as regular users work with others who work with Microsoft Windows, you'll have to make sure the archives they create are compatible with Microsoft-based tools.

Some Microsoft-based tools can handle Linux *tar* archives with ease. Others, including the native tool associated with Windows XP, can handle only Linux archives created with the ZIP-compatible utility.

The following is one example of instructions that you can share with your users. It can can help your users create a *.zip* archive compatible with Microsoft and Linux *zip* tools.

If you want to create a Microsoft-compatible *zip* archive for your files, follow these instructions:

- If the files you want to zip up (archive) are in your home directory, you can just add them to the zip file of your choice. For example, if you want to add a couple of pictures to a zip file named *mypics.zip*, run the following command:

      zip mypics picture1.tif picture2.tif

- If the files you want to zip are in a subdirectory, add an *-r* to the line and cite the subdirectory. For example, if you want to archive all of the files in your *lageeks/* subdirectory in a file named *geeks.zip*, run the following command (the *-r* makes *zip* recursively save all files in deeper subdirectories):

```
zip -r geeks lageeks/
```

- If you want an archive of your home directory, such as for backup purposes, the following command can place all visible and hidden directories into a file named *michael.zip*. This command includes hidden files, which contain configuration information rather than your own data:

```
zip -r michael .
```

- If you don't want to back up hidden files or directories, change the period to an asterisk:

```
zip -r michael *
```

- If you want to create an archive of files with similar names, you can use patterns that combine different kinds of characters. For example, if you want to archive all of your *.doc* files in your home directory, run the following command:

```
zip mydocs *.doc
```

You can now use the zipped archive file that you've created. You can copy it to another computer as a backup. You can even transmit this archive by email to other users.

You may want to create an alias for the *zip* command to automatically include files in lower-level directories. To modify the alias for all users, add a command such as alias zip='zip -r' to the global alias file, which is */etc/bash.bashrc* for Debian and SUSE, and */etc/bashrc* for Red Hat and Fedora.

Zipping with the Archive Manager

Many users are just more comfortable with the GUI. For those users, you can use (or, better yet, modify) the following directions to help them work with the Archive Manager, also known as the File Roller. I'll show you how to create a zipped archive of your documents in Linux, which you can share with your colleagues who use Microsoft Windows. If any of these instructions do not work, you may not have the required software installed and should contact your administrator.

The actual location of the Archive Manager in the GNOME and KDE GUI menus varies by distribution. If all of your users work with one desktop environment on one distribution, you can substitute appropriate directions from the GUI menu. Even if they work with more than one distribution or desktop, you may want to include directions anyway, in separate lists. After all, these are desktop users.

To create a zipped archive with the Archive Manager, follow these steps:

1. Press Alt-F2, enter `file-roller` in the Run Application text box, and click Run.

2. To create a new zipped archive, click New. This opens the New window. In the Name text box, enter the name you want for your archive—for example, *mydocs*. In the archive type, click the Archive Type drop-down menu and select Zip. Click New when you're finished. This returns you to the main Archive Manager window. You should now see the name of the archive you've selected—in this case, *mydocs.zip*—in the window title.

3. Click Add. This opens the Add Files window. You can now add the files of your choice to the archive. Click Add to return to the main Archive Manager window. Repeat the process as desired.

4. Choose Archive → Test Integrity. This tests the archive for errors.

5. Choose Archive → Quit. Your archive is now ready for use. Unless you've specified otherwise, the archive is in your home directory.

6. You can now share the archive. For example, when you're sending an email, you can attach the archive to your email in the same way as you attach any ordinary document or image.

In my opinion, these tools and the associated instructions are still awkward for regular users. They do not match the conveniences associated with Win-Zip or Windows XP Zip in a file manager such as Windows Explorer. However, there is another alternative.

Archiving and Zipping with Nautilus

As long as you have the packages mentioned earlier in "Installing the Components" installed, you can create zipped archives with current versions of the Nautilus File Browser. It's a fairly straightforward process, which you might document to your users with the following instructions.

I'll show you how to create a zipped archive of your documents in Linux, which you can share with your colleagues who use Microsoft Windows. If any of these instructions do not work, you may not have the required software installed and should contact your administrator:

1. If you're running the GNOME Desktop Environment, click on the file cabinet on the upper taskbar. If you're running the KDE Desktop Environment, press Alt-F2, type *nautilus*, and press Enter. You'll see the File Browser open, showing your home folder.

2. Select the files and/or folders you want to add to your archive. As with Microsoft Windows Explorer, you can use the Shift, Ctrl, and arrow keys to help you select more than one file and folder.

   If you're interested in making your own backups, press Ctrl-A. See how that selects all files in the local directory. (The instructions that follow allow you to create an archive of all regular files in your home directory.)

3. Once you've selected the desired files and/or folders, right-click. In the pop-up menu that appears, click Create Archive. There may be a slight delay as Nautilus collects the list of files and subdirectories from any directories you've selected.

4. In the Create Archive window that appears, enter the archive name of your choice. Make sure it has a *.zip* extension; otherwise, the archive manager may compress your files with a protocol unreadable to users of Microsoft Windows. Click Create. The process is automatic from here.

5. Once the process is complete, you can inspect your new archive. In the File Browser, navigate to the name of the archive, such as *mydocs.zip*. When you double-click on the archive file, the File Browser opens a new window with the files and folders that you just saved in this archive.

6. You'll now have an archive of your files that you can share with your colleagues who use Microsoft Windows or Mac OS (as well as Linux). For example, when you're sending an email, you can attach the archive to your email in the same way as you attach any ordinary document or image.

If your user is interested in creating a backup of his own home directory, give him some guidelines. If the backup is relatively small and your organization allows such transfers, your user can transmit the backup to a remote system via email. If the backup is larger, you should direct the user to any directories that you've shared over your network. If the user is more capable, direct him to the associated with "I'm Afraid of Losing Data," at the beginning of this chapter. If you allow DVD recording (and the hardware is available), direct the user to the instructions you publish related to "That Command Doesn't Write to My DVD," earlier in this chapter.

## CHAPTER 3

Optimizing Internet Applications

In this chapter, I'll address some of the annoyances associated with further customizing workstations for regular users. As most of these users are not comfortable with Linux, you'll have to configure a number of features and tools to ensure that your users' desktop environments "just work."

In the world of Linux, there are often several choices, even on the GUI, for key applications. Linux, after all, is about freedom of choice. For example, you can navigate around the World Wide Web with Firefox, Balsa, Epiphany, and Opera—among other browsers. You can manage email with Evolution, Thunderbird, KMail, etc.

As an administrator, you could well find that freedom of choice is not best for users. In fact, it can be helpful to standardize key applications. There is less to keep up-to-date, and fewer tools at which you'll have to become "the expert." In this chapter, I've arbitrarily selected what I believe are the most appropriate tools as of this writing. For example, I've assumed that Firefox is the most popular browser and Evolution is the most appropriate Personal Information Manager (PIM). While you may disagree with these decisions, the steps you take to standardize equivalent applications are similar.

Firefox Isn't Working as It Should

Mozilla's Firefox is perhaps the hottest web browser on the market. With a reputation for convenience, robust code, and fun plug-ins, Firefox is one way to avoid the virus, worm, and spyware problems associated with Microsoft's Internet Explorer. With these advantages, Firefox is quickly gaining market share. It is almost certainly the preferred browser for most regular users on a Linux workstation; in addition, perhaps tens of millions have loaded it on their Microsoft Windows computers at home.

However, installing Firefox with appropriate plug-ins on Linux is not a task for newbies. As of this writing, when you upgrade Firefox, you have to reinstall associated plug-ins. Therefore, it's important that you document what you do. Briefly, I'll show you how you can:

- Install the latest appropriate version of Firefox
- Select the plug-ins you need
- Customize Firefox for your organization

Installing the Latest Version of Firefox

In practice, you may not want to install the absolute latest version of Firefox. Instead, it's generally preferred to install Firefox as *customized* for your distribution. Even if it doesn't have the latest features, you'll know that a Firefox package customized for your distribution will at least place key configuration files in the appropriate directories.

I'll show you how you can install Firefox on our selected distributions, and then how you can make the absolute latest version of Firefox work, if you can't wait for the latest hot feature.

SUSE installations

If you run SUSE's YaST Online Update on a regular basis, you may already have the latest version of Firefox. However, SUSE updates are not automatic and occur only if there are security issues associated with an application. Even automatic updates don't upgrade your browser just because new features were added.

If you want to just install and/or upgrade the Firefox browser on your SUSE workstations, take the following steps:

1. Start the GUI version of YaST with a command such as *yast2* (you can also start it from a GUI menu).
2. Run the Online Update system and let it retrieve information about available updates. (Alternatively, you can jump directly to this screen with the *yast2 online_update* command.)
3. When you see available updates, click the Filter drop-down text box and select Search.
4. Enter firefox in the Search text box and click Search. You'll find appropriate SUSE packages that you can upgrade online—in this case, *MozillaFirefox*.
5. Proceed with the upgrade. Pay attention to any dependencies, especially if you're going to upgrade more than one SUSE workstation.

6. You can use the downloaded RPMs on the other SUSE workstations on your network. In this case, you'll find the *MozillaFirefox* RPM, as well as any dependencies, in the */var/lib/YaST2/you/mnt/i386/update/9.3/rpm/i586/* directory (substitute your version of SUSE for *9.3*).

Naturally, you can always download and install the latest *MozillaFirefox* RPMs directly from SUSE repositories or mirrors. For example, if I wanted to upgrade to the latest version of the Firefox browser using the Oregon State download servers, I'd run the following command:

```
rpm -Uvh http://suse.osuosl.org/suse/i386/update/9.3/rpm/i586/
MozillaFirefox-1.0.6-4.1.i586.rpm
```

Naturally, this command won't work if the Firefox RPM depends on other packages that aren't installed yet.

Red Hat/Fedora installations

With Red Hat/Fedora distributions, it's easy to install or update to the latest version of the Firefox browser. As long as you're properly connected to the Internet and appropriate repositories, all you need to do is to run the following command:

```
up2date -u firefox
```

The Red Hat *up2date* system automatically installs any dependent packages along with the latest version of the Firefox browser. As of Fedora Core 5, *up2date* is no longer installed by default, so you'll have to run the following command:

```
yum update firefox
```

Debian installations

If you've installed Debian Linux on your workstation computers, you've probably already installed Firefox. Even if you haven't already done so, the command is the same; the following command installs or upgrades Firefox on Debian Sarge:

```
apt-get install mozilla-firefox
```

If this doesn't work, remember that, with Debian and allied distributions, the name of the package can vary by version or distribution (Debian Etch uses *firefox*). If you want a bit more information on the available Firefox browser package options, run the following command:

```
apt-cache search firefox
```

When you use *apt-get* to install or upgrade any package, you may see a number of "grave bugs" before you're asked to confirm the installation. In that case, one option is to install the Firefox browser as released by the Mozilla Foundation. I describe the installation process from the Mozilla package in the next section.

Tarball installations

Sometimes, the package system of your distribution doesn't offer the absolute latest version of Firefox you need. Sometimes, the version of a distribution-specific update package does not work. In either case, you can download and install Firefox from the associated tarball package.

The latest version of Firefox is available from *http://www.getfirefox.com*, which redirects you to *http://www.mozilla.com/firefox*. Naturally, not all systems include web browsers. In that case, you can also download the latest version of Firefox from Mozilla's FTP server at *ftp.mozilla.org/pub/mozilla. org/firefox/releases/*.

 The following steps vary by Firefox version. For example, Firefox 1.5 supports direct installation from tarball to the desired directory. If you have a previous version of Firefox on your system, you'll want to use the directory associated with your distribution, as noted near the end of these steps.

I've downloaded the package built by the Mozilla Foundation in tarball format, and have installed it using the following steps:

1. Log in to the Mozilla FTP server, which supports anonymous access. You can do so using any standard text or GUI FTP client. Navigate to the appropriate subdirectory. As of this writing, it's */pub/mozilla.org/ firefox/releases/*.

2. Review available directories and navigate to the one with the latest available official release.

3. Navigate to the directory with the appropriate operating system and language—in my case, *linux-i686/en-US/*.

4. Download the package with the Firefox installer—in my case, *firefox-1.0.6.installer.tar.gz*.

5. Save a copy of the installer package for use on other workstations.

6. Unpack the downloaded package; in my case, I ran the following command (your version number will probably be different):

   ```
   tar xzvf firefox-1.0.6.installer.tar.gz
   ```

7. Navigate to the directory this created—in this case, *firefox-installer/*—and run the Firefox installer. You may find two executable files in the *firefox-installer/* subdirectory: *firefox-installer* and *firefox-installer-bin*. Run the

first of these files, as it configures directories and environment variables, and then serves as a frontend to the second executable. From the *firefox-installer/* directory, run the following command:

```
sudo ./firefox-installer
```

Note how I use the *sudo* command to run the Firefox installation script. This allows the Firefox installer to run in the GUI with the environment variables associated with a regular user, and with the root permissions needed to write files to the common directory that you're about to create.

8. Follow the instructions associated with the Firefox installer, which told me to close all currently running instances of Firefox and then accept the License Agreement (which cites the Mozilla Public License and other open source licenses).

9. When prompted for a Setup Type, select a Custom Setup and a more standard Destination Directory. While I selected */usr/local/firefox* (which is a good generic directory), you may prefer a different directory better suited to your distribution. For example, SUSE specifies */opt/ MozillaFirefox*, Red Hat/Fedora specifies */usr/lib/firefox-versionum*, and Debian specifies */usr/lib/mozilla-firefox/*.

However, installing a Firefox tarball in a distribution-specific directory includes risks, if you install a distribution-based version of Firefox in the future.

Don't forget to delete firefox-installer from the Selection text box, or that will become part of the directory where Firefox is installed.

If you don't choose a standard directory that's on every user's default PATH, the browser you install may be executable only by one specific user on that workstation.

10. Depending on how much responsibility you want to burden your users with, you may want to disable the Firefox Quality Feedback Agent. Developer tools are appropriate for web developers but generally not for end users.

11. Once you've completed the installation process, the Firefox browser starts. You can proceed to the next sections to add Firefox plug-ins to your system.

If you've installed Firefox directly from the generic package from the Mozilla Foundation, you may not get an appropriate entry in your GUI menu. For more information on how you can customize GUI menus, see Chapter 1. For most Linux distributions, you'll want to add a menu entry for Firefox in the Internet submenu; SUSE uses the Internet → Web Browsers submenu.

Firefox Plug-ins

There are a wide variety of plug-ins available for Mozilla Firefox. While the size of this book does not allow me to show you how to install every plug-in, I can provide some examples.

In this section, I'll show you how you can install and activate Adobe Acrobat Reader and the Java Runtime Environment. While they're almost certainly not the only plug-ins that you'll want or need for your users, they will establish a pattern. If you know how to make these plug-ins work on Firefox, you have the skills to make other plug-ins work as well.

To see what plug-ins are already installed for Firefox, open the browser and type the following in the address bar:

    about:plugins

For a detailed review of plug-ins that you can install for the Firefox browser, see *http://plugindoc.mozdev.org/linux.html*.

It's possible that Firefox will make it easier to install plug-ins on the Linux version of its browser in the future, perhaps even as easy as it is in Microsoft Windows. At that point, if your users have a reasonable skill level on Microsoft Windows, they may be able to handle plug-ins on their own. But then again....

Installing Acrobat for Firefox

Acrobat has become an essential tool online. A huge number of documents are available in PDF format, and it can be a terrific convenience to view such documents directly in the Firefox browser.

As with other applications, it's generally best to install the plug-in packages built for your distribution. I list the packages associated with our selected distributions in Table 3-1.

Table 3-1. Adobe Acrobat packages

Distribution	Packages	Notes
Red Hat Enterprise Linux	*acroread, acroread-plugin*	Requires access to the Extras channel; also applies to rebuilds such as CentOS-4; automatically includes the *nppdf.so* plug-in in the Plugin registry file, *pluginreg.dat*
SUSE	*acroread*	Updating to the latest packages automatically includes the *nppdf.so* plug-in in the Plugin registry file, *pluginreg.dat*.

Table 3-1. Adobe Acrobat packages (continued)

Distribution	Packages	Notes
Debian	*mozilla-acroread,* *acroread-plugins*	Updating to the latest packages automatically includes the the *nppdf.so* plug-in in the Plugin registry file, *pluginreg.dat*

Adobe makes Acrobat Reader available for Linux/Unix workstations in both RPM and tarball formats. As of this writing, the downloads are available from *http://www.adobe.com/products/acrobat/readstep2.html*.

If you want the latest and greatest version of the Acrobat Reader, or your distribution's current version of Acrobat Reader has bugs, you may want to install directly from the tarball package available from Adobe. To do so, take the following steps:

1. Download the tarball (in *.tar.gz* format) from the aforementioned web site.
2. Unpack the tarball with a command such as:

   ```
   tar xzvf AdbeRdr701_linux_enu.tar.gz
   ```
3. Navigate to the directory where files were unpacked:

   ```
   cd AdobeReader
   ```
4. Start the installation process; as of this writing, it's available in the *INSTALL* script:

   ```
   sudo ./INSTALL
   ```

   Running the installation script in this manner allows you to take advantage of regular user environment variables required for GUI installers, while supporting installations into directories that require administrative permissions.
5. Scroll through the agreement and type accept to accept the license conditions.
6. Enter the installation directory; unless you have another version of Adobe Acrobat in the specified directory, the default is generally acceptable.
7. Run the *install_browser_plugin* script, in the */usr/local/Adobe/Acrobat7. 0/Browser* directory. If the *firefox-installer* directory is in a standard system directory, you probably need to use *sudo* to run the script as *root*.
8. Confirm the installation directory for Acrobat, normally */usr/local/ Adobe/Acrobat7.0/*.
9. Select a global installation to apply to all users on this workstation.
10. Type in the directory where Firefox is installed, such as */usr/local/ firefox*.

11. If it's the right directory, you'll see the following message:

```
Installation successful. Added the file /usr/local/firefox/plugins/
nppdf.so
```

12. If Firefox is currently open, you'll have to close and reopen it before the plug-in takes effect.

Installing Java for Firefox

Java is a key component of many web sites. If you allow your users to browse online, they'll need you to enable Java on their browsers. As of this writing, one relatively minor annoyance is how Firefox makes users believe that Java can be automatically installed. Unfortunately, that's not true. And until you install Java for your users, all they'll see is the message shown in Figure 3-1.

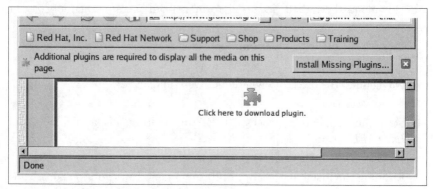

Figure 3-1. Java not properly installed for Firefox

The message in the browser suggests that all a user needs to do is click the Install Missing Plugins button. Yes, that starts the Plugin Finder Service and identifies the Java Runtime Environment. But most will be discouraged when they see the message requiring a manual installation. The few who proceed probably won't know which version of Java for Linux to install (if they even realize they're running Linux). Then the complaints will begin.

To avoid this annoyance, you should install Java on your users' workstations. The following steps work for the Java Runtime Environment on Firefox, as of this writing:

1. Download the appropriate package from the Sun Microsystems web site at *http://www.java.com/en/download/linux_manual.jsp*. The RPM is designed to work on Red Hat/Fedora; the other "self-extracting file" is designed to work on Debian Linux.

   If you're running SUSE Linux, the required RPM should already be available from your installation DVD/CDs; for example, SUSE Linux

Professional 9.3 uses the *java-1_4_2-sun-plugin* RPM. In that case, don't bother with the download from the Sun web site.

2. Whichever package you've download, you'll first have to make it executable. To do so, run an appropriate *chmod* command such as:

   ```
   chmod u+x /tmp/jre-1_5_0_04-linux-i586.bin
   ```

   If you're running Debian Linux and have downloaded the self-extracting file, navigate to the */usr/java* directory. Create it if required.

3. Run the download as a script. If you're using the *-rpm.bin* file, the script automatically installs the RPM on your system.

4. Accept the license terms; next, you can link to the appropriate plug-in file.

5. If you want to enable Java only for specified users, link the plug-in file, *libjavaplugin_oji.so*, to each user's *~/.mozilla/plugins/* subdirectory. For example, I use the following command to create the link to my own home directory:

   ```
   ln -s /usr/java/jre1.5.0_04/plugin/i386/ns7/libjavaplugin_oji.so \
   /home/michael/.mozilla/plugins/libjavaplugin_oji.so
   ```

   You can create the link for each user individually, or you can create a script for this purpose.

   Alternatively, you can create a link for all users on a workstation. For Java, the standard plug-in directory is */usr/lib/mozilla/plugins*; the required link command is:

   ```
   ln -s /usr/java/jre1.5.0_04/plugin/i386/ns7/libjavaplugin_oji.so \
   /usr/lib/mozilla/plugins/libjavaplugin_oji.so
   ```

6. Now, you'll have to enable Java in the Firefox Preferences. Click Edit → Preferences to open a window of the same name. In the left pane, click Web Features and then activate the "Enable Java" and "Enable JavaScript" options.

7. If you're currently running Firefox, you'll have to close all instances and restart to make sure it works.

8. You can verify the installation of Java plug-ins; type about:plugins in the Firefox address text box. When I do, I see the locally configured web page shown in Figure 3-2.

Customize Firefox for Your Organization

While I can cover only a few of the many useful ways to customize the Firefox browser, there are a few key settings that can help your users. If you need more information on customizing this browser, see *Firefox Hacks* by Nigel McFarlane (O'Reilly).

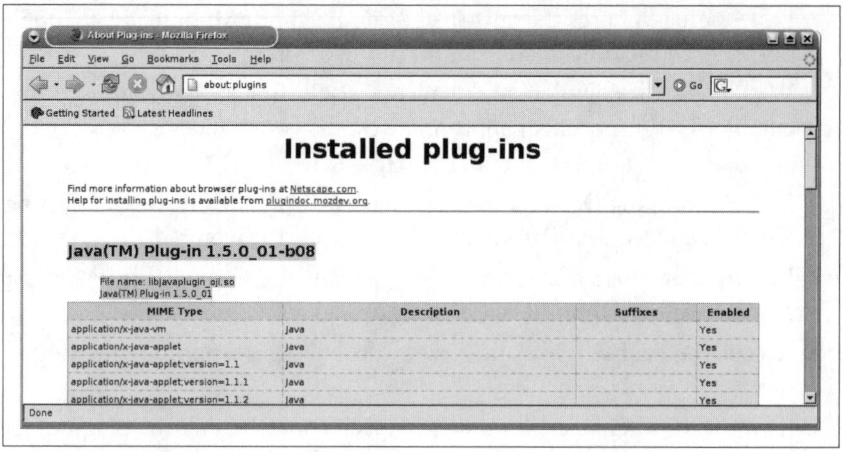

Figure 3-2. Java installed as a Firefox plug-in

As with many browsers, you can customize key settings in the associated preferences. Select Edit → Preferences to access the Preferences window. You can navigate between sections in the Preferences by clicking the desired option in the left pane. In the following sections, I highlight a few key settings that can help you avoid annoyances.

General Preferences

Under General Preferences, you may want to customize several settings, including:

Home Page
> You may want to configure all users' browsers to start from a specific location, such as your internal or external corporate web site.

Fonts and Colors
> You can set up different fonts and colors for a specific corporate "look and feel" for your browsers.

Languages
> If you've installed an appropriate version of Firefox associated with more than one language, you can specify defaults. Many web servers allow you to choose whether home pages for more than one language are available.

Connection Settings
> If you've configured a proxy server for your network, you'll definitely want to configure connection settings. Unless you point your users' browsers to your proxy server, you won't get the money-saving benefits associated with reduced traffic on your corporate Internet connection.

Privacy Preferences

Depending on the function and location of the workstation, you may want to vary the level of privacy associated with Firefox. Under Privacy Preferences, you can regulate what Firefox saves on your system, including:

- The history of previously viewed pages
- Previously entered information in web forms
- Passwords
- Downloaded files
- Cookies
- Cache

Web Features Preferences

The Web Features of Firefox allow you to manage the functionality associated with different web sites. For example, this section allows you to:

- Block (most) pop-up windows
- Support installation of software from a web site prompt
- Load images
- Enable Java
- Enable JavaScript

Download Preferences

The Download Preferences of Firefox allow you to manage how downloads are run through this browser, including:

- Download directory location
- Download manager supported users
- Plug-ins associated with specific download file types

Advanced Preferences

The Advanced Preferences associated with Firefox allow you to manage accessibility, browsing characteristics, tabs, software updates, security, certificates, and more. Details are beyond the scope of this book; for more information, see the aforementioned *Firefox Hacks* by Nigel McFarlane (O'Reilly).

Copying Preferences

Once you've configured preferences for the Firefox browser, you can share them with the rest of your organization by copying the directory where Firefox stores your preferences to the same location in other users' home directories. Your preferences are contained within your *~/.mozilla/firefox* subdirectory, in a random subdirectory named with a *.default* extension, such as *ev2junio.default/*.

I'm Drowning in Good Email

I spend a lot of time every morning sifting through email. A lot of it comes from various Linux mailing lists. Many of you may receive several hundred messages every day, just from the Fedora mailing lists.

Luckily, you can use the capabilities of your mailer to search through headers, email addresses, message bodies, and more to prioritize your good email. Because this book is for geeks, I've chosen a slightly advanced topic: how to set up virtual folders on Evolution. This lets you view mail in many different ways. For instance, you can view all the mail regarding a particular project from different people and then with a single click view all the mail from a particular person on all projects. The same mail messages will appear in different folders, matching whatever criteria you specify.

To understand virtual folders, consider a quick comparison of mail messages to files. If you move a file, it's no longer accessible in the old directory. If you want to access the file in two different directories, you can copy it, but then anything you do to one has to be repeated on the other. How can you access a single file in two different directories and make sure that anything done to a file in one directory is reflected in the copied file in the other directory?

The solution for files is links. The same solution in Evolution is virtual folders. Mail remains in one real folder, but it can show up simultaneously in any number of virtual folders, and if you delete it or mark it in some way, the action takes place everywhere it appears.

In this section, I'll show you step by step how to set up a virtual folder. To help you understand how they work, I've cited the specific steps I used to identify all emails to and from my agent:

1. Open Evolution.
2. If you're not already in the email manager, click the Mail button, or press Ctrl-F1 or Ctrl-1.

3. Choose File → New → Mail Folder, or Shift-Ctrl-F, to open the Create Folder window.

   If the desired Virtual Folder already exists, right-click it and select Properties from the pop-up menu, and then skip to step 5.

4. In the Folder Name text box, enter the name you want to use. In this case, I've entered Agent. Highlight VFolders and click Create to open the New VFolder window.

5. Click Add to start adding filtering rules.

   One choice you have is to make the folder group messages together with the following messages that answer them; this is called threading. Because the rules will search through all email messages in my Inbox and Sent mail folders, I do not need to include threads. However, it might be useful for threads on mailing lists such as those related to the Fedora Project.

6. If you're going to specify more than one rule, you'll want to choose the appropriate option in the Execute Actions drop-down menu: "if all criteria are met" or "if any criteria are met." In my case, I want all criteria to be met.

7. Under the Add button, select the search criteria of your choice in the lefthand drop-down text box. What you select determines the options that follow. In this case, I select Sender, and then "contains" in the next drop-down menu. I then enter the name used by my agent in her email addresses.

8. I want more than one search criterion, so I click Add. I want to make sure the message is from my agent, so I specify Message Body in the first drop-down menu and "contains" in the next drop-down menu. I enter the first name of my agent, fairly secure in the knowledge that Carole is a somewhat uncommon spelling.

9. Since I want a listing of all communication to and from my agent, I select "all local folders" under the VFolder Sources in the drop-down text box.

   Evolution won't search through the Junk folder.

10. Alternatively, if you want to limit the search to the Inbox, select the "specific folders only" option in the drop-down menu. Click Add, and then navigate to and select the Inbox folder. You'll see the "mbox: Inbox" listing.

    Even if you specify "mbox:Junk", Evolution won't search through the Junk folder.

11. Alternatively, if you want to search through remote folders, such as those available from an IMAP server, you can change the drop-down menu to "with all active remote folders" or "with all local and active remote folders."

12. Once complete, click OK. It may take a bit of time to collect the messages in virtual folders, especially if you've created filters that search within messages or from remote servers.

Filtering Spam with Evolution

There are several excellent email managers available for Linux, including Thunderbird, Kmail, Evolution, and pine. My selection of Evolution is somewhat arbitrary, based on how it closely resembles Microsoft's Outlook and how it can be integrated with the Microsoft Exchange email server. While KOrganizer also supports much of the same functionality, it does not have the same level of popularity. Evolution is the default email manager for both Red Hat and SUSE distributions.

SUSE has only recently moved toward GNOME and Evolution, to reflect its ownership of Ximian, the developers of Evolution.

However, Evolution is a big package. If you do not need the non-email features associated with a Personal Information Manager (PIM), you may want to use a a simpler email manager, such as Thunderbird, Kmail, or pine.

Because spammers don't label their email as undesirable, some trial and error is required to manage this problem. Filters are not 100 percent reliable; you may need to accept some spam for the sake of making sure that you do see important email.

Once you activate the Evolution spam filter, you'll need to check your junk mail folder periodically, to make sure that important messages aren't accidentally classified as spam.

The kind of spam that users want to filter may vary. For example, one user may appreciate discount ticket offers on Airline X; another may have a fear of flying and would therefore never want to see any airplane-related email. Associated features in Evolution allow individual users to customize their junk email filters.

Installing SpamAssassin

Before you can activate junk mail filtering on Evolution, you need to install the SpamAssassin package on your workstations. It's available for each of our selected distributions, under an RPM or DEB package of the same name.

SpamAssassin includes Bayesian filtering, an algorithm that uses probabilities to calculate the likelihood that a specific email is junk. For example, *Viagra* is a common word in junk email; however, if you work for the company that produces Viagra, related emails may be serious business.

SpamAssassin includes a substantial number of tests for junk email, as documented at *http://spamassassin.apache.org/tests_3_0_x.html*. These tests are associated with configuration files in the */usr/share/spamassassin* directory.

The details of how you can customize SpamAssassin covers an entire book of the same name, *Spam Assassin* by Alan Schwartz (O'Reilly). One tip from that book is that SpamAssassin supports whitelists and blacklists for specific email addresses or domains. You can include directives such as:

```
whitelist_from guru@linuxexam.com
blacklist_from *@spamisus.abc
```

Activating spam filtering

Spam filters are available on email servers, and they can be quite helpful. But they may not be enough for you or your users. Evolution includes a customizable spam filter, which takes advantage of SpamAssassin features. Set it up as follows:

1. Access Evolution Settings by choosing Tools → Settings (or for some versions of Evolution, Edit → Preferences).
2. In the lefthand pane of the window, select Mail Preferences.
3. In the righthand pane of the window, select the Junk tab.
4. Activate the Check Incoming Mail For Junk option.

   The Check Incoming Mail For Junk option checks against a database of known junk messages as well as anti-spam blacklists.
5. If you have ample speed on your Internet connection, you may choose to activate the Include Remote Tests option.

   The Include Remote Tests option checks against a SpamAssassin-compiled list of blacklisted message senders and ISPs. This option can slow down email delivery and, in some cases, slow your effective Internet connection. It can lead to other problems; for example, the IP address used by my domain was for a while also used by a known spammer. Some of my emails were automatically filtered as junk by several ISPs.

6. Click Close. Your Junk folder should now be active.

While the Junk folder is now active, you still need to add messages to the junk filter. You'll also need a spam folder for the detailed filters. In the main Evolution screen, click the Mail button. Right-click on a folder and select New Folder from the pop-up menu that appears. Enter an appropriate name for a folder; I've created a folder named *Spam*. In the Specify Where To Create This Folder window, highlight On This Computer and click Create.

You now have a Spam folder for your filters.

Junk filters

Filtering is a routine feature of most modern mailers. You can configure a mailer to put mail from certain sources in certain folders, delete certain types of messages automatically, or even send messages to a program to do some automated processing, such as generating a reply. In this section, we use this powerful feature in Evolution to send the messages you predict to be spam to their own folder.

The easiest way to start filtering spam is to mark it as such. For example, check your Trash folder. You probably have a lot of spam there. One popular type of junk email is "phishing" for your personal financial information. Naturally, if you don't have an account from that institution, you'll know it's spam.

To add a spam email to your filters, highlight the message and click Junk. If the Junk button is grayed out (and the Not Junk button is active), it's already been recognized as spam by your filter criteria.

Spam filters

You can also create your own rules, such as whitelists and blacklists. To do so, click Tools → Filters to open a window of the same name. Any filters already in this list were created by others. Make sure Incoming (and not Outgoing) is selected in the top drop-down menu. Click Add. This opens the Add Rule window shown in Figure 3-3.

As you can see in Figure 3-3, I have created a simple rule for emails from the *spammer@spam.spm* email address. All email from that address will be transferred to the Spam folder. But spam isn't that simple. You can add as many rules as you need for your test. In place of Sender, you can specify a number of different conditions, shown in Table 3-2. As you can see in the "Execute actions" drop-down menu, you can classify a message as spam if any or all of your conditions are met.

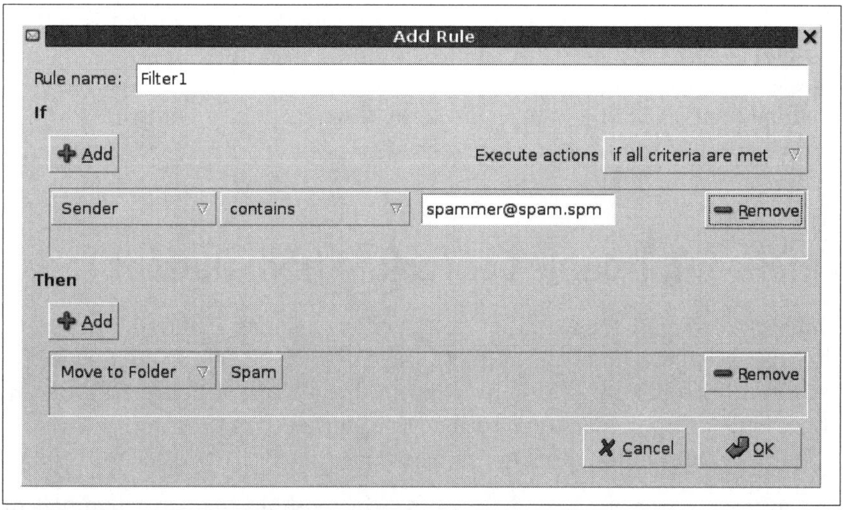

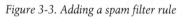

Figure 3-3. Adding a spam filter rule

Table 3-2. Spam conditions

Condition	Description
Sender	The email address associated with the `From:` directive.
Recipients	The email addresses in the `To:` and `cc:` directives.
Subject	Information in the `Subject:` directive.
Specific Header	Supports selections from any header you choose.
Message Body	Uses text you supply to search through a message.
Expression	Allows programmers to filter in the Scheme programming language (related to LISP).
Date Sent	Supports filtering based on actual or relative time.
Date Received	Supports filtering based on actual or relative time.
Label	If you have labels for your emails—e.g., Work, Personal, or To Do—you can add that criterion to your filter here.
Score	Assigns a message score for further filtering.
Size	Helps you filter out messages that may be suspiciously large.
Status	If you already have a message in an existing folder such as Drafts or Junk, you can add the messages to the filter list.
Follow-Up	Checks if message is flagged for a follow-up.
Attachments	Checks if attachments are included with the email.
Mailing List	Supports filtering based on a mailing-list address.
Regex Match	Allows the use of *grep* to search through a message header or body.
Source Account	Filters the account based on the source email server.
Pipe To Program	Supports the use of piping to an external program, such as another spam filter.
Junk Test	Filters based on the results of the test.

If you're not satisfied with SpamAssassin, one alternative is Bogofilter (*http://bogofilter.sf.net*). Whatever spam-filtering tool you select, you can use the Pipe to Program rule to filter your email through its filter; if the message is identified as spam, you can set its status to Junk. Once configured, email that meets the conditions identified by your spam filter is sent to your Junk folder.

I'm Having Trouble Converting from Outlook

One key advantage for Evolution is its ability to act as a client on networks that use Microsoft Exchange. As an Exchange client, it can help ease the transition for organizations converting to open source software. If you are converting to open source software, you may need to convert your users from Microsoft Outlook to Evolution at some point.

Unfortunately, if your systems are not Microsoft Exchange or equivalent Novell OpenExchange clients, Novell has no easy way to convert data from Microsoft Outlook to Evolution. However, there are alternatives.

 If your users' information is on a Microsoft Exchange server, you do not have to convert data from Microsoft Outlook. Once you connect your users' Evolution systems to Microsoft Exchange (or perhaps the alternative Novell OpenExchange, *http://www.novell.com/products/openexchange/*), the data should be downloaded as easily to Evolution as it is to Outlook.

Preparing Outlook

Unfortunately, the standard methods for converting email from Microsoft Outlook are labor-intensive. While there are several utilities available, none are currently maintained. The developers behind the KMail package appear to have the most current list of conversion utilities at *http://kmail.kde.org/tools.html*.

Novell, which is most interested in helping users convert from Outlook to Evolution, actually recommends the use of Mozilla Mail for Windows to facilitate the conversion process. It seems at best strange to use the email application of a third party in order to convert a Microsoft application, but that's the best available process as of this writing.

If your users will be performing the conversion, you'll need to keep the process as simple as possible.

The Conversion Process

There are three basic options for converting data from Microsoft Outlook to Novell Evolution:

1. You can implement a Microsoft Exchange or Novell OpenExchange mail server to move the data to a central server. Evolution can take data from either mail server.

2. Novell recommends using a third-party PIM to support the conversion—such as Mozilla Mail, Netscape Mail, or Eudora—within Microsoft Windows. You can then import the converted files into Evolution on your Linux workstations.

3. Resolvo's MoveOver allows you to convert data into a format usable by Linux. Its tools can convert data from Outlook, Internet Explorer, and even User Environment settings to provide a more complete conversion (Resolvo is a strategic partner of CodeWeavers, the company behind CrossOver Office). For more information, see *http://www.resolvo.com*.

Configuring Evolution for Exchange

If you've configured a Microsoft Exchange server for your network, you can configure Evolution on each workstation as a Microsoft Exchange (or Novell OpenExchange) client. But the default version of Evolution does not communicate with Exchange.

As of this writing, connections to a Microsoft Exchange server from Evolution require the *evolution-exchange* package. Once installed, you'll see an Exchange button in the lower-left corner of Evolution. Click it to see the status of the connection with the Exchange server. If it's active, your workstations should automatically download your users' data from the server.

I'm Having Trouble Chatting on AIM, Yahoo!, or MSN

If you want to communicate via Instant Messaging (IM), you need to understand how most people use networks built on Microsoft tools. Fortunately, you do not have to install AOL, Yahoo!, or Microsoft Network (MSN) software to IM with others online.

IM is more than just a social tool. It is an important means of communication in business, as it facilitates teleconferences and more. When you work with others using IM, you need to be able to communicate on the major IM networks. Regular users can configure open source tools to communicate on each of these networks. Naturally, this may lead to another annoyance if your users waste their time on social IM networks; however, you can block IM messages to and from your LAN by blocking appropriate TCP/IP ports.

There are a wide variety of IM systems available. The IM systems native to the GNOME and KDE desktop environments are Gaim and Kopete, respectively. Either IM can act as a client on many different networks, including those described in Table 3-3.

Table 3-3. Gaim and Kopete Instant Message systems

System	Description
AIM/ICQ	America Online Instant Messenger and ICQ. ICQ, for "I seek you," is based on the first IM service. (A Linux version of AIM is available from *http://www.aim.com/get_aim/ linux/latest_linux.adp*.)
Gadu-Gadu	An IM system based in Poland; for more information (in Polish), see *http://www. gadu-gadu.pl*.
Novell Groupwise	This PIM system developed by Novell also supports IM; see *http://www.novell.com/ products/groupwise/*.
IRC	Internet Relay Chat; for a global server list, start your search at *http://www.irchelp. org/irchelp/networks/servers/*.
Jabber	The standards-based version of IM, secure and ad-free; for more information, see *http://www.jabber.org*.
MSN	Microsoft Network. Gaim can communicate seamlessly with these users; for more information, see *http://messenger.msn.com/*.
Napster	The original Napster client includes a chat service; Gaim can still facilitate IM communications between these users.
SILC	Secure Internet Live Conferencing (SILC), a secure IM protocol. For more information, see *http://silcnet.org*.
Yahoo!	Yahoo!'s IM system; downloads for Red Hat/Debian are available from *http:// messenger.yahoo.com*.
Zephyr	An IM system popular at universities, developed by MIT; for more information, see *http://itinfo.mit.edu/product.php?id=85*.

For more information (and a longer list) of different IM systems, see *http:// en.wikipedia.org/wiki/Comparison_of_instant_messengers*.

In the following sections, I'll show you how you can configure Linux IM clients on three different IM networks: AOL, Yahoo!, and the Microsoft Network. Before you can connect, you'll need accounts on each of these networks. Be aware that some of these networks have eligibility requirements; for example, AIM requires users to be at least 13 years of age.

Links to IM registration pages are available from *http://gaim.sourceforge.net/faq. php#q15*. You'll have to record your account, or screen name and password.

The process is straightforward. You may want to adapt the instructions shown here for your users.

First, you'll need to create an account on the desired IM network. These are basic instructions; details will probably change in the future:

- To create an AOL IM account, navigate to *http://my.screenname.aol. com*. Under the Need An Account window, click Create One Free Now. You'll need to confirm your request using the instructions that AOL emails to you.

- To create a Yahoo! account, navigate to *http://edit.yahoo.com/config/ eval_register*. If you already have a Yahoo! account, such as for their email or auction services, you can skip this step.

- To create an account on the Microsoft Network, you'll need to create a Microsoft Passport. Navigate to *http://accountservices.passport.net*. If you don't want to give Microsoft your email address, I suggest that you create an email account from a free service such as Hotmail for this purpose. Microsoft won't send you any email that you need to log in to the Microsoft Network.

Once you create an account, you can proceed to configure Gaim or Kopete with your account information.

Gaim

Gaim is the default IM client on the GNOME desktop. It can also be used on KDE. According to its developers at *http://gaim.sf.net*, despite the resemblance to AIM, Gaim is an acronym with no meaning. You can configure Gaim as a client on a wide variety of networks, including those listed in Table 3-3. I'll show you how to configure a Gaim client for the networks I've selected earlier:

1. Open Gaim. From the GNOME Applications menu, select Internet → GAIM Internet Messenger. (In SUSE Linux, it's Internet → Chat → GAIM Internet Messenger.)

2. Click the Accounts button to open the Accounts window.

3. Click Add to open the Add Account window.

4. Select your desired IM network (AIM/ICQ, MSN, Yahoo) in the Protocol drop-down menu.

5. Enter the Screen Name, Password, and Alias (Display Name) you created for your account.

6. If you want to select a different authentication host (such as one dedicated to your organization) or configure communication through a proxy server, click Show More Options and make the appropriate changes.

7. Once complete, click Save.

8. Click Close in the Accounts window.

9. In the Login window, select the AIM account you've configured in the Account drop-down menu. Enter your password, and click Sign On.

10. To send an instant message, click the IM button. In the New Instant Message window that appears, enter the desired screen name.

11. Alternatively, click the Chat button. In the Join A Chat window that appears, enter the desired room name.

12. You should now be able to start your IM or chat session.

The next time you start Gaim, you should find your User ID in the Account drop-down menu. Select your account (if you have more than one), enter your password, and you're good to go! Automatic startup and login can also be configured, so you can start IMing without doing anything more than logging in to your system.

Kopete

Kopete is the default IM client on the KDE desktop. It can also be used on GNOME. The strength of Kopete is in its configuration wizard. One drawback, however, is that it does not support direct access into chat rooms (although you can invite or be invited into sessions with as many users as you desire). For more information on Kopete, see *http://kopete.kde.org*. You can configure Kopete as a client on a wide variety of networks, including those listed in Table 3-3. I'll show you how to configure a Kopete client for the networks I've selected:

1. Open Kopete. From the KDE Main menu, choose Internet → Internet Messenger (Kopete). (In SUSE Linux, it's Internet → Chat → Internet Messenger [Kopete].)

2. The first time you start Kopete, you'll see the Configure Kopete window, where you can add any IM accounts that you've created.

   If you've run Kopete before, select Settings → Configure Kopete to get to the configuration window.

3. Highlight Accounts in the left pane. Click New to start the Welcome To The Add Account Wizard. Click Next.

4. In the next pane, select the IM service you need, and click Next. I cover the procedure for AIM, MSN, and Yahoo!; if you're using another service, the procedure is similar.

5. In the next pane, you'll be able to enter the IM account information that you've created. Some services have different names for the username, such as the AIM Screen Name or Microsoft Passport ID.

   If there's more than one tab, the second tab allows you to override the authentication server location. If you're creating an MSN account, you'll see four tabs; however, you can't modify information in the last two tabs until you've signed in to the service.

6. Next, you can select a custom color for the account. This feature is useful if you have to IM on more than one type of network. Select a color if desired and then click Finish.

7. Click OK back in the Configure Kopete window.

8. To start the connections you've configured, choose File → Connection → Connect All.

9. If you haven't configured passwords earlier, you're prompted for them as contact is made with appropriate servers. Once configured, Kopete can log users in to IM accounts automatically without prompting.

10. Before you can start a chat, you'll need to add contacts. To do so, click File → Add Contact to start the Add Contact Wizard.

11. Enter the name of the contact, as you want it seen on your Kopete client. You can add that contact to the Top Level group or create a group of your choice.

12. Associate the new contact with the appropriate IM account.

13. Add the username for the desired contact (on the Microsoft Network, it's the user's Passport ID).

14. When one or more of your contacts are online, you should be able to start your IM session. Right-click on the contact, and run the desired command to start the chat or send a message.

The next time you start Kopete, select File → Connection → Connect All and then enter the passwords for your accounts, if prompted. When your contacts come online, you're good to go!

I Need a Simple Web Browser

Not all Linux desktops have the firepower needed for the GUI. Even if you have enough memory for a simple GUI, your system may not be able to handle a fully featured browser such as Firefox. Alternatively, you may want a GUI browser other than Firefox so you can avoid the effects of its known bugs in that browser.

 While the Firefox browser avoids many, perhaps most, of the problems associated with Microsoft's Internet Explorer, as time goes on, crackers will create problems for Firefox (as they have already).

Fortunately, there are web browsers of many types available for the Linux desktop. Most distributions include more than one application that can be used as a web browser. I'll review some of the alternatives in this annoyance.

Text Browsers

Yes, in Linux you can browse the World Wide Web from the text console. Several major options are described here:

Elinks

Elinks is a fully featured, text-based browser and an enhanced version of Links. It supports many GUI-style features, such as downloads of images and Cascading Style Sheets. It is currently available from the Fedora/Red Hat and Debian repositories. Once it's installed, you can start the browser with the *elinks* command. You can then access menus with the Esc key. You can move between links with the up and down arrows; you can move to a highlighted link with the right arrow; and you can move back in your link history with the left arrow. Developed in the Czech Republic, this tool is documented at *http://www.elinks.or.cz/*.

Links

Links is a browser with pull-down menus; SUSE and Debian have customized versions on their installation CDs. For more information, see *http://links.sf.net*. When you run the *links* command, you can access menus with the Esc key. You can move between links with the up and down arrows, you can move to a highlighted link with the right arrow, and you can move back in your link history with the left arrow.

 If you have both Elinks and Links installed, the *links* command opens the Elinks browser.

Lynx

Lynx is a browser that lets you move the cursor between links. SUSE and Debian make this browser available from their repositories. You can move between links with the up and down arrows, you can move to a highlighted link with the right arrow, and you can move back in your link history with the left arrow. Menu keys are listed at the bottom of the screen. For more information, see *http://lynx.isc.org*.

W3m

W3m is a browser with *more/less* command-style pager capabilities. Only Debian makes this browser available from its repositories. You can move to links with the arrow keys, you can move to a linked page with the Enter key, and you can access menus with the Insert key. For more information, see *http://w3m.sf.net*.

Assuming you're connected to the Internet, you can call the web site of your choice with a command such as:

```
lynx www.yahoo.com
```

Other Graphical Browsers

Linux supports a wide variety of graphical browsers; Firefox is just the most prominent. I've compiled an incomplete list below, based on some of the browsers I'm able to install on my Linux desktops. I do not include Mozilla and Galeon, as their developers have used the associated code to create the successor browsers Firefox and Epiphany. Mozilla (in suite form) is still available and currently at 1.7.12.

Epiphany

Epiphany, the successor to Galeon, is a web browser designed for the GNOME desktop. Development seems to have slowed as of this writing, perhaps due to its shared use of the Gecko rendering engine (with Firefox). For more information, see *http://www.gnome.org/projects/epiphany/*.

Konqueror

Konqueror is a web browser designed for the KDE desktop. As a file manager and browser, it is functionally similar to GNOME's Nautilus. However, it is more customizable through the KDE Control Center (current versions of Nautilus are at best difficult to use for web browsing). For more information, see *http://konqueror.kde.org*.

Netscape

Believe it or not, Netscape still provides a viable web browser. At one time, it was the leading browser on the Internet, with a market share far greater than Internet Explorer. Now it is built on Firefox, with a focus on securing user systems against untrusted sites. For more information, see *http://browser.netscape.com/*.

Opera

Opera is an excellent alternative to Firefox. In fact, until the advent of Firefox, Opera was my preferred browser. Opera still does a better job at blocking pop-up windows. If you choose to download Opera, just be careful with the download site. The default download server is in Norway (the home country of Opera), and if you're in the U.S., it's most efficient to download from a U.S. server. For more information, including downloads, see *http://www.opera.com*.

I Keep Having to Start an FTP Download from Scratch

In many cases, Internet connections are less than reliable. The latest DVD for your favorite Linux distribution or a DVD-length video of your friends' wedding in Las Vegas requires several gigabytes of data. Even with broadband connections, such downloads can take many hours. If you're downloading over a wireless network associated with the 802.11b/g protocols, you may experience interruptions from ordinary devices such as microwave ovens and some cordless telephones, because they operate on the same range of frequencies.

 Cordless telephones may be the most common problem for wireless networks. To avoid interference with either my 802.11a (5.8Ghz) or my 802.11b/g (2.4Ghz) networks, I have a 900Mhz cordless phone.

Even if you're using a wired Internet connection, there are a number of ways your download may get interrupted. If there's a thunderstorm anywhere between you and your download server, if there's electromagnetic interference near a cable, or if someone flips a switch in the wrong place, you may experience interruptions during your download.

There are many good applications that can help you restart connections after a download. I explore only two options in this annoyance: *lftp* from the command line and gFTP from the GUI.

Whichever you choose, there are other things you can do. If you have doubts about the integrity of a download, many services provide a checksum file you can use to verify it. If you administer an FTP server from which users download CD-length files, you can provide these same checksums for your users.

lftp

One reason I focus on *lftp* is that it is the FTP client of choice, at least as listed in an older version of the Red Hat Certified Engineer (RHCE) Exam Prep guide.

 For more information on RHCE certification, see *http://www.rhce.com.*

The *lftp* client is a flexible file-transfer program that supports downloads from more than just FTP services. In fact, it can handle downloads from regular and secure web services (HTTP, HTTPS), Secure FTP services (SFTP, FTPS), and more. In this annoyance, I show you how you can access, start, and resume a download using this client. For more information on *lftp*, refer to its home page (it was developed in Russia) at *http://lftp.yar.ru/.*

To access a server such as *kernel.org*, you can run the following command:

```
lftp mirrors.kernel.org
```

Alternatively, if you've already started the *lftp* client and see the associated *lftp* :~> prompt, you can connect to the desired FTP server with the following command:

```
open mirrors.kernel.org
```

If you're familiar with FTP and bash shell commands, *lftp* should be easy. For example, you can check your current directory with *pwd*, list files and directories with *ls*, navigate to different directories with *cd*, download the file of your choice with *get*, and so on.

The *lftp* service also supports a command history, as well as tabbed command completion. For example, if you want to see what's in the *fedora/* subdirectory, you can navigate with a double tap on your Tab key, as far as you need in the directory tree. In that way, you can easily find the appropriate subdirectory with the DVD ISO file that you need with the following command:

```
lftp mirrors.kernel.org:/> cd fedora/core/4/i386/iso/
```

Then you can review available downloads and use standard FTP commands to get the ISO file you need. For example, if you want to download the Fedora Core 4 DVD, you can run the following command:

```
get FC4-i386-DVD.iso
```

Now, if you were interrupted while doing this download and a partial file was left in your local directory, you can resume the interrupted download by adding the -c switch (otherwise, the download starts from scratch):

```
get -c FC4-i386-DVD.iso
```

If you're downloading more than one file, you can *mget* those files; for example, if you really want to download all of the CD-based ISO files, you can run the following command:

```
mget -c FC4-i386-disc?.iso
```

If you're not sure what's already available on your system, you don't have to exit *lftp*. With the *!* prefix, you can use the shell commands of your choice; for example, the following command at the *lftp* prompt lists files in the current local directory:

```
!ls
```

gFTP

While gFTP is the GNOME FTP client, it also works well on the KDE desktop environment. As a GUI client, it is fairly easy to use, so it's suitable for your regular users. If you want to provide instructions, you might start with the following. It's best if you modify these instructions to use downloading examples that are of practical use to people in your organization. In addition, the location of gFTP in your GNOME and KDE desktop menus may vary. This case describes how regular users can download aircraft-related documents from the NASA FTP server.

To download one or more documents on airplanes from the NASA FTP server, use the following instructions:

1. Open gFTP. In GNOME, select Applications → Internet → gFTP. In KDE, click the K menu → Internet → gFTP.

   In SUSE Linux, gFTP is in the Internet → Data Exchange submenu.

2. When gFTP opens, type the following in the Host text box, and press Enter:

   ```
   ftp.hq.nasa.gov/pub/
   ```

   As you run gFTP, messages in the bottom box monitor the success or failure of what you do.

   If you see an Enter Username window, type anonymous in the text box.

3. If your connection is successful, you'll see a list of files and directories in the righthand listbox.

4. Navigate to the *pub/* directory and then to the *aircraft/* subdirectory. You can do so with appropriate double-clicks, or by entering /pub/aircraft in the righthand text box.

5. Highlight the documents you need. To start the transfer, you can click and drag these documents, click the left-facing arrow, or click Transfers → Retrieve Files.

6. If your download is interrupted before completion, you can restart the transfer or start where you've left off. If you have a transfer that has been interrupted, when you start a transfer, you'll see a Transfer Files window. If you click Overwrite, the transfer starts from scratch; alternatively, if you click Resume, the transfer continues from the point of interruption.

7. When you're finished, exit from gFTP. Choose FTP → Quit, or press Ctrl-Q.

For more information on gFTP, review its home page at *http://gftp.seul.org/*.

Checksums

Those who provide large downloads would do well to provide checksums. They can help users make sure that the download will work as intended. Perhaps the most popular option for checksums is MD5, the message-digest algorithm designed by Ronald Rivest of MIT and documented in RFC 1321 (*http://www.ietf.org/rfc/rfc1321.txt*).

Checksums are commonly available for ISO file downloads associated with Linux distribution CDs and DVDs. For example, if you download the Fedora Core 4 ISO for a DVD, you should find a SHA1SUM text file in the same download directory.

When your download is complete, run the *sha1sum* command on the downloaded ISO file. For the Fedora Core 4 DVD ISO file, the specific command is:

```
sha1sum FC4-i386-DVD.iso
```

The *sha1sum* command calculates a 128-bit checksum based on the noted file. The output from the command should match the checksum provided by the supplier—in this case, in the SHA1SUM text file. As an example, the following is an excerpt from this file in the Fedora Core 4 ISO download directory:

```
2f151a7329846da685c2a72fcb40eba3e8a355a0  FC4-i386-DVD.iso
3fb2924c8fb8098dbc8260f69824e9c437d28c68  FC4-i386-disc1.iso
31fdc2d7a1f1709aa02c9ea5854015645bd69504  FC4-i386-disc2.iso
032455cdf457179916be3a739ca16add75b768b7  FC4-i386-disc3.iso
f560f26a32820143e8286afb188f7c36d905a735  FC4-i386-disc4.iso
```

If the checksums do not match, there may have been a problem with the download. The CD or DVD that you create from that ISO will almost certainly be faulty. In that case, it's best to try the download again.

If you're responsible for an FTP server from which users download CD-length files, you may want to provide checksums. It may be a SHA1SUM or MD5SUM checksum. All you need to do is run the *md5sum* or *sha1sum* commands on the files in question and add the checksums to a text file similar to the SHA1SUM file shown above.

I Need to Connect via Modem (GUI Tools)

As of this writing, still over half of those in the U.S. who connect to the Internet use telephone modems. While the availability of broadband service is increasing, it is not always affordable or available in the user's geographic area. With the problems associated with the digital divide, those with less money are more likely to connect via telephone modem. And with the lower costs associated with Linux, you as a Linux geek are more likely to have to support home users on single computers with telephone modems.

As a Linux geek, you've probably raved about the advantages of Linux to your friends and relatives. But as a Linux geek, you may be annoyed when they ask, "How do I get on the Internet?"

You'll have to remember that in many cases, these users may not even know that they're using a telephone modem, except for noticing that they can't use the phone.

As of this writing, there is no universal GNOME-based GUI tool to connect to the Internet via telephone modem on our selected distributions. If you need a GNOME-based tool, I personally recommend GNOME PPP. It's available on Debian-based repositories and can also be download and compiled from its current developer home page (in Serbia): *http://www.icmreza.co.yu/blogs/vladecks/en/?page_id=4*.

The best available tool for regular users who connect via telephone modems, in my opinion, is KPPP. It works equally well on the GNOME and KDE desktop environments. Unfortunately, KPPP does not work for all ISPs; I describe some workarounds available in "The AOL Problem" section later in this annoyance.

Key Tools

Linux GUI tools are frontends to command-line tools. KPPP is no exception. Before you can connect via a telephone modem, you first need to make sure it's accessible via Linux. One handy tool for this purpose is *wvdialconf update*, which detects installed modems and documents associated settings in */etc/wvdial.conf*. If KPPP has problems, you can cross-check its settings against the updated version of this configuration file.

 If *wvdialconf* can't detect a modem on your system, you may have a dreaded "winmodem." For more information, see "I'm Having Trouble with Microsoft-Dependent Hardware" in Chapter 5.

However, you don't have to install the *wvdial* package before installing KPPP. The only packages you need are the ones containing KPPP, its dependencies (which sometimes include some basic KDE packages), and *ppp*. It's best to use your favorite update tool (*apt-get*, YaST, *up2date*, *yum*) to install the right package, as it detects and installs any needed dependencies. For example, the following command installs KPPP and dependencies on Red Hat/Fedora distributions, respectively (KPPP is part of the Red Hat/Fedora *kdenetwork* RPM):

```
up2date -u kdenetwork
yum install kdenetwork
```

On Debian Linux (Sarge), KPPP is part of its own package, so you can install it with a command such as:

```
apt-get install kppp
```

Like Red Hat/Fedora, later versions of Debian Linux (Etch) include KPPP in the *kdenetwork* package. (Naturally, I use similar commands to install the *wvdial* package on each distribution.) Unfortunately, in SUSE Linux, unless you've configured a connection to an up-to-date *apt* repository, you can't run package updates from the console. To install the noted packages, you'll have to access YaST to install SUSE's *wvdial* and *kdenetwork3-dialup* packages.

Scanning for Modems

In many cases, modems are automatically detected during the installation and boot process. Generally, the device file associated with detected modems is linked to */dev/modem*. In other words, when you run the following command:

```
ls -l /dev/modem
```

you'll see a link to the actual port associated with the modem, such as → */dev/ttyS0*.

If there is no link, it's appropriate to run the *wvdialconf update* command. It's available with the *wvdial* package. Run it on your system. It scans available ports for a modem. For example, when I run the command on my Debian laptop, I see the following output:

```
Found a modem on /dev/ttySHSF0.
Modem configuration written to update.
ttySHSF0<Info>: Speed 460800; init "ATQ0 V1 E1 S0=0 &C1 &D2 +FCLASS=0"
```

While you can specifically point KPPP to this */dev/ttySHSF0* device file, many modem configuration tools assume there's a link to */dev/modem*. If there is no link, you can create one—in this case with the following command:

```
ln -s /dev/ttySHSF0 /dev/modem
```

If you need to recheck settings detected by the *wvdialconf* command, you'll find them in your */etc/wvdial.conf* configuration file.

 If *wvdialconf* does not work, try the scanModem utility. Instructions and download links are available from *http://linmodems.technion.ac.il/#scanmodem*. Once scanModem is unpacked, with executable permissions, run the script. It detects most telephone modems (including Winmodems), with directions on downloading and installing drivers. As the directions vary widely by modem, it's beyond what I can cover in this book.

Configuring KPPP

Now, with your modem detected, the next step is to configure KPPP for your user's Internet Service Provider (ISP). But before you begin, you'll need to configure KPPP permissions to support access by all regular users, just in case they start KPPP from the command line. The steps vary by distribution:

Configuring KPPP on Debian
When you install the kppp package on Debian Linux, the key script isn't even executable by regular users. You can make it so with the following commands:

```
chmod 755 /usr/bin/kppp
chmod u+s /usr/bin/kppp
```

Alternatively, you could combine these commands:

```
chmod 4755 /usr/bin/kppp
```

You may also need to add KPPP to the appropriate GUI desktop menu. While it's automatically included in the KDE menu, it's not included in the Debian GNOME Applications menu. For more information on how

---

to add it, see "I Want the Advantages of Both KDE and GNOME" in Chapter 1.

Configuring KPPP permissions on SUSE

When you install the *kdenetwork3-dialup* package on SUSE Linux, it automatically adds KPPP to appropriate GNOME and KDE menus. To make sure all users can start KPPP from the command line, run the following command:

```
chmod u+s /opt/kde3/bin/kppp
```

Configuring KPPP permissions on Red Hat/Fedora

Red Hat and Fedora regulate access to KPPP using pluggable authentication modules. The KPPP utility is regulated in the */etc/pam.d/kppp* configuration file. That means you'll need to replace the auth sufficient pam_rootok.so directive in that file with:

```
auth sufficient pam_permit.so
```

To start configuring KPPP, take the following steps:

1. Verify the availability of a telephone modem, as described earlier in this annoyance.

2. Make sure you have the needed information from the user's ISP, at least the connection telephone number. To make sure the connection works, you'll need an account and password on that ISP.

3. Click the K menu (or Applications) → Internet → KPPP.

   If you're working with SUSE, KPPP is under the Internet → Dial-Up submenu. In some cases, KPPP may also be known as the Internet Dial-Up Tool.

4. Click Configure to start the configuration process; this action opens the KPPP Configuration window.

5. Under the Accounts tab, click New. This opens the Create New Account window.

   If you're editing an existing account, select it and click Edit; then skip to step 7.

6. While KPPP offers a wizard, it's not helpful unless you're configuring an ISP in one of several countries in Europe, or in New Zealand or Taiwan. If you're elsewhere, click Manual Setup to open the New Account window.

7. In the New Account window, on the Dial tab, enter a name for the connection, such as "Local ISP."

8. Click Add. Enter the full phone number required to dial via the telephone to the ISP. If you have to enter a prefix such as 9 for an outside

line, add a comma. That tells KPPP to wait a couple of seconds, normally sufficient to get a dial tone.

In most cases, no other changes are required. If there is a problem, you may need to check with the ISP to ask what authentication protocol it uses. Some ISPs, especially those connected with some secure organizations, call your computer back after verifying a connection.

Generally, you won't have to change settings in any of the other tabs, as they are configured for a dynamic IP address, a default gateway, and DNS servers as assigned by the ISP. If you require a specialized login script, commands to be executed during the connection and disconnection process, or accounting based on the amount of time online, you may be interested in some of these tabs.

Click OK when you're finished configuring the account for this ISP. Return to step 5 if you want to configure another connection.

9. Navigate to the Modems tab. If a modem isn't already configured, select New; alternatively, highlight the modem and select Edit. Under the Device tab, make sure the settings correspond to what was detected and recorded, as described earlier in this annoyance, by the *wvdialconf update* command to the */etc/wvdial.conf* file.

10. Navigate to the Modem tab. Click Query Modem. KPPP sends a series of commands to your modem; if they're successful, you'll see a series of messages in a Modem Query Results window. (For some modems, you may need to have a physical connection to a telephone line.) Click Close.

If your modem isn't properly configured, you'll get a message like Modem Query Timed Out or Unable To Open Modem.

11. Click OK to exit from the KPPP Configuration window. You should be back in the main KPPP window.

12. Now you can test your connection. Make sure your configured ISP (and, in some cases, Modems) is shown in the Connect To drop-down menu. Enter your login ID and password for the ISP, and click Connect. If your modem is configured for sound, you should hear the modem in action.

13. If your connection is successful, you should see a message to that effect in a Connecting To window.

If successful, you can now pass on this configuration to your users. You can copy the configuration file, *~/.kde/share/config/kppprc*, directly to your users' workstations.

The AOL Problem

If you're working with users who insist on connecting to the Internet via telephone modem to America Online (AOL), standard Linux PPP connections don't work and the solutions aren't easy. If the users are geeks, they may be able to download and install solutions such as those associated with the PengAOL project (available for download from *http://sourceforge.net/project/showfiles.php?group_id=32335*). However, as the associated home page is not active as of this writing, I cannot recommend it as a solution for you or your users. If you have problems, and developers are not available to help, you could be out of luck.

One other solution is the AOL Dialer, available as part of the Linspire Linux distribution. While officially it's still "beta" software, it is a GUI solution available for a Linux-based desktop distribution. Unfortunately, there are costs associated with Linspire, available from *http://www.linspire.com/*. Alternatively, Linspire comes preinstalled on several desktop PCs—and even on a $500 laptop PC from Wal-Mart.

CHAPTER 4

Setting Up Local Applications

The variety of tasks associated with user support may seem endless. If you've read the first three chapters, you've worked through some of the gymnastics required by your users. In this chapter, I'll show you how you can help your users manage applications, especially how they can work with files created by Microsoft Windows–based applications.

Linux is about choice. There are many viable options for just about everything a user needs to do. However, too many choices can be overwhelming. And in some cases, it may be difficult to find the application that can help your user read files created on a Microsoft operating system—with all of the macros and functions that users want.

So Many Options for Applications

Linux includes an incredible variety of applications. The number of choices may annoy some users, as it can be difficult to glean the wheat from the chaff. Just browsing through what's available takes time. In this annoyance, I introduce some of the libraries of Linux applications. I provide some guidelines that you can use to find the gems in the forest. Then I'll provide an example of how you can find the application most suited to the needs of your users.

Linux Application Libraries

There are a number of excellent Linux application libraries available. The ones I find most useful are:

The Linux Online library
> The Linux Online library is a database with rich features. While you can browse its categories and subcategories from the Applications web page

at *http://www.linux.org/apps*, the strength of the library is its search engine. If you have a specific need, such as video editing, office suites, or money management, use the Linux Online search engine. You may be pleasantly surprised with the results.

The Freshmeat project trees

The people behind Freshmeat host the home pages for a substantial number of projects. Developers add their contributions to Freshmeat all the time, supplying software updates, messages, and more. Projects in the Freshmeat database are organized into several levels. Once you find the appropriate subcategory, projects are ordered by popularity.

For example, if you want to find the most popular Linux chat programs that can connect to the AOL Instant Messenger service, navigate to the Freshmeat libraries at *http://freshmeat.net/browse/18/* and click Communications → Chat → AOL Instant Messenger. As of this writing, there are 85 projects in this area, and the most popular application is Gaim, which is covered in "I'm Having Trouble Chatting on AIM, Yahoo!, or MSN" in Chapter 3.

One caution for Linux users: some software from Freshmeat projects is designed only for operating systems other than Linux.

The SourceForge Software Map

In its own words, SourceForge is "The world's largest development and download repository of Open Source code and applications." It is well indexed. Like Freshmeat, projects are listed in order of popularity. Like Linux Online, it has a powerful search engine that can help you find the application that you need.

You can search its applications engine directly from the home page at *http://sourceforge.net*, or search through its application categories starting with the Software Map tab. For example, if you wanted to search through applications associated with AOL Instant Messenger, you would click Communications → Chat → AOL Instant Messenger for the 247 related projects.

 Both Freshmeat and SourceForge are maintained by the Open Source Technology Group; nevertheless, their project databases are different.

When you examine a project, know what you need. Some less popular projects may be perfect for you and your users.

Selection Criteria

I recommend that you use the following guidelines when selecting an application:

Availability for preferred distribution

Linux applications generally work best when built and tested on your target distribution.

Cost

Naturally, cost is always a key factor when selecting an application. While most Linux applications are freely available under an open source license, some are not. Some companies provide two versions of an application: one is open source, and a second includes additional features for a price. Some companies who have released open source applications sell support contracts.

Licensing

The license associated with an application determines what you can do with it. Open source licenses allow you to freely modify the application to meet your needs. If you develop features that you're willing to share, you can release your changes to the community.

Support

There are at least two levels of support to consider with any Linux application: support direct from the company, for which you pay, and support from fellow users (and often some of the developers), available through mailing lists.

Development status

Many applications are "not ready for prime time." If you find that an application is in *alpha* development, it generally has not been tested with any rigor on most Linux distributions. However, many (but not all) *beta* projects, which are nominally still in testing, are as stable as any Microsoft application that you can purchase today.

As described on SourceForge, there are seven levels of development: planning, pre-alpha, alpha, beta, production/stable, mature, and inactive. In most cases, you should not install planning, pre-alpha, and alpha applications on production computers. Beta software may or may not be ready for production computers and should be tested rigorously before installation. Production/stable software can generally be installed on production computers without as much testing. Mature and inactive applications may not have the latest features, or may be superseded by other applications.

Activity

Generally, it's best to use applications with a lot of activity, as defined by popularity and message traffic. Freshmeat and SourceForge list projects by their popularity, and most projects have a mailing list that you can peruse to check experiences of others. If the mailing list associated with an application hasn't seen a new message for months, it's probably inactive.

Self-tests

Whatever you install, even if it is stable production software, should be tested on your systems. What you do may be unique. The new application may have unanticipated effects. Only when you're confident of a positive result should you install the new application on a production system.

Sample Applications Search: Office Suites

If you need an office suite, the obvious choice on Linux is OpenOffice.org. As you'll see in the next two annoyances, the applications in the Open-Office.org suite work well with Microsoft Office files—even those that have complex embedded templates and macros. However, the OpenOffice.org suite may not be best for all Linux users. It takes up a lot of room. Every time you update the suite, you may download several hundred megabytes of packages.

If your users have uncomplicated Microsoft Office files, one of the other Linux Office Suites may be better for you. In this section, I'll guide you in a search of office suites through the Linux Online applications database, using the following steps:

1. Navigate to the Linux Online applications database at *http://www.linux. org/apps/*.

2. Under the Office category, click on the Office link.

3. Read through the available options. If none are satisfactory, search through the databases of the other application libraries described in this annoyance.

4. Pick an option. Evaluate it based on the criteria described in the previous section (except self-tests):

   • To find out its availability for your selected distribution, search for the package from your distribution's repositories. For a Debian-based distribution (or a distribution enabled with an *apt* repository), you can search with the following command (substitute the name of the package for *searchterm*):

```
apt-cache search searchterm
```

Alternatively, for distributions with *yum*-based repositories (such as Fedora Linux), you can search with the following command:

```
yum list | grep searchterm
```

In other cases, you can use the package search engines most closely associated with the distribution, such as SUSE's YaST or the Red Hat Network at *rhn.redhat.com*.

Alternatively, the developers behind a distribution may have built packages for specific distributions and made downloads available from their home pages. Or you can build the package from source code; however, that makes installation more difficult and suggests that the application may not be fully tested on your preferred distribution.

- Check for a price or a fee. The listing for the application should list any direct costs associated with the application.

- Inspect the license. The "free" versions of many applications may have limited functionality or may expire after a certain amount of time.

- Find out about support. You (or your users) may need it. Your management may demand it. All applications are associated with some sort of learning curve. Support may be available for a fee from the developers (or third-party consultants); details should be available from the application's web page. Support may also be available online; it can help to search through the mailing lists for the application.

- Make sure you're comfortable with the development status of the application. Generally, production applications should have a production/stable development status. There are risks associated with alpha software. Conversely, mature or inactive software may not be up-to-date, may not work with the latest distributions, and may not address the latest security issues.

- Check the current level of activity associated with an application. It's best if you see a relatively regular revision history, as well as discussion on mailing lists. These measures suggest that the software is up-to-date and relatively popular.

Once you're satisfied with these steps, consider downloading and installing the application. Start with a test computer, configured with the same components as you would find on production workstations.

Download the application. Unpack and compile it if required. Install the application. Configure it as you would want your users to see it. Test it as it would be run by your users, with a variety of other applications. Inspect the results, including the additional messages you might find in related logfiles.

Only after you're satisfied with the results should you install the application on the production computers on your network.

Microsoft Word Documents Don't Work on Linux

One objective of many Linux gurus is to help as many users as possible convert from Microsoft Windows. The process may not seem that difficult to you or me. But we are Linux gurus, and all we see is that most users just use their computers as a word processor. However, Microsoft Word includes features that can make the conversion process annoyingly difficult.

Microsoft Word is a complex application. It supports macros, stylesheets, embedded comments, and more. It supports complex templates, it supports revision marks, it supports collaboration. Making Microsoft Word documents work on many Linux word processors can be annoying.

If you can overcome these problems, you can go a long way toward helping Microsoft users to convert seamlessly to Linux. Users who try Linux and are unable to do what they've done before on Microsoft Word get frustrated. Productivity suffers. And worst of all, users begin to demand that you reinstall Microsoft Windows on their systems.

Some Linux word processors are supposed to work seamlessly with Microsoft Word files. Sometimes this is true. But do not blindly follow the claims of any developer. Even with the best intentions, they might not address some specific need of you or your users.

In any case, you need to know for sure. You'll want to test files with the features desired by your users. Get copies of their files (with their permission, as required by your company/organization policy) and test them on the Linux word processor of your choice.

Don't force your users into something with which they're not comfortable. While many Linux geeks are comfortable with word processor scripting languages such as TEX, Microsoft users haven't worked with this type of word processor since WordPerfect 5.2, which was last popular over a decade ago.

Finally, any change in word processor can be difficult for many, perhaps most, users. You have to be prepared to take positive steps to promote interest. In other words, after you select a GUI word processor for your Linux system:

- Test the installation on a production-ready system.
- Make sure the word processor works seamlessly with your users' most demanding files.
- Find users who are willing to test the word processor. Provide incentives such as extra support for other applications.
- Monitor the results after installation; continue monitoring until you're confident that your users have confidence that the new word processor can do everything they expect from Microsoft Word.
- Find specialty commands popular with your users and test their equivalents on the Linux-based word processor that you select. Create cheat sheets for these commands. Sometimes appropriate cheat sheets may already be available for purchase.

For those users still on Microsoft operating systems, you may be able to ease their transition by installing appropriate versions of open source office suites. For example, you can install the latest version of the OpenOffice.org office suite on Microsoft Windows or the Apple Macintosh operating systems.

Linux Word Processing

As you can see from the application libraries described in the previous annoyance, there are a large number of Linux word processors. As of this writing, there are around 100 different projects related to office suites listed at *http://freshmeat.net*. Based on the criteria described earlier in this chapter, you'll want to do your own searches. In my opinion, the following are the major Linux-based alternatives to Microsoft Word:

AbiWord
>   AbiWord is the default word processor associated with the GNOME desktop. It can read and write several document types, including Microsoft Word, Rich Text Format, and more. To ease user transitions, it is also available for Microsoft Windows and Apple Macintosh operating systems. Unfortunately, its developers seem to be slowing down; the latest available packages as of this writing are configured for Fedora Core 3 and Mac OS X. Its abilities are somewhat limited, as it cannot import files native to OpenOffice.org/StarOffice Writer.

KWord
>   Part of the KDE Office Suite, KWord can handle many different kinds of Microsoft Word documents. When I test KWord with Microsoft Word

documents that I've used for various publishers, the results are not always satisfactory. Although KWord packages have been created for Apple Macintosh, it is not available for Microsoft Windows.

OpenOffice.org Writer
Part of the OpenOffice.org office suite, OpenOffice.org Writer is the word processor that is most compatible with Microsoft Word. I describe my success with this word processor in the next section.

StarOffice Writer
While current versions of StarOffice are built from OpenOffice.org source code, you can also purchase the StarOffice suite, with commercial support. For more information, see *http://www.sun.com/software/star/staroffice/*.

Microsoft Word on CrossOver Office
Later in this annoyance, I'll show you how you can install Microsoft Word on Linux, with the help of CrossOver Office.

OpenOffice.org Writer Document Formats

OpenOffice.org was originally developed from Sun Microsystems' StarOffice. However, development has proceeded full circle; the latest versions of StarOffice are now developed from OpenOffice.org code.

OpenOffice.org Writer adapts well to document templates written for Microsoft Word. You can open Microsoft templates as well as native Microsoft Word 6.0/95 and 97/2000/XP document files, with full template functionality.

You can add to your templates in OpenOffice.org Writer. To do so, select Format → Styles → Catalog. In the Style Catalog window that appears, click New to open the Character Style window. You can then customize the style in the tabs that appear. For more information, consult OpenOffice.org Help under the style catalog.

 If you don't see OpenOffice.org Help, you may have forgotten to install the associated package. Debian organizes English-language OpenOffice.org help files in the *openoffice.org-help-en* package.

OpenOffice.org Writer Capabilities

I've written this book with OpenOffice.org Writer. The templates provided by O'Reilly include a complex level of functionality. If needed, I can save files in various Microsoft Word document formats. The OpenOffice.org developers are still working on compatibility with Microsoft Office macros; it's a difficult issue because of the viruses associated with these macros.

I've used OpenOffice.org Writer in the past to write books for other publishers. Some of these publishers require that I save book files in Microsoft Word format. The results, even when translated to publishing software such as Corel's Ventura, have generally been seamless.

> If you're using OpenOffice.org Writer in place of Microsoft Word, and your downstream customers need to transform the files into other formats, let them know. Make sure to save your files in the format they need. You can use Open-Office.org Writer to save files in the latest Microsoft Word or Rich Text formats. Your customers may need to watch out for differences in behavior. With a little luck, they won't find any (or actually prefer the functionality of OpenOffice. org Writer) and will gain confidence in the OpenOffice.org suite.

One moderate annoyance relates to embedded comments. As of this writing, OpenOffice.org limits the size of the highlight box. If your users work with embedded comments, you may want to encourage your users to explore alternatives, such as re~~ordered~~corded changes, which are displayed in the document in a different color (as shown here), with properties that identify the person who made the change.

> If you have to use embedded comments, you can review them in OpenOffice.org Navigator. Select Edit → Navigator or press F5 to open the Navigator window, shown in Figure 4-1.

OpenOffice.org Writer on Microsoft Operating Systems

One way to help users become comfortable with open source tools is to install them on their Microsoft Windows computers. Then, when they start working on Linux workstations, they'll recognize some of the applications that they've used before. To this end, you can install the latest version of the OpenOffice.org suite on Microsoft operating systems.

Installing Microsoft Word on Linux

As of this writing, Microsoft has not ported its Office Suite or Microsoft Word to Linux. Nevertheless, there are two major ways to install Microsoft Word on a Linux computer:

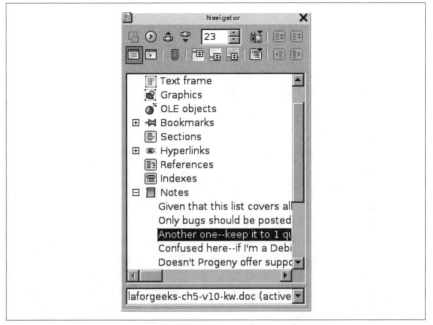

Figure 4-1. Navigating OpenOffice.org Writer embedded comments

Wine or CrossOver Office

Based on the work of the Wine Is Not an Emulator (Wine) project, CodeWeavers (*http://www.codeweavers.com*) has developed CrossOver Office in part from Wine code. While you can install Microsoft Word on Linux with either Wine or CrossOver Office, the latter is more efficient and therefore more likely to meet with the approval of regular users. For more information on how to install Microsoft Word on Linux with Wine, see "I Need Those Microsoft Applications on Linux" in Chapter 8. I'll explain how to install Microsoft Word on CrossOver Office shortly.

A Virtual Machine

There are several different Virtual Machine (VM) options available. The market leader is VMWare (*http://www.vmware.com*). Other options include Win4Lin (*http://www.win4lin.com*) and Bochs, the open source 32-bit emulator (*http://bochs.sf.net*). When you install a VM on Linux, you're installing a second operating system inside Linux. Thus, the drawback of a VM is the delay associated with booting the second operating system. You already wait long enough for Linux to boot; if your users also have to wait for Windows to boot inside a VM, it might test their patience.

There are other alternatives, such as a thin client. With a thin client, a user on a Linux computer can log in to and access the GUI of a Microsoft computer on the same network. There are several options for thin clients, including rdesktop, TSClient for Windows Terminal Services, and VNC. All are described in detail in the latest edition of O'Reilly's *Running Linux* by Matthias Kalle Dalheimer and Matt Welsh.

To install Microsoft Word on CrossOver Office, take the following steps:

1. Install CrossOver Office on your system. Download the latest version of this emulator from *http://www.codeweavers.com*. While there are three versions of CrossOver Office available, all you need is CrossOver Office Standard edition, which costs $39.95 and includes six months of support and updates. If you prefer, you can download and install the trial edition, good for 30 days.

   CodeWeavers has compiled DEB packages designed for Debian-based distributions such as Xandros, Knoppix, and Ubuntu, as well as RPM packages for related distributions such as Red Hat, SUSE, and Mandriva. Alternatively, if you want to install from source, CodeWeavers offers a Loki installer.

2. Once CrossOver Office is installed, run the associated CrossOver Office setup program. In the GUI, start the menu (using KDE's K menu or GNOME's Applications menu, followed by CrossOver → Office Setup).

3. In the CrossOver Setup window, select Install to start the CrossOver Installation Wizard. (If you've previously installed one or more component of Microsoft Office, select it from the Installed Software menu and click Repair/Remove.)

4. Select Show All Supported Applications, and then select the version of Microsoft Office that you're using. If you have only Microsoft Word, treat it as if it were Microsoft Office.

5. Follow the instructions, which will prompt you to insert the Microsoft Office CD.

6. Proceed with the same steps that you would use to install Microsoft Word on a Microsoft Windows system.

7. When you're prompted to reboot, it's OK to accept. CrossOver Office simulates a reboot cycle for Microsoft Windows, without rebooting Linux.

8. You can now find Microsoft Word (as well as other Microsoft Office programs that you may have installed) in the GNOME Applications or the KDE K menu's Windows Applications → Programs submenu.

I Need My Microsoft Office

Microsoft Word is only the most commonly used (and, in my opinion, the most annoying) of the Microsoft Office applications. While there are different Microsoft Office suites, they generally include a series of integrated applications, including Excel for spreadsheets, PowerPoint for presentations, Access for databases, and Outlook for email/personal information management.

For more information on helping users convert from Microsoft Outlook to Evolution on Linux, see "I'm Drowning in Good Email" in Chapter 3. This annoyance is focused on the other components of Microsoft Office, and the Linux applications that can replace them.

To evaluate each of these applications, follow the selection criteria listed in "So Many Options for Applications," earlier in this chapter, I evaluate the components of the OpenOffice.org suite as alternatives to Microsoft Office.

Evaluating the OpenOffice.org Alternative

Using the selection criteria described in "So Many Options for Applications," here are some general comments on the OpenOffice.org suite:

- It's available for all major Linux distributions.
- It's free.
- The license allows you to use OpenOffice.org in just about any way you want. If you improve it and want to release those improvements, you just have to make the source code publicly available.
- Official support is available from a variety of consultants, as well as Sun Microsystems. For more information, see *http://support.openoffice.org*.
- OpenOffice.org development continues at a brisk pace; 2.0.1 was just released as this chapter was being written.
- The OpenOffice.org suite is large; the package itself is around 100 MB. If you have an older system, performance might be an issue.

Naturally, if OpenOffice.org (or another Linux-based alternative) is not satisfactory, you can install Microsoft Office on Linux, with any or all of the associated applications, using one of the techniques described in the previous annoyance.

Excel Spreadsheets Are Not Readable

Spreadsheets often incorporate complex calculations, normally implemented with the help of macros. Spreadsheets are often published with document templates. Both macros and templates are customized on Microsoft Excel. From the previous annoyance, this may sound familiar; these are the same factors that make Microsoft Word documents difficult for alternative word processors.

However, OpenOffice.org Calc is highly compatible with Microsoft Excel. While Calc works well with templates, it does not yet work with macros developed for Microsoft Excel. Once installed, start it in your system by clicking KDE K menu (or GNOME Applications) → Office → OpenOffice.org Calc. In SUSE, OpenOffice.org Calc is in the Office → Spreadsheet submenu.

This annoyance is not meant to denigrate alternative Linux spreadsheet programs, most notably Gnumeric Spreadsheet and KOffice KSpread. These alternatives are also excellent and may also suit your needs. Unfortunately, neither of these programs are available for Microsoft Windows, so you can't ease user transitions in that fashion. (However, a Microsoft port of Gnumeric Spreadsheet is being tested as of this writing.)

OpenOffice.org Calc works with spreadsheets from Microsoft Excel, as well as a number of other spreadsheet programs, including StarOffice Calc, Lotus 123, comma-separated text files, and more.

However, as with any application, you should test it with your users' spreadsheets. Make sure it is compatible with the templates and macros that are run in their files. Don't introduce OpenOffice.org Calc until you're confident that it won't create undue hardship for your users.

I Need My Microsoft Access

While Linux works with several excellent database managers, including MySQL and PostgreSQL, it has been lacking a database client, specifically one with features familiar to those who use Microsoft Access.

OpenOffice.org 2.0 is the first version of this suite with a database tool, known simply as OpenOffice.org Base. If you've installed OpenOffice.org 2.0, Base is available in the same GUI menus as other OpenOffice.org applications (except in SUSE, where it's available in the Database submenu).

As of this writing, when you try to start OpenOffice.org Base, you may get an error message associated with installing the Java Runtime Environment (JRE). To address this issue, take the following steps:

1. Download and install JRE. A Java package may be available for your distribution; for example, SUSE Linux Professional 9.3 includes the *java-1_4_2-sun-plugin* RPM. Alternatively, download and install the appropriate package from *http://www.java.com/en/download/linux_manual.jsp*. For detailed instructions, see "Installing the Latest Version of Firefox" in Chapter 3.

2. In OpenOffice.org, select Tools → Options to open the Options - OpenOffice.org window. In the lefthand pane, under OpenOffice.org, select Java.

   If you don't see a Java suboption, your version of OpenOffice.org may not support OpenOffice.org Base.

3. If you've installed JRE and it's recognized by OpenOffice.org, you'll see that the "Use a Java runtime environment" option is active, as shown in Figure 4-2. Select the latest available version and click OK.

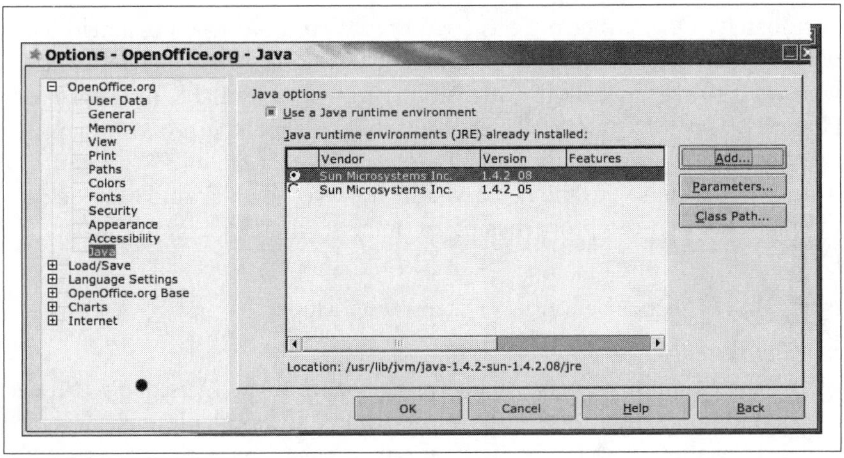

Figure 4-2. Adding JRE

If no version is visible in the window, click Add and navigate to the JRE directory that was installed. The actual location varies by distribution and by package. Once complete, you can select the latest JRE version.

You may have already installed JRE for Firefox, as described in "Firefox Plug-ins" in Chapter 3.

I Want My PowerPoint

One staple of the office is the screen presentation. While many just use bullet points with OpenOffice.org Writer (or Microsoft Word), there are a number of high-powered professionals who are dependent on Microsoft PowerPoint.

Fortunately, OpenOffice.org Impress is a great alternative to Microsoft PowerPoint. It can import PowerPoint presentations, and can help your users create the presentations they need to impress their managers with a variety of innovative tools. In our target distributions, including SUSE Linux, OpenOffice.org Impress can be started from the Office menu.

I Miss My Front Page

With the focus of the Linux geek on the command-line interface, there has been less demand for a GUI web page developer. Many Linux geeks are comfortable writing pages directly in HTML. But that's too much for many regular users to handle. Conditioned by Microsoft Front Page, they expect a GUI web page developer for their web sites.

Fortunately, OpenOffice.org has its Writer/Web tool, which can help users develop their web pages in a GUI, with a second screen available for users who want to see the HTML code, similar to what's available in Front Page. However, OpenOffice.org Writer/Web does not include the same level of functionality as Microsoft's Front Page with respect to links. Yes, you can include hyperlinks with the HTML code; however, with Front Page, it's easy to create links in the properties of an item, such as highlighted text or an image.

Alternatives to OpenOffice.org Writer/Web include:

Mozilla/Netscape Composer
> Mozilla Composer was originally created from the Netscape web page development tool and is the most commonly available web development tool on most Linux distributions. It has many of the same features as Microsoft Front Page. You can also install Netscape Composer on Linux. Standard Mozilla Composer packages are available for the distributions discussed in this book.

Nvu
> Nvu, pronounced "New View," was developed from an older version of Mozilla Composer. It is easy to use and includes most features in Front Page as well as Macromedia's Dreamweaver. Because the first stable version was released in mid-2005, it is not yet in the repositories for our preferred distributions. However, you can build it easily from the source code. For more information and downloads, see *http://nvu.com*.

Quanta Plus

Quanta Plus, built on the KDE development environment, provides one more feature-rich option for web developers. For more information and downloads, see *http://quanta.kdewebdev.org/*.

Another advantage to Mozilla Composer and Nvu is that both applications are available for Microsoft Windows, which can help you ease your users' transition to Linux. Depending on your Linux distribution, you may be able to start these tools from the Office or Internet menus.

I Can't Read PDFs or PostScript Documents

Microsoft users need access to documents in specialized formats. If you expect to convert them to Linux, you have to accommodate these needs. Two of the more important formats are PDF and PostScript. The standard for reading PDFs on Microsoft operating systems is Adobe Acrobat Reader. There is no standard for reading PostScript files on Microsoft Windows, yet it is an important standard for documents because of its compatibility with PostScript printers.

For many regular users, it is best to install Adobe Acrobat on their workstations. I've described the process in "Installing the Latest Version of Firefox" in Chapter 3.

Many Linux geeks do not like the license associated with Adobe Acrobat. Fortunately, there are a number of alternatives to Adobe Acrobat Reader available. In addition, several Linux applications can easily read PostScript files.

 To create PDF documents, you can export to PDF directly from your OpenOffice.org applications, as described in "Creating Acrobat Files," later in this annoyance.

Alternatives to Adobe Acrobat Reader

There are several alternatives to Adobe Acrobat Reader available to Linux users, which I've summarized in this section. Their locations may vary in desktop menus; generally, you can find them under the Office or the Graphics menu:

Xpdf

Xpdf is an open source viewer for PDF files. It's a simple viewer; once the application starts, a right-click opens the menu, and you can highlight and copy data to a text editor. The Xpdf project includes a separate text extractor as well as a PDF-to-PostScript converter. For more information, see *http://www.foolabs.com/xpdf/*.

GNOME PDF

GNOME PDF, naturally, is the PDF reader designed for the GNOME desktop environment. It is based on Xpdf. While it has regular GUI menus, I find it less capable than Xpdf. Although it is still popular, the developers do not appear active, as is apparent on their home page at *http://www.inf.tu-dresden.de/~mk793652/gpdf/*.

Evince

The latest distribution releases include the Evince document viewer, which is intended to be GNOME's all-in-one document reader. It supports documents in PDF, PostScript, DVI formats, and more. For more information, see *http://www.gnome.org/projects/evince/*.

KPDF

KPDF is a reader with excellent potential. It includes views with thumbnails, and it's highly configurable. KPDF version 0.41, included with SUSE Linux, is better than the version of KPDF included with Red Hat Enterprise Linux, as it supports text copying, under the Mouse Mode menu.

If you've already installed the *xpdf* package on SUSE Linux, you'll have to uninstall it first and then install the *kdegraphics3-pdf* RPM, which includes both the KPDF and Xpdf applications. For more information on KPDF, see its home page at *http://kpdf.kde.org/*.

KGhostView

The KGhostView application supports both PDF and PostScript documents. It does not include the text-capture capabilities associated with Xpdf and later versions of KPDF. While it is part of a separate *kghostview* package on Debian Linux, it is part of the *kdegraphics* RPM on Red Hat/Fedora and the *kdegraphics3-postscript* RPM on SUSE Linux. For more information, see the KGhostView documentation at *http://docs.kde.org/development/en/kdegraphics/kghostview/*.

Creating Acrobat Files

You do not need the full version of Adobe Acrobat to create your own PDFs. You can create your own PDF documents with the OpenOffice.org Writer. All you need to do in this application is choose File → Export as PDF. OpenOffice.org Writer takes your document and saves it, including embedded graphics, in PDF format.

Microsoft Office still does not support file exports to PDF format. If you're running the OpenOffice.org suite, you can save the costs associated with Adobe Acrobat.

Reading PostScript Documents

There are PostScript viewers associated with both the GNOME and KDE desktops. The GNOME PostScript reader is known as GGV; the KDE PostScript reader is KGhostView. Both applications are essentially just readers; they do not include any specialized text-capture capabilities. For more information on GGV, see *http://directory.fsf.org/print/misc/ggv.html*; for more information on KGhostView, see the documentation described in the previous section.

I Want My Quicken

As with Microsoft's Office, Intuit's Quicken is another reason regular users hesitate to convert to Linux. They suggest that Quicken isn't available for Linux, and they're right. As of this writing, Intuit has no plans to port Quicken (or its tax software) applications to Linux. Naturally, the same can be said for the main rival to Quicken, Microsoft Money.

In this annoyance, we'll explore some of the open source alternatives to Quicken. In addition, we'll install Quicken with the help of CrossOver Office. You can also install Quicken with Wine, using steps similar to those described for Microsoft Word in "I Need Those Microsoft Applications on Linux" in Chapter 8.

One problem with these open source alternatives is that they're not available for Microsoft Windows. Therefore, if you want to help your users transition to Linux, you may want to install Quicken (and even TurboTax or TaxCut) on an emulator such as CrossOver Office or a VM such as VMWare.

As I am not an accountant, I've avoided detailed evaluations of the open source personal finance programs. However, one of the leaders of the open source movement, Bruce Perens, has openly described his use of Quicken and TurboTax on his Microsoft Windows computer, once per year. So there is no dishonor in using a Microsoft Windows program, even as a Linux geek, if you are not satisfied with the current open source personal finance applications.

With personal finance applications, there are references to QIF and OFX formats. QIF is the original Quicken Interchange Format for downloading transactions from financial institutions, as well as exchanging data between personal finance applications. You can export files in QIF format from older (pre-2005) versions of Quicken and Microsoft Money. Newer versions of Quicken use the Open Financial Exchange (OFX) format, and the open source personal finance tools are doing the same.

KMyMoney

KMyMoney is a full-featured, double-entry accounting application, designed for the K Desktop Environment. As of this writing, KMyMoney states that it's "striving to be a full-featured replacement for your Windows-based finance software."

Stable development packages may be significantly more advanced than what may be available from your distribution repositories. As of this writing, you can download KMyMoney version 0.8 from its home page at *http://kmymoney.sf.net*; the version available from the Debian repositories is 0.64.

Incidentally, KMyMoney has created a number of distribution-specific packages for Fedora, SUSE, Xandros, and Ubuntu Linux (but not Debian). While Fedora and SUSE are popular distributions on the desktop, Debian is not. However, Xandros and Ubuntu are popular consumer-level alternative distributions based on Debian. If you install the source package for KMyMoney, you'll have to unpack the tarball and then follow the instructions as described in the *INSTALL* text file, which is unpacked in the same directory as the rest of the package.

KMyMoney allows you to manage investments, create reports, pull real-time stock quotes, and more. It also supports over 170 different currencies. It even supports the Value Added Tax (VAT) systems common in Europe. In addition, it can help you convert files from GNUCash and Quicken (OFX format).

GNUCash now supports OFX imports, but not directly from U.S. financial institutions, as they do not make the URLs for their download servers publicly available. KMyMoney requires a separate OFX plugin. Unfortunately, neither is nearly as convenient as the click-and-import capabilities associated with Quicken.

By default, on our selected distributions, KMyMoney is available only in the K menu's Office submenu.

GNUCash

The first time you run GNUCash, you'll be prompted either to import files in Quicken QIF format or to create a new set of accounts.

GNUCash supports Quicken-style transaction entry, allows you to schedule future transactions, helps configure loan payments, and supports customer/vendor tracking, invoices, and bill payments. It can help you manage your stock portfolios, reconcile your financial statements, create reports, categorize income and expenses, print checks, and more.

Personal Finance via CrossOver Office

You can install Quicken and even QuickBooks on Linux with the help of CrossOver Office. The procedure is similar to that described in "Microsoft Word Documents Don't Work on Linux," earlier in this chapter, for the installation of Microsoft Word on Linux. If you've installed CrossOver Office, you can see both personal finance applications listed in the Cross-Over Office installation wizard. For more information, see the CrossOver Office compatibility list at *http://www.codeweavers.com/compatibility/*.

 The latest versions of software, especially those updated on a yearly basis, may not be tested on CrossOver Office. While they may work fine, if they're not on the compatibility list, they won't be officially supported by CodeWeavers. However, if an earlier version of a popular application has been supported, they may be quite interested in your installation experiences. This annoyance is based on CrossOver Office Standard version 5.

Installing Quicken via CrossOver Office is fairly easy. Just take the following steps:

1. Insert the Quicken CD/DVD (or record the location of the associated installation files, such as on a shared network directory).

2. Start the CrossOver Office setup tool, available in the GUI from the K menu (GNOME Applications menu) → CrossOver → Install Windows Software.

3. In the CrossOver Standard Setup window, click Install Software.

4. Select Quicken in the window and click Next.

5. Verify installation files on the CD/DVD device (such as */media/cdrecorder*) or another directory that you can specify.

6. Follow the prompts for installation. If you have problems with installing from the CD, you may need to mount it from the command line.

7. Once installation is complete, accept the prompts associated with a CrossOver reboot. Linux keeps running; the CrossOver simulation of a Microsoft system reboots.

8. Open Quicken. In the GUI from the K menu (GNOME Applications menu), select Windows Applications → Programs → Quicken → Quicken (year). Quicken opens in your Linux system, as shown in Figure 4-3.

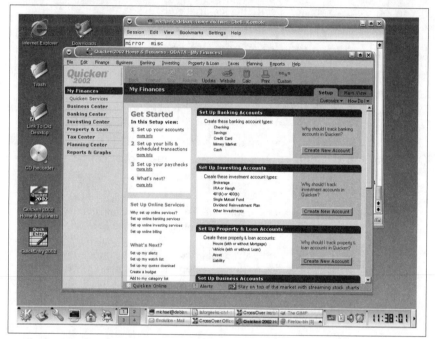

Figure 4-3. Quicken in Linux

Tax Software

Tax software goes hand in hand with personal finance software. Those of us who manage our finances electronically have an easier time doing our taxes. Unfortunately, while it's fairly easy to install personal finance software such as Quicken on CrossOver Office (and even Wine), as of this writing, CodeWeavers does not support U.S. tax software.

Applications such as TurboTax and TaxCut are updated every year, and their releases are time-sensitive. It would be difficult for CodeWeavers to provide the level of support expected by users who are anxious about their taxes.

The installation of TaxCut 2004 worked well for me on CrossOver Office. However, since I had already done my taxes for that year, the copy of Cross-Over Office that I used came after TaxCut 2004 was released. I do not know if TaxCut 2004 would have worked on the previous version of CrossOver Office on a timely basis.

If you try a later version of tax software such as TaxCut or TurboTax 2005, it may work. If not, you may be able to find the problem based on the associated logfile, *Unsupported*.log*, in the *~/.cxoffice/dotwine/dosdevices/c:/Windows/Temp* directory. It's a huge file; when I installed TaxCut 2004, the log was over 300kb.

If you have to support Linux users who need personal tax software, there are several options:

- Virtual machine software such as VMWare or Win4Lin
- A dual-boot configuration with Microsoft Windows
- Remote access to a Microsoft computer, with a service such as rdesktop or Windows Terminal Services
- Web-based tax software (TurboTax for the Web is available at *http://www.turbotax.com*, and TaxCut for the Web is available at *http://www.taxcut.com/tcforweb/*)

If you or your users run a personal finance program such as Quicken on a Linux system, you can still export the datafiles to wherever you've installed your tax software, even a Microsoft Windows system.

I Need a Screenshot

When you just need to document what's happening, a picture is worth a thousand words. To create that picture, many Microsoft Windows users run Corel's Paint Shop Pro and Adobe's Photoshop. These programs support extensive graphics capabilities and allow you to take screenshots of your desktop.

There are several Linux applications that can help you get that screenshot you need. I'll explore a few of them here. More importantly, these Linux applications can meet any other graphics needs of those who rely on Microsoft-based graphics programs.

Perhaps movie studios have the most intensive needs for quality graphics. According to *http://linuxmovies.org*, Linux has become the operating system of choice for Fox, Disney, DreamWorks, Universal, and others. While some of these studios have shown antagonism toward open source licenses in the past, our information suggests that they recognize the superiority of graphics applications on Linux.

If Linux graphics applications are not good enough for you or your users (or if your users are just dependent on Windows-based applications), Cross-Over Office supports the installation of Adobe Photoshop. The procedure is as simple as those described previously in this chapter with respect to the installation of Quicken and Microsoft Word.

 If you're creating instructions for your users, you'll be interested in the screenshot capabilities of many of these programs. The screenshots you can create can help you provide more effective directions.

The GIMP

Perhaps the most commonly used graphics-manipulation program on Linux is the GIMP, also known as the GNU Image Manipulation Program (*http://www.gimp.org*). As described on its web site, you can use it for such tasks as photo retouching, image composition, and image authoring.

The GIMP is also commonly used for screenshots. It is what I've used to capture the figures that you see in this book. Taking screenshots is an excellent way to illustrate the steps your users can take to do their work, easing their transition to Linux.

If you want to take a screenshot, choose File → Acquire → Screenshot from the GIMP menu. In the Screen Shot window that opens, you can select a single window or the whole screen. If you want to depict a menu that requires a mouse click, use the Grab After __ Seconds Delay option. This allows you to open the menu options you want to depict before the screenshot is taken.

Eye of GNOME

If you just need a graphics viewer on the GNOME desktop, all you need is the Eye of GNOME and the Nautilus file browser. For example, after you open Nautilus in a screen similar to Figure 4-4, just double-click on the desired image to open it in the Eye of GNOME. As you can see, image thumbnails in Nautilus help you identify the image that you need.

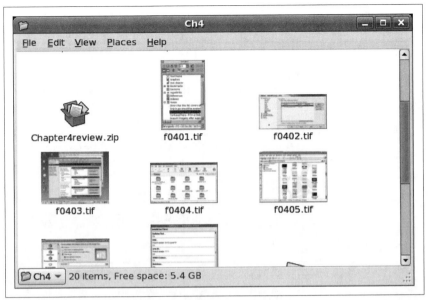

Figure 4-4. Nautilus displays image thumbnails

GNOME Panel Screenshot

If you just need a screenshot without complications on the GNOME Desktop, click Desktop → Take Screenshot. (On older versions of GNOME, click Actions → Take Screenshot.) This activates the GNOME Panel screenshot utility. On Red Hat/Fedora and Debian distributions, it's part of the *gnome-panel* package. On SUSE Linux, it's part of the *gnome-utils* package.

From the command line, this utility is surprisingly versatile. For example, if you want a screenshot of a specific window, take the following steps:

1. Open a command-line console, or a command window with Alt-F2.

2. Enter the *gnome-panel-screenshot --window --delay=5* command. You'll have five seconds to perform step 3; if you need more time, change the *--delay* switch as needed.

3. Open the desired window, and hover the mouse pointer over that window.

4. In the Save Screenshot window that opens, specify a filename for the screenshot that you want to save. While the default format is *.png*, other formats are possible, including *.gif* and *.tif*. Just save the screenshot in the desired file format.

KDE Viewers

The K Desktop Environment includes a number of viewers, integrated with the Konqueror file browser. To see how this works, open Konqueror on your K Desktop Environment. On our preferred distributions, click the K menu → Home. This opens Konqueror, displaying the files in your home directory.

Assuming you have graphics files in your home directory, you'll be able to view thumbnails by default in Konqueror without any additional configuration. In Figure 4-5, I show a view of some of my graphics files in my *~/lageeks* subdirectory.

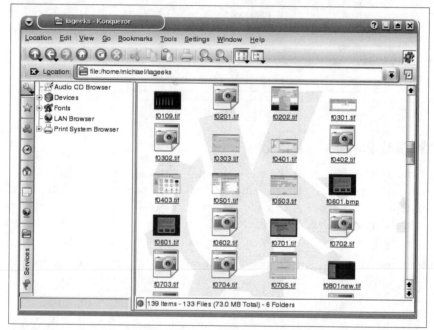

Figure 4-5. Viewing graphical thumbnails in Konqueror

Double-click the graphical file of your choice, and the graphic will be shown full size in Konqueror. You can also open the graphic in another viewer. Under the Konqueror Location menu, you can open the graphic in KView, the Eye of GNOME, or the GIMP (assuming these graphical viewers are installed). Just right-click on the item and select the Open With option to make your choice.

KDE Snapshot

If you need a simple graphical screenshot program on the KDE desktop, install the KSnapshot program. On Fedora/Red Hat Enterprise Linux, it's part of the *kdegraphics* RPM. On SUSE Linux, it's part of the *kdegraphics3* RPM. On Debian Linux, it's part of the *ksnapshot* DEB package.

The menu steps required to start the KDE Snapshot program vary by distribution. The one way to start it on all distributions is to open a command line in the GUI, or a command window with the Alt-F2 command, and then type in *ksnapshot*.

The KDE Snapshot program starts by taking a snapshot of your desktop. You can take a snapshot of an individual window, with a delay, by using the following instructions. In these steps, I'll take a screenshot of a command-line interface in the GUI:

1. Open a command-line window on the KDE desktop. On SUSE Linux, you can do so by clicking the K menu → System → Terminal → Konsole; on Red Hat/Fedora, click the K menu → System Tools → Terminal; and on Debian, click K Menu → System → Terminal.

2. Hide the scrollbar, the tabs, and the menu bar. In the KDE terminal window that appears, choose Settings → Scrollbar → Hide; then select Settings → Tab Bar → Hide; and finally, select Settings → Hide Menubar.

3. Run a simple command; for this exercise, I run *ls -l*.

4. On a GUI desktop, open a command line with the Alt-F2 command.

5. Enter the *ksnapshot* command in the text box.

6. Under the Capture Mode text box, scroll to Window Under Cursor. Select an appropriate snapshot delay; you'll have this amount of time to perform step 7.

   If you don't want the window frame, deselect the "Include window decorations" option.

7. Click New Snapshot, and open the window that you want in your image. Make sure to hover the cursor over this window before the snapshot delay has expired.

8. Save the snapshot. You may already be able to see how the snapshot resembles a command-line console, without the GUI. Even better, the screenshot includes black text on a white background, which is easier to read.

Making GUI File Managers Work for You

Both the KDE and GNOME desktops have their own file managers. Nautilus is built for GNOME, and Konqueror is built for KDE. If you've read the previous annoyance, you've seen how these file managers can help you work with graphics. They can help you (and regular users) manage the files on their systems. In this annoyance, I describe how you might configure these file managers for regular users.

KDE Konqueror

KDE's Konqueror is a versatile file manager. It should normally be installed by default, when you install the K Desktop Environment on your computer. Just in case, it's a part of the Red Hat/Fedora *kdebase* RPM, the SUSE *kdebase3* RPM, and the Debian *konqueror* package.

To configure Konqueror, click Settings → Configure Konqueror. As you can see from Figure 4-6, it's a highly customizable file manager. As you can also see, there are several categories of customizations in the lefthand pane. I'll cover each of these options in the following subsections.

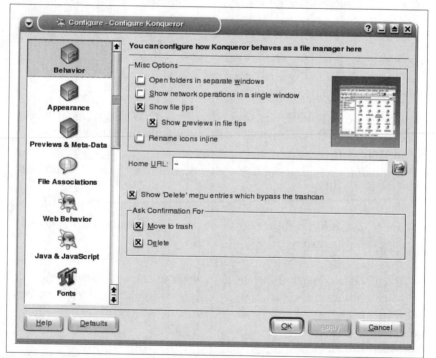

Figure 4-6. Konqueror is highly customizable

Any changes you make are saved in the *konquerorrc* configuration file, in each user's *~/.kde/share/config* directory. If you want to save your changes as default settings for each of your workstations, place them in the appropriate directory; on Red Hat/Fedora, it's */usr/share/config*, and on SUSE, it's */etc/opt/kde3/share/config*. Debian does not include a default directory for this configuration file.

Behavior

Under Behavior settings, you can configure several Konqueror functions, including:

- Opening folders locally or in a separate window
- Browsing network shares locally or in a separate window
- Showing file tips
- Supporting renaming of filenames (icons) inline
- Setting a default home page
- Managing file deletions

Appearance

Under the Appearance settings, you can define the standard font, size, and color Konqueror uses. You can also define the height of icon text, whether filenames are underlined, and the units used to display file sizes.

Previews & Meta-Data

Under the Previews & Meta-Data settings, you can define the maximum size of previewed files, whether previews are magnified, and whether Konqueror can use thumbnails already embedded in files.

File Associations

Here, you can define the applications associated with different filename extensions. Konqueror includes a wide variety of categories, from images to messages to video. It allows you to add preferred applications for different types of files, as well as what is done when users select those files.

Web Behavior

Konqueror also works as a web browser. It allows you to configure bookmarks, behavior for completing forms, tabbed browsing, responses to mouse behavior, links, and animations, as well as the loading of images and redirects.

Java & JavaScript

If you want to enable Java and JavaScript options for your web browsing, you can enable it here. However, you'll also have to install a compatible Java release environment. Unfortunately, according to the current Konqueror HOWTO for Java (*http://www.konqueror.org/javahowto/*), the Java you may have downloaded for Firefox in "Firefox Isn't Working as It Should" in Chapter 3 or for OpenOffice.org Base in "I Need My Microsoft Office," earlier this chapter, may not work for Konqueror. Alternatives are listed on the HOWTO page.

Fonts

Under the Fonts settings, you can do more than define standard fonts, as previously discussed in the "Appearance" section. You can define font sizes, the fonts associated with different web page settings, and the default encoding, which can help if you regularly browse non-English pages.

Web Shortcuts

Web shortcuts allow you to enter abbreviations for a number of commonly used web sites. For example, by default, the RPM Find service at *http://www.rpmfind.net* is associated with the *rf* web shortcut. If you want to search for RPM packages associated with the kernel, enter the following in the Location text box:

```
rf:kernel
```

Based on the default settings under Web Shortcuts, Konqueror translates this to the following URL:

```
http://rpmfind.net/linux/rpm2html/search.php?query=kernel
```

History Sidebar

Under the History Sidebar settings, you can specify the number of URLs retained in the Konqueror history, as well as their time in the cache (90 days by default).

Cookies

Under the Cookies settings, you can specify browser policies in response to cookies offered by different web sites. If you accept cookies on a permanent basis from a site, it's added to the Site Policy window shown in this section.

Cache

Under the Cache settings, you can specify the size of the cache associated with your browsing. Konqueror will take from the cache when possible, if you activate the "Use cache" option.

Proxy

If you have a proxy server for your network, you can specify whether and how you use the proxy. You can also enable SOCKS support to allow users to access FTP sites and more through a firewall.

Cascading Stylesheets (CSS)

You can customize the stylesheets used to render web pages. It is also one way to help make the Web more accessible for those who are visually impaired.

Crypto

You can specify access to web sites through a wide variety of cryptographic protocols. You can also specify access to OpenSSL shared libraries. If you have SSL certificates, such as for your email, you can specify or configure them here.

Browser Identification

You can specify how Konqueror is seen as a browser. Such data is collected by web servers to identify the browsers used to connect to their sites. This setting is also used to render different formats for web pages, and thus may have to be set manually because some web sites refuse to display pages to browsers not tested by the developers. You can set Konqueror to be identified as Netscape, Opera, or even Microsoft's Internet Explorer.

Plugins

You can configure Konqueror with plug-ins, such as what you may have configured for Firefox in "Firefox Isn't Working as It Should" in Chapter 3. In fact, if you've added Firefox plug-ins, many of them may also work for Konqueror. Under these settings, you can click "Scan for New Plugins." If detected, Konqueror may work well with them. For example, I've been able to work on Konqueror with the Adobe Acrobat Reader plug-ins described in "Firefox Isn't Working as It Should" in Chapter 3.

Performance

Under the Performance settings, you can configure memory usage as well as the number of preloaded threads associated with the Konqueror web browser.

GNOME Nautilus

GNOME's Nautilus is also a versatile file manager. It should normally be installed by default, when you install the GNOME desktop environment on your computer. Just in case it's not, it's a part of the *nautilus* package on all of the distributions covered in this book.

 Older versions of Nautilus had web browser capabilities. You can still use it as a remote file browser—for example, to browse an FTP server.

To start Nautilus, browsing in your home directory, click Places → Home Folder (or, in older versions of GNOME, Applications → Home).

Configuring Nautilus

When you configure Nautilus, not all options are available, depending on what you have installed. You may need a more advanced version of GNOME to get all of the options described in this subsection.

To configure Nautilus, select Edit → Preferences. This opens a File Management Preferences window with five tabs:

Views
> Under the Nautilus File Management Preferences Views tab, you can configure whether files and folders are shown as icons or names, whether icons and lists are shown in a zoom mode, and whether directory trees are shown.

Behaviour
> Under the Behaviour tab (which is shown with the British spelling), you can configure single- or double-clicks, actions on executable files, and how deleted files are managed with respect to the Nautilus wastebasket.

Display
> Under the Display tab, you can configure three items to display with icon captions, as well as the date format used.

List Columns
> Under the List Columns tab, you can change the amount of information associated with each item.

Preview

Under the Preview tab, you can configure thumbnails, sound clips, items in folders, and text in icons.

Nautilus as an Internet file browser

Although Nautilus no longer works as a web browser, you can still use it as an Internet file browser, such as for FTP servers. For example, if you want to browse the *kernel.org* FTP server, take the following steps:

1. Open Nautilus. In addition to the options described earlier, you can also press Alt-F2 and enter the *nautilus* command.
2. In Nautilus, click File → Connect to Server to open a window of the same name.
3. In the "Service type" drop-down menu, select Public FTP.
4. Enter the URL for your chosen FTP server—in this case, *ftp.kernel.org*. If special information is required for Port or a Folder, enter it in the appropriate text boxes, and click Connect.
5. Start browsing the FTP server!

I Need a Movie Viewer

Linux supports several different multimedia applications that can play DVDs. (In "That Command Doesn't Write to My DVD" in Chapter 2, I showed you how you can copy DVDs that you've created.) However, if you try to play a DVD movie that you've rented from the video store, the DVD players probably won't work. The difference is that commercial DVDs, such as those with commercial movies, are encrypted. DVDs aren't supposed to be playable in computers, at least without copy protection. They are protected using a 40-bit-encryption-stream cipher algorithm, the Content Scrambling System (CSS).

I'll show you what you need to install to bypass this encryption—specifically the decryption package that uses a brute-force decryption routine to read commercial DVDs encrypted via CSS. Then I'll show you how you can install and run several different movie viewers.

Several major entertainment companies discourage the use of decryption on Linux, as it facilitates free (and illegal) copying of commercial DVDs. As Linux companies exercise an abundance of caution to minimize the risk of lawsuits, most Linux distributions do not include DVD decryption packages with their packages. However, they can be easily downloaded from third-party sources, and they integrate seamlessly with the major Linux movie viewers. To address some of the fears that may be associated with software for commercial DVDs on Linux, I address the decryption issues in the next section.

 As there are no movie-player packages included with Red Hat Enterprise Linux, I do not cover the installation procedure on that distribution. If you require a movie player on Red Hat Enterprise Linux, the procedure is similar to that for Fedora.

SUSE is perhaps more cautious about its users playing encrypted DVD movies. The movie players included with the SUSE distributions do not support reading commercial DVDs, even with appropriate DVD decryption software. If you want to play a DVD movie on SUSE Linux, you'll have to download the players from a third party, such as *http://packman.links2linux.org*.

 Movie players and automatic mounters don't play very well. If you want to configure a movie player on your system, I recommended that you disable any Autostart or other defaults that may automatically mount an installed DVD, as described in Chapter 7.

Decryption Issues

The Motion Picture Association of America (MPAA) and the Recording Industry Association of America (RIAA) have worked to discourage decryption of commercial DVDs. After the decryption program DeCSS was developed in 1999, the MPAA filed an international complaint, which prompted the Norwegian authorities to place one of the reported developers, Jon Johansen, on trial. Johansen was eventually acquitted of all charges.

As CSS provides only 40-bit encryption, the decryption of CSS-encoded DVDs is not rocket science. However, one legal issue regarding DeCSS is how it was reportedly developed with a reverse-engineered encryption key from a DVD player. The MPAA and RIAA have resorted to various lawsuits to prevent distribution of DeCSS, citing this reverse engineering. In 2004, a related lawsuit against the distribution of DeCSS was dropped, and a previous ban was overturned as a violation of free speech.

In other words, it's probably legal to distribute DeCSS; however, reverse-engineering a proprietary decryption key is another question.

Alternatively, current Linux media players can use the *libdvdcss* package to decrypt CSS-encoded DVDs. As this package does not use a reverse-engineered key from a DVD player, it might not be subject to the same legal risks associated with DeCSS. However, with the history of legal action on the subject, it's understandable that Linux companies would hesitate to include DVD decryption packages with their distributions.

Current DVD Decryption Software

To decrypt commercial DVDs, you'll need the *libdvdcss* package. You can download the latest version from the VideoLan developers at *http://download. videolan.org/pub/libdvdcss/*. As of this writing, the VideoLan developers also provide packages in RPM and DEB format.

 The developers behind *libdvdcss*, at least those listed on the VideoLan web site, are all located in Europe, which makes legal action from the MPAA and RIAA more difficult.

The *libdvdcss* packages are also available from third-party repositories, including:

- The *ftp.nerim.net/debian-marillat* repositories for Debian distributions.
- Standard third-party repositories for Fedora Core and Red Hat Enterprise Linux—from *http://dries.studentenweb.org*, *http://dag.wieers.com*, and *http://atrpms.net*, among others.
- Repositories maintained by individual SUSE developers; for my SUSE 9.3 computer, I downloaded the *libdvdutil* package from *ftp://ftp.gwdg. de/pub/linux/misc/suser-sbarnin/suse92/i586/RPMS/*. When I upgraded to SUSE 10.0, I used the *libdvdutil* package from almost the same URL, except I substituted *suse93* for *suse92* (yes, the updates are one revision behind). When you install *libdvdutil* from this repository, you're actually installing *libdvdcss*.

Once *libdvdcss* is installed, run the DVD player of your choice. When you start the DVD player, you may have to wait a few extra seconds while the decryption algorithm breaks the 40-bit CSS key.

Totem Movie Player

The Totem Movie Player is a standard application for playing DVDs on Linux systems (along with audio formats and streaming media) and is designed for the GNOME desktop environment. Installation is a straightforward process; all it requires is the package of the same name.

Once Totem is properly installed, it's easy to open and run. On Fedora or Debian Linux, select Applications → Multimedia → Totem Movie Player. In

SUSE Linux, select Applications → Multimedia → Video Player → Totem Movie Player. Generally, all you need to do is insert the DVD into the drive, select Movie → Play Disc, and you're good to go! The volume and play controls are intuitive; if you want to view your movie in full-screen mode, choose View → Fullscreen; you can use your mouse to control the standard DVD movie menus.

If you see an "Are you trying to play an encrypted DVD without libdvdcss?" message, you may have forgotten to install the decryption package described earlier, or the package may not be appropriate for your system. On rare occasions, it may be due to a DVD that is somewhat worn or warped, which makes the movie more difficult for *libdvdcss* to handle.

If you see a "Please check that a disc is present in the drive" message, Totem is having trouble mounting the DVD. Try mounting the DVD with a command such as *mount /media/ cdrecorder*, and then try again.

If you want to run encrypted DVD movies on SUSE Linux, you'll need to download and install the Totem Movie Player from a third party. As recommended earlier, I downloaded and installed the Totem Movie Player from *http://packman.links2linux.org/*. One advantage of that site is that it also includes the packages that are required as dependencies.

For details on how the Totem Movie Player works, refer to its home page at *http://www.gnome.org/projects/totem/*.

MPlayer

Developed in Hungary, MPlayer has recently won the TUX Magazine Readers' Choice award for Favorite Media Player. However, if you're using MPlayer to run commercial DVD movies, you won't be able to get to the standard movie menus associated with subtitles, episodes, special features, and so on.

Once MPlayer is properly installed, it's easy to open and run. On Fedora or Debian Linux, select Applications → Multimedia → MPlayer. In SUSE Linux, select Applications → Multimedia → Video Player → MPlayer.

One small annoyance when you start MPlayer for the first time on Debian is an error message relating to "New_Face." and *subfont.ttf* in the ~/.mplayer subdirectory. If this occurs,, find the *.ttf* font file of your choice and copy it to that location.

To start a DVD movie in MPlayer, right-click on the screen for a pop-up menu, and then click DVD → Open Disc. Once MPlayer has connected to the DVD, you can select titles, chapters, audio languages, and subtitle languages from the pop-up menu's DVD submenu. In many cases, titles correspond loosely to episodes, and chapters to scenes.

You can also adjust the size of the video on the screen with the pop-up menu to "normal size," "double size," and "full screen." Once in full-screen mode, you can access controls by moving your mouse pointer toward the bottom of the screen.

If you want to run encrypted DVD movies on SUSE Linux, you'll need to download and install the MPlayer from a third party. As recommended earlier, I downloaded and installed the MPlayer from *http://packman.links2linux.org/*. One advantage of that site is that it also includes the packages that are required as dependencies.

For details on how MPlayer works, refer to its home page at *http://www. mplayerhq.hu/*.

Kaffeine

The first time you start the KDE Media Player, also known as Kaffeine, it starts the associated Installation Wizard. You can do so from the K Desktop Environment by clicking the K menu → Multimedia → Kaffeine (in SUSE, Kaffeine is in the Multimedia → Video Player submenu). The wizard does not prompt for any input; it tells you what it found in a screen similar to Figure 4-7.

It checks for:

- Proper installation of the Kaffeine package.
- An appropriate version of the K Desktop Environment.
- A current version of the *xine-lib* package (which is the *libxine1* package on SUSE and Debian).
- Win32 codecs, which can allow you to play *.wma* files associated with Windows Media Player. If you want to download these files, see the sidebar "Other Codecs."
- Proper installation of *libdvdcss* for decryption.
- An available DVD drive. (It also checks for access to DMA mode for smooth playback and may suggest you run an *hdparm* command; for more information, see "My Hard Drive Is Too Slow" in Chapter 8.)

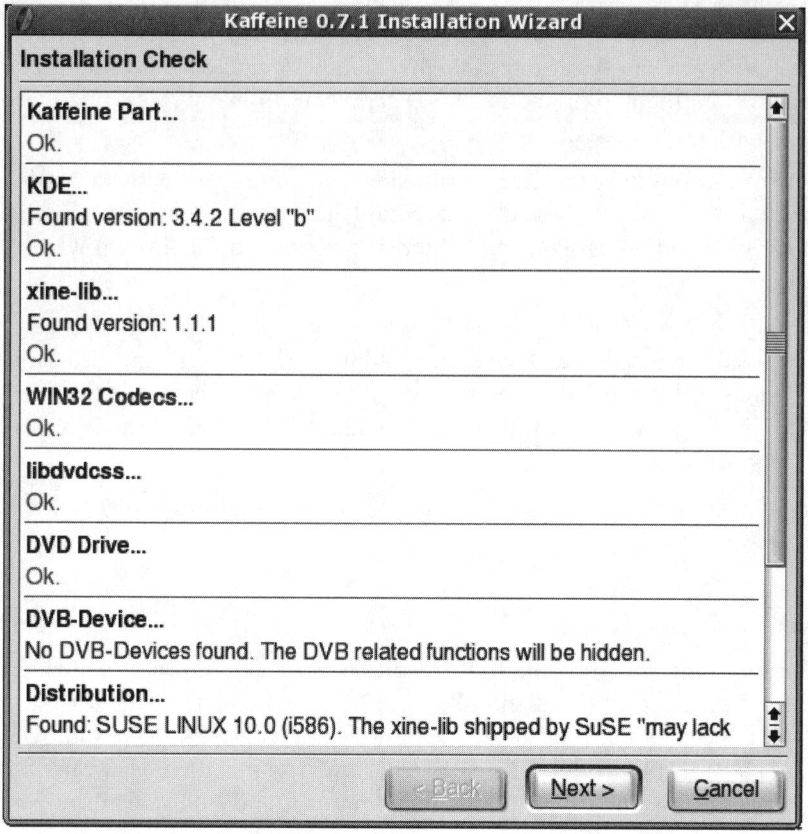

Figure 4-7. Kaffeine Installation Wizard results

- An available DVB device, associated with Digital Video Broadcasting (*http://www.dvb.org*).

- An appropriate distribution; as you can see from Figure 4-7, the Kaffeine viewer installed with SUSE does not support movies.

In the following step, you're prompted whether you'd like to configure Kaffeine to work with Microsoft or Real Media streams. If you want to do so, you'll also need the codecs described in the "Other Codecs" sidebar.

Like Totem, Kaffeine supports mouse access to standard DVD movie menus associated with episodes, subtitles, special features, and so on.

To start a DVD movie in Kaffeine, double-click on the Open DVD icon under the Go tab. Once Kaffeine has connected to the DVD, you can use your mouse to select titles, chapters, audio languages, and subtitle

Other Codecs

If you want to use Kaffeine to view additional media formats, including those associated with Windows Media Player and Real Player, you'll have to download the "essential codecs." One source for these codecs is the home page for MPlayer, whose codecs also work for Kaffeine. For more information, point your browser to the MPlayer home page at *http://www.mplayerhq.hu*, and navigate to the download pages. The packages that you can download and install from this site include appropriate codecs that you can copy to a directory such as */usr/lib/win32*.

languages. You can also move to full-screen mode with the Ctrl-Shift-F command.

If you want to run encrypted DVD movies on SUSE Linux, you'll need to download and install Kaffeine from a third party. As recommended earlier, I downloaded and installed Kaffeine from *http://packman.links2linux.org/*. One advantage of that site is that it also includes the packages that are required as dependencies.

For details on how Kaffeine works, refer to its home page at *http://kaffeine. sf.net/*.

CHAPTER 5

Installation Annoyances

A "macho" Linux user might just jump in and install a random Linux distribution on any available hardware. In contrast, a real Linux geek uses hard-learned knowledge to plan a Linux installation. A quality plan can help the geek manage the system throughout its life cycle. Once tested, that system can be replicated in the enterprise, saving cost and time. In this chapter, I provide guidance that can help you harness your experience before you install.

The latest Linux distributions are easy to install on most modern hardware. I've found few annoyances within the installation routines for the Linux distributions I know. But there are related topics that merit careful attention. Ideally, every hardware component that you own is certified by the Linux distribution of your choice. But we live in the real world. For example, many geeks have to deal with bosses who want Linux installed on the cheapest possible laptops (translation: hardware that depends on Microsoft driver libraries with few available Linux drivers) with all the latest features, such as wireless support and working high-resolution displays.

The choice of Linux distributions can be difficult. Your manager may not have heard of your favorite distribution. If you choose a cost-free version of Linux, you generally have to download gigabytes of data, and "everyone" wants the latest distribution when it's released. While there are brand-name distributions that may get a corporate stamp of approval, they may also break your budget. Unless you can afford to rely exclusively on support from Red Hat or Novell/SUSE, you need to know how to interact with the Linux community in order to solve some of the annoyances I touch on in this book. While flames may seem to be the norm to many, there are several principles that can maximize the quality of response from the community, which I'll list at the end of the chapter.

Linux Won't Work with All My Hardware

One common "annoyance" is the literature that warns of dire consequences if you don't record every detail of your hardware before starting the installation process. You've probably installed Linux on a variety of computers. While you may never have had a problem with hardware, trouble does happen. For this reason, some Linux vendors, including Red Hat and Novell, do test and certify hardware components as well as entire systems. They offer more extensive support if you use such hardware. Even if you're using another distribution, their certified hardware is more likely to work reliably with Linux.

Classifying Hardware

Any A+ certified hardware technician can list the hardware components on a computer. A Linux geek can cite the compatible components, such as the chipsets associated with a specific wireless card. He can use this information to compile the most efficient kernel for his system.

 The A+ certification was developed by CompTIA, primarily as an entry-level exam for Microsoft computer hardware technicians. As someone comfortable with Linux, you know so much more about computers. The entry-level CompTIA Linux+ exam (*www.comptia.org/certification/linux/*) includes a significant hardware component. Other Linux certifications include those released by the Linux Professional Institute (*www.lpi.org*), Novell (*www.novell.com/training/certinfo/*), and Red Hat (*www.redhat.com/training/certification/*).

If you're installing Linux at home, consider whether your system has any of the common components in Table 5-1, and ensure you know at least the make and model of each component. If time is limited, focus on the components that you configure during the installation process: the size of the hard drive(s), CPU(s) type, amount of RAM, and video card chipset.

Table 5-1. Common hardware components

Component	Key information to learn	Additional information
Motherboard/BIOS	Integrated support (e.g., video)	A BIOS upgrade may add useful options.
CPU	Type (x86 [e.g., i386, i586, i686], ia-64, Itanium)	Some distributions may be built for your CPU.
RAM	Amount	Minimums vary by distribution. Some BIOSes can detect only a limited amount of RAM.

Table 5-1. Common hardware components (continued)

Component	Key information to learn	Additional information
Video card	Chipset	If Linux can't detect your chipset, get the Horizontal and Vertical refresh rates.
Hard drive controller	IDE, SCSI, SATA, RAID support	SCSI and SATA can support more than the standard 4 IDE drives.
Network adapters	Chipset, revision	If Linux doesn't detect your adapter, knowing the chipset and revision level can help you find alternative drivers.
Sound	Chipset	Most have MIDI/ALSA support.
Hard drive	Size	A few drives are not supported; avoid the same IDE cable for multiple drives.
Pointing device	Mouse protocol	Most two-button mice can imitate the middle (third) button.
Keyboard	Keyboard type	Usually associated with a language.
Modem	Connection (PCI/USB/ISA)	Microsoft-dependent hardware discussed later.
Printers	Parallel/USB	Microsoft-dependent hardware discussed later.

What follows are solutions to the most common hardware annoyances, with general guidance that you can follow for unspecified hardware problems. Ideally, you should classify your systems or hardware in the following categories:

- Certified hardware by a distribution company
- Compatible hardware, as classified in one of the Linux hardware databases
- Additional Linux-compatible hardware, which requires additional research, including the Linux Hardware HOWTO
- Linux hardware in the works, with pre-release drivers
- Incompatible hardware, awaiting development

Certified Hardware

The first thing to check is the web site for your Linux vendor. They maintain lists of hardware and systems that they've tested. You can find Red Hat's list at *http://bugzilla.redhat.com/hwcert/*; Novell/SUSE currently maintains their list (English version) at *http://hardwaredb.suse.de/?LANG=en_UK*. If you're lucky, you're working with complete hardware systems certified for a specific distribution. Red Hat and SUSE have tested a number of complete servers, workstations, notebooks, and more. If you are installing a Linux distribution on certified hardware, you should have no problems, and you may be able to get additional support for your systems.

One implied category of certified hardware consists of computers where Linux is already preinstalled. There are a number of vendors, including big names such as HP and Dell, who sell systems where they install a major Linux distribution for you. They support their systems with the originally installed operating system. All you need to do is keep it up-to-date. However, if you add hardware or a new Linux distribution, you may be on your own.

Compatible Hardware

Red Hat and SUSE, among others, maintain a database of compatible hardware. Such hardware has been tested, often by employees associated with that distribution. This is known by Red Hat as "compatible hardware" and by SUSE as "ready for SUSE Linux." While distributor companies may provide limited support for such hardware, there may be interactions such as IRQ conflicts beyond their control.

 Red Hat has recently changed their hardware database to focus on compatible hardware systems. As of this writing, there are very few individual hardware component compatible with Red Hat Enterprise Linux 4.

As Debian is built by volunteers, they do not have a program of certified hardware. But as with any Linux distribution, you can start your hardware checks with the Linux Hardware HOWTO, available from *http://www.tldp. org/HOWTO/Hardware-HOWTO*.

Additional Linux-Compatible Hardware

The databases provided by the Linux distributors can't keep up with the torrent of new hardware. They may not have updated their databases for the latest Linux drivers. So if you don't see your hardware on a compatibility list, don't give up! I'd look in five areas:

- Check the web site associated with your hardware. You might just find a new set of Linux drivers, ready for download. If you're lucky, you may get an RPM or DEB package that you can install directly on your system. Alternatively, if you have to compile drivers from their source code, you may need to install the Linux kernel source code for your system. Watch the *Makefile* associated with such source code; you may need to modify its settings.

- At other times, Linux compatibility may be there where you least expect. The chipset associated with a component may be produced by a third company.

- Third, Linux drivers for earlier versions of a component may provide partial compatibility. For example, the drivers associated with a version 1000 scanner may provide sufficient functionality if you're working with a version 1100 scanner.

- Fourth, there are developers who enjoy cloning drivers for new hardware. Just as the original Linux developers cloned the functionality of Unix, the Linux hackers of today create new source code that emulates the functionality of proprietary drivers. Sometimes hackers build the functionality with original code; other times they may build wrappers that allow use of drivers built for other operating systems. As open source developers want to share their work, their progress is usually available online. Some are organized into SourceForge groups, which are listed at *http://www.sourceforge.net*.

- Finally, you sometimes may be able to extract the drivers by recompiling the kernel. I describe the recompiling process in "Recompiling the Kernel" in Chapter 7.

Linux Hardware in the Works

Linux hackers are constantly at work on incompatible hardware. They lobby hardware vendors to release their source code. They clone drivers for desirable peripherals. The open source nature of Linux means that the development work is transparent. If you have the time, there are a multitude of projects where you can help. SourceForge is the home of a number of Linux hardware projects.

The people behind Linux distributions are often cautious. Many won't include a developmental driver until it is tested and proven to work, without causing trouble with other systems. But if you absolutely need that wireless card, that scanner, that memory stick, etc., developmental drivers may be your only choice. And if you have to compile the driver into your kernel, that's another annoyance we'll work through in "I Need to Add a Custom Kernel Module" in Chapter 7.

Any developmental software that you install may be less than complete. For example, you may need to configure a script to load the appropriate drivers the next time you boot Linux. If you want to run the script during the boot process, you can make it part of the appropriate boot script from the following table:

Distribution	Script
Debian	/etc/init.d/local
Red Hat/Fedora	/etc/rc.local
SUSE	/etc/init.d/boot.local

These files are often empty; when you add the commands of your choice, they're run automatically during the boot process. You'll actually have to create /etc/init.d/local on Debian Linux; all you need is to start the script with the first line to use the bash shell interpreter, followed by the full path to the commands you need:

```
#!/bin/sh
/path/to/command switch
```

You'll need to make sure the command starts in the appropriate runlevels, preferably after other scripts, with the following command:

```
update-rc.d local defaults 99c
```

Incompatible Hardware

The resources of the Linux community are limited. They may not be working on the hardware that you need. There are third parties who can help, for a fee. For example, Xi Graphics' DeXtop (*http://www.xinside.com*) and SciTech's SNAP graphics (*http://www.scitechsoft.com*) provide proprietary drivers for many otherwise incompatible graphics cards. Linuxant (*http://www.linuxant.com*) provides a wrapper that uses Microsoft Windows driver software for network cards.

If you're brave and dedicated, you can start your own Linux hardware project. A good place to start is SourceForge, where you may ask for help from those working on related projects. Alternatively, *Linux Device Drivers* by Jonathan Corbet et al. (O'Reilly) is also an excellent resource, as it can help you identify starting points from related hardware.

I'm Having Trouble with Microsoft-Dependent Hardware

In typical desktop and laptop systems, a number of components depend on Microsoft Windows driver libraries. The most well known of these is the *winmodem*. Trouble with Microsoft-dependent devices is not limited to Linux; there are a wide range of Microsoft-dependent devices that do not work on Windows XP/2003. While most of these devices are modems and older printers, don't be surprised if you find other Microsoft-dependent hardware. Many of the initial "hacks" that support this hardware are based on the Wine project, which allows Linux to use Microsoft driver libraries.

 As strange as it sounds, about half of U.S. Internet connections are still made via telephone modem. While this seems almost "third world" in contrast to broadband connections in other industrial nations, it means that telephone modems are still a common fact of life in the U.S., and a key skill set for the well-rounded Linux geek.

The winmodem

In principle, it's best to find and install hardware that does not depend on Microsoft driver libraries. In practice, that's not feasible, as many computers come preloaded with winmodems.

In many cases, Linux detects winmodems straight out of the box. To see if that applies to your system, run the *lspci* command. Linux has detected winmodems on all three of my computers. The *lspci* output is straightforward; I've isolated the key lines for the detected internal modems:

```
01:0e.0 Communication controller: Conexant HSF 56k Data/Fax Modem (rev 01)
0000:00:08.0 Modem: Ali Corporation M5457 AC'97 Modem Controller
```

When I ran a *cardctl ident* command, Linux also detected the PCMCIA winmodem on my third computer, a Motorola ModemSurfr, as shown here:

```
Socket 1:
    product info: "Motorola", "MobileSURFR 56K", "021", "A"
    manfid: 0x0109, 0x0505
    function: 2 (serial)
```

 cardctl is being replaced on the latest Linux distributions with *pccard ctl*.

If you have an ISA modem, you might try a *pnpdump* or *isapnp* command. If a modem is installed when you start Linux, you might be able to find a related message in the */var/log* directory, in the *dmesg* or *messages* files.

But even when your winmodem is supported by the kernel, configuring the modem might require extra effort on your part. With the latest Linux distributions, working winmodems are linked to the */dev/modem* device file; for example, the following output from *ls -l /dev/modem* tells me that */dev/modem* is ready and linked to */dev/ttyS1*, also known in the Microsoft world as port COM2. (Microsoft numbers ports starting at 1, while Linux starts at 0; COM1 is *ttyS0*, and so forth.)

```
lrwxrwxrwx   1 root root 10 2004-11-19 07:12 /dev/modem -> /dev/ttyS1
```

If you don't see this link, you'll need to create it. If you know the port device associated with your modem (such as from a dual boot with Microsoft Windows), you can do so with the *ln* command. For example, if Microsoft suggests that the modem is connected to port COM3, use the following command:

```
ln -s  /dev/ttyS2 /dev/modem
```

If you want winmodem support, you'll need to enable kernel modules. This is a good practice that I think every Linux geek follows in a regular PC, because enabling modules lets you load the drivers and other modules that you need, depending on the type of modem that you have.

Plug and Play ISA

One problem Linux has in a Microsoft-dominated world is default Plug and Play settings. Left alone, Linux does well with Plug and Play. However, any Plug and Play settings in a computer BIOS can keep Linux from detecting an otherwise Plug and Play device.

If you have an ISA winmodem, run the *pnpdump* command. This looks through all of your ports for ISA attachments. Look at the output in the */etc/isapnp.conf* file. SUSE 9.3 still has *pnpdump* in the *isapnp* package. The current version of Debian Sarge includes *pnpdump* in the *isapnptools* package.

 ISA cards are sufficiently rare that some distributions (including Red Hat/Fedora) no longer include the *isapnp* package, which includes the *pnpdump* command. If you have a newer distribution without *isapnp*, you should be able to install an older version of the package on your system. Alternatively, you can download and install the appropriate packages from *http://www.roestock.demon.co.uk/isapnptools/*.

Plug and Play PCI

If Linux detects a PCI card on your system, you should find it in the output to your *lspci* or *scanpci* commands. You may get additional information if you run *lspci* in verbose mode—i.e., *lspci -vv*. Some distributions (such as Red Hat) store this information in */proc/pci*.

Testing your winmodem

If you're fortunate, your winmodem is ready to go. Your */dev/modem* device is linked to the actual modem device (alternatively, you can substitute the actual modem device file, such as */dev/ttyS1*). You can test your modem from the command-line interface with the minicom utility. I open it with the *minicom -s* command, which starts the configuration menu, where you can modify modem settings as needed through the Serial Port Setup menu. When you run the "Save Setup As Dfl (default)" command, and then exit, *minicom* takes you to the main menu with a basic Attention (AT) command similar to:

```
AT S7=45 S0=0 L1 V1 X4 &c1 E1 Q0
OK
```

This confirms that Linux can communicate with your winmodem. You can configure the Internet connection tool of your choice, such as KPPP or Red Hat Internet Configuration Wizard, to connect to the Internet via modem. Alternatively, you could connect directly on a touch-tone line with a command such as:

```
ATDT 555-654-3210
```

If your modem is connected to the telephone network, this will dial a number. If successful, it connects you to the system on the other side. If the call is not free, you may see additional charges on your telephone bill.

Finding the driver for your chipset

If minicom shows no response to your commands, Linux is having trouble communicating with your modem. The first step is to make sure your phone line is securely connected to your modem.

The next step is to find the chipset associated with your winmodem. You may already see it in the output to the *lspci -vv* command or in the */proc/pci* file, both described earlier in this annoyance. Alternatively, you can use the *scanModem* tool available at *http://www.linmodems.org* to find most chipsets. Just make sure to make the *scanModem* tool executable (*chmod +x scanModem*).

You can then connect to additional resources for your system through links at *http://www.linmodems.org*, or with a Google search. The options are too varied to list here. In general, you will need to install the source code for your active kernel, make sure to enable modules, and then add the driver modules you need.

If you have a Conexant/Rockwell winmodem, you may be able to use the drivers available through Linuxant. While their work does not fully comply with the GPL (see the Linuxant HSF Driver License Agreement), it can save significant amounts of time. If you're willing to live with 14.4 Kbps, they have drivers that you can download for free. Alternatively, full 56k drivers are available on a trial basis for a month, and then for a one-time fee of $20.

 If you use the Linuxant drivers (or any other drivers where the source code is not available and licensed under the GPL), they "taint" the Linux kernel with non-GPL code. For many, this is not a big deal; it's just incorporating code that helps Linux work better. But if you're building a new version of Linux, tainted code can't be released under the GPL. In addition, some Linux enthusiasts are ideologically opposed to non-free drivers and refuse to help people on mailing lists if they use such drivers.

The winprinter

The other major hardware item that depends on Microsoft Windows driver libraries is the GDI printer, also known as the winprinter. Naturally, most winprinters are found on older (pre–year 2000) systems. As these printers generally depend on older driver libraries, newer Microsoft operating systems such as 2000/XP also have trouble printing to winprinters.

There are three basic categories of winprinters. Two are associated with specific brands (HP and Lexmark). The third includes a variety of printers that are designed to convert Windows printer output into the PostScript language that newer Microsoft operating systems can understand. Unfortunately, that by itself does not make such printers usable on Linux. However, many Linux distributions include the work described at *http://linuxprinting.org* to help many winprinters work on Linux.

Sometimes winprinters are already supported through the new standard Linux print system, CUPS. Before you try any other techniques, try configuring your printer through CUPS (or *system-config-printer* in the latest Red Hat/Fedora distributions). You may be pleasantly surprised.

Briefly, the HP winprinters use Printing Performance Architecture. If you have one of these printers, you can download the *pnm2ppa* print filter. If there is no package available for your distribution, you can download it from the associated SourceForge project home page at *http://sourceforge.net/projects/pnm2ppa/*. As it was last updated in 2002, there is no guarantee that it will work with the latest distributions.

A few older Lexmark printers also relied on Microsoft Windows driver libraries; these printers were effectively ported by 2000. A number of the associated Linux drivers are available from *http://bimbo.fjfi.cvut.cz/~paluch/l7kdriver/*.

Making That Laptop Sing with Linux

The sales of laptop computers are rapidly approaching those of desktops. According to the NPD Group (*http://www.npd.com*), the dollar sales of laptops exceeded those of desktops for the first time in 2003. Computer users want mobility. Linux geeks want to be in the forefront of this trend.

Weight, form, and function are critical on laptop computers. Many manufacturers rely on unique proprietary systems to reduce even a few grams from each system. Fortunately, a lot of hackers have shared their Linux experiences on a wide variety of laptops. A lot of this information has been collected on two web sites, *http://www.linux-laptop.net* and *http://www.tuxmobil.org*. The same principles apply when you install Linux on Personal Digital Assistants (PDAs) and even mobile phones.

Laptops provide additional hardware challenges. Components such as PCMCIA cards, LCD displays, infrared ports, and more were first commonly used on laptops. They normally require drivers that you won't find for desktop computers.

Laptop computers include more specialty hardware than desktops. For example, laptops have PCMCIA adapters. They may have mini-PCI cards. They may not even include CD/DVD drives, which makes network cards more important for installation. Their graphics systems often include customized chipsets.

Laptops That Just Work

There are a few manufacturers who sell laptops with Linux preinstalled. Besides HP's nx5000, there are a number of smaller companies who sell laptops with Linux preloaded. The skill sets of these manufacturers, and thus the levels of support, vary.

Most laptops still come with Microsoft Windows preinstalled. If you overwrite the Microsoft operating system, you may partially or completely void the warranty for your computer. Nevertheless, many Linux geeks appreciate the challenge of installing Linux on a laptop designed for Microsoft Windows. However, that can lead to a number of annoyances, including the dreaded winmodem (a modem designed to work with Microsoft drivers; see the previous annoyance) as well as proprietary hardware without Linux drivers. If you see your laptop (or a similar model) at *http://www.linux-laptop.net* or *http://www.tuxmobil.org/mylaptops.html*, read through people's experiences with it. For example, I had trouble installing Red Hat Enterprise Linux 3 on an HP laptop until I read the experience of another Linux geek on how

Anaconda (Red Hat's installer) has trouble detecting the HP keyboard. All I had to do was tap on the keyboard at the right time, and Anaconda recognized the keyboard.

 Many Linux geeks believe that the preloading of Microsoft Windows on most personal computers is essentially a tax. There have been several efforts in recent years to get refunds on preloaded Microsoft operating systems. Unfortunately, these efforts have been less than successful.

As a Linux geek, one more annoyance (for some) is a responsibility to share with the community. If you've installed Linux on a laptop that you don't see on the list, post your experience online. Submit your experience to one of the aforementioned Linux laptop sites. Once you've done so, you can cite your contribution and increase your credibility in the Linux community.

Laptop Hardware Challenges

When you're planning a Linux installation on a laptop computer, you'll generally want to pay particular attention to the hardware components noted in Table 5-2. Focus on the details you need for installation.

Table 5-2. Laptop hardware annoyances

Component	Key information	Additional data
BIOS	Boot order	Some BIOS settings—such as legacy USB, Plug and Play, and hibernation—can prevent installation.
Monitor	Resolution, refresh rates	Find the maximum refresh rates to avoid overloading the monitor.
Graphics card	Memory, chipset, options	If there is no Linux driver available, be prepared to accept a minimal SVGA configuration.
No CD/DVD drive	Is there room for a portable drive?	A portable drive requires PCMCIA (Cardbus) / USB / IEEE 1394 (FireWire) drivers during the installation process.
Wireless card	PCMCIA, USB, or mini-PCI	Check the availability of the driver for your wireless card. More information is available in a related annoyance, "My Wireless Card Works on Another Operating System, but Not Linux," later in this chapter.
Power management	APM or ACPI	Linux drivers depend on power-management scheme; better managed in Kernel 2.6.

Finessing a Laptop Installation

If you have a 1.44" boot floppy and CD/DVD drive integrated into the laptop, you're set. You should be able to install Linux on your laptop even if your BIOS doesn't detect the Linux installation CD. But what if your laptop doesn't meet these requirements? While I can't cover all possible scenarios, I have some basic suggestions:

- If you're having problems booting from a CD despite the right BIOS configuration, check it on another CD drive. Make sure the *md5sum* or *sha1sum* value matches that of the download or the associated text file listed on the CD. If you're still having problems, re-create the CD, preferably on the same drive. Also, some laptops can't handle the more common compressed *bzImage* kernels.

- If you're having problems booting from a DVD, try booting from a CD. Some drives that won't boot from a DVD will boot from a CD. This is one reason why both SUSE and Fedora provide bootable CDs and DVDs.

- If you can't boot from a CD/DVD or floppy, there are other options. If your network card supports the Pre-boot eXecution Environment (PXE), you can boot and install Linux via a TFTP network installation server. For more information on a PXE-based Red Hat installation, see *http://www.stanford.edu/~alfw/PXE-Kickstart/PXE-Kickstart.html*.

- If your laptop BIOS supports booting from a USB key drive, you can set up a network boot from that device. Generally, you can write boot disks to a USB key drive almost in the same way as you would to a CD. This is important for Fedora/Red Hat distributions, where the alternative boot image is now designed for a USB key drive.

- Alternatively, you can set up installation files on a different laptop partition. For details, see the documentation for your distribution.

Display Issues

Display issues are common when installing Linux on a laptop. Key to managing a display on Linux is the frame buffer, where your current screen image is stored, pixel by pixel. You can manage how the frame buffer functions during the Linux installation process. Help screens are often available when you press a function key—such as F1, F2, etc.—from the installation boot screen. There are two basic problems you may have with the display.

- The installation screens may not be readable. No instructions are visible. You are forced to restart the process. In this case, you can disable frame buffer acceleration. Some distributions allow you to do so by adding *linux nofb* to the installation prompt.

- The display may be out of proportion. For example, I've seen a 320×200 display that shows a useless fraction of a graphical installation screen. In this case, you can restart the installation process, with the frame-buffer video modes shown in Table 5-3. For example, if you add *vga=791* to the installation boot prompt, you're setting 16-bit color with 1024×768 resolution. This is a translation of the hex code, which is described in the Frame-buffer HOWTO at *http://www.tldp.org/HOWTO/Framebuffer-HOWTO.html*.

Table 5-3. VESA video modes

Bits	640 × 480	800 × 600	1024 × 768	1280 × 1024	1600 × 1200
8	769	771	773	775	796
16	785	788	791	794	798
32	786	789	792	795	799

 Here's another tip: if you can't get the built-in screen to display properly, plug an external monitor into the laptop.

Post-Installation Laptop Configuration

Just because you've installed Linux on a laptop doesn't mean that it's useful, at least to someone who is experienced with Linux. Installation routines install software and drivers only for detected hardware. Linux can't install software for what it doesn't see.

A better Linux kernel?

The Linux 2.6 kernel is generally superior in the way it handles laptop hardware. Unlike the Linux 2.4 kernel, it incorporates the code required to handle different PCMCIA adapters. The extra steps in older books to make sure that PCMCIA drivers are loaded during the installation process no longer apply. But there are problems. For example, some of the earlier 2.6 kernels have power issues with respect to PCMCIA cards. A number of these issues have been collected at *http://pcmcia.arm.linux.org.uk*.

 Cardbus is the 32-bit version of the PCMCIA bus. Current laptops should have Cardbus controllers. If you see such a listing in the output of the *lspci* command, Linux has detected your PCMCIA controller.

If you have problems with PCMCIA cards, the first place to start is the controller. Generally, you can identify the associated PCMCIA/Cardbus controllers (and installed cards) with the *lspci* command. Kernel modules associated with the controller should show up in the output to the *lsmod* command. Typical PCMCIA controllers are associated with the *yenta_socket* and *i82365* modules.

 If you're having trouble with the PCMCIA controller, make sure you have the appropriate PCMCIA package installed. For Debian and Red Hat, it's *pcmcia-cs* (naturally, in their native DEB and RPM package formats). For Fedora, it's now *pcmciautils*. For SUSE, it's *pcmcia*. Make sure the *pcmcia* service script (which is normally started from */etc/init.d*) is running and that it starts in the appropriate runlevels. It should also load the appropriate modules; you need not include them in */etc/modules.conf*, */etc/modprobe.conf*, or related files.

Once you have your PCMCIA controller working, you can now run the aforementioned commands to check for the card. In addition, you can use various *cardctl* or *pccardctl* commands to check whether cards have been properly detected by your laptop PCMCIA controller. If your kernel recognizes your card, you should see it listed in the output of the *cardctl ident* command. I show you how this process works in the next annoyance, which discusses wireless network cards

Laptop CPUs

There are a number of different CPUs designed to save power on laptop computers, controlled on modern Intel-style systems through the Advanced Configuration and Power Interface (ACPI). Power management allows ACPI to adjust the CPU to lower speeds. Throttling allows ACPI to lower the CPU clock speed when the temperatures are too high. The *limit interface* option allows ACPI to regulate both power management and throttling. They generally works as follows: the bus master allows ACPI to tell your RAM to stop accessing the CPU, which allows the CPU to enter a sleep or suspend state. This in turn lowers the power consumption of the CPU and lets the battery run longer.

If ACPI does not save battery power or otherwise help you regulate power on your laptop (*http://www.tldp.org/HOWTO/ACPI-HOWTO/*), disable ACPI through your bootloader. Linux interfaces work well with the older Advanced Power Management (APM) service. It's normally part of the *apmd* package, which is available on most distributions. To disable ACPI, add the following command to the kernel command line in your bootloader configuration file (such as */boot/grub/grub.conf*, */boot/grub/menu.1st*, or */etc/lilo.conf*):

```
acpi=off
```

You may already have optimal power-management settings. If you've activated the Advanced Configuration and Power Interface (ACPI) daemon for Linux, check your kernel processor settings. For the first CPU, it's located in the */proc/acpi/processor/CPU0* directory. Check the *info* file in this directory. If you have full ACPI power management configured, you should see:

```
bus mastering control:   yes
power management:        yes
throttling control:      yes
limit interface:         yes
```

For power management, ACPI also may use the SpeedStep or PowerNow! modules. Both are normally compiled into the kernel:

- SpeedStep is associated with the Intel Centrino CPU. It's configured as a module on most Linux distribution 2.6 kernels. To check, run the following command:

  ```
  grep CENTRINO /boot/config-`uname -r`
  ```

- PowerNow is associated with the AMD K6, K7, and K8 CPUs. It's configured as a module on most Linux distribution 2.6 kernels. To check, run the following command:

  ```
  grep POWERNOW /boot/config-`uname -r`
  ```

If the associated kernel settings are not set to *m* or *y* (modular or included in the kernel), you may need to make changes. I guide you through the annoyance of recompiling the kernel in "Recompiling the Kernel" in Chapter 7.

To manage these systems, Debian supports the *cpufreqd* or *cpudyn* DEB packages, which you can add with the *apt-get install* command. Alternatively, you can install the *cpufreq* package from a SUSE installation CD. If you have a Red Hat/Fedora distribution, you can get the *cpudyn* RPM from Dag Wieers's repository at *http://dag.wieers.com/packages/cpudyn/*.

Laptop batteries

If your laptop battery is not performing as it should, check the battery state. It's available in the */proc/acpi/battery* directory. Each battery, *BAT1* and *BAT2*, includes an *info* file. When fully charged, the design capacity should equal the last full capacity. The first few lines of my HP laptop's state file show a problem:

```
present:               yes
design capacity:       4400 mAh
last full capacity:    3840 mAh
```

This suggests I may not have followed good battery-management practices, which include discharging and recharging the battery completely during the first few uses. Most Linux desktop GUIs include a battery-management applet, which you can use to monitor your system. I describe how you can configure desktop GUI applets in Chapter 1.

My Wireless Card Works on Another Operating System, but Not Linux

Personally, I'm rather annoyed with the current state of wireless connections from Linux. With precious few exceptions, you can't just plug and play an 802.11g card on a Linux laptop computer. As we move toward Intel's "World Without Wires," Linux is going to have to handle 802.11a/b/g and even "WiMAX" (802.16) network cards seamlessly. But for the immediate future, Linux geeks will often have to download and compile experimental drivers. If you take this approach, you'll have to recompile the kernel with modules every time you upgrade the kernel.

Fortunately, the need for Linux wireless card drivers has the attention of the hacker community. As of this writing, 4 of the top 10 Linux kernel projects listed on SourceForge are focused on specific wireless chipsets. I've managed to download and install "alpha" drivers on my laptop computer fairly easily. But it did require that I recompile my kernel. If this is too time-consuming, proprietary help is available from Linuxant (which happens to taint your kernel). A number of the hacking approaches are based on using an NDIS wrapper around an existing Windows XP driver. You'll need to configure your kernel source code with loadable modules. I cover recompiling the kernel in "Recompiling the Kernel" in Chapter 7.

As for packages, make sure you've loaded the appropriate wireless-tools RPM or DEB package. If you're working with a wireless PCMCIA card on a Linux 2.4 kernel, you'll also need the *kernel-pcmcia-cs* associated with your current kernel. If you're running a Linux 2.6 kernel, the PCMCIA tools are integrated into the kernel source code.

 Some wireless card drivers are also integrated into the latest kernels. For example, after I drafted this chapter, the drivers for the internal laptop Centrino wireless cards were integrated into Linux kernel 2.6.14.

The main sponsor of Linux wireless network cards is Absolute Value Systems. You can browse the work they've collected online at *http://www.linux-wlan. com*. The basic database of wireless cards and their Linux status is available online at *http://www.linux-wlan.org/docs/wlan_adapters.html.gz*. Another great resource is maintained at *http://www.hpl.hp.com/personal/Jean_Tourrilhes/Linux/Wireless.html.*

As of this writing, precious few cards support the *linux-wlan* project. If possible, purchase these cards. Your budget will go toward companies that support Linux, and you're more likely to have trouble-free installations; many of these cards are described in the aforementioned databases.

If you're willing to use Microsoft Windows drivers, one more alternative is the NdisWrapper project, available online at *http://ndiswrapper.sourceforge.net.*

 If you're having problems with an installed wireless card, refer to "I'm Having Trouble Connecting to an Existing Network" in Chapter 7.

Identifying the Wireless Card

If Linux doesn't automatically detect your wireless card, you'll first need to identify it. What you see on the package may not correspond to the actual chipset in the card. When you find drivers for your card, you need to know the chipset.

If detected, you should be able to find the card in the output from the *lspci -v* or *scanpci* commands. If you have a Red Hat distribution, you might also find it in the */proc/pci* file. The output is fairly straightforward; for example, the *lspci -v* command on my desktop computer gives me the following information about my wireless card:

```
01:0d.0 Network controller: Texas Instruments ACX 111 54Mbps Wireless
Interface
          Subsystem: Abocom Systems Inc: Unknown device ab90
          Flags: bus master, medium devsel, latency 64, IRQ 9
          Memory at f4102000 (32-bit, non-prefetchable) [size=8K]
          Memory at f4120000 (32-bit, non-prefetchable) [size=128K]
          Capabilities: [40] Power Management version 2
```

As you can see, this is an 802.11g wireless card, based on the Texas Instruments ACX 111 chipset. It's actually a card from another manufacturer, who uses the TI ACX 111 chipset, which I got at a discount store. (As of this writing, that particular chipset is proprietary.) Shortly, I'll show you what I did to install open source drivers for this card.

If you have a PCMCIA card, you should see it detected in the output from the *cardctl ident* or *pccardctl ident* command. You may not be so fortunate. As described earlier in the "Linux Won't Work with All My Hardware" annoyance, older Linux 2.6 kernels have had trouble with respect to managing power and some wireless network cards. In that case, you might not even see output from the card. If your kernel and card are not affected by this problem, you may get specific output. For example, I got specific output from one laptop:

```
Socket 0:
    product info: "Realtek", "Rtl8180"
    manfid: 0x0000, 0x024c
    function: 6 (network)
```

But less output from another:

```
Socket 0:
    no product info available
    manfid: 0x0007, 0x0082
```

Fortunately, if you can identify the controller and chipset from the PCI interfaces, you're set. If Linux doesn't detect your card at all, there are alternatives.

- Make sure the card is physically secure in its slot. If the card is internal, such as with a regular or mini-PCI card, turn off your computer first.

- If available, check detection in another operating system, such as Microsoft Windows.

- Use the documentation for your card. Chipsets are often listed in paper documentation, or even on the physical hardware. But be careful; manufacturers have been known to change chipsets at different revision levels of the card.

Finding Drivers

If you're fortunate, the drivers for your wireless card are included with your Linux distribution and were detected during installation of the native network configuration tools. But this is not the case for the majority of wireless network cards. In this case, you'll need to find and probably install drivers on your own. There are several basic steps to this process:

1. Check to see if your network card is detected and/or configured; the most straightforward method is with the *ifconfig -a* command. In some cases, you'll see your network card as device *wlanx*, *athx*, or *ethx*. If you don't see an IP address, all you may need to do is configure IP addressing for your card, which you can do with the same basic commands (such as *ifconfig*) as with a regular network card.

2. If your network card is not configured, Linux may have still detected it. You'll need the manufacturer and chipset. You may be able to get this information from your documentation, with the *lspci -vv* or *scanpci* commands, or from data in */proc/pci*. If it's a PCMCIA card, try the *cardctl ident* or *pccardctl ident* command.

3. Once you find a manufacturer and chipset, search through available databases. Start with the database available from *http://www.linux-wlan.com*.

4. If this doesn't help, you can check for Linux support from the manufacturer's web site. You may be able to download driver modules, which you can install with the appropriate *insmod* or *modprobe* commands and configure to install automatically upon rebooting in */etc/modules.conf*. Sometimes complete open source drivers are available online. A web search is usually the best bet for finding such drivers.

> The Debian Sarge version of */etc/modules.conf* loads modules from different configuration files in the */etc/modultils* directory. The default versions of the major configuration files in this directory provide guidance in their comments. Add the module command that you need to the appropriate file in this directory.

5. Some Linux distributions (e.g., SUSE) support access to binary drivers without source code. If you accept, you will "taint" your kernel with non-GPL code. Unless you're a Linux purist or otherwise need a consistently licensed kernel, this just makes it easier to manage your system.

6. If all else fails, you're now in the realm of developmental drivers: alpha and beta drivers associated with your wireless network card's chipset. If Linux drivers are in work, they may be available through Source Forge (*http://www.sf.net*).

Installing Developmental Drivers

In many cases, if you want to get a wireless network card working on your Linux computer, you'll need to install developmental drivers. Often, these beta- (and even alpha-) level drivers work as well as any stable kernel module. I've installed alpha drivers from a TI ACX100 SourceForge project to enable wireless "no name" cards with this chipset on my laptop and desktop computers.

Generally, you'll need the tools associated with compiling the kernel to install developmental drivers. I go into detail on basic requirements in Chapter 7. While most software for the major Linux distributions is compiled into binary RPM and DEB packages, test software is often available only as compressed archives in *tar.gz* or *tar.bz2* formats. You need to know how to decompress such packages. For example, when I downloaded drivers for the ACX100 chipset, I downloaded a package named *acx100-0.2.0pre8_plus_fixes_37.tar.bz2*, which I then unpacked in my home directory with the following command:

```
tar xjvf acx100-0.2.0pre8_plus_fixes_37.tar.bz2
```

Alternatively, if the package were in *tar.gz* format, I'd use a command such as *tar xzvf acx100-0.2.0pre8_plus_fixes_37.tar.gz*. But I won't go into detail, as these are basic skills for the Linux geek. The result is unpacked to a subdirectory with the same filename. For example, if I downloaded to the */home/michael* directory, I'd find the source for the wireless drivers in the */home/michael/acx100-0.2.0pre8_plus_fixes_37* subdirectory.

 Sometimes your distribution may support special drivers. SUSE offers a download for using wireless cards with the ACX100/ACX111 chipsets. It's downloadable through YaST Online Update (YOU), and it's based on the work of the SourceForge project that I describe in this section.

Compiling the Drivers

If you've installed the source code associated with the current kernel and configured loadable modules, you should be able to compile the downloaded wireless drivers into your kernel. The basic steps vary and should be documented in a file such as *INSTALL* or *README* in the driver package. There are three basic steps:

1. Remove the modules associated with older versions of the same driver. For example, if you've installed drivers with *abc* in their names, you can find them in the active kernel module directory with the following command:

    ```
    find /lib/modules/`uname -r` -name "*abc*"
    ```

2. Prepare the package with the new drivers. Follow the directions in the applicable *INSTALL* or *README* files.

3. Install the package per instructions; normally this is done with a *make install* or *make* command.

Starting the System

Next, you'll have some sort of script to activate your wireless card. If you've installed drivers from an RPM or a DEB package, the script commands may already be installed. Run the script as documented in the package. To make sure the script runs the next time you boot Linux, you'll need to add it to a user start script. Standard administrator configurable start scripts vary by distribution; start scripts for our three distributions are shown in Table 5-4.

Table 5-4. Startup scripts for user commands

Distribution	Script filename
Red Hat/Fedora	/etc/rc.d/rc.local
SUSE	/etc/init.d/boot.local
Debian	/etc/init.d/local

If the file in question does not yet exist, you'll need to create it. Start with the command for your preferred shell; the following works for the default bash shell:

```
#!/bin/sh
```

Then proceed with the full path to the script that activates your wireless card. Alternatively, if you've loaded modules, you'll want to make sure they load the next time you boot, by adding desired modules to */etc/modules.conf* or */etc/modprobe.conf*. Debian discourages direct editing of this file; you can configure modules in this distribution in one of the files in the */etc/modutils* directory.

So Many Distributions, So Little Time

At last count on *http://www.linux.org*, there were over 350 different Linux distributions. In an annoyance-free world, everyone could download her favorite distribution and get courteous and free support from the wide variety of Linux geeks dedicated to support online. So much for the perfect world!

Many people think of Linux as a free operating system. Linux geeks know that isn't quite true. Support takes time, which is valuable. Many Linux distributions, including Red Hat and SUSE, provide fee-based support for licensed installations of their distributions. If you're willing to get your support directly from the community, there are alternatives to the well-known licensed Linux systems.

Red Hat network entitlements are expensive. They start at $179 for Red Hat Enterprise Linux WS (workstation) and can reach above $2,500 per system for Red Hat Enterprise Linux AS (advanced server). While Red Hat is the "name brand" Linux distribution, there are ways to get the same software for the cost of support. Novell's support fees for SUSE are similar: they start at $60 for SUSE 10.0 and can reach $14,000 for SUSE Linux Enterprise Server 9 for IBM Z Series servers.

Red Hat's move away from standard supported distributions has dismayed a significant part of the Linux community. However, Red Hat continues to release the source code for all but the proprietary packages of their Enterprise distribution. This means the Linux community has access to the same software that Red Hat is licensing. Similarly, SUSE releases many of the binary packages for its latest workstation and server distributions, with ISOs available some weeks later.

Alternative Distributions

As a Linux geek, you probably already know something about the variety of available Linux distributions. You may already have your favorites. In most cases, distributions organize packages in one of two camps: RPMs or DEBs. In other words, they work with the RPM Package Manager or the Debian package system.

In this book, we've focused on Red Hat/Fedora, Novell/SUSE, and Debian. This is patently unfair to the wide variety of available distributions. I've included in Table 5-5 an arbitrary sample of alternative distributions that include some level of support, assuming you've purchased an official version of their product. The list is less than fair, as it does not mention many of the benefits of distributions such as Knoppix and Ubuntu (both derivatives of Debian). A more complete list is available from *http://www.linux.org/dist/list.html.*

Table 5-5. Alternative Linux distributions

Name	URL	Support	Comments
Gentoo	www.gentoo.org	Mailing lists	Focused on developers and power users; uses *portage* for package management
Mandriva	www.mandriva.com	Support incidents	Based on the merger of Mandrake and Conectiva
Knoppix	www.knopper.net/ knoppix/index-en.html	From *knopper.net* in Germany	Based on Debian Linux
Slackware	www.slackware.com	Support providers listed on web site	From Patrick Volkerding
Yellow Dog	www.yellowdoglinux.com	Phone, install, and mailing list	For PowerPCs; home of *yum*
Turbolinux	www.turbolinux.com	Limited installation support	Largest distribution in Asia
Linspire	www.linspire.com	Email and on-call support	Formerly known as Lindows; sold with Wal-Mart PCs
Ubuntu	www.ubuntu.com	Focused on usability in all languages	Based on Debian Linux

Table 5-5. Alternative Linux distributions (continued)

Name	URL	Support	Comments
Xandros	www.xandros.com	Email support	Also known for compatibility with Microsoft Windows; based on Debian

Red Hat Enterprise Rebuilds

Red Hat builds the software for its distributions from source code, organized in source RPMs. Red Hat releases this enterprise-quality source code on public FTP servers. When others compile this source code into a distribution, it is known as a "rebuild." The process is considerably more complex than just compiling source RPM files.

Several groups have sprung up to provide "rebuilds" based on Red Hat Enterprise Linux source code. I personally prefer the cAos rebuild (*http://www.caosity.org*), as the cAos Foundation keeps its rebuilds up-to-date with the latest Red Hat Enterprise Linux 3/4 updates. (Its rebuilds of these distributions are officially known as CentOS-3/CentOS-4.) While others have also kept their "rebuilds" up-to-date, cAos at this time appears to have the most active community. But even with volunteers, maintenance and download servers are expensive, and cAos has requested that users contribute $12/year per system.

I've found the cAos updates are available about a month after Red Hat releases its updates. While cAos has modified the icons and other graphics to avoid Red Hat trademarks violations, the software is identical to what is released in Red Hat Enterprise Linux 3/4 in almost every respect. One exception is that it uses the *yum* (Yellow Dog Updater, Modified) for updates, as is done with Fedora Linux. Others follow a similar model. Table 5-6 lists a few Red Hat clones, along with their web sites.

Table 5-6. Rebuilds of Red Hat Enterprise Linux

Name	URL	Notes
CentOS	www.caosity.org	Author preference
White Box Linux	www.whiteboxlinux.org	First with an official rebuild
TaoLinux	www.taolinux.org	From Alfred University, New York
Lineox	www.raimokoski.com/lineox	European distribution; CDs/*apt*-based support available from its web site
Scientific Linux	www.scientificlinux.org	Based on a consortium of labs and universities
Rocks	www.rocksclusters.org	Configured for cluster management; CDs available through CheapBytes

If you need an official level of support, there are alternatives to Red Hat. Progeny supports the most recent versions of Red Hat Linux (8 and 9), released before 2003. cAos has links to corporate levels of support at *www.caosity.org/support/commercial*. But if you are a Linux geek, you may be able to support your Red Hat Enterprise Linux 3/4 rebuild installations on your own, with a little help from the community, as described in the next annoyance.

 The third-party rebuilds of Red Hat Enterprise Linux are an inexpensive way to practice for the Red Hat certifications. For more information, see *http://www.redhat.com/training/certification*.

Downloading New Distributions Takes Too Long

So many distributions, so little time. What makes downloading new distributions more difficult is the lack of high-speed connections. Even in the U.S., half of all users still primarily use telephone modems. I once tried to download the ISO files associated with an older Red Hat distribution over a telephone modem. After three days of stops and starts, the ISO I downloaded was corrupt and unusable.

For those of us without a T3 level (45 Mbps) connection to the Internet, downloads can take hours. Standard DSL connections may be barely satisfactory for some. When I had a DSL connection, it typically took three hours to download the data for a single CD. Cable modem connections are often faster; if I downloaded at an optimum time, I might be able to download the data for a CD every hour. But God help me if others in the neighborhood are downloading music or movies.

One option is to wait until your favorite distribution is available on CD from a third party such as *http://www.cheapbytes.com* or *http://www.linuxcentral.com*. They often have the most popular distributions available for purchase within a week of release. If you don't have the time or bandwidth, this is a viable option.

Use a Mirror

If you're downloading SUSE Linux on DVD in the USA, don't download all 7 GB from the SUSE servers in Germany. You're pulling traffic over routers and heavily used backbones between yourself and Germany. Data slows down when it runs into traffic. It may have to wait for other data with people who've paid more for Quality of Service (QoS). It's best to find a mirror where you can download closer to where you are (or use BitTorrent, described in the next section).

Every major Linux distribution has a list of mirrors. As long as the mirror is up-to-date, it's best to pull your distributions from it for two reasons:

Speed

> The closer you are to what you're downloading, the less chance there is for a delay due to traffic at an intermediate router.

Cost

> Downloads are billed to the repository. Several popular volunteer sites (including Debian) limit direct downloads to keep their costs down.

 When you have a subscription to Red Hat Enterprise Linux, you can download the CDs only through your Red Hat Network account, and updates through the official Red Hat Update Agent server.

Linux distributions include updates. Whether you have a subscription to the Red Hat Network, or are using a participatory distribution such as Debian or Fedora, updates are frequent. You may be able to upgrade critical components for new features or security. Most distributions allow you to update through a mirror site. Be sure to keep your */etc/apt/sources.list* or */etc/yum.repos.d* files up-to-date with the latest update repositories.

Getting BitTorrent Help

A number of distributions support downloads via BitTorrent, which is a peer-to-peer protocol for file transfers. As more clients download a specific file, there are more peers available. With BitTorrent, you can set up a download from multiple sources, which can maximize the speed of the download. More popular downloads support faster BitTorrent speeds.

If it isn't available for your distribution, you can download the basic Bit-Torrent software from the associated home page at *http://www.bittorrent.com*. The BitTorrent commands are written in Python. Versions are also available for Microsoft Windows and Apple Macintosh. Once installed, the applicable commands on several distributions have *.py* extensions.

If you have a firewall on your network, you'll need to open a range of TCP ports for BitTorrent: 6881–6999. You'll need to open these ports before starting any BitTorrent download.

Once you start a BitTorrent download, you'll need to be patient. It takes time to find clients who have already downloaded a desired file with this system. But once you've connected to a group of others, your BitTorrent speed can be impressive. For example, the following download of a Debian Sarge CD is proceeding at about three times the speed of a standard midday download through my cable modem, as shown in Figure 5-1.

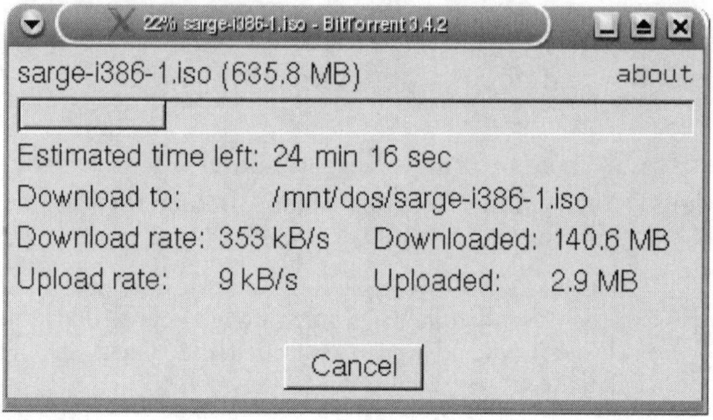

Figure 5-1. Fast BitTorrent download

You can use a GUI such as Azureus to help you monitor your downloads. Some BitTorrent packages include a *btdownloadgui* script that makes the process easy, as shown in Figure 5-2.

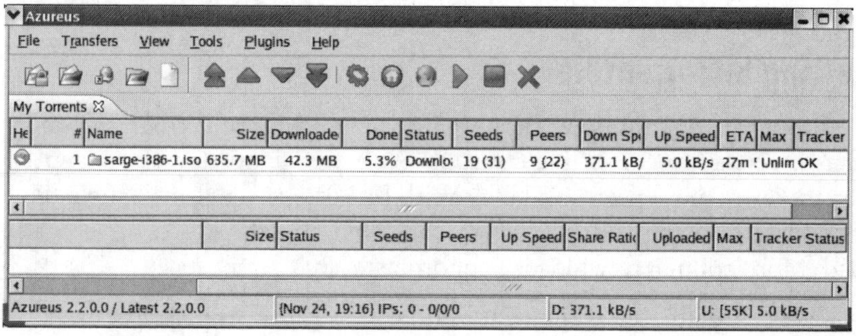

Figure 5-2. Another fast BitTorrent download

Alternatively, you can open a download directly from the command-line interface. For example, I've downloaded the first Sarge CD torrent file to my */tmp* directory. If I then wanted to join the "Torrent" for the first Debian Sarge CD, I'd run the following command:

```
btdownloadheadless /tmp/sarge-i386-1.iso.torrent
```

Once you've downloaded the CD, keep BitTorrent open as long as possible. The BitTorrent system does not work unless you share—in other words, unless you allow others to download parts of the file from your system.

 One popular alternative to BitTorrent is Jigdo, the Jigsaw Download tool, which is supported by Debian Linux. Download the *jigdo* or *jigdo-lite* packages. Make sure you have version 0.6.8 or above. The *jigdo-lite* command is straightforward; it prompts you for a *.jigdo* file, which is available from *http://cdimage.debian.org*. It follows up with a prompt for a Debian mirror site. Jigdo works in the background and takes care of the rest.

Too Many Computers on Which to Install Linux

As a Linux geek, you have to be ready in case the people you're working with want to install Linux on a substantial number of computers. And it would be supremely annoying to be up all night running installation programs on each individual computer. There are four sensible steps that you should take before installing Linux on a large number of computers:

1. Test the desired configuration on one computer. Document any changes that you make.

2. Create or use an existing configuration file to automate a new installation. Modify to match any changes you make to the test computer.

3. Test the new configuration file, by using it to install Linux on a second computer. Document any problems. Modify the configuration file to make required changes.

4. Repeat step 3 until the configuration file allows you to install Linux automatically on the computer of your choice.

Different Linux distributions include tools that can help. Red Hat has Kickstart. SUSE has AutoYaST. Debian uses the Fully Automatic Installation (FAI) tools. While some of these tools can work with bootable network cards, you may not be lucky enough to have them in your environment.

With these tools, you can automate the installation of Linux on other computers. If you have 100 identically configured computers and a DHCP server on a network, you can set up a single installation process that works automatically for those computers. Test your favorite Linux on one computer, configure it to your needs, and replicate this process on other computers. Yes, you could use disk mirror tools as well, but that requires you to physically move the disks, etc. If there is a hardware defect on one of the 100 systems, you may not know it until you get a user complaint.

As a Linux geek, you may already be familiar with Progeny Linux (*http://www.progeny.com*). Ian Murdock (one of Debian's founders) created Progeny to bring Linux, and primarily Debian Linux, to more people. Progeny uses open source tools; they're in the process of porting Red Hat's Anaconda and Kickstart tools. Thus, in this section, we'll limit our solution to the basic procedures for Kickstart and AutoYaST.

Kickstart is still a work in progress for Progeny Debian as of this writing. Progeny has announced that Kickstart will be a part of its next release. It is consistent with Progeny's decision to adapt Anaconda as the primary installation program. Hopefully Kickstart for Debian will be ready by the time you read this book, possibly for the Debian-based enterprise distribution. (Ubuntu already uses Kickstart.) Alternatively, you might consider SystemImager (*http://www.systemimager.org*) or the aforementioned FAI (*http://www.informatik.uni-koeln.de/fai/*).

Configuring Kickstart

Kickstart is a straightforward tool. If your test computer is perfect and does not need tweaking, you can almost take your original Red Hat (or Debian) configuration Kickstart file, add it to a boot disk, and install away on the computers of your choice. When you install a Red Hat distribution on a computer, it includes the current configuration in */root/anaconda-ks.cfg*. We'll take a brief look at my version of this file, with things you may need to modify for your situation. Here are the first few commands:

```
install
nfs --server=server.example.com --dir=/mnt/fedora
lang en_US.UTF-8
langsupport --default=en_US.UTF-8 en_US.UTF-8
keyboard us
```

The second command, which specifies a network installation, is critical. NFS has the advantage over FTP and HTTP; besides being most efficient, you can copy the Red Hat installation CDs to the directory that you're sharing over the network as *.iso* files. Alternatively, if you use *cdrom* on this line, you'll need installation CDs for each computer.

```
xconfig --card "Intel 810" --videoram 16384 --hsync 31.5-37.9 --vsync 50-70
--resolution 800x600 --depth 24 --startxonboot --defaultdesktop gnome
network --device eth0 --bootproto dhcp --hostname Fedora3
rootpw --iscrypted $1$2l6AeSZr$54N4e4kuMQFYiZnuxDdxwO
```

The *xconfig* command appears on two lines in this book because it's long. It specifies an automatic boot into the GUI by setting the id variable in */etc/inittab* to runlevel 5. The network command could be annoying; it sets up *Fedora3* as the hostname of every computer. You could leave out the *--hostname Fedora3*

---

option if your DHCP server assigns hostnames. The *rootpw* command can carry an encrypted password, which you can copy from */etc/shadow*, assuming you've configured the shadow password suite on your computer. For more information on how you can use the shadow password suite, see the "Too Many Tasks, Too Few Qualified Administrators" annoyance in Chapter 10.

```
firewall --disabled
authconfig --enableshadow --enablemd5
timezone America/Los_Angeles
bootloader --location=mbr --append="rhgb quiet"
```

Most administrators disable a firewall on a computer within a LAN. In any case, a computer that serves as a firewall should get special attention and not be configured using Kickstart. The *authconfig* command enables the shadow password suite, with MD5 encryption. The computers on your network are probably all in the same time zone. Unless you have another bootloader, the MBR is the best place for it. Red Hat now appends the *rhgb quiet* command to the kernel; regular users might be confused by standard kernel messages. This configuration is for systems with SCSI disks; the *sda* name below is the standard name for the first SCSI drive.

```
#clearpart --linux --drives=sda
#part /boot --fstype "ext3" --size=100 --ondisk=sda
#part pv.8 --size=0 --grow --ondisk=sda
#volgroup VolGroup00 pv.8
#logvol / --fstype ext3 --name=LogVol00 --vgname=VolGroup00 --size=5024
#logvol swap --fstype swap --name=LogVol01 --vgname=VolGroup00 --size=256
--grow --maxsize=512
```

You can't use this file to automate installation until you activate the preceding commands. This particular set of commands configures a standard *ext3* partition for the */boot* directory, with logical volumes and given sizes for the root directory (/) and swap partitions.

```
%packages
@ office

...

@ graphical-internet
kernel
e2fsprogs
grub
lvm2
```

The package selection list is straightforward; I've abbreviated it to save space. In the preceding lines, I see the Office and Graphical Internet package groups, which are defined in Red Hat's *comps.xml* file. Red Hat organizes its RPM packages in groups in a file named *comps.xml*, in the first installation CD's */Package/base* subdirectory, where *Package* is *Fedora* or

RedHat. As the file's name suggests, it's in XML format. During the installation process, Red Hat's Anaconda installer presents these package groups to the administrator so you can choose which you want to install.

For example, here is an excerpt from *comps.xml* for Red Hat Enterprise Linux 3. A number of intermediate XML comments and commands have been omitted for brevity. As you can see, Red Hat's Office group includes several packages over and above *openoffice.org*:

```
<group>
    <id>office</id>
    <name>Office/Productivity</name>

......

    <grouplist>
      <groupreq>base-x</groupreq>
    </grouplist>
    <packagelist>
      <packagereq type="default">openoffice.org</packagereq>
      <packagereq type="default">xpdf</packagereq>
      <packagereq type="default">ggv</packagereq>
      <packagereq type="default">mrproject</packagereq>
      <packagereq type="optional">kdepim</packagereq>
      <packagereq type="optional">kdegraphics</packagereq>
      <packagereq type="default">tetex-xdvi</packagereq>
    </packagelist>
  </group>
```

We also see the kernel, *e2fsprogs*, *grub*, and *lvm2* packages listed separately because they are not a default part of any Red Hat package group.

If you've added software while testing your Linux system, you'll need to add that information to this list. Red Hat also provides a GUI configuration tool for *ks.cfg*: *system-config-kickstart* or *redhat-config-kickstart*.

Once you've configured the Kickstart file with desired settings, save it to *ks.cfg*. Next, you'll want to copy this file to a shared directory. You can use the same shared directory that the installation files are in.

Now you can test the result on a new computer, with the following steps:

1. Make sure the computer properly connected to your installation server via the network.

2. Set it to boot from the CD.

3. When you see the boot: prompt, you can get Kickstart to read from your *ks.cfg* file.

4. Once you've copied it to the installation server, you can use the following command:

```
boot: linux ks=nfs:server.example.com:/mnt/fedora/ks.cfg
```

Similar options are possible from *ks.cfg* files on a floppy disk or embedded on the CD.

Note the *%post* tag at the bottom of the Kickstart configuration file. You can add commands to further configure servers. For example, you might use it to copy key configuration files, such as for Samba servers.

SUSE AutoYaST

SUSE also has a tool for automated installations called AutoYaST. It's available through YaST2, SUSE's Yet another Setup Tool. You can start it from the command line with the */sbin/yast2 autoyast* command, or by selecting "autoinstallation" from the miscellaneous options in the graphical YAST tool. Unless you're familiar with SUSE's XML tags, I recommend that you use AutoYaST to configure the autoinstallation file.

If you don't see the AutoYaST module, you probably need to install the associated RPMs: *yast2-trans-autoinst*, *yast2-config-autoinst*, and *yast2-module-autoinst*.

As with Kickstart on Red Hat, you can configure a reference profile based on the local computer. To do so, open YaST. Navigate to the Misc menu, where you can start the Autoinstallation tool. Then click Tools → Create Reference Profile. It opens the Create a Reference Control File menu shown in Figure 5-3. Select the services that you need, and the appropriate settings will be copied to the Reference Control File.

Once created, you can modify the Reference Control File or save it via the File menu.

Setting up AutoYaST installation media

To set up your AutoYaST installation media, you'll need to make sure that you copy all of the CDs to the installation server. To make sure the client sees the server as a single installation source, run the following Perl command, where *inst* is the directory with the SUSE installation files:

```
perl -pi -e 's/InstPath: \t\d+/InstPath: \t01/' /inst/suse/setup/descr/
common.pkd
```

Now you can share the */inst* directory. NFS is usually best for this purpose. Then, to configure a network installation, copy the *autoyast.xml* file to the boot media. To make sure the client looks at the installation server, configure an info file. You can include this information within the <init> tags, with an <info_file> tag:

```
<init>
 <info_file>
install: nfs://192.168.0.1/inst/suse
```

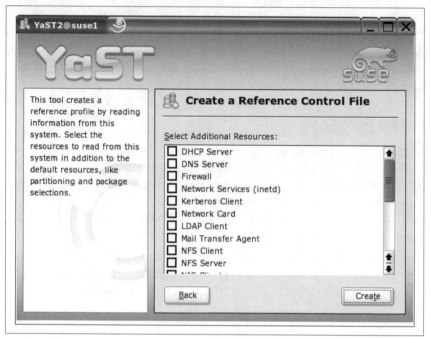

Figure 5-3. Creating a SUSE Autoinstallation file

```
netdevice: eth0
server: 192.168.0.1
serverdir: /inst/suse
autoyast: 192.168.0.1/inst/autoinst.xml
  </info_file>
</init>
```

Then when you boot the SUSE installation program, enter the following command, where *autoyast.xml* is on the shared NFS directory from *server.example.com*:

```
linux autoyast=nfs://server.example.com/inst
```

I Need Help and Am Afraid of Asking Online

I believe that Linux geeks are helpful. They'll take time that they don't have to help you with an interesting problem. They love good questions, as they can help them learn more about Linux. On the other hand, many Linux geeks are strong-willed. They are not known for social graces. In short, Linux geeks (other than yourself) can be annoying. But if you do your homework and treat the Linux community with dignity and honor, you can keep annoyances with Linux geeks to a minimum. While there are no guarantees, you'll probably get a better response from the Linux community if you follow these principles:

- If you're learning to do something, read the associated HOWTO. Learn the associated manpages. If you're having a problem, read the appropriate logfiles in your */var/log* directory. For example, if you're having a problem with Windows file sharing, review the newest files in the */var/log/samba* directory. Examine the error messages. Use Google and Google Groups (*http://groups.google.com*) to search the Web and associated newsgroups for others who've had the same problem. I often search quoting the same or similar error messages. I've found at least a few others who've had similar problems almost every time. There are other sites with Linux-dedicated message boards, which may also be helpful. Be prepared. Know (and be able to cite) your relevant hardware. Have key configuration and logfiles handy.

- Use your favorite Linux book! Many are available from O'Reilly and other reputable publishers. Even this author has written other Linux books with more detailed information.

If you've done your homework and still need help, there are several options:

- If your Linux distribution comes with support for your problem, use it. You've paid for it!

- If your Linux distribution has mailing lists or IRC channels, ask your question there, using the guidelines described in the next section.

- If you're working with a specific service, there may be a mailing list or newsgroup associated with that service. For example, Samba has their own mailing lists, and there are several newsgroups focused on that service.

Selecting a Newsgroup or Mailing List

There are perhaps thousands of mailing lists and newsgroups available on different subjects associated with Linux. Selecting the right newsgroup or mailing list can save time and help you get the answers as quickly as possible. When looking for answers, follow these guidelines:

- Look for the right group. For example, it's not a good idea to ask a question about the DEB packaging system on a Red Hat newsgroup. Most of the readers (and even many of the gurus) won't have the experience that you're looking for to answer your question. And they will not hesitate to tell you so, sometimes in less-than-polite terms.

- Make sure the group is active. There are a lot of inactive newsgroups. If few people see your question, you're not likely to get a response. Review the latest newsgroup headers, and check the dates.

- Read over previous messages on the newsgroup. If you're comfortable with the level of expertise, proceed with your message. See "Posting Guidelines for Newsgroups and Mailing Lists," later in this annoyance, for some posting rules of thumb.

Signing Up for a Mailing List

There are a substantial number of mailing lists dedicated to Linux. Many are organized by distribution (see the following table). When you sign up for a mailing list, you're getting an account on that list. Remember, these lists are by and large staffed by volunteers. If you want to unsubscribe, use your account. Alternatively, check the bottom of the message. Unsubscribe information is often also available there.

Distribution	Mailing list
Red Hat	http://www.redhat.com/mailman/listinfo
SUSE	http://www.suse.com/us/private/support/online_help/mailinglists/
Debian	http://lists.debian.org

Users often get frustrated with the volume of messages on some mailing lists, such as the main Fedora Linux list. Many have asked the Fedora group, in a message to the whole list (thousands of people), for instructions on how to unsubscribe. The Fedora lists put instructions on how to "unsubscribe" at the bottom of each message. Unless you've tried and are having problems with the instructions (which may indicate a problem with a server), and cannot identify a mailing list administrator, it is bad form to ask the group to unsubscribe you from any mailing list.

Almost as annoying are the mailing-list subscribers who inadvertently send their vacation messages to the entire mailing list. Without the proper settings, a user's vacation message is sent as a reply to every mailing-list message. Don't get caught with this problem.

Organizing a Newsgroup or Mailing-List Message

Linux users and geeks ask for help all the time. It is axiomatic; the only stupid question is the one that is not asked. However, there are unhelpful ways to ask a question, many of which will irritate the average Linux geek. Some (sanitized) examples include:

- "I can't hear sound after installing Fedora. What do I do?"
- "cdrecord doesn't work."
- "I am a beginner who wants to get RHCA."

These are examples of unspecific generic questions, which make it difficult for others to help. If they're peeved enough, a likely answer is an admonishment to "Do your homework before asking another question!" Less chastising would be a link to standard documents such as the Sound and CD-Writing HOWTOs, available from *http://www.tldp.org*. The thought of a Linux beginner who wants to pass the Red Hat Certified Architect (RHCA) exams might lead to derisive laughter, or a link to the Red Hat home page for this newest and most advanced certification.

There are correct ways to ask a question on a newsgroup or mailing list. What I cite certainly isn't the only way. You may already be experienced with newsgroups. But remember, there are a whole army of Linux geeks who have trouble with newsgroups and commonly end up in flame wars.

- When you have a new problem, start a new thread. Direct your message directly to the mailing-list address.

- Stay focused on one topic. For example, if you ask unrelated questions about Samba and DVD movies on one thread, it will be more difficult for others to respond.

- Summarize your topic or problem in the subject line. Keep it short. Subject lines that are too long are more likely to be deleted.

- Provide a brief description of your problem. If there's a service involved, include key lines from the appropriate configuration file. Don't overdo it. For example, the contents of */var/log/syslog* would overwhelm most readers with irrelevant info; most will avoid your message. And if you have personal information and/or encrypted passwords, do leave them out of your message.

- List the versions of the applicable software or services. Others need to know what you're working with.

- State what you've done to try to solve the problem.

- List the resources that you've read—such as HOWTOs, FAQs, and documents—in your efforts to solve the problem.

- If you're seeing errors, include key lines from logfiles. Boot messages can be found in the *dmesg* output. Service messages are normally listed in specific logfiles or directories. Other errors can be found in */var/log/messages*. Don't include the entire output of your */var/log/messages* file; mine are typically text files with tens of thousands of lines (which corresponds to several MB of data).

There is also a right way to answer questions on a newsgroup or mailing list. As a Linux geek, you are part of a community. You have a responsibility to share what you know. It's like participating in a democratic society. If you can help someone who needs help with Linux, you're contributing to the success of this operating system:

- Just as you should keep your questions as short as possible, keep your responses short. If you know that the answer is available in another document, such as a HOWTO, it's appropriate to cite that document.

- Don't feel obligated to answer all questions associated with the message. If you only know the answer to one of the questions, it's OK to just answer that question. Edit out the other issues, and include your answer inline or after the end of the message.

- By convention, Linux users post responses at the bottom of a message. This allows others to read archived messages with the problem at the top and the solution at the bottom.

Posting Guidelines for Newsgroups and Mailing Lists

There are a number of basic guidelines that can help you cope in the world of Linux geeks. Some are well known, such as avoiding the use of caps so others don't think you're shouting. Here are some additional guidelines:

- Don't post in HTML. A number of Linux geeks use text-based messaging solutions. HTML email can foul up such clients.

- Don't hijack the threads of others. Mailing lists are organized in threads. When you have a new topic, it's best to start with a new message. For example, new messages to the main Fedora mailing list should be sent directly to *fedora-list@redhat.com*. As an example, assume there's a current thread on sound cards, and you want to ask the group about graphics settings. If you use the "Reply" function on an email client such as Kmail, Evolution, or (heaven forbid!) Outlook Express, your reply will show up as part of the sound card thread, even if you change the subject line.

- Avoid cross-posting where possible. Cross-posting is when someone posts the same message on multiple mailing lists. Many Linux gurus often subscribe to a large number of mailing lists. If they see your message multiple times, they're less likely to help.

- Limit the length of your lines. More than 72 characters per line can make it difficult for some to read your message in their email readers.

- When you answer a message, edit it and leave the relevant questions. This minimizes the size of the email. Answer the message inline. This makes it easier for the reader to associate your answer with the question at hand.

- If you must have a signature line, keep it short. Start them with a delimiter; a standard is a couple of dashes followed by a space (--). Many newsreaders take this delimiter to strip out the signatures.

Flame Wars

A *flame war* is when deliberately hostile messages are posted on a mailing list or discussion board. It's easy to say "Don't get involved in flame wars." It can be difficult to put into practice, especially if you feel passionate about a topic. And many Linux geeks are passionate about their beliefs. There are several principles you can follow that can help keep a flame war from becoming personal:

- Don't be afraid to step away. Online discussions move quickly, and anything that you may have said is usually quickly forgotten.

- Focus on the subject. Do not attack the person.

- Keep looking at how to solve the problem at hand.

- State your opinions clearly. Experiences differ. You can speak to your own experience. Do not try to speak for others.

- Avoid discussions beyond your expertise or experience. For example, it's usually not helpful to say "copying this software breaks the law" unless you are a lawyer with expertise in that particular area of the law. And if you do have that kind of expertise, you should know that expressing such opinions could get you into a different kind of trouble.

- And again, don't be afraid to step away from a flame war. There are more important things in life.

Not all flame wars are bad. Many become serious academic discussions about software—for example, the important discussions between Andrew Tannenbaum (the creator of Minix) and Linus Torvalds on the use of micro-kernels and monolithic kernels in the operating system. If you get involved in a flame war expecting a serious academic discussion, be careful. Not everyone can conduct a debate like Tannenbaum and Torvalds—or, for those of you familiar with U.S. history, Lincoln and Douglas.

Abraham Lincoln and Stephen Douglas conducted a series of debates in the mid 1800s, a few years before the American Civil War, that stand in the annals of political history. Each of their debates lasted several hours and held the interest of the many thousands who watched it live (and out of doors). Even though they were vigorous political rivals, they remained friends throughout. Douglas supported Lincoln after he became president of the United States in his efforts to keep the U.S. together. If you think you can manage a debate like Lincoln or Douglas....

Posting in Bugzilla

If you are a Linux geek, there will be times where nobody will be able to answer your question. If the previous steps have failed, it's time to post a bug report, more commonly known as a Bugzilla. A Bugzilla is a single bug or feature request, documented on an appropriate list of bugs for a Linux distribution, application, or service. There are guidelines to Bugzilla reports as well:

- Check the current Bugzilla database. Someone may have already reported the problem.

- Make sure your problem is reproducible. A hacker can't help you if he can't reproduce the problem on his own PC. Document the steps you took when you encountered the problem.

- Report the issue to the proper developers. If you're having a problem with the functionality of OpenOffice.org Writer, it's generally less helpful to report it on the Debian bug list. The people who need to see it are the developers of OpenOffice.org Writer.

- Note the distribution and packages in question. Linux distributions are large. Different developers have responsibility for different packages. Bugzilla procedures often prompt you in this process.

Some Bugzilla reports are feature requests. If you want action, be realistic. Don't ask for a service that creates world peace. Do ask for features that can improve a product. One simple example of a feature request that I made was to Red Hat's X Configuration tool. I asked that the associated configuration file note whether it was created by Anaconda (the Red Hat Installation tool) or the post-installation configuration tool (*system-config-display*).

## CHAPTER 6

Basic Start Configuration

Just as the best mechanics tinker to improve the performance of an automobile, the best Linux geeks tinker to improve the security and speed of the operating system on their computers. When a Linux geek tinkers with the start sequence, he changes the configuration of his system, starting with the boot process, and continues with user logins.

There are a number of potential annoyances that affect the speed and security of a Linux system. Default configurations start too many services. We show you how to minimize this risk.

I spend a lot of time on passwords in this chapter because it's important to get them right at the very start, and because problems with *root* passwords can require you to reboot the system. In this chapter, I show you ways to require users to choose strong passwords. I also show you how to recover if you've lost your *root* password. Unfortunately, the same method that allows you to bypass the *root* password may allow a cracker to take control of your system. Therefore, this chapter also discusses physical and system boot security.

Defaults in terminal and service configurations allow too many people to log in, even with blank passwords. All of this work may be for naught unless you remember to keep your systems physically secure.

It Takes Too Long to Boot

Current versions of Windows boot fairly quickly, faster than most Linux configurations. But the reason Linux is slower to boot is that most distributions install, by default, a lot of software that few users need—and to make things worse, the distributions are configured to have them start automatically. If you can get rid of this software, you have a win all around: the system boots faster, demands less of your hardware, and is more secure.

Many users don't know, for instance, that they are running a sendmail or Postfix mail daemon all the time. (One system I tried takes more than a minute just to get the sendmail daemon started.) For all except a handful of servers in a larger network that really deliver mail, running such a daemon is a waste of time and perhaps a security risk.

Several distributions (notably SUSE and Red Hat/Fedora Linux) hide the startup messages associated with the Linux kernel and Linux services when their systems boot. Many feel that hiding these messages (as is done during the Microsoft boot process) is less intimidating to novice users. But as a Linux expert, you need to know what's happening during the boot process. In this section, I'll show you how to find out what's running, decide what you need, and shut down the rest.

There are two approaches to this annoyance: uninstall services that you'll never need, and deactivate services that you aren't currently using. Both approaches are straightforward and should be familiar to most Linux geeks. Once you complete this process, you've reduced the time required to boot and improved the security of your systems.

Uninstalling Services

The commands for uninstalling a service are straightforward; the dpkg -r *packagename* or rpm -e *packagename* command removes the specified package from the system. But that leaves support packages and libraries on the system that you don't need. You can use command-line or GUI tools to uninstall them.

 If you're annoyed by dependencies, read the related annoyances in Chapter 8.

Uninstalling at the command line

If you don't share directories and printers with Microsoft Windows computers, you don't need Samba on your Linux computers. In this case, you can uninstall Samba. However, if you want to disable all connections to Microsoft Windows computers, you'll also need to uninstall related packages such as *samba-common*.

You can uninstall Samba packages from the command line. First, you need to know what to uninstall. To find Samba-related packages on Red Hat/ Fedora or SUSE, just run:

```
rpm -qa | grep samba
```

Alternatively, to find Samba-related packages on a Debian-based distribution, run:

```
dpkg -l | grep samba
```

Either command provides a list of installed packages associated with Samba, which you need to uninstall to remove Samba from your system.

When you manage packages from the command line, Debian goes one better. The *apt* series of commands allows the Linux geek to clean packages and associated dependencies. For example, the following command deletes not only the *samba* package but also the SWAT configuration package that accompanies it:

```
apt-get remove samba
```

If you've installed the *yum* (Yellowdog Updater, Modified) package management tool, you can remove all related packages with a similar command:

```
yum remove samba
```

But among the major distributions analyzed in this book, *yum* is installed by default only for Fedora Core. For more information, see "Avoid Dependency Hell with apt" and "Avoid Dependency Hell with yum" in Chapter 8.

Uninstalling with a GUI tool

Most systems have several hundred packages installed. If that's bewildering, a visual overview of related packages can help. The GUI tools from Debian, Red Hat, and SUSE organize packages in groups. With the embedded comments, these tools can help you review the purpose of each package.

GUI tools can help define, review, and uninstall packages by groups, which makes it less likely that you'll leave an orphaned package. Unfortunately, just about every distribution uses a different GUI tool: Debian offers Synaptic, SUSE offers YaST2, and Red Hat–based distributions offer the Package Management tool, also known as *system-config-packages* (Red Hat is moving toward *pirut*, at least on Fedora Core, as it integrates well with *yum*.) One advantage of the Red Hat, SUSE, and Debian GUI package-management tools is that they highlight any dependencies associated with packages you might want to uninstall. Thus, when you remove a tool, you can also remove these dependencies (libraries or other related software), assuming that they're not required for other packages you want to keep. Unfortunately, this is not foolproof. The GUI tools may not be able to identify dependencies if you've installed packages *not* built for your distribution.

Both command-line and GUI tools are effective in managing installed packages. Whether you use the command line or the GUI is a matter of personal taste.

Simplifying your system

On a Red Hat Enterprise Linux 3 computer I administer, I've uninstalled the mail, web, and DNS server package groups because I don't normally run those servers. This cleanup alone reduced the boot time for this computer by two minutes.

Uninstalling services built from a tarball

As a Linux geek, you've probably installed packages from a *tarball*. This is commonly associated with a package organized and compressed into a single file archive. Common tarball formats include *.tar.gz*, *.tgz*, and *tar.bz2*. All can be unpacked with the *tar* command; the *-z* and *-j* switches apply the *gunzip* and *bunzip2* commands to these compressed formats.

When you unpack a tarball, the packaged files are opened in a subdirectory that is easy enough to clean up. But when you compile the files and install the software, the installation process often distributes the files to a number of different directories. Cleaning up these files is generally more trouble than it's worth. That's one reason the RPM and DEB package-management systems are preferred.

Package Databases and Tarballs

If you want your package database to include everything that you've installed, you should create an RPM or DEB package from any tarballs that you want to use. Then when you install the package, it becomes a part of your installation database. If you later choose to uninstall that package, you'll know that you've removed all associated files. You may not have full functionality, however, as the package may not list all dependencies for your distribution.

I don't describe the package creation process in detail, as the process is long, and it is not an annoyance, per se. Section 6 of the RPM HOWTO (*www.rpm.org/ RPM-HOWTO/build.html*) describes how you can create an RPM *.spec* file, which you can then use to create an RPM binary from a tarball of source code. Alternatively, the Debian New Maintainers' Guide (*http://www.debian.org/doc/ manuals/maint-guide/*) can help you to create a DEB package from source code.

If you already have a package associated with another system, you may be able to convert between formats with the *alien* command.

Disabling Services

Generally, it's best to just remove any services that you don't need. Once you uninstall a service, you almost eliminate the risk that a cracker will use that service to break into your system.

However, if you're starting to configure a service such as vsFTP, you may want the service installed during the test process. In that case, you should disable that service to make sure it is not currently running and doesn't start up automatically the next time you boot Linux.

We've described how you can remove packages associated with a service. But if you want to deactivate a service, the process is a bit more complex.

First, list installed regular services. In Red Hat/Fedora, Debian, and SUSE, you can do so with the following command:

```
ls /etc/init.d
```

There are also other services associated with the so-called Internet "super server." By default on Red Hat/Fedora and SUSE, the super server is *xinetd*, which controls services in the */etc/xinetd.d* directory, and individual scripts can be listed with:

```
ls /etc/xinetd.d
```

In Debian Linux, super-server services are configured directly in the */etc/inetd.conf* configuration file. The way you deactivate a service varies between the Red Hat/Fedora/SUSE and Debian distributions.

With Red Hat/Fedora and SUSE, the simplest solution is to turn off the noted service. For example, if you're in the process of configuring Samba, you want to keep the packages installed, but you want to keep the daemons inactive. The following commands deactivate the Samba daemon and make sure that it doesn't start the next time you boot Linux:

```
/etc/init.d/smb stop
chkconfig smb off
```

Once you've configured Samba, you'll want to make sure it starts in appropriate runlevels. The following command makes sure Samba starts in at least runlevels 3 and 5 in Red Hat/Fedora and SUSE Linux:

```
chkconfig smb on
```

 Red Hat/Fedora and SUSE use the same defaults for text console (3) and GUI login (5) runlevels.

Managing scripts in Debian distributions is similar. In these cases, it's easiest to turn a service off in all runlevels. The following command deactivates Samba and then makes sure it does not start the next time you boot Linux:

```
update-rc.d -f samba remove
```

You can then restore Samba service in the runlevels of your choice. The following command restores it in the standard runlevels:

```
update-rc.d -f samba start 20 2 3 4 5 .
```

> The *20* in the above command determines the order in which services are started and stopped in each runlevel. Lower numbers are run first. For example, my Debian */etc/rc2.d* directory starts the *S15bind9* service before *S21sendmail*, as sendmail may depend on DNS.
>
> Debian handles runlevels differently from Red Hat/Fedora or SUSE. If you've installed a GUI for Debian, it automatically boots into the GUI login screen, unless you choose to boot into single-user mode. Unlike Red Hat/Fedora and SUSE, Debian runlevels 2 through 5 normally start and stop the very same services.

Major distributions provide GUI tools for managing runlevels and services. Like the package-management GUI tools described earlier in this chapter, the tools vary by distribution: Debian can use *ksysv*, Red Hat provides the Service Configuration tool, and SUSE embeds its runlevel editor in YaST. Unlike the package-management tools, the tools for managing services are usually considered eye candy and not as convenient for system administrations as doing things by hand on the command line, but you are free to try them and see whether they do the trick for you.

> As most Linux tools are licensed under the GPL, you may find tools developed for a different distribution on your system.

4G/4G Kernel Issue

Developers are adapting the Linux kernel for larger amounts of RAM. Traditionally, a 32-bit address space (4 GB) has been divided so that user-space applications have access to 3 GB and the kernel has access to 1 GB of memory. The so-called 4G/4G patch is designed so that both the kernel and user space can make full use of more than 4 GB of RAM on 32-bit systems.

The developers believe that this patch is not worth the overhead for 32-bit systems with less than 16 GB of RAM (*http://lwn.net/Articles/39283/*). I agree.

I've found that the 4G/4G kernel slows down the boot process significantly on my systems (all with 1 GB of RAM or less). I therefore use Linux kernels without this feature and suggest that you do not install this patch unless you have appropriate levels of RAM.

Network Mounts

One more problem that can slow the boot process is a remotely mounted network directory. Certainly, remote mounts are valuable in many LANs; it is common practice to mount critical directories—even the users' home directories—from a central server. However, if you have connectivity problems on your network or if the server is prone to going down (hint: replace your Windows server with Linux), the systems mounting the directories can experience slow boots or even complete system hangs during the boot process.

The problem is most significant with shared NFS directories. If a server or network is down, Linux keeps trying to mount a remote NFS directory. If you've configured a hard mount, connectivity problems can stop your boot process for minutes—or even, in some cases, stop it cold. In contrast, while NFS soft mounts are slower under optimal conditions, they expire by default after 60 seconds. If you have network problems, a NFS soft mount won't stop your boot process. However, soft mounts can lead to data corruption on some programs.

 For a description of hard- and soft-mounted NFS directories, see the NFS HOWTO at *http://nfs.sourceforge.net/nfs-howto/client.html*.

Rooting Out the Bootloader

There are two major bootloaders associated with Linux: GRUB and LILO. If you have a problem with a bootloader, it's important to know how to go through the associated configuration files with a fine-tooth comb.

Managing GRUB

The Grand Unified Bootloader (GRUB) has become something of a standard in Linux. It's the default for Red Hat/Fedora, SUSE, and Debian. As you might expect, there are differences in the way it's configured on different distributions. For example, while Red Hat/Fedora uses *grub.conf*, SUSE and Debian use *menu.lst*. In either case, the file is stored in the */boot/grub* directory.

GRUB typically comes in three stages, known as 1, 1.5, and 2. Stage 1 is a pointer from the MBR to the boot sector of the hard drive. Control is transferred to stage 1.5, associated with */boot/grub/*1_5 files. Control is then taken by stage 2, which displays the menu and options as defined in the main GRUB configuration file.

When you read the GRUB configuration file, be aware that many GRUB numbers start with 0. For example, the first partition on the first SCSI or SATA hard drive is known as sd(0,0), the second partition on the first SCSI or SATA hard drive is sd(0,1), and so on. In addition, default=0 defers to the first kernel stanza in the file. Because we're just diagnosing the standard versions of this file, I won't examine too many special directives within GRUB.

Both Red Hat/Fedora and SUSE include special directives that go over and above the standard GRUB directives as defined by its author, the Free Software Foundation. For more information, see *http://www.gnu.org/software/grub*.

 Fedora Linux now adds rhgb quiet to the kernel directive line. SUSE Linux adds splash=silent to the corresponding line. These directives substitute a relatively blank splash screen for the hardware-detection and service start messages associated with previous versions of Red Hat–type distributions. You can still monitor these messages by pressing the Esc key during the boot process.

Red Hat's GRUB

The following is an excerpt from my Red Hat Enterprise Linux 3 version of the GRUB configuration file, with comments:

```
password --md5 $$1$7/P7gO$eJKez1Tddjfl498.!kd.
default=0
timeout=10
```

This GRUB menu is password-protected. If the user doesn't select an available option, GRUB boots the operating system associated with the first stanza (default=0) after 10 seconds. If you have a second stanza and wanted to make that the default, you'd set default=1.

```
splashimage=(hd0,1)/grub/splash.xpm.gz
```

Red Hat displays its own version of the GRUB menu as a *splash image*. It's located in the */boot* directory, which happens to be on the first IDE hard drive, on the second primary partition (hd0,1).

```
title Red Hat Enterprise Linux ES (2.4.21-15.EL)
    root (hd0,1)
```

It's easy to get confused here. The root directive has two meanings in GRUB. By itself, it refers to the partition associated with the /boot directory. When used with the kernel or initrd directives, root refers to the actual root directory (/) on your filesystem.

```
kernel /vmlinuz-2.4.21-15.EL ro root=LABEL=/ hdd=ide-scsi
initrd /initrd-2.4.21-15.EL.img
```

The kernel directive defines the kernel to load. In this case, it's the /boot/ vmlinuz-2.4.21-15.EL.img file. The Initial RAM disk (initrd) file loads a read-only filesystem (ro) into RAM, before Linux loads drivers and other modules.

If you have multiple kernels, you may have more than one Linux stanza. Here is a sample alternative stanza:

```
title Red Hat Enterprise Linux ES (2.4.21-20.EL)
    password --md5 $1$9U66g0$nFbkwahtdojv2JXLIEj7i1
    root (hd0,1)
    kernel /vmlinuz-2.4.21-20.EL ro root=LABEL=/ hdd=ide-scsi
    initrd /initrd-2.4.21-20.EL.img
```

You'll note that the contents of this stanza are nearly identical to the directives shown at the start of this section; besides the password protection, only the version number of the kernel and Initial RAM disk have changed. A Linux geek who is testing a new kernel on a user's workstation may want to protect that new kernel with a password. I'll show you how you can create an encrypted password shortly.

SUSE and GRUB

If you're unfamiliar with GRUB, read the previous section on the Red Hat GRUB configuration file for basic information. In general, SUSE discourages manual configuration of files such as the GRUB configuration file. Nevertheless, understanding the directives in the file can help you diagnose any problems that may arise. SUSE uses a slightly different set of configuration files. It starts with the /boot/grub/device.map file, which translates the GRUB name for the hard drive (hd0) to the Linux device name for that drive (/dev/ hda):

```
(hd0)   /dev/hda
```

SUSE continues with a simplified /etc/grub.conf configuration file, designed to set the stage for installing the bootloader. My version includes the following directives:

```
root (hd0,6)
```

In this case, (hd0,6) refers to the main root directory, associated with partition device /dev/hda5.

```
install --stage2=/boot/grub/stage2 /boot/grub/stage1 (hd0) \
    /boot/grub/stage2 0x8000
(hd0,6)/boot/grub/menu.lst
quit
```

The `install` directive takes control from the bootloader. Once the filesystem files in */boot/grub* are installed, the file hands over control to the *menu.lst* configuration file. The following are the basic directives from my version of this file:

```
color white/blue black/light-gray
default 0
timeout 8
```

These directives set up a color scheme. They also configure the first stanza as the default, which is started automatically if there's no user input within eight seconds.

```
gfxmenu (hd0,6)/boot/message
password linux4me
```

The SUSE-designed splash menu is known as *gfxmenu*. If you use YaST to edit GRUB, you won't be able to enter an encrypted password. You can still use the *grub-md5-crypt* command to encode an MD5-encrypted password, as I described in "Password-protecting GRUB," earlier in this chapter.

 SUSE disables the gfxmenu menu if you configure GRUB with a password. The alternative menu looks similar to the Red Hat GRUB menu.

```
title SUSE LINUX 9.2
    kernel (hd0,6)/boot/vmlinuz root=/dev/hda7 vga=0x314 selinux=0 \
        splash=silent resume=/dev/hda6 desktop elevator=as showopts
    initrd (hd0,6)/boot/initrd
```

This stanza configures the default SUSE 9.2 installation. The kernel root directory is (hd0,6), also known as */dev/hda7*. The Linux kernel is associated with the */boot/vmlinuz* file (which happens to be linked to the actual kernel). The `vga=0x314` option forces 800×600 resolution (easier on my eyes). As shown by `selinux=0`, security-enhanced Linux policies are disabled.

As with the latest Red Hat installations, SUSE hides the hardware detection and service start messages (`splash=silent`). The `resume` option specifies the swap partition. The `elevator=as` option defines a kernel access algorithm to the hard disk. (For more information on this algorithm, load the kernel source code and read the *as-iosched.txt* file in the */usr/src/linux/Documentation/block* directory.) The `showopts` option lists boot options on the GRUB command line.

Finally, the initrd directive starts the Initial RAM disk. It's listed on partition /dev/hda7, in the /boot directory.

SUSE includes a fail-safe stanza by default:

```
title Failsafe -- SUSE LINUX 9.2
    kernel (hd0,6)/boot/vmlinuz root=/dev/hda7 showopts ide=nodma \
      apm=off acpi=off vga=normal noresume selinux=0 barrier=off \
      nosmp noapic maxcpus=0  3
    initrd (hd0,6)/boot/initrd
```

The kernel command line includes additional options that are straightforward. DMA is disabled for IDE devices. APM and ACPI power management are both disabled. No special VGA options are noted. No applications are suspended to the swap partition (noresume). Symmetric multiprocessing, APIC (Advanced Programmable Interrupt Controller), and the use of multiple CPUs are disabled. Finally, the kernel is set to start in runlevel 3.

Debian's GRUB

Debian's GRUB bootloader is quite similar to SUSE's. Both use the /boot/grub/menu.lst configuration file. Just as you can configure the SUSE GRUB bootloader with YaST, you can configure the Debian GRUB bootloader with the update-grub command, which reads kernels listed in the /boot directory.

But a Linux geek learns the code within the configuration files. The standard Debian (Sarge) menu.lst file is well commented. For this annoyance, I'll examine a portion of the directives from my own Debian menu.lst file. It starts with the same standard commands as other GRUB bootloaders:

```
default 1
timeout 5
color cyan/blue white/blue
password --md5 $1$7/P7g0$eJKez1Tddjfl498.!kd
```

If you've read the previous two sections on the Red Hat and SUSE versions of GRUB, you should be familiar with these directives. The default 1 directive points to the second stanza; it's automatically booted if there's no user input within five seconds. A typical blue color scheme is defined for the boot menu, and the menu is password-protected.

If you want to make the user's previously selected boot option the default, change default 1 to default saved. It works with the savedefault directive later in the file.

```
title       Debian GNU/Linux, kernel 2.6.8-1-386
root        (hd0,4)
```

This illustrates a /boot directory on the first IDE hard drive, on the fifth partition, which is also known as /dev/hda5.

```
kernel          /vmlinuz-2.6.8-1-386 root=/dev/hda6 ro
```

The kernel directive cites the kernel to load from the */boot* directory, followed by the partition with the real top-level root directory.

```
initrd          /initrd.img-2.6.8-1-386
```

The initrd directive loads the Initial RAM disk from */boot/initrd.img-2.6.8-1-386*.

```
savedefault
```

The savedefault directive works only in conjunction with a default saved directive earlier in this file. With savedefault, if a user selects this operating-system stanza, it becomes the default the next time this computer is rebooted.

```
boot
```

The boot directive, which uses all defaults because it bears no options, proceeds to boot Linux with the given parameters in the stanza.

Working with LILO

The LILO bootloader has fallen out of favor. It's not as easily customizable as GRUB, and it doesn't offer a command interface during the boot process. It does not support encrypted passwords. However, it's often the only bootloader that works with many different SCSI disks, so it is still in fairly common use.

LILO can be protected with two commands:

```
password=somepass
restricted
```

The first command, when alone, requires users to enter a password to boot an operating system. When you add the second directive (restricted), it keeps crackers from entering a command such as init=/bin/sh at the boot prompt, where they could then change the root password.

As LILO can recognize only passwords in clear text, you should limit read and write access to the *root* user with a command such as:

```
chmod 600 /etc/lilo.conf
```

Once you've added the commands of your choice to */etc/lilo.conf*, you'll need to write it to the MBR with the */sbin/lilo* command.

Red Hat and Fedora distributions try to make it easy to convert from GRUB to LILO. They include a template configuration file, which you can find in */etc/lilo.conf.anaconda*, based on the operating systems detected during installation.

Dual Boots Can Be Troublesome

Most Linux systems actually offer multiple boot options. The most common dual-boot configuration allows you to boot either Linux or Microsoft Windows. And in fact, most modern Linux distributions automatically detect a pre-existing Windows operating system during the installation process. The Windows partition is left alone, and the installation program adds a stanza to the bootloader to facilitate booting into Windows.

You don't have to have a second operating system to have a dual boot. If you've installed new kernels from an RPM or DEB package, it has set up alternate kernel selections in GRUB or LILO. Alternatively, if you installed a new kernel from a tarball, you need to know how to configure a new kernel selection in your bootloader.

In this annoyance, I'll show you the basics of configuring a dual boot for multiple Linux kernels, as well as a configuring a dual boot on GRUB and LILO for Linux and Microsoft Windows. This annoyance provides fundamental bootloader basics for the one that follows.

Configuring a Linux Kernel Dual Boot

If you have just configured a new Linux kernel, you'll want to be able to boot both the old and the new kernel. At least until you've completely tested the new kernel, you need access to the old one just in case something goes wrong.

If you install (not upgrade) a Linux kernel from a modern RPM or DEB package, the process automatically adds the new kernel to your current bootloader. If you're using a distribution with one of these systems, you generally should use the kernels as compiled by the distribution company. This helps make sure that drivers get to the right directories. In addition, Red Hat (and others) often include "backports" from more advanced kernels, especially in its enterprise series of distributions.

 Do not use the "upgrade" option for kernel RPM or DEB kernels. It overwrites your existing kernel. If the new kernel doesn't work on your system, you'll have to boot into some rescue or Knoppix recovery system in order to download and reinstall the original kernel. And that can be annoying.

However, if you want the latest in functionality, you may need to use the latest kernel, in tarball format, from *http://www.kernel.org* or one of its mirrors. When you unpack and compile the kernel from the source code, it does not automatically upgrade your bootloader, so you'll need to upgrade it yourself. For more information, see "The Kernel Needs an Upgrade" in Chapter 7.

Fortunately, GRUB and LILO stanzas associated with the former kernel can help. Generally, all you need to do is modify the version numbers associated with the kernel and initial RAM disk.

For example, if you've upgraded from a Debian 2.6.8-1-386 kernel to a *kernel.org* 2.6.11 kernel, you'll need to set up another stanza in your bootloader. When you compile a new kernel, it's useful to modify the EXTRAVERSION variable in the *Makefile*, which you can find linked from the */usr/src/linux* or */usr/src/linux-2.6* directories.

 Starting with Fedora Core 3 and Red Hat Enterprise Linux 4, Red Hat no longer includes a binary kernel source code package. You'll have to install from the kernel source code *.src.rpm* package. The resulting *Makefile* can be found in the */usr/src/redhat/BUILD/kernel-2.6.9/linux-2.6.9* directory (the version numbers will vary). For details, see Chapter 7.

For instance, if you set:

```
EXTRAVERSION=-new
```

before you compile a kernel, you'll get a file with a name such as *vmlinuz-2.6.11-new*. Take a kernel with the following stanza in a GRUB configuration file:

```
title       Debian GNU/Linux, kernel 2.6.8-1-386
root        hd(0,5)
kernel      /vmlinuz-2.6.8-1-386 root=/dev/hda7 ro
initrd      /initrd.img-2.6.8-1-386
savedefault
boot
```

After you've compiled the new kernel from source and created an associated Initial RAM disk, you can set up a new stanza for that kernel. I'm assuming that you're storing the kernel and Initial RAM disk files in the standard location, */boot*. The new stanza would look almost identical to the previous stanza:

```
title       Debian GNU/Linux, kernel 2.6.11-new
root        hd(0,5)
kernel      /vmlinuz-2.6.11-new root=/dev/hda7 ro
initrd      /initrd.img-2.6.11-new
savedefault
boot
```

Generally, if you've created a new kernel, you should create a new Initial RAM disk using the new kernel version number. For example, if your new kernel is *vmlinuz-2.6.11-new*, you'd use the following command:

```
mkinitrd 2.6.11-new
```

The changes in a LILO configuration file follow the same pattern, and the modifications are elementary.

Configuring a Dual Boot with Microsoft Windows

There are several annoying reasons why you might have to rebuild GRUB or LILO in a dual-boot configuration. A junior administrator might have deleted the file. Hard drive corruption might have made the file unusable. Someone else might have edited the bootloader incorrectly.

 In the next section, we'll examine a bigger annoyance: what happens to the bootloader (and what you can do about it) when someone reinstalls Microsoft Windows.

Fortunately, the Linux bootloader directives associated with Microsoft Windows are fairly simple.

If you need to set up Microsoft Windows in a dual boot, you need to know the partition with the basic Microsoft Windows system filesystem. If you're in Linux, you can make a good guess with an *fdisk -l* command. That will show the partitions with Microsoft-based filesystems. Some examples include:

```
Device Boot    Start      End       Blocks    Id    System
/dev/hda1   *      1    20012    10929039+    7    HPFS/NTFS
/dev/hda2       20012    77520    30453674+    f    W95 Ext'd (LBA)
/dev/hda5       20012    40024    10929039+    c    W95 FAT32 (LBA)
```

fdisk recognizes the format of each partition and displays it in the final column. Yes, the System label associated with the first partition is vague. HPFS is short for the High Performance File System, which is associated with IBM's OS/2 operating system. I don't have one of these operating systems available, so I haven't tested it. But as it's designed for partitions of 200–400 MB and can't be read by Windows NT 4 and above, you're unlikely to encounter it today. The alternative is NTFS, Microsoft's New Technology File System. Linux's *fdisk* does not distinguish between Microsoft's NTFS standards, which have changed as Microsoft operating systems have evolved from NT 4 to 2000 and then XP/2003.

A simple GRUB stanza for Windows begins with a title, which can specify anything you'd like to jog your memory:

```
title Windows
```

Because the first partition is bootable, it should contain an operating system. In GRUB, this can be associated with the following directive. While it points to the first partition on the first IDE hard drive, it does not attempt to mount it in a Linux fashion:

```
rootnoverify (hd0,0)
```

A GRUB pointer to a Microsoft operating system requires one more directive. The chainloader directive points to the first sector (+1) of the noted partition, from where just about any operating system continues the boot process:

```
chainloader +1
```

The results are straightforward. A typical GRUB stanza for a Microsoft Windows operating system is:

```
title       Windows NT/2000/XP
root        (hd0,0)
chainloader +1
```

A LILO stanza for Windows also contains a line for a title, such as:

```
label = Windows
```

To specify the bootable partition containing Windows, you need two directives. The first indicates you're booting a non-Linux operating system located on the */dev/hda1* partition, and the second keeps LILO from looking for a Linux boot image:

```
other=/dev/hda1
     optional
```

All together, a typical LILO stanza pointing to a Microsoft Windows operating system looks like:

```
other=/dev/hda1
     optional
     label = Windows
```

Other Bootloaders

There are other commercial bootloaders that can load Linux on a computer. Some aren't directly related to any operating system. The leaders in this area include Partition Magic (*http://www.symantec.com/partitionmagic*) and Partition Commander (*http://www.v-com.com*). The alternative is to boot Linux with the Microsoft Windows bootloader, NTLDR.

If you want to use NTLDR, most documents strongly recommend that you do so with a boot disk. In NTLDR, the basic menu is associated with the *C:\boot.ini* file. Normally, it includes commands such as:

```
[boot loader]
timeout=5
default=multi(0)disk(0)rdisk(0)partition(1)\WINNT
[operating systems]
multi(0)disk(0)rdisk(0)partition(1)\WINNT="Microsoft Windows XP
Professional" /fastdetect /NoExecute=OptIn
```

If you're familiar with Linux bootloaders, you may recognize the basic format of this file. Essentially, these commands boot Microsoft Windows XP Professional from the first IDE hard disk, after a five-second delay. To configure a pointer to Linux, you need two things. First, add the following line to *boot.ini*:

```
c:\linux.bin="Linux"
```

Next, create a *linux.bin* file. One method of doing so is with a disk dump from the */boot* partition. For example, if */dev/hda7* is mounted on */boot*, you can create *linux.bin* with the following command:

```
dd if=/dev/hda7 of=linux.bin
```

Then copy *linux.bin* to the partition associated with the Microsoft C: directory on your hard drive.

Just remember, Linux bootloaders are designed for multiboot environments, especially with Microsoft Windows. NTLDR is not. You're less likely to be annoyed if you use GRUB or LILO.

Dual-Boot Recovery

One thing some advanced Microsoft users do when their systems slow down is reinstall their version of Windows. Microsoft filesystems do get fragmented frequently, which can affect key Microsoft system and library files. Installations and removals of various applications can also overwrite and even delete these files. Users are frequently annoyed.

But therein lies the problem. If a user reinstalls Microsoft Windows on a dual-boot computer, he or she automatically overwrites any existing non-Microsoft bootloader. Microsoft installation programs do not detect Linux installations. The user loses access to any Linux installations on that computer.

That brings us to the annoyance—what do you do when a user installs Microsoft Windows on a Linux computer? He may have bypassed your security, and he may have installed Microsoft on a computer previously configured in a dual boot with Linux. And now, the Linux bootloader is gone, as well as regular access to the Linux operating system. But that does not necessarily mean you have to reinstall Linux.

If you find that the reinstallation of Windows has overwritten the Linux partitions, then you have no choice. You'll have to reinstall Linux. But chances are good that the Linux partitions are still there, just hidden, and you can recover your Linux system. But you won't know if that's the case until you boot your computer with a rescue disk, as described in the following sections.

 I recently tried Symantic's Partition Magic without reading the instructions. It rearranged the order of partitions on my computer, which led to an error when I tried writing my GRUB configuration to my MBR. Improper use of other partition-configuration tools can lead to the same problem. I'll show you how to deal with this problem in the last part of this annoyance.

Rescuing with Red Hat or SUSE

For now, we'll assume that your Linux partitions are still there. In this case, recovering a Linux bootloader is a straightforward process. If you're running Red Hat/Fedora or SUSE Linux, the associated installation CDs automatically search for existing Linux installations. If a Red Hat/Fedora or SUSE rescue disk detects its own distribution, it will mount your partitions automatically.

The objective is to reload your GRUB or LILO bootloader. Therefore, you need access to the associated configuration files on the */boot* directory, as well as the executable (*/sbin/grub-install* or */sbin/lilo*), which writes the appropriate part of the bootloader to your MBR.

A Red Hat/Fedora rescue installation, if it finds Linux on your computer, mounts your Linux partitions on the */mnt/sysimage* directory. Otherwise, you may be able to check for Linux partitions with the *fdisk -l* command. If there are no Linux partitions on your computer, you're probably stuck. The reinstallation of Microsoft Windows has overwritten your Linux system, and you'll have to restore from backup or reinstall Linux.

But let's assume that Linux is still on your system. After going through the Red Hat/Fedora rescue installation process described in "My Server Is So Secure I Can't Log In as Root," later in this chapter, you'll see a command prompt. Run a *df* command at the prompt. You'll see output similar to:

```
Filesystem      1K-blocks     Used Available Use% Mounted on
rootfs              4151       848     3066  22% /
```

```
/dev/root.old       4151      848    3066  22% /
/tmp/cdrom        132160   132160       0 100% /mnt/source
/dev/hda3        6756712  5323020 1090468  83% /mnt/sysimage
/dev/hda2         102486    18902   78292  20% /mnt/sysimage/boot
```

The appropriate partitions are already mounted. To restore the original file-system hierarchy, run the following command. Then you can run standard Red Hat/Fedora commands to repair your system:

```
chroot /mnt/sysimage
```

If the Linux installation is still there, the bootloader configuration files should be intact. You can then run the command to restore the appropriate Linux bootloader to your computer's MBR. For example, if your system uses the first IDE hard drive, run the following to recover GRUB:

```
/sbin/grub-install /dev/hda
```

 If you see an error message, the *grub-install* command is having trouble finding your boot partition. See the last part of this annoyance for a solution.

or the following to recover LILO:

```
/sbin/lilo /dev/hda
```

A SUSE rescue installation is not quite as straightforward. It looks for existing Linux partitions. If it finds a SUSE installation, it boots your system in runlevel 3. You'll then need to mount the appropriate partitions. In my case, I have SUSE on just one partition, */dev/hda7*. If I needed to rescue my system, I'd mount the partition with my root directory (/) on */mnt* with the following command:

```
mount /dev/hda7 /mnt
```

The *mount* command allows you to specify the format of the filesystem, but I don't need to do so for this ReiserFS filesystem because the SUSE rescue system includes *reiserfs* in */etc/filesystems*. If */boot* were on a separate partition, I would need to mount that as well.

I then run the following command to set up my original SUSE filesystem:

```
chroot /mnt
```

After making sure that my bootloader configuration file is in the right place, I can then run the appropriate command, shown earlier in this section, to write the GRUB or LILO bootloader to the MBR.

Rescuing with Debian or Knoppix

Debian and Knoppix rescue systems are quite similar. As described in "My Server Is So Secure I Can't Log In as Root," later in this chapter, a Debian from Scratch CD loads an abbreviated command-line version of Linux, while Knoppix loads a fully functional operating GUI from a CD. However, as Knoppix is based on Debian, they include many of the same tools.

> As described later in this chapter, you can download John Goerzen's Debian from Scratch CD at *http://people.debian. org/~jgoerzen/dfs/*.

When you boot from the Debian from Scratch CD, it loads a basic Debian operating system. While it's designed just to install Debian over a network, it has nearly full functionality at the command line. It allows you to log in as the *root* user without a password.

A Knoppix CD loads many of its own systems on a RAM disk. It lists, but does not mount, the appropriate partitions as GUI icons. It provides default mount points in its */etc/fstab*. For example, if you have a */dev/hda2* partition, it detects the filesystem format and configures a mount point of */mnt/ hda2*. If you have directories mounted on different partitions, you may not want to accept the defaults.

For example, when I use Knoppix to boot my Debian installation, the screen shown in Figure 6-1 appears. You can see the available partitions on the left side of the screen. None of the partitions on your hard disks are mounted.

When you open a command-line interface in the Knoppix CD–based desktop, what you can do is similar to your options when you boot from the Debian from Scratch CD. You can *su* into *root* without a password. This is necessary, as commands such as *mount* and *grub-install* require *root* privileges.

Normally, you want to mount the partition associated with your root directory (*/*); in my case, that's located on */dev/hda7*. Depending on the rescue system, it may also be */mnt* or */mnt/hda7*. Once mounted, check the associated files. Make sure it's the right directory. If you have multiple partitions configured for Linux, some trial and error may be required.

Next *chroot* to the associated directory mount point. Then mount the partition with the */boot* directory—in my case, */dev/hda6*. So on my Knoppix rescue system, I run the following commands:

```
mount /dev/hda7 /mnt/hda7
chroot /mnt/hda7
mount /dev/hda6 /boot
```

Figure 6-1. Knoppix rescue

This assumes I want the bootloader on the MBR of the first IDE hard drive. After making sure that my bootloader configuration file is in the right place, I can then run the appropriate command, shown in the previous section, to write the GRUB or LILO bootloader to the MBR.

Before rebooting into your standard operating system, don't forget to remove the CD. You might also want to change your BIOS boot order so that you boot first from hard disk, not from CD.

Finding the Boot Partition

When you use *grub-install* to write your GRUB configuration to the MBR, it works only if it can find your GRUB configuration files. If you see an error message, you may be able to use the grub> shell to write GRUB to the MBR.

As suggested earlier, because I did not read the instructions for Partition Magic, I had trouble with it. It renumbered the partitions on one of my laptop computers. I was booting four operating systems on that laptop (Windows, SUSE 10.0, Ubuntu, and RHEL 4 Workstation). I had three partitions with Linux */boot* files.

Partition Magic changed the numbers on my partitions. For example, while I configured SUSE 10.0 on */dev/hda7*, Partition Magic changed it to */dev/hda8*.

Partition Magic designated Windows as the active partition. The other partitions were renumbered in a similar fashion; I could not boot with GRUB.

In my case, I used a Knoppix CD to boot my system. I mounted a couple of partitions, in a similar fashion to the previous section. When I ran the *grub-install* command, I received the following error message:

```
The file /boot/grub/stage1 not read correctly.
```

I repeated the process with a SUSE installation CD and got the same result. To address this problem, I took the following steps:

1. I booted my system with a Knoppix CD, which mounted all partitions on my hard drive.

2. I searched through the partitions, and found the directory with my desired GRUB configuration file. After reading through the files on the other partitions, I edited GRUB to incorporate the partition settings to point to the four operating systems on that computer.

3. I selected the */boot* and root directory (/) partitions for one of my Linux installations.

4. I mounted them on appropriate directories. For example, I found the root directory partition of my RHEL 4 Workstation on */dev/hda8*, and the */boot* partition on */dev/hda7*, and ran the following commands:

```
mount /dev/hda8 /mnt/hda8
mount /dev/hda7 /mnt/hda8/boot
chroot /mnt/hda8
```

5. I navigated to the */boot/grub* directory, and started the GRUB shell:

```
cd /boot/grub
grub
grub>
```

6. At the grub> prompt, I looked for the aforementioned */boot/grub/stage1* file, and GRUB directed me to the right partition:

```
grub> find /boot/grub/stage1
(hd0,7)
```

7. Then I defined the partition with the bootloader configuration files. A space is required between root and the partition, (hd0,7). The output tells me that GRUB has found the bootloader files:

```
grub> root (hd0,7)
Filesystem type is ext2fs, partition type 0x83
```

8. Finally, I wrote GRUB to the MBR; don't forget the space between setup and (hd0).

```
grub> setup (hd0)
```

9. I rebooted my computer to make sure GRUB was properly written to my MBR.

My Computer Won't Stop Rebooting

Newer Linux users are fascinated by the chance to experiment with different components. For the most part, careful experiments should be encouraged in a test environment. How else can we learn Linux? But there are mistakes that can annoy the heck out of us, including the Linux computer that won't stop rebooting.

Grouped in this section are three low-level annoyances associated with the boot process:

- The computer starts and then proceeds to shutdown without allowing a login.
- The computer starts and then proceeds to reboot, continuously.
- Something weird happens during the boot process.

These annoyances are normally associated with configuration problems in boot files. The first two of these annoyances are straightforward, as they relate to the default runlevel on your computer. In each of these cases, you'll almost certainly have to boot with a rescue disk or a system such as Knoppix, as described in the previous annoyance.

On occasion, these annoyances may be related to hardware issues. In those cases, you'll see similar behavior when you use a rescue disk or a system such as Knoppix to boot your system.

 Red Hat has the elite certifications in the world of Linux, including that of the Red Hat Certified Engineer. One of the RHCE skills listed on the Red Hat web site suggests that RHCEs need to "diagnose and correct boot failures arising from bootloader, module, and filesystem errors." Does that sound like it addresses some of the annoyances in this chapter?

The Computer Starts and Then Shuts Down

This annoyance is often easy to fix. Once you've booted with a rescue disk and mounted the root directory (/), the first thing to check is the default runlevel as defined in /etc/inittab. If it's 0, as shown here, all you need to do is restore the proper default runlevel, such as 2 for Debian, or 3 or 5 for Red Hat/Fedora or SUSE:

```
id:0:initdefault
```

If the id directive isn't set to 0, you may have a different problem that's described later in this annoyance.

The Computer Starts and Then Reboots

This annoyance is also often straightforward. Again, boot with an appropriate rescue disk. Proceed by checking the default runlevel in /etc/inittab. If it's 6, as shown here, restore the proper default runlevel, such as 2 for Debian or 3 or 5 for Red Hat/Fedora or SUSE:

```
id:6:initdefault
```

If the id variable isn't set to 6, you may have a different problem described in the next section.

Something Weird Happens During the Boot Process

When Linux boots, it goes through more than just the /etc/inittab file. It reads the default runlevel and then starts the service scripts as defined in the associated /etc/rcx.d directory. While a problem here normally is associated with a configuration problem with a service, it's probably not serious.

If you want to add a program or script to the boot process, each distribution has a dedicated script in the /etc directory for this purpose.

Alternatively, most distributions have a user-definable script. You can use this script to add commands that you want applied to the computer during the boot process. For example, if you've configured a wireless network card using experimental code, you can add the command to start this card to the script. Various distributions define this script differently:

Red Hat/Fedora
  Commands in the /etc/rc.local file run after all other init scripts.

SUSE
  Commands in the /etc/init.d/boot.local file run after all other init scripts.

Debian
  Debian Sarge includes a pointer to /etc/init.d/local in all runlevels. Interestingly enough, this file is missing from the default Debian configuration. But you can create it and add the commands that you need.

User Passwords Are Too Weak

One thing that annoys me about Linux is how the default configurations allow simple passwords. Yes, there are warning messages against dictionary words or passwords shorter than six characters. But these are just warnings. By default, most Linux distributions allow simple passwords. SUSE even allows blank passwords.

Fortunately, modern versions of Linux have put some barriers in the way of malicious intruders. For instance, passwords are no longer stored in */etc/passwd*, which is world-readable. Instead, they are stored in */etc/shadow*, which is readable only by the *root* user. Still, passwords are subject to dictionary attacks and social engineering (such as when a cracker tries a pet name or favorite term used by the victim). In this section, I'll show how to enforce strong passwords.

One way for an administrator to battle weak passwords is to take on the role of a cracker and run a command such as *crack* on user passwords. If a password is cracked, the user can be warned, his account can be disabled, or the user can be disciplined in some appropriate fashion. (Of course, management often provides the worst offenders.) But this section focuses on techniques to require strong passwords in the first place.

 Keep in mind that the rules we set to protect the security of our passwords probably annoy most users. If the rules are too difficult, users may post their current passwords in the open, next to their workstations.

You can use the *chage* command to make users change their passwords periodically. You can even set *chage* to lock out users if passwords aren't changed within a certain period of time. For example, with the following command, you can restrict user *michael*. If he doesn't change his password every week, he will be unable to log in after that time:

```
chage -M 7 -I 7 michael
```

This command sets the maximum number of days (*-M*) for which the password is valid. In this case, user *michael* is prompted to change his password after seven days. If *michael* doesn't log in for another seven days, the account is rendered inactive (*-I*), and *michael* is locked out.

PAM Password Administration

One way Linux distributions define effective password policies is through Pluggable Authentication Modules (PAM). One example of poor security is provided by the default SUSE configuration, which allows blank passwords with the following commands in */etc/pam.d/login*:

```
password   required   pam_pwcheck.so   nullok
password   required   pam_unix2.so     nullok use_first_pass use_authok
```

The first command allows users to enter blank passwords (nullok). The second command supports logins with blank passwords, then checks the first and last time the user logged in for passwords.

Naturally, null passwords are not good when you want a strong password policy. Therefore, if you're running SUSE, I recommend you change the password directives shown to the more secure ones described later in this section.

Linux includes a password strength checker with the *cracklib* or *cracklib2* packages. When combined with PAM and the shadow password suite, this can force your users to choose stronger passwords. All you need is the right PAM module for the *passwd* command. In Red Hat and SUSE, PAM *passwd* modules are installed in */etc/pam.d/passwd*; in Debian, they refer to */etc/pam.d/ common-password*.

The key directive in this file is password; the following example from the Debian file checks the password against the *cracklib* libraries, allows the user to try three times, requires a minimum length of six characters, and allows a group of three characters to be in common between old and new passwords:

```
password required pam_cracklib.so retry=3 minlen=6 difok=3
```

Naturally, you can make this more complex. The following directive gives the user credit for two characters toward the minimum length of the password for each digit or uppercase character she includes; it gives the user credit for three characters if she includes a punctuation character such as an "!":

```
password required pam_cracklib.so retry=3 minlen=10 difok=3 \
     dcredit=2 ucredit=2 ocredit=3
```

In other words, this module command would allow the following passwords:

```
acprksgtlm
acp2rgk3
Acp2rgsm
Ap2gr!
```

By default, when users are required to choose a password, the prompt "New UNIX password" appears. It's a nice enhancement to make the prompt more appropriate for a Linux system by changing "UNIX" to "Linux." Do so by adding the type=Linux option to the password directive just after the pam_ cracklib.so entry. For example, the previous command would now be:

```
password required pam_cracklib.so type=Linux retry=3 minlen=10 difok=3 \
     dcredit=2 ucredit=2 ocredit=3
```

The Red Hat/Fedora version of this file refers to the *system-auth* PAM configuration file, as shown here:

```
password    required    pam_stack.so service=system-auth
```

When you open */etc/pam.d/system-auth*, you can add type=Linux to the following password directive:

```
password requisite /lib/security/$ISA/pam_cracklib.so type=Linux retry=3
```

Debian has an excellent guide to this process, which is available online in Chapter 4 of *http://www.debian.org/doc/manuals/securing-debian-howto*.

PAM Options Related to Strong Passwords

To explore the standards you can enforce using the password directive, let's examine each option in more detail:

debug
> Adds information to the kernel's logfile, which may be */var/log/messages* or */var/log/auth.log*.

type=*xxx*
> Configures a new password prompt. The default prompt is "New UNIX password:". I use type=Linux, which creates a "New Linux password:" prompt.

retry=*n*
> Prompts the user *n* times before returning an error.

difok=*n*
> Defines the degree of similarity between old and new passwords, defined by a group of characters they hold in common; if difok=3, you're allowed to use three of the same characters between passwords.

difignore=*n*
> If the password is at least n characters, the PAM module ignores the difok variable.

minlen=*n*
> Defines the minimum number of characters in the password. This minimum, however, is affected by the dcredit, ucredit, lcredit, and ocredit variables.

dcredit=*n*
> Defines the weight of digits in a password. For example, if dcredit=2, a number in a password gets credit for two characters against the minlen variable.

ucredit=*n*
> Defines the weight of uppercase characters in a password. For example, if ucredit=2, a capital letter in a password gets credit for two characters against the minlen variable.

lcredit=*n*

Defines the weight of lowercase in a password. For example, if
lcredit=2, a lowercase letter gets credit for two characters against the
minlen variable.

ocredit=*n*

Defines the weight of other characters (basically punctuation) in a password. For example, if ocredit=3, a character other than a letter or number gets credit for three characters against the minlen variable.

I Lost the Root Password

As Linux geeks, we have a responsibility to set a good example and avoid easy passwords. However, if you have to change your password frequently, there's a chance that you'll forget it.

Single-User Mode

If you've misplaced your *root* password but can reboot your system, recovery is simple:

1. Boot your computer into single-user mode, which logs you in as the *root* user, without network connections or server services.

2. Linux mounts only the root filesystem (the / directory) in single-user mode, but you can mount other filesystems manually with the *mount* command if you need them.

3. Use the *passwd* command to reset the *root* password.

This useful workaround unfortunately allows a cracker with physical access to your system to get access to the *root* account. In the next section, I'll show you what you can do to at least slow a cracker in his attempts to break into your system.

To boot your computer in single-user mode, you need to access the kernel command line from your Linux bootloader. I'll show you how you can add your option to the kernel command line in Red Hat/Fedora and SUSE shortly.

 The Debian Linux boot menus include a "recovery mode" option, which automatically boots the system in single-user mode. The SUSE "recovery mode" boots into runlevel 3, which normally includes full functionality without the GUI.

Any of the following commands, if added to the kernel command line, boot into single-user mode:

```
single
s
1
```

These three options boot Linux into runlevel 1, which is associated with single-user mode.

Some distributions, however, require the *root* password in order to boot into single-user mode. So the options just shown won't help you if you don't know the *root* password. However, another option you can add to the kernel command line bypasses the password check, along with all other activities associated with the init process, and immediately puts you into a shell in single-user mode:

```
init=/bin/sh
```

 Red Hat distributions do not require the *root* password to log in using the single, s, or 1 options. I consider this a security hazard, and therefore an annoyance. SUSE and Debian both require the *root* password to log in using these commands. However, the *root* password is not required if you boot with init=/bin/sh.

When you boot with init=/bin/sh, the *passwd* command is disabled by default. But it's easy to get around this. Just remount your root directory (/). For example, if */dev/hda2* is mounted on /, run the following command:

```
mount -o remount /dev/hda2 /
```

You can then change the *root* account password with the *passwd* command. While some might consider this to be a flaw, you'll be grateful to know it when you forget a *root* password or have to do emergency administration on a system where you haven't been told the *root* password.

Protecting Single-User Mode

Because it's possible to change the *root* password on our major Linux distributions via single-user mode, additional security is wise. You can take the following steps to further secure your system:

Set a BIOS password
Modern BIOS systems support passwords, which can keep a cracker from bypassing your bootloader with a boot disk. One drawback is that there are methods to reset a BIOS password. Some of these methods

require removing the BIOS battery, which requires opening up a computer case. That may be enough to discourage an attack. For details, see the documentation for your BIOS.

Set a password on your bootloader
The GRUB and LILO bootloaders also support passwords, which can prevent single-user-mode logins.

Keep the timeout on your bootloader to a minimum
If you have a minimal timeout on your bootloader, it can prevent a cracker from starting your system in single-user mode, where he or she can then change your *root* account password.

Password protection for the bootloader may not be enough. If a cracker has access to the reset button and can set your BIOS to boot from a CD/DVD or floppy drive, she can insert a boot disk or even a Knoppix CD to crack your system. We'll describe some of the physical methods you can use to prevent this crack in "The Boss Told Me to Secure the Server Without Locking the Room," at the end of this chapter.

Password-protecting GRUB

You can add encrypted passwords to GRUB with the *grub-md5-crypt* command, as follows:

1. As *root*, run *grub-md5-crypt*.
2. At the command prompts, type the password you want to use to log in, and confirm.
3. With your mouse, highlight the encrypted password printed by *grub-md5-crypt* and paste it into the GRUB configuration file. There are two places where you can paste the GRUB password:
   - If you want to protect the GRUB menu from changes, enter the password as the first line in the GRUB configuration file.
   - If you want to protect a specific boot option, paste it after the title line of the stanza.

In either case, the password directive will appear as follows; the --md5 switch tells password to expect an MD5-encrypted password.

```
password --md5 $1$cg36g0$HgArcGTyynzZhPidnlTe.o
```

Password-protecting LILO

You can add a password to the LILO bootloader to protect the menu or specific operating-system options. Unfortunately, LILO does not support encrypted passwords; you'll have to enter the password of your choice in clear text. Be aware of the security risk. The directive that you'll add to *lilo.conf* is straightforward:

```
password=mysecret
```

As with GRUB, if you want to protect the LILO menu, place the `password` directive in the first part of *lilo.conf*. If you want to protect a specific boot option, place the password command after the `label` directive in the associated stanza.

My Server Is So Secure I Can't Log In as Root

If you've forgotten your GRUB and *root* passwords, you're not stuck. You do not have to reinstall Linux. The problem may be as simple as a misconfigured bootloader, a mislabeled kernel, or an incorrect partition. Or the problem may be more complex, such as a bug-laden kernel or problematic files associated with the boot process. I describe some of these issues in Chapter 7.

The techniques described in this annoyance can help you solve all of these problems. Rescue disks can help you get around boot problems and get into your system. Once you've booted into Linux, you can repair any problems that you see.

You should also read this annoyance from the point of view of the cracker. If you need a really secure system, you need to think like someone who enjoys breaking into computers. It will help you understand the reasons behind the last annoyance in this chapter.

Rescue Disks

Every Linux distribution that I've used includes some sort of rescue-disk system. It can help you recover from problem kernels, lost *root* passwords, misconfigured installation files, and more. In this annoyance, I show you how to use the basic rescue disks. I cover how you might use these rescue disks for a troubled system in Chapter 7.

Some rescue disks are more self-contained than others. The Red Hat/Fedora rescue system works from the first installation CD. As shown in Figure 6-2, it can boot your system in several ways, which I'll describe shortly.

Rescue disks load minimal systems onto a RAM disk. The tools contained on those systems are often quite limited. At least the *vi* text editor (which should be all that a Linux geek needs) is included so you can edit key configuration files after booting.

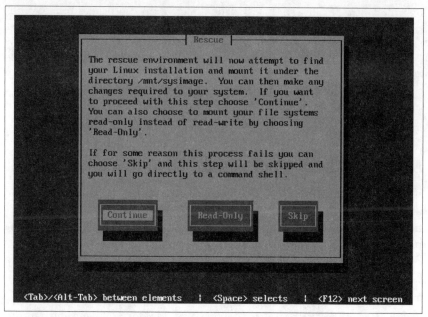

The rescue environment will now attempt to find your Linux installation and mount it under the directory /mnt/sysimage. You can then make any changes required to your system. If you want to proceed with this step choose 'Continue'.
You can also choose to mount your file systems read-only instead of read-write by choosing 'Read-Only'.

If for some reason this process fails you can choose 'Skip' and this step will be skipped and you will go directly to a command shell.

Continue   Read-Only   Skip

<Tab>/<Alt-Tab> between elements   <Space> selects   <F12> next screen

Figure 6-2. Fedora rescue screen

Rescue systems support password-free *root* user access. Once you've mounted your root directory (/) in read-write mode, you can recover (or change) the *root* password. The first step is to restore the standard filesystem hierarchy. Normally, this is possible with the *chroot* command. The directory that you use depends on the rescue disk, which I'll describe shortly.

> Because of the capabilities of a rescue disk, security-conscious Linux geeks will have a physical lock on critical server CD/DVD drives—and disable USB boot access. We'll detail the importance in "The Boss Told Me to Secure the Server Without Locking the Room," at the end of this chapter.

Creating a Red Hat/Fedora rescue disk

There are two different kinds of rescue disks that you can create on Red Hat/Fedora distributions. The best kind is customized for your system, and you can create it with the *mkbootdisk* command. The alternative is already available as part of the first Red Hat/Fedora installation CD, and I describe how you can use that as a rescue disk shortly.

To customize a rescue disk for your system, all you need is the active kernel version number, which you can check with the *uname -r* command. Insert a floppy disk, and you can create a customized rescue disk with the following command, which takes the output from *uname -r*, the active kernel version number, and applies it as input to *mkbootdisk*:

```
mkbootdisk `uname -r`
```

In most cases, the boot image is too big for a 1.44 MB floppy drive; most PCs no longer have floppy drives. If you don't have a floppy drive but do have a CD burner, you can create a customized rescue CD with the following command, which writes at standard (1x) speed:

```
mkbootdisk --iso --device rescue.iso `uname -r`
cdrecord -v speed=1 rescue.iso
```

Naturally, if your CD writer can handle faster rates, you can increase the value of speed. Alternatively, you can use the first Red Hat/Fedora installation disk as a rescue disk.

Rescuing a Red Hat/Fedora system

The procedure for rescuing the latest Red Hat/Fedora distributions is straightforward. If you have a rescue disk, you can use it to boot your system directly. Otherwise, all you need is the first installation CD, using the procedure described here.

At the installation boot screen, enter the *linux rescue* command. You're taken through the first few steps associated with installation, including language and keyboard. Once you reach the screen shown in Figure 6-2, you have three choices:

Continue

> The rescue system tries to mount your partitions, as defined in your */etc/fstab*, on the */mnt/sysimage* directory. For example, if you have a separate */boot* partition, you'll find those files in the */mnt/sysimage/boot* directory. You can then restore your original filesystem configuration with the *chroot /mnt/sysimage* command and then fix your bootloader or reset your *root* password as needed.

Read-Only

> The rescue system tries to mount your partitions as listed in */etc/fstab*, as read-only. While you can still restore your original filesystem configuration with the aforementioned *chroot* command, it does not allow you to write to the associated directories. You'll need to remount the appropriate directories in read/write mode with a command such as *mount -o remount /dev/hda2 /mnt/sysimage* before you can fix your bootloader or reset your *root* password.

Skip

The rescue system takes you to a bash shell prompt. None of your standard partitions are mounted; it's as if you started in single-user mode with the init=/bin/sh directive. You can then mount your partitions, one at a time, until you isolate a problem. Make sure to mount in read/write mode; then you can fix your bootloader or reset your *root* password.

After you make your choice, no login is required. You have *root* privileges on this system.

Rescuing a SUSE system

In a similar fashion, you can rescue a SUSE system by booting from the first installation CD or DVD. For example, with SUSE 9.2/9.3/10.0, the procedure is easy: just highlight and run the Rescue System command from the first GUI boot menu. But if you have fatal problems with hardware or drivers, you may need to run the manual rescue method:

1. From the installation boot menu, run the Manual Installation command.
2. Select the appropriate language and keyboard when prompted.
3. From the Linuxrc Main Menu, run the Kernel Modules command.
4. Load only the drivers that you need to start your system, and then go back to the Linuxrc Main Menu when you're finished.
5. Select the Start Installation or System command. Select the Start Rescue System command from the menu that appears. Select the source for the installation files (CD, Network, or Hard Disk).

At the Rescue login: prompt, you can log in as the *root* user. A password is not required. None of your existing partitions are mounted. But if the partitions are error-free, you should be able to mount them on a directory such as */mnt*. Make sure to check that you're mounting the right partition; remember, you can list the current partitions on the first IDE drive with the *fdisk -l /dev/hda* command. If you've read the previous section on Red Hat/Fedora, its rescue mode automatically mounts your configured directories.

Once you've mounted appropriate directories, you can restore your original filesystem with the *chroot* command. If you've made a mistake, you can always return to the rescue filesystem with the *exit* command.

Now you can repair your bootloader or reset your *root* password as needed.

The Debian from Scratch rescue

The Debian from Scratch CD was developed by John Goerzen as an alternative to the standard Debian installer. When you boot from this CD, it loads a not-too-minimal version of this operating system.

 When using the Debian from Scratch CD as a rescue disk, don't use the partition tools associated with the installation menu, unless you are ready to lose all your data and reinstall Debian from scratch.

Once loaded, Debian from Scratch includes a wide variety of tools, including *fdisk*, parted, development environments, full networking support, CD/DVD burning tools, print tools, and even the mutt mail reader.

As I described in the previous section on SUSE rescues, you should be able to mount your root (/) partition on a directory such as */mnt*. Make sure to check that you're mounting the right partition; remember, you can list the current partitions on the first IDE drive with the *fdisk -l /dev/hda* command.

Once you've mounted appropriate directories, you can restore your original filesystem with the *chroot* command. If you've made a mistake, you can always return to the rescue filesystem with the *exit* command.

Now you can repair your bootloader or reset your *root* password as needed.

Using Knoppix

The Knoppix CD (*http://www.knoppix.org*) is gaining popularity as the universal rescue disk. It boots a complete Linux system from the CD with an array of excellent tools that you can use to rescue almost any PC. As you can see in Figure 6-3, Knoppix loads a complete Linux operating system from the CD.

Knoppix can even help you rescue Microsoft operating systems. As with any Linux distribution, it includes native support for FAT-style formats (FAT16, FAT32, VFAT). If you have an NTFS-formatted partition with Microsoft Windows, Knoppix can load the associated Microsoft NTFS drivers, which can make the associated partitions writable from this Linux system.

 At present, file transfers to an NTFS system with available Linux drivers are very slow.

Figure 6-3. Knoppix GUI

USB boot

You can configure many PCs to boot from a USB device, including floppy, CD, and key drives. If USB boot options are not available in your BIOS, look for an upgrade. You may be pleasantly surprised.

If you can boot from a USB drive, there are several Linux distributions customized for USB keys. They include:

Feather Linux

A fully featured embedded operating system based on Knoppix that takes up about 60 MB. You can download this distribution from *http://featherlinux.berlios.de*.

Flonix

A complete Linux operating system (*http://www.flonix.com*), which is sold on a 256 MB key drive. While it is built with GPL components, it does not appear to be available for download. It's currently sold only within the European Union.

Flash Puppy

Another complete Linux operating system, which boots completely into a RAM disk. For more information, see *http://www.goosee.com/puppy/index.shtml*.

If your system can't natively boot via USB, some distributions have 1.44 MB boot floppies that can help you boot from the USB drive. With the advent of 1 GB and larger USB keys, you can configure a complete bootable distribution such as Knoppix or SUSE Live CD on a USB key.

There Are Too Many Ways to Log In

Linux computers are designed as multiuser, multiterminal systems. Multiple users can log in to a Linux computer simultaneously, from different physical terminals. A person can normally log in as *root* on any terminal, or remotely, which makes Linux relatively easy to fix when a problem requiring superuser privileges comes up—but it can also be a security risk.

 Ubuntu Linux actually disables *root* logins by default. I'll show you how you can adapt the Ubuntu technique on the distributions covered in this book.

Don't forget the other ways to log in to a Linux computer. There are a number of secure services for remote logins. Generally, SSH, which I describe in "My Other Computer Has No Monitor" in Chapter 11, is the most secure way to log in to and administer remote computers. As discussed in "I'm Afraid of Losing Data" in Chapter 2, *rsync* is an efficient way to maintain backups. The vsFTP server, described in "Users Need to Download Files" in Chapter 9, is a secure option used by Red Hat and SUSE to share their distributions. But remember, any remote access, even in encrypted format, may be a security risk.

And then there are the insecure ways to connect to a Linux computer. Telnet allows crackers to see user passwords in clear text. TFTP is not secure either. In addition, some Linux computers include terminals configured for modem and serial-line connections.

Restricting Remote Internet Services

There are three services associated with remote logins to a Linux computer: Telnet, FTP, and SSH. The safest option is to delete or disable these services if they aren't needed. But they are useful services that you sometimes don't want to disable.

 Many distributions include standard commands in their default configuration files. In many cases, commands that you see commented out are defaults for that service. Many configuration files include their own manpages.

Limiting Telnet access

The use of Telnet is strongly discouraged in Linux because associated messages, including passwords, are sent in clear text. All a cracker needs is a simple protocol analyzer (a.k.a. packet sniffer), and he can read users' passwords directly on his screen.

However, there are users who are more comfortable with Telnet, and there is a Kerberos version of Telnet in use. For more information, see "Users Are Still Demanding Telnet" in Chapter 9.

Unless you use the secure version of Telnet, it is important to disable this protocol. For the distributions associated with this book, Telnet is a "super server," configured in */etc/inetd.conf* or an appropriate file in the */etc/xinetd.d* directory.

If you're using Red Hat/Fedora or SUSE, you can disable Telnet with one of the following commands (depending on the associated script in the */etc/xinetd.d* directory):

```
chkconfig telnet off
chkconfig krb5-telnet off
```

If you're running Debian, you can disable Telnet in the */etc/inetd.conf* file. Just comment out the command that would otherwise start this service. By default, the line in Debian is:

```
telnet stream tcp  nowait root /usr/sbin/tcpd /usr/sbin/telnetd -a user
```

The users on some networks demand Telnet. I discuss the more secure Kerberos version in Chapter 9.

Limiting FTP access

If you're going to share serious amounts of data, you've probably considered FTP. Despite its age, it's still the most efficient protocol for transferring files. There are several different FTP servers available for Linux. Unfortunately, FTP can also leave you vulnerable to attack. If you need an FTP server, the best approach is to limit access. Specifically, you should consider whether to:

- Limit access to anonymous or real users
- Prohibit access to the *root* user
- Disable uploads/writes to the FTP server
- Log all access attempts
- Set a timeout in case someone walks away and another person uses that login

- Prevent access to higher-level directories (configure a *chroot jail* for the server)
- Specify users who are allowed to access the server

Not all FTP servers allow you to regulate logins in these ways. For more detailed information, consult the manuals associated with the FTP server of your choice. I describe how you can configure the vsFTP server securely in "Users Need to Download Files" in Chapter 9.

Limiting SSH access

The key file for limiting access through SSH is the */etc/ssh/sshd_config* file. There are two SSH protocols in general use, 1 and 2. As you might expect, SSH2 is more secure. However, both protocols are enabled by default. You can change this setup by adding the following directive to the SSH configuration file:

```
Protocol 2
```

A commonly recommended secure policy for remote logins is to add the following directives to this file:

```
IgnoreRhosts yes
IgnoreUserKnownHosts yes
```

At minimum, you should disable *root* logins over a network. Sending a *root* password over a network is never a good idea. Even if encrypted, anyone who intercepts the *root* password can eventually decrypt it and log in to the administrative account. With the following directive in *sshd_config*, you can still log in as a regular user and then log in as *root* with *su* using SSH encryption.

```
PermitRootLogin no
```

 One might think that a cracker could decipher the *root* password when an administrator runs the *su* command remotely. But with SSH encryption, there is no easy way to know when *su* is run.

Other directives can limit allowed users and groups; see the AllowUsers and AllowGroups directives as listed in the *sshd_config* manpage. For example, if *michael* is the only user who should be authorized to access a server via SSH, just add the following directive:

```
AllowUsers michael
```

There are a few other directives worth considering. For example, you may not want to use this directive, as it would let users log in without a password:

```
PermitEmptyPasswords yes
```

One of the strengths of the X Window System is that users can log in to a remote system, run a program on it, and interact with it from their terminal on the local system. As an administrator, this is particularly useful to you because you can gain access to remote GUI tools. On the system where the programs run, you can enable remote users to get access to them (known as *X forwarding*) by including the following directive in the *sshd_config* file:

```
X11Forwarding yes
```

On SUSE, this line is included by default.

Once X forwarding is enabled on the system running the program, it's easy to set up remote access to GUI tools. All you need to do is log in to the remote system with the *-X* switch. For example, if I access my desktop named *enterprise4a* with the following command:

```
ssh -X michael@enterprise4a
```

I can then run GUI applications from the remote system. For example, if I'm running the Evolution email manager from the remote *enterprise4a* computer, I can then use the *evolution* command to display this email manager on the local computer.

Preventing Access via RADIUS, Modems, and Serial Ports

Internetwork access services such as SSH and FTP aren't the only remote ways to log in to a Linux computer. You also need to pay attention to access options over modems and serial ports.

Modem servers, which are commonly installed on servers to which users connect from remote locations, are a potential security risk. There are several different Linux modem servers based on RADIUS, which you should make sure are not installed with a command such as:

```
rpm -qa | grep radius
dpkg -l | grep radius
```

Check also for the existence of */usr/sbin/radiusd*; it's possible that another administrator installed this daemon from a tarball. For more information, see *http://www.freeradius.org*.

But RADIUS isn't the only way to enable modem access on a Linux computer. The modem getty service (*mgetty*) is already partially configured in */etc/inittab* with a directive such as:

```
T3:23:respawn:/sbin/mgetty -x0 -s 57600 ttyS0
```

This command includes four fields, separated by colons. It starts with a command label (*T3*). It continues with the active runlevels (*23*) for this command. The third entry, *respawn*, reruns the *mgetty* command after every disconnect. Finally, the *mgetty* command is run, with no logging (*-x0*), at a port speed of 57600 bits per second (*-s*), on the first serial communications port (*ttyS0*).

Not many modern networks are connected through serial ports. But they're still available on many computers. If a cracker gets physical access to your computer, he can connect through a null modem serial cable unless you disable commands in */etc/inittab* such as:

```
T0:23:respawn:/sbin/getty -L ttyS1 9600 vt100
```

This particular command supports a VT100-style connection at 9600 bits per second through the second serial port.

Limiting root logins via terminal

It's also important to limit remote logins with the *root* account. If a cracker has found your *root* account, you may be able to frustrate her efforts to gain access by minimizing the *root*-capable terminals on your system.

You can limit the consoles where the *root* user can log in through the */etc/securetty* configuration file. Depending on your distribution, you'll see a number of lines, such as tty1, tty2, vc/1, vc/2, and so on. It's a good idea to prevent direct logins to all but the first console, by commenting out or deleting all but tty1 and vc/1 in this file (these terminals are required to support *root* access in single-user mode). You can still log in to other consoles as a regular user and then use the *su* or *sudo* commands to access the *root* account.

Alternatively, you can disable *root* logins by disabling the account. If you have an */etc/shadow* file, passwords are stored there in encrypted format, in the second column. Replace the encrypted password for the *root* user with an asterisk (*) to disable that account, as shown in the following command. You can still access the administrative account with the *su* or *sudo* commands:

```
root:*:13089:0:99999:7:::
```

If you don't have an */etc/shadow* file, you're not using shadow passwords, and you can disable the *root* account by substituting the asterisk in the second column of the *root* user's account directive in */etc/passwd*.

Using PAM to Control the Console

One key contemporary skill for a Linux geek is the Pluggable Authentication Module (PAM) feature. Red Hat, SUSE, and Debian all store associated files in the */etc/pam.d* directory. They each manage logins to the console through directives in */etc/pam.d/login*. The details vary widely by distribution. But the default versions of this file share commonalities:

Standard console logins
> With the *pam_unix* or *pam_unix2* module, PAM allows text-mode console logins, which are essential if you have not configured a GUI.

Console restrictions for root
> With the *pam_securetty.so* module, PAM limits logins to consoles specified in */etc/securetty*. You can make a cracker's life more difficult by limiting the consoles in this file.

Red Hat and SUSE include *README* files associated with most PAM modules. For example, *pam_securetty* is documented in *README.pam_securetty*. The directory varies by distribution.

In contrast, Debian organizes PAM-related packages differently. While Red Hat and SUSE have all-encompassing packages with most PAM modules, Debian has a series of *libpam* packages that you can browse with the *apt-cache search libpam* command. Install the ones you need; the packages are individually documented.

The Boss Told Me to Secure the Server Without Locking the Room

Security is a balancing act. For example, you can reduce the risks to your network by disconnecting it from the Internet. But that network would no longer be useful to most users.

As annoying as it may seem, physical security is sometimes appropriate and even required for servers. For example, it's a fairly common practice to limit access to servers in locked rooms. But what if others need access to this room? There are other things you can do to physically secure your server. Some of them have been noted as part of other annoyances in this chapter. I list them here for your convenience:

- Consider a card-key system, which would track users in the server room.

- Add passwords to your BIOS and bootloader.

- Disable detection/access to USB drives in the BIOS (if possible). Linux can detect them after it boots.

- Lock or remove any floppy, Zip, or CD/DVD drives on your server. With the availability of network installations, such hardware isn't absolutely necessary. (The exception is if you want to use the rescue modes described in "My Server Is So Secure I Can't Log In as Root," earlier in this chapter.)

- Restrict physical access to network equipment. Open physical ports on a hub are like open doors in a bank vault. With a capable Trojan horse, a cracker could connect a laptop computer, collect data such as usernames and passwords, and have the data sent outside your network.

- Limit access to wiring, especially network cables, and keep wiring and network equipment organized so it's easier to spot unauthorized equipment. Shield equipment from electromagnetic monitoring, if possible.

- Secure any removable drives.

- Disable or remove any telephone modems.

- Consider removing the monitor and keyboard. As you're not using the server as a workstation, you can administer it remotely using a secure communications protocol such as SSH.

- Consider a closed-circuit camera to monitor and identify unauthorized users.

- Don't forget other aspects of physical security, such as windows, ducts, thin walls, etc.

If you're not allowed to take some of these steps, document what you can and cannot do, and write up a proposal on how you would increase security. It may get some attention if there's actually a break-in!

CHAPTER 7

Kernel Itches and Other Configuration Annoyances

Even when you get a thoroughly tested and supposedly user-friendly distribution of Linux, things may not work the way you want out of the box. Superficial problems such as file shares that you can't access on other computers, or Microsoft partitions you want to read on your own computer, can usually be fixed with helper programs. But sometimes serious upgrades are required, which may include a new kernel module or even a new version of the kernel. A lot of this chapter, therefore, covers kernel configuration and compilation.

This chapter is rounded out with a couple of annoyances that don't fit into other chapters: allowing regular users to mount the CD, and configuring access to Microsoft-formatted VFAT and NTFS partitions.

The Kernel Needs an Upgrade

You don't need to change the kernel on your system often, but any Linux geek should be comfortable installing a new kernel without having to upgrade the entire distribution. The difficulty of the job depends on the reason you're upgrading. If a security flaw or other bug is found that merits an upgrade (which doesn't happen often), you may be able to simply download a package from your distributor with the new kernel. Support for new hardware may require the compilation of a new module, but usually not the entire kernel. The one major job you may run into—recompiling the whole kernel—is usually necessary only when you want to add some major feature, such as a new networking protocol, and even that isn't so hard.

A new kernel may have unexpected effects on your system, and you may accidentally leave out a feature that was in the previous kernel, so make sure an upgrade is absolutely necessary before you go whole hog. Any time you upgrade a kernel, you're taking a risk. Kernel upgrades can change the way your operating system works with your hardware, services, and more. Be prepared to back off and return to the previous kernel until you have run the new one for quite some time and are sure it's robust.

When you upgrade the Linux kernel, you have several other decisions to make: how to add the new kernel to your system, selecting a source, and whether to patch the existing kernel. These options require you to consider a number of factors:

Upgrading from a package
> Do you use the binary package provided by your distribution? If not, are you aware of the possible risks, such as changes in configuration defaults, incompatibilities with other software, or differences in default directories?

Selecting a source
> Should you work from the source code provided by your distribution, or generic source code from *kernel.org*?

Patching the kernel
> When should you patch the kernel? When should you avoid kernel patches?

Sharpen your tools
> Do you have the tools you need to modify or recompile your kernel?

I explain each of these factors in detail in the following sections.

Kernel Numbering

The official version of the Linux kernel now has four numbers, such as 2.6.15.1. The first number is the kernel version, which is only revised with the most major changes to the kernel; the last revision (to 2.0) was in 1996. The second number is the major revision of the kernel; even numbers are associated with stable releases. The third number is the minor revision of the kernel; it is revised only to incorporate new drivers or features. The fourth number is revised for bug fixes or security patches.

When Linux kernels had three numbers, the third number incorporated new drivers, features, bug fixes, and security patches.

As of this writing, most Linux distributions use the old three-number system; however, they include additional characters associated with the way distributions customize the kernel. For example, a Fedora kernel might have a version such as 2.6.14-1.1688_FC5, and a Debian kernel might have a version such as 2.6.12-9-386. All distributions may include options that differ from the stock kernel available from *http://www.kernel.org*.

Upgrading from a Package

Red Hat, SUSE, and Debian all create binary kernel packages to incorporate security updates, add new features, address problems documented in bug reports, and more. When you install an updated binary kernel package, it automatically updates your active bootloader. You'll then have two kernels available, side by side, in your /boot directory.

Installing a new kernel is simple. For Red Hat and SUSE, use the -i or --install option associated with the rpm command:

```
rpm -i kernel-newversion
```

Alternatively, you can use the update tool associated with each distribution (up2date, yum, YaST); when you select an updated kernel with those tools, by default they apply the install (and not the upgrade) option.

For Debian, connect to the network and use apt-get install to retrieve and install the new kernel:

```
apt-get install kernel-image-newversion
```

Debian is moving from kernel-image to linux-image as the name of their kernel packages.

Red Hat, SUSE, and Debian design their current binary kernel packages to add appropriate stanzas to GRUB or LILO bootloaders.

Use the install option instead of the upgrade option when you add binary kernel packages to your system. If you use the upgrade option, you'll overwrite your existing working kernel. In that case, you'll burn your bridges behind you. You'll be gambling that your system will work immediately with a new kernel, but that's very risky. There might be a hardware issue or other aspects of your particular system configuration that cause the kernel to fail. If your new kernel does not work, you may have to restore your system from backup. In contrast, if you save the old kernel by using the install option, you can simply choose the old one at the boot prompt and then try to fix the new kernel and recompile it.

Selecting a Source

There are a couple of situations when you can't depend on a binary package but have to download and compile source code.

The first situation is when the feature you need, such as the right modules for your hardware, is not available in your current kernel. You may need to download the modules as a part of another package. Especially if the package is available as a tarball, you may need to apply the instructions in any embedded script. Typical script names include *Makefile* and *INSTALL*, and may be detailed in a *README* file. One example of how this works is the "My Wireless Card Works on Another Operating System, but Not Linux" annoyance in Chapter 5.

The other situation is where the driver is already available as part of the kernel, either embedded in the kernel itself, or available as a module in the appropriate */lib/modules/`uname -r`* directory. In that case, you'll need to download the source code for your kernel, use a menu to activate the appropriate features, and then recompile that kernel.

If at all possible, use the kernel source code developed specifically for your Linux distribution. While you may want to use the latest features available in the latest "stock" Linux kernel *http://www.kernel.org*, be careful. Each distribution compiles kernels with specific features that can interact and impact one other in subtle ways.

Several distributions work with special kernel sources. Some even include "backports" from more advanced kernels. So if you download a new version from *http://www.kernel.org*, you could lose the backports with other features that you need. It's therefore best to work with kernel sources provided for your distribution. For example, Red Hat Enterprise Linux 3 uses a specially configured Linux kernel that's nominally built from version 2.4.20, but includes backports from version 2.6. So if you install version 2.4.21 from *http://www.kernel.org*, you may actually lose features that you need.

Most distributions make the source code available in easily downloadable packages with names such as *kernel-source*. As we'll see shortly, though, Red Hat changed this convention starting with Fedora Core 3 and RHEL 4.

Patching the Kernel

If you download the original source code for a kernel from *http://www. kernel.org*, you can also use patches from that site. For example, if you've compiled and installed kernel version 2.6.15, you can upgrade to version 2.6.16 by downloading and installing *patch-2.6.16*—and compiling the combined source code.

At *www.kernel.org*, you can see patches labeled *ac* and *mm*. These are developmental patches released for general testing. The *ac* patches are released by Alan Cox; the *mm* patches are released by Andrew Morton. These patches include features not yet accepted by Linus Torvalds for the stable kernel.

If you choose to patch a kernel, the process may be more complex than you expect. Patches are applied to the kernel source code. Installing the patch is not enough. You still have to compile the combined source code into a new kernel.

Patches incorporate improvements between minor kernel revisions. In this section, I'll offer directions that work with most generic patches from *http://www.kernel.org* as well as patches provided by most distributions. However, the directories are different for Fedora Core 3 or later (we'll discuss this in the next annoyance). In general, here's what you do:

1. Install the source code for the current kernel (in this case, for version 2.6.15) in the */usr/src/linux-2.6.15* directory.

2. Download the desired patch (in this case, *patch-2.6.16.gz* or *patch-2.6.16.bz2*); make sure the patch is in the */usr/src* directory.

3. Unpack the desired patch with the appropriate command (*gunzip* or *bunzip2*).

4. Navigate to the current kernel source directory—in this case, */usr/src/linux-2.6.15*.

5. Apply the desired patch, using in this case the command:

```
patch -p1 < ../patch-2.6.16
```

Minor problems can arise when you try to apply a patch. Watch the output carefully for error messages. You may be able to diagnose a problem such as a compiler that is too old or a patch on a wrong directory.

It may help to back up a kernel when you apply a patch, by adding the *--backup* option:

```
patch --backup -p1 < ../patch-2.6.16
```

You can also create a log of error messages; the following command saves errors in the *patch.log* file:

```
patch --backup -p1 < ../patch-2.6.16> patch.log 2>&1
```

Some of you may know more efficient ways to run these commands, such as combining them on one line with pipes, and so forth. However, I think it's important to break out commands on something as important as kernel patches in detail.

Now you're almost ready to configure and recompile your new kernel. However, you need to make sure your tools are suitable for the software you're compiling.

Because Fedora Core 3 is the development platform for Red Hat Enterprise Linux 4, new features that you see for Fedora Core 3 normally also apply to Red Hat Enterprise Linux 4. This includes new conventions for kernel sources discussed in this chapter. Fedora Core 5 is reportedly the development platform for Red Hat Enterprise Linux.

Sharpen Your Tools

If you need to recompile your kernel, the source code is not enough. You also need the right tools. First, there are the tools that do the actual work, such as the GNU C Compiler. They vary by distribution and by major kernel version (2.4 and 2.6). More information is available in the *Changes* file, in the *Documentation* subdirectory of your kernel source directory.

Linux kernel 2.4 is still in common use on the Red Hat Enterprise Linux 3 series of distributions. Although that may seem dated, Red Hat has included appropriate "backports" of various kernel 2.6 features, and they have committed to support their customized kernel through the year 2008.

Then there are the packages that allow you to customize the kernel using graphical menus. Generally, these include the *ncurses-devel* library in the *libncurses5-dev* package for the lower-end *menuconfig*, and the TCL and TK libraries for the higher-end *xconfig* and *kconfig* menus. We'll look at these menus briefly in the next annoyance.

The *ncurses-devel* library is a good choice for a system that isn't running the X Window System, which is the case with many servers. Alternatively, there are three different menu configuration systems that take advantage of the X Window System GUI. If you use the GNOME desktop, find and install the

GTK+ 2.0, Glib 2.0, or *libglade* 2.0 development libraries. The actual packages and their names vary by distribution. Alternatively, if you use the KDE desktop, download the QuickTime development libraries.

Recompiling the Kernel

The thought of recompiling the kernel strikes fear into far too many Linux geeks. While you have to perform each step in order and wait for the process to finish, and while mistakes can force you to try again or backtrack to an earlier kernel, the process is not as bad as it seems. Assuming that you have the source code and tools installed, as described in the previous annoyance, you can just follow the basic steps I describe here. Variations are possible, depending on your kernel version and distribution. For more information, see the *README* file in the directory with your source code, usually */usr/src/ linux*. (For Fedora Core 3 and above, the standard source code directory is a subdirectory of */usr/src/redhat/BUILD*.)

Configuring the Kernel

The following are general steps associated with getting to the kernel customization menu. Depending on your configuration, there may be variations:

1. Navigate to the directory with the kernel source. If you've compiled your kernel in the past, you should have a *.config* file in this directory. If you want to start over, you can delete this *.config* file and make sure that the source code is clean with the following command:

    ```
    make mrproper
    ```

2. Create a *.config* file in the local directory. If you're recompiling the current kernel, just copy it from the *config-`uname -r`* file in the */boot* directory. For example, if your current kernel is version 2.6.11, run the following command:

    ```
    cp /boot/config-2.6.11 /usr/src/linux/.config
    ```

 When you include the `uname -r` string in another command, it embeds the version number of the current kernel. It's useful, as many kernel-related files and directories use the version number of the current kernel.

Customize the *Makefile* in the directory with your source code. Modified correctly, this helps identify the new kernels that you create. The key is the fourth variable in the *Makefile,* EXTRAVERSION, which gets appended to the end of the new kernel files. On my Debian computer, I've set EXTRAVERSION to -mj1; when I modified my 2.6.8 Linux kernel, the new kernel was named *vmlinuz-2.6.8-mj1.* If I recompile this kernel again for different features, I'd change *EXTRAVERSION* to -mj2; that kernel would be named *vmlinuz-2.6.8-mj2.*

3. Now you can modify the kernel as needed. With the thousands of options available, it's more efficient to make modifications with a graphical interface. If you have the proper *ncurses* development libraries installed, you can start a menu similar to Figure 7-1 with the *make menuconfig* command.

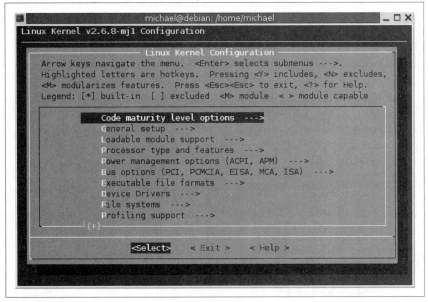

Figure 7-1. The ncurses kernel menu

If you're running GNOME and have one of the libraries described in the previous section installed, you can start a menu similar to that shown in Figure 7-2 with the *make gconfig* command.

If you use the KDE desktop and have the QuickTime libraries, you can open the *qconf* kernel configuration menu shown in Figure 7-3 with the *make xconfig* command. (The *xconfig* menu had a substantially different look and feel for kernel version 2.4.)

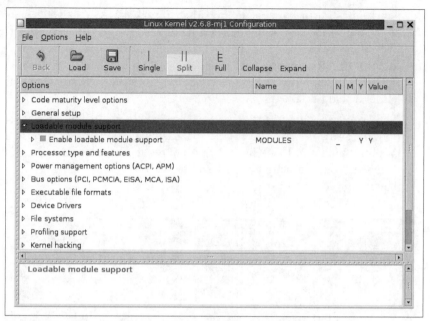

Figure 7-2. The gconfig kernel menu

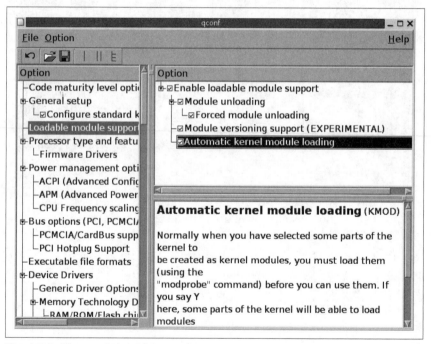

Figure 7-3. The xconfig kernel 2.6 menu

With SUSE, you need to set the environment and display defaults to correspond to the *root* account before opening a kernel configuration tool with the *make xconfig* or *make gconfig* commands. If you've logged in to the SUSE GUI with a normal account, open a command-line terminal interface and log in to the *root* account with the following command, which transfers your account's X environment directives to *root* for this session:

sux - root

4. Now you can customize the kernel with the settings of your choice. Unless you're working with an embedded device, you should almost always enable loadable module support. You then have three choices for many features: to exclude it, compile it into the core kernel, or compile it as a module.

The variety of options in kernel configuration is annoying, and unfortunately beyond the scope of this book. An advantage of reusing the */boot/config-`uname -r`* file is that you can probably get away with just adding a single module or making a few limited changes (hopefully well documented by a *README* file when you downloaded the kernel or patch). When you save your settings, you're creating a new *.config* file. Once compiled, the result should be saved to the */boot* directory.

This is where the Debian process diverges from the commands you can use on Red Hat/Fedora and SUSE; I'll describe both processes in the following sections. In either case, the commands required to compile the kernel can take several minutes, or even hours, depending on your hardware.

Preparing the Source for Fedora/Red Hat

Starting with Fedora Core 3, Red Hat has eliminated the *kernel-source* package. But you can build the source code from the source RPM, which is called *kernel-`uname -r`.src.rpm* in the SRPMS directory.

For example, if you download the original kernel source *.src.rpm* for Fedora Core 3 (version 2.6.9-1.667), you need to take the following steps to get to the kernel customization menu:

1. Install the source RPM with the *rpm -ivh kernel-2.6.9-1.667.src.rpm* command.

2. Navigate to the directory with the kernel SPEC file—normally, */usr/src/redhat/SPECS*.

3. Build the source code. The following command builds it in an appropriate directory. The `uname -m` option provides the architecture associated with your system:

```
rpmbuild -bp --target=`uname -m` /usr/src/redhat/SPECS/kernel-2.6.9-2.6.
spec
```

4. Install the development tools. The easiest way to do so is by installing the Development Tools package group via the *system-config-packages* or *pirut* utility.

5. Install the graphical tools required for the kernel configuration tool of your choice. Generally, if you use the GNOME Desktop Environment, run *make gconfig*, which requires the GNOME Development Tools package group. If you use the KDE Desktop Environment, run *make xconfig*, which requires the KDE Development Tools package group.

 Whatever distribution you use, many packages assume that your source code is in the */usr/src/linux* directory. If your distribution uses a different directory, it can help to create a symbolic link from */usr/src/linux* to the directory with the kernel source code.

Processing a Red Hat/Fedora or SUSE Kernel

Once the kernel is configured, you can start the build process. Once you've customized your *.config* kernel configuration file, the following are basic steps associated with recompiling the kernel. Depending on your configuration, there may be variations:

1. The following command checks your *.config* settings against any dependencies and processes your kernel source code accordingly:

```
make dep
```

2. Before you start compiling the source code, it's a good idea to make sure no files exist from previous builds with the following command. Otherwise, they might get mixed in with your new build and cause havoc:

```
make clean
```

3. Now you can compile your source code into a binary kernel. The following command creates a binary kernel in the *arch/i386/boot* subdirectory. If you have something other than a 32-bit CPU, the directory name will contain a string denoting that processor in place of *i386*:

```
make bzImage
```

4. Assuming you've configured loadable modules, you'll need to process and install the modular drivers associated with your new kernel:

```
make modules
make modules_install
```

You should find your newly customized modules in the */lib/modules/* `uname -r` directory.

5. Finally, you're ready to process your new kernel. The following command creates an Initial RAM disk, copies it and the new kernel to your */boot* directory, and updates the active bootloader:

```
make install
```

Naturally, you should check the result in the */boot* (and in some cases, the top-level root) directory, as well as in your bootloader configuration file. If the bootloader configuration was not updated, you can do it yourself using the information in Chapter 6.

Processing a Debian Kernel

The Debian kernel build process is relatively simple because it involves making your own custom Debian package; most of the grunt work is done for you automatically by this package. This section of the chapter assumes you've modified your *.config* file with one of the kernel configuration tools described earlier. The following are basic steps associated with recompiling a Debian kernel:

1. Install the Debian package known as *kernel-package*, which includes a number of scripts that can help process the Debian kernel. Then run the following command to create a Debian kernel package:

```
make-kpkg buildpackage -rev mine kernel-image
```

If this is successful, you'll find your package with a *.deb* extension in your */usr/src* directory. In my case, I found the *kernel-image-2.6.8-mj1_mine_i386.deb* package in that directory. (Debian Etch uses the *linux-image* package name.)

2. Install the kernel package with the following command:

```
dpkg -i kernel-image-2.6.8-mj1_mine_i386.deb
```

3. Make sure this command updates your active bootloader in the appropriate configuration file. Alternatively, you can update the bootloader configuration file yourself using the information in "Rooting Out the Bootloader" in Chapter 6.

4. Make sure this command updates the soft links from the top-level root directory (*/*) for the Initial RAM disk and the kernel (*vmlinuz*). As an example, the following lines are excepts from an *ls -l* command on my Debian computer (dates have been removed due to line space constraints):

```
lrwxrwxrwx  1 root root 22 vmlinuz -> boot/vmlinuz-2.6.8-mj1
lrwxrwxrwx  1 root root 24 vmlinuz.old -> boot/vmlinuz-2.6.8-1-386
```

If any of these files point to the wrong kernel, that can lead to one of the most annoying problems of all, a kernel panic. This is the subject of the following annoyance.

I Can't Boot Because of a Kernel Panic

One of the most feared problems in the world of Unix or Linux is the kernel panic, when the system stops completely during the boot process. The computer won't respond to any input, save the power switch. This is where your backups, rescue modes, or rescue media can be a lifesaver—see Chapter 6 for how you can prepare for this situation.

A number of problems can cause a kernel panic, many of which occur when you try to recompile or install a new kernel. During the boot process, if Linux can't find the hard drive, the partitions, or initial RAM disk files, you'll get a kernel panic. But kernel panics aren't limited to these issues.

Unless there's corruption on your disk or some problem with your hardware, kernel panics generally come from some recent change to key components in the boot sequence, driver problems, or boot issues, such as:

- The bootloader (GRUB or LILO)
- A recompiled kernel
- A new Initial RAM disk
- Partition changes associated with the root (/) or /boot directories
- Power problems
- Troublesome drivers, especially those created for other systems

Record the messages that the console displays immediately before your kernel panic. Review what you did just before the kernel panic, especially with respect to the preceding list. These actions can give you hints to your problems. If you still can't figure out the problem, use these messages as keywords for a search for similar problems with search engines such as *http://www.yahoo.com* or *http://groups.google.com*.

Sample Panic Messages and Their Possible Meanings

Here's a typical example of a kernel panic:

```
VFS: Cannot open root device "hda6" or unknown-block(0,0)
Please append a correct "root=" boot option
Kernel panic: VFS: Unable to mount root fs on unknown-block(0,0)
```

This problem is caused by an error in the bootloader configuration file. The Virtual File System (VFS) could not find some filesystem such as root (/) or /boot.

One possible cause is the confusing nature of the GRUB configuration file. For example, if you see the following directive in /boot/grub/grub.conf or /boot/grub/menu.1st:

```
root (hd0,5)
```

You might think this points to the /boot directory on /dev/hda5. But as you should know from "Rooting Out the Bootloader" in Chapter 6, this directive actually tells your computer to look for the /boot directory on /dev/hda6.

Another example shown here is slightly misleading. This error message might suggest that there is a problem with the /sbin/init command, which is the first process (process 1) always run by the system:

```
Warning: unable to open an initial console
Kernel panic - not syncing: No init found.
Try passing init= option to kernel
```

In fact, this problem is not directly related to init. My computer could not find init because the bootloader pointed to the wrong partition for the top-level root (/) directory. The root directory on my system was on /dev/hda7, but the bootloader configuration file pointed to /dev/hda6, as shown here.

```
kernel   /vmlinuz-2.6.8-mj1 root=/dev/hda6
```

If you have a separate partition for the /boot directory, a mislocated partition could lead to a similar kernel panic message.

Another possible cause of panics in Debian are the links from the /vmlinuz and /initrd.new files. Debian links these files from the top-level root (/) directory. If the links are broken or point to the wrong locations, you might get the following message:

```
pivot_root: No such file or directory
/sbin/init: 426: cannot open dev/console: No such file
Kernel panic: Attempted to kill init!
```

Naturally, you can address this problem either by linking the noted files from the top-level root (/) directory to the right locations in the /boot directory or by revising the menu.lst configuration file to point directly to /boot.

Another panic is related to the following message:

```
Kernel panic - not syncing: VFS: Unable to mount root fs on unknown-
block(3,7)
```

While this appears similar to previous messages related to misplaced partitions, it actually is based on a missing Initial RAM disk file. Look at your *menu.lst* file. It should point you to an *initrd* file in the */boot* directory. If you don't find the cited *initrd* file, you may need to re-create it with the *mkinitrd* command.

From these examples, we see that the cause may not be directly related to the error message. If you have some experience, you may recognize some of these messages. Otherwise, the best approach is to analyze the files and directories associated with the boot process, with the help of books such as this one.

 If you haven't made any recent changes to your kernel, check your power supply and fans. Hardware doesn't last forever, and the lack of sufficient ventilation could cause your system to stop with a kernel panic. Dust can also affect ventilation and heat transfer, especially in non-clean room environments.

Reviewing the Rescue Process After a Panic

"Dual-Boot Recovery" in Chapter 6 describes how to use a rescue CD or other medium to boot a system; after a system panic, the process is straightforward. Try each of the following steps to boot a system. They're ordered by increasing levels of difficulty:

- If you have more than one kernel configured in your bootloader, try them all. If a different kernel works, you may have a corrupt kernel, initial RAM disk, or an error in the bootloader configuration file.

- If you have a rescue disk or CD customized for your system, try that next. Such disks are designed to boot your system in your current configuration. At that point, you can connect to any backups that you might have to recover a previously working configuration.

- Use the rescue mode customized for your distribution. If you have the Red Hat/Fedora installation CD, it searches for and mounts your existing partitions. SUSE's installation disk and the Debian from Scratch CD install familiar tools that can help you mount and diagnose any problems you may have.

- Boot with a CD-based Linux distribution such as Knoppix. It includes a complete Linux distribution, including specialized tools designed to help you rescue a system.

"I Lost the Root Password" in Chapter 6 describes booting into single user mode. Unfortunately, if you have a kernel panic, your system has usually stopped before it could boot into this useful runlevel.

Rescuing from a Kernel Panic

Once you've started your system using some emergency or rescue disk, review what you've done since your last successful boot. If you've changed a kernel, revised a bootloader, created a new initial RAM disk, or revised the partition associated with your root (/) or /boot directories, that could be the cause of your kernel panic.

The cure, then, is to reverse what you've done recently. If applicable, restore the original kernel, initial RAM disk, /boot or root (/) partition, or bootloader. Alternatively, restore the key parts of your system from a backup. Once you've gone back to your previous working configuration, test the result.

 If you revise a key part of the boot system, you should test the result as soon as possible by rebooting Linux. If there are problems, you can restore your system while your memory of the changes you've made is fresh. You should also document the changes you've made.

I Can't Boot Because of Some "File Not Found" Error

Closely related to the kernel panic is a "File not found" error that stops the boot process. While not as severe as a kernel panic, it is still a fatal error that prevents booting into Linux. As with panics, the primary causes of "File not found" messages are errors in files related to the boot process. And the error messages are relatively straightforward, so you can usually figure out how to specify the proper filename and directory.

One example of a "File not found" error is the following, where the root(hd0,0) directive points to the wrong partition. It's pretty clear what the problem is in this case, because the filesystem is listed as FAT:

```
root (hd0,0)
 Filesystem type is fat, partition type 0xb
kernel /vmlinuz-2.4.21-15.EL ro root=LABEL=/ hdd=ide-scsi

Error 15: File not found
```

The noted partition is (hd0,0), also known as */dev/hda1*. It's formatted to the FAT filesystem. Your Linux boot files are almost certainly not located on a partition formatted to a Microsoft filesystem. You may need to do some searching to find the partition with your Linux boot files. Then you can revise your bootloader to point to the right partition.

In the following case, the problem is less clear. While the message is almost identical to the previous error, the problem is actually a missing Linux kernel:

```
root (hd0,0)
 Filesystem type is ext2fs, partition type 0x83
kernel /vmlinuz-2.4.21-15.EL ro root=LABEL=/ hdd=ide-scsi

Error 15: File not found
```

The solution may be as simple as correcting a typo in the name of the file you specified as the kernel.

The following error message illustrates a boot process that proceeded a bit further. As the messages stop at the Initial RAM disk message, you might (correctly) conclude that the problem is related to a missing, mislinked, or misnamed Initial RAM disk file:

```
root (hd0,0)
 Filesystem type is ext2fs, partition type 0x83
kernel /vmlinuz-2.4.21-15.EL ro root=LABEL=/ hdd=ide-scsi
   [Linux-bzImage, setup=0x1400, size=0x12dae6]
initrd /initrd-2.4.21-15.EL.img

Error 15: File not found
```

The following error message says that Linux can't find /etc/inittab:

```
INIT: No inittab file found
```

Another error message indicates that the /boot filesystem is mislabeled:

```
Couldn't find matching filesystem: LABEL=/bot
```

A closely related error may indicate that the runlevel field has been omitted or incorrectly specified in the id directive in /etc/inittab:

```
INIT: /etc/inittab[20]: fault unknown action field
Enter runlevel:
```

At the prompt just shown, if you can enter the number associated with your preferred runlevel, there may be a problem with the id directive in /etc/inittab. Otherwise, there may be a different problem with the /etc/inittab file.

Finding That File

If you see a "File not found" message, focus on the filename associated with the message. Usually, a file or directory specified in /etc/inittab or /etc/fstab is the source of the problem. A Linux guru should know these files well—or at least be able to refer to them on other Linux computers as models.

Commands related to those files include *mount* and *init*. If either of those commands is corrupted, or perhaps replaced by a cracker, you'll see characteristic symptoms. A missing */sbin/init* leads right to a command shell prompt such as:

```
sh-3.00#
```

A missing *mount* command, on the other hand, leads to unexpected errors. In SUSE, you'll see a number of "failed to mount" errors. In Red Hat, you'll see something simpler:

```
Is /proc mounted?
```

With Red Hat and SUSE, you can see whether one of these files became corrupted by checking it against the associated RPM:

```
rpm -Vf /bin/mount
```

If you don't see any output, the file is verified as the original. Otherwise, you may have a problem, depending on the output. The options you might see are shown in Table 7-1.

Table 7-1. rpm output for files that are unverified

Output	Description
S	Mismatched file size
M	Different permissions or file type (Mode)
5	Incorrect MD5 checksum
L	Bad symbolic link
D	Wrong device number
U	Ownership (user) wrong
G	Ownership (group) wrong
T	Mismatched file modification time
c	Identifies a configuration file

If you're checking files on Debian-based packages, use the *debsums* command. It uses the MD5 checksum for each file to verify its authenticity. This requires you to get the Debian package from a CD or download. I've downloaded and installed my Debian packages with the *apt-get* command, and they're stored in the */var/cache/apt/archives* directory. Thus, if I wanted to check the MD5 checksums of the files from the *smbclient* package, I'd run the following command:

```
debsums -ag /var/cache/apt/archives/smbclient*
```

Any MD5 checksum for a specific file that does not match returns a message such as:

```
usr/bin/smbtar                    FAILED
```

For a more comprehensive and preemptive approach to detecting the malicious replacement of critical system files, install Tripwire on your system as soon as you install the operating system (and before connecting to a network). Tripwire works on most modern Linux distributions. For more information on the open source version of this tool, refer to *http://www.tripwire.org*.

I Need to Add a Custom Kernel Module

Sometimes, the module associated with an item of your hardware is not included with your distribution. That's an annoyance every Linux geek should know how to fix.

In "My Wireless Card Works on Another Operating System, but Not Linux" in Chapter 5, we stressed the importance of knowing the make, the model, and, in many cases, the chipset associated with each hardware component. With this information, you can identify available Linux modules associated with your hardware.

To find the right hardware module, try the following in order:

1. Check loaded modules. If the *lsmod* command shows a module for your hardware, it has been detected and installed by your distribution.

2. Check compiled modules. If you're lucky, the right module for your hardware is already available in your */lib/modules/`uname -r`* directory.

3. Check the kernel source code. If it contains the module for your hardware, the kernel probably supports it and you can compile and install the module yourself.

4. Check your hardware manufacturer. Increasing numbers of hardware vendors support Linux. You may be able to download drivers direct from the manufacturer's web site, just as you might download Microsoft Windows drivers.

5. Check for experimental drivers. As discussed in the annoyances in Chapter 5, experimental Linux drivers are often available for testing. While these are not "production-ready," they may work well enough for your needs.

I'll describe what you do if one the first four steps yields results. Refer to "My Wireless Card Works on Another Operating System, but Not Linux" in Chapter 5 if you have to resort to developmental (alpha or beta) drivers.

Check Installed Modules

The module that you need may already be properly installed; in this case, the operating system is ready and you may just have to do something hardware-specific to activate the hardware. (It may be as simple as checking that the cable is plugged in.)

As an example, assume you're looking for the Linksys Tulip driver. Based on the module name that you've found in your documentation or online web search, identifying the right driver is a simple:

```
lsmod | grep -i tulip
```

 Sometimes the case of a driver varies; the *grep -i tulip* command searches for tulip in upper- and lowercase.

If the driver turns up in your list of modules, the problem may be with the hardware. If you're sure the hardware is working (perhaps because you've tried it under another operating system), you may have a defective module; you may try recompiling from a fresh copy of the driver software, using the techniques we've described in "Recompiling the Kernel," earlier in this chapter.

Check Compiled Modules

If you're fortunate, the module for your new hardware is part of your distribution's module directory. The right compiled module should be in the */lib/modules* directory associated with your active kernel (you might have more than one kernel). This directory is defined by:

```
/lib/modules/`uname -r`
```

If the module is available only in a different directory, try copying it to the directory associated with the active kernel. It might work if you're fortunate. Otherwise, use the source code to recompile the module for your running kernel.

Check the Kernel Source Code

When you recompile your kernel, you can incorporate drivers of your choice. Assuming you've enabled loadable modules, there are three options for most drivers during kernel configuration:

- Incorporate the driver directly into the kernel (the y option).
- Configure the driver as a module, which will be loaded as needed (the m option).
- Leave the driver out of your kernel altogether (the n option).

The notes associated with a driver are often quite specific. For example, the HCI UART driver shown in Figure 7-4 is directly associated with several specific Bluetooth cards.

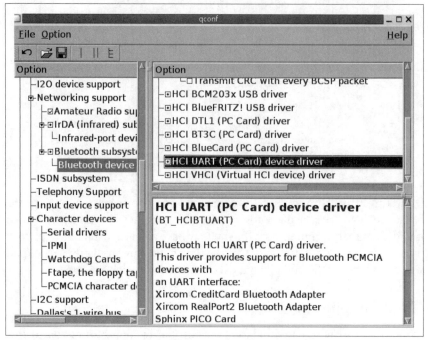

Figure 7-4. A Bluetooth driver in the kernel

The particular tool shown in this figure lists modules with dots, and notes drivers that are compiled directly into the kernel with check marks. Other tools may be more straightforward. For example, with the *ncurses*-based *make menuconfig* tool, *y* incorporates the driver into the kernel, *m* configures the driver as a module, and *n* excludes the driver from your kernel and list of modules.

Check Your Hardware Manufacturer

An increasing number of hardware manufacturers provide Linux drivers. If you haven't found a module for your component yet, try their web sites. You might be pleasantly surprised. Unfortunately, loading a driver is a bit more difficult than downloading and running an executable file.

While details vary, there are five basic steps associated with setting up a downloaded driver for Linux:

1. Download the driver. Process it per the vendor's instructions. If they suggest that you don't need to recompile your kernel, and they include a driver customized for your specific kernel, skip to the next section of this annoyance.

2. Place the driver's source code file (if it is not compiled, it normally has a *.c* extension) in the appropriate kernel source code directory. The vendor instructions may suggest a directory.

3. Navigate to your kernel directory. Use the kernel configuration tool of your choice, such as *make menuconfig*, *make xconfig*, or *make gconfig*. Configure the driver either as a module or directly into the kernel.

4. If the only change that you've made is to add the driver, you can try just reinstalling the modules with the *make modules* and *make modules_install* commands. But the safer option is to recompile the whole kernel. The documentation from your driver vendor may provide more information.

5. Reboot and start Linux using the new kernel. Find the appropriate module in the */lib/modules* directory. If found, you may be able to install it, using the options described in the next section.

Making Sure Your Kernel Is Loaded

Once you have a working driver, Linux might automatically detect it the next time you reboot. If not, make sure the driver module is available from the correct directory, specifically a subdirectory of */lib/modules/`uname -r`*. See if you can load it with the appropriate *insmod* or *modprobe* commands.

Assuming that works, you'll need to add the driver, with configuration options, to a module configuration file. The next time you boot Linux, driver modules are loaded based on instructions in this file. For distributions associated with Linux 2.4 series kernels, the file is */etc/modprobe.conf*. For Linux 2.6 series kernels, the file name varies by distribution.

For example, Debian includes some generic drivers in */etc/modules*. Specialty drivers are loaded via scripts in the */etc/modultils* directory. Standard module aliases are listed in different files in the */etc/modprobe.d* directory.

In SUSE and Fedora Core 3, standard modules are listed in */etc/modprobe. conf*. SUSE User-defined modules can be loaded via */etc/modules.conf*. Specific options can be added to appropriate files in the */etc/modprobe.d* directory.

My Files Are on That Other Computer

What's the point of a network if you can't share files? Linux provides several different protocols for file sharing. Two of the most common are the Network File System (NFS) and Samba.

NFS is the most efficient way to share directories between Linux and Unix computers. Unfortunately, if you have connection problems, shared NFS directories can hang up a client computer.

Samba supports sharing between Linux/Unix and Microsoft Windows computers. It's almost up-to-date with the latest developments in the Server Message Block/Common Internet File System (SMB/CIFS) protocols. While you can configure a Samba server as a Primary Domain Controller (PDC) or as a member server of an Active Directory (AD) network, Samba cannot yet act as a Domain Controller on an AD network.

The process of configuring NFS and Samba shares is a complex topic; a complete discussion is beyond the scope of this book. We assume in this section that you know the basics of installing and activating the appropriate NFS and Samba packages on your system. For more information, see *Managing NFS and NIS* by Hal Stern and *Using Samba* by Jay Ts et al. (both published by O'Reilly).

The annoyances that we'll deal with are:

- Configuring NFS directories risks hangs when the network is down.
- Connecting to shared Samba directories normally requires *root* account access.

Connecting with NFS

The process of configuring a regular NFS share is elementary for the Linux geek. However, if you want to minimize the risk of hangs when a client tries to mount an NFS directory, you'll need to follow these instructions carefully.

Under NFS, the system on which a shared directory physically resides permits other systems to mount the directory by listing it in */etc/exports*. Access can be further limited with the */etc/hosts.allow* and */etc/hosts.deny* files. Given the NFS security issues, such as no provision for encryption over the network, *root* access is prohibited by default.

It's common to configure a shared directory good for all users, such as */home*, from a central server. For example, you might see the following line in */etc/exports*:

```
/home    192.168.0.0/24(rw,sync)
```

This line exports the directory /home to all systems on an internal Class C network, allowing read/write access and making the application that writes a file wait until the data is stored on the remote disk.

On the client side, there are two basic ways to mount a shared NFS directory: with a hard mount or a soft mount. A hard mount is more resistant to dropped connections, which can corrupt your data. In contrast, a soft mount can keep your system from hanging if there's a network problem when your system attempts to connect to a NFS directory. So if you need reliability when writing to a shared NFS directory, consider a hard mount. If you have trouble connecting to NFS server systems, consider a soft mount.

Default mounts through NFS are hard mounts. So if you choose a hard mount, you can configure it with a line such as this one in the client computer's /etc/fstab:

```
192.168.0.10:/home    /server    nfs    nfsvers=2    0    0
```

The /home directory on 192.168.0.10 will be hard-mounted on /server. To use a soft mount, configure it explicitly on the client:

```
192.168.0.10:/home    /server    nfs    soft,nfsvers=2    0    0
```

Naturally, this isn't the only way you can configure a mount from a client. You can mount the remote /home directory on the local /home directory. You can also use the fully qualified domain name of the NFS server, as long as forward and reverse DNS pointers are available for that server.

There is one more way to mount a shared NFS directory: the automounter, which we'll describe at the end of this annoyance.

Connecting with Samba

One of the annoying things about Samba is that you have to be the *root* user to connect to a shared Samba or Microsoft directory—at least under the defaults for some distributions. Regular users need to connect to shared directories all the time. I'll show you some ways around this problem in this section.

To support access, users need an account on the Samba server or on the corresponding PDC. Just as you can configure a single database of Linux/Unix usernames and passwords on a NIS or LDAP server, you can configure a single database of Microsoft usernames and passwords on a Domain Controller. You can configure a Microsoft Windows server or a Linux server configured with Samba as a PDC.

Let's start with the simplest solution to the user account problem—but the solution that requires the most manual work for you. This solution is to configure a user account for every user to whom you want to give access to a share on your Linux system. This works fine in a small environment where only one server offers files or printers.

For example, I've configured my own account with the following command, which prompts for a password.

```
smbpasswd -a michael
```

If you're using a Samba 2.x system, the corresponding command is *smbadduser*.

To browse the shares from a Samba (or a Microsoft Windows) server, *smbclient* can help. For example, if you want to view the shares on a computer named sunshine, run the following command:

```
smbclient -L sunshine
```

If you're familiar with Microsoft operating systems, you may recognize the output. It's similar to what you see through the Network Neighborhood or My Network Places tools, or from a *net view \\sunshine* command.

Most of the latest Linux GUI desktop environments make it easy to browse a Samba/CIFS network. Current GNOME desktops support network browsing with Nautilus, while KDE desktops can access the network via Konqueror. Just enter the following in the address bar of one of these tools:

```
smb:///
```

If you don't see the address bar in either browser, press Ctrl-L (Nautilus) or Ctrl-O (Konqueror). You can then enter *smb:///* in the Location text box.

The standard Samba configuration file, *smb.conf*, supports access by regular users to their home directories. The following commands in the file serve up the home directory for each user:

```
[homes]
        comment = Home Directories
        valid users = %S
```

But therein lies a problem. Regular users aren't normally allowed to use the *mount* command. On many Linux distributions, they aren't even allowed to use the Samba mount commands such as *smbmount*.

Debian alleviates this problem by configuring two key commands as SUID *root*, supporting access by regular users: *smbmnt* and *smbumount*. If you're running Samba on another distribution, you can set SUID permissions with the following commands:

```
chmod u+s /usr/bin/smbmnt
chmod u+s /usr/bin/smbumount
```

Non-*root* users can now use *smbmount* and *smbumount* to access their home directories on other Linux computers. The first command mentioned in the previous sentence is not a misprint; because *smbmount* uses the *smbmnt* command, regular users can work with either one, as long as they have set the noted SUID permissions.

It's possible that other distributions will adapt Debian's settings for *smbmount* and *smbumount*. At that point, user connections to remote home directories shared via Samba will be less of an annoyance.

 As described shortly, you can use the automounter to mount shared Samba directories. However, unless the share is not password-protected, that means you'll have to add a password in clear text to an automounter configuration file.

Regular users now have access to their home directories. In this configuration, as user *michael*, I can access my home directories on other computers. For example, to mount the */home/michael* directory on a directory named *test/* on my SUSE laptop, I'd run the following command. Commands such as *smbmount* prompt for passwords as required (the password on the server or Microsoft Domain Controller, not the user's local system), so I'll need to enter the password that I created on the Samba server when prompted:

```
smbmount //suse1/michael test
```

Then I can unmount this share with the following command:

```
smbumount test
```

One user can also log in as a different user on the Samba server. Assuming Samba passwords have been assigned, I could log in to Donna's account with the following command:

```
smbmount //suse1/donna test -o username=donna
```

Once again, I'm prompted for Donna's password. I could add the password to the command line, but it would appear in clear text on the terminal, where a "shoulder surfer" (someone who looks over your shoulder for information) might read the password.

Automating Mounts with the Automounter

If your network is less than reliable, network mounts can cause trouble. Mount attempts to inaccessible NFS servers can even cause your computer to hang.

This is where the automounter can help. It is invoked by the kernel when someone accesses a remote directory in any way—such as by issuing an *ls* command or opening a file in that directory in a text editor—and performs the necessary mount over NFS or SMB/CIFS. The behavior is impressively fast and really makes networking seamless.

The automounter is available by default on most modern Linux systems. It requires the *autofs* service and is configured through the */etc/auto.master* configuration file. In most cases, the file you configure is */etc/auto.misc*. Most distributions include commented sample commands that you can use. We'll show simple examples here. For more information, see *http://www. tldp.org/HOWTO/Automount.html*.

NFS automouter share

In this example, I've set up an NFS share of the */home* directory from the *suse1* server. I've also configured the following command in my */etc/auto.misc* file:

```
linux     -rw,soft,intr     suse1:/home
```

I can then access the NFS share as a regular user with the following command:

```
ls /misc/linux
```

Samba automouter share

In this example, I can use the standard Samba share of my */home/michael* directory from the *suse1* server. All I need is the following command in my */etc/auto.misc* file:

```
michael -fstype=smbfs,username=michael,password=michael ://suse1/michael
```

I can then access the Samba share with the following command:

```
ls /misc/michael
```

Notice that configuring the automounter this way stores your password in clear text, which is a big security hazard because this file is readable by default by all users. If you choose to share Samba directories in this way, limit access to this configuration file to the *root* user:

```
chown 600 /etc/auto.misc
```

Regular Users Can't Mount the CD/DVD Drive

The CD/DVD drive is a critical part of modern personal computers, allowing users to access music, movies, backups, and more. While you may find it best to lock the CD/DVD drive on Linux servers, you need to support it on users' systems. And that is precisely where Linux makes trouble: it generally allows only the *root* user to mount a filesystem. When a user inserts a CD or

DVD, the filesystem associated to the CD/DVD drive has to be mounted before the user has access.

There are two options for giving users access to their drives: running the automounter, or making revisions to the *mount* command and */etc/fstab* file to let non-*root* users mount the pertinent directories.

 Closely related is the "My CD/DVD Is Locked" annoyance in Chapter 1, which includes instructions on how to disable automatic CD/DVD mounting via KDE's *autorun* and GNOME's *gnome-volume-properties*.

Configuring the Automouter

The automounter runs as *root* when the kernel detects that a new filesystem has appeared and mounts it as *root* so that it magically appears for the user. As discussed in the previous annoyance, the automounter relies on the */etc/auto.master* and */etc/auto.misc* configuration files. When you activate the following directive in */etc/auto.master*, you'll get a link to */etc/auto.misc*:

```
/misc     /etc/auto.misc    --timeout=60
```

Open the */etc/auto.misc* file. You'll see a default directive for the CD/DVD drive, such as:

```
cd        -fstype=iso9660,ro,nosuid,nodev :/dev/cdrom
```

Make sure the automounter reads your revised configuration files by restarting the associated service:

```
/etc/init.d/autofs restart
```

Put the two files together. You've configured the */misc* directory in */etc/auto.master* and the *cd* subdirectory in */etc/auto.misc*. Test the result. Insert a disk in the CD/DVD drive and run the following command:

```
ls /misc/cd
```

Setting Up Mounts by Regular Users

The alternative to the automounter is to configure your */etc/fstab* configuration file to allow regular users to mount your CD/DVD drive. Because there is a single group to represent all users in SUSE, the following command works on that distribution.

```
/dev/hdc /media/cdrecorder  users,umask=000    0 0
```

The *users* group is available on most distributions, and you can assign the users of your choice to that group. The default Linux Group ID for users is 100.

You'll also need to configure the *mount* command with SUID permissions, to support access by regular users. It's already configured that way in SUSE and Fedora Core.

I'm Having Trouble Connecting to an Existing Network

Unfortunately, there are so many ways networks can go wrong that they're hard even to categorize, much less describe and solve. With the development of wireless networks, potential problems have multiplied.

When diagnosing network problems, the first thing to remember is that most problems are physical. If you rush to change your networking software when the problem is just a hub without power, you could make things worse. As wireless networks have their own physical and software issues, we discuss this issue separately at the end of this annoyance.

 This annoyance assumes you're using TCP/IP networking, which is the standard on the Internet. Because Unix was developed concurrently with the foundations of the Internet, and Linux is in many ways a clone of Unix, Linux is built for TCP/IP.

Some companies use other networking protocols to promote security or for legacy reasons. Linux can support other networking protocols, such as AppleTalk and IPX/SPX. For more information, see the applicable HOWTOs at *http://www.anders.com/projects/netatalk* and *http://www.tldp.org/HOWTO/IPX-HOWTO.html*.

After you fix a network problem, you may need to revise a configuration file to keep the problem from happening again the next time you boot. Generally, most modern distributions store these configuration files in the */etc/sysconfig/network* or similar directories. If you have trouble finding the right file, Red Hat/Fedora, SUSE, and Debian all have excellent GUI utilities that can help you configure basic network interfaces.

 While this is a relatively long section, I still cover only a few of the basic networking issues. Unfortunately, a complete list of annoyances and solutions is beyond the scope of this book. For more information, start with the Networking HOWTO at *http://www.tldp.org/HOWTO/Net-HOWTO*.

Isolating the Problem

Chances are good that you already have a working LAN. But trouble is sure to happen from time to time. Cables can fray or become loose. Heat can cause network cards to work their way out of their slots. Power may cycle on your hub, switch, or router. And the first symptom you see may be network trouble on your Linux system.

In this section, I list potential problems to check step by step. As you gain experience, you may be able to isolate the problem more quickly.

Basic loopback connections

Check whether networking is operational by looking at the status of your loopback connections, one that doesn't depend at all on networking hardware. Output from the *ifconfig* command should list active network adapters. As long as network software is installed, you should see output at least from your loopback adapter, similar to:

```
lo        Link encap:Local Loopback
          inet addr:127.0.0.1  Mask:255.0.0.0
          inet6 addr: ::1/128 Scope:Host
          UP LOOPBACK RUNNING  MTU:16436  Metric:1
          RX packets:533496 errors:0 dropped:0 overruns:0 frame:0
          TX packets:533496 errors:0 dropped:0 overruns:0 carrier:0
          collisions:0 txqueuelen:0
          RX bytes:75134145 (71.6 MiB)  TX bytes:75134145 (71.6 MiB)
```

If you don't see a loopback interface, it may be down. You can try to activate it with the following command:

```
/sbin/ifconfig lo up
```

You should also be able to verify the loopback interface with the following command:

```
ping 127.0.0.1
```

Now try the *ifconfig* command again. If this doesn't work, the problems are deeper than I can address in this annoyance.

Checking network interfaces

Assuming you have network adapters on your system, you should also see their output from *ifconfig*. If you don't, try activating the associated interfaces. Assuming they're Ethernet or wireless adapters, try the following commands:

```
/sbin/ifconfig eth0 up
/sbin/ifconfig wlan0 up
```

Then run *ifconfig* again. You should see output such as:

```
eth0      Link encap:Ethernet  HWaddr 00:0D:9D:86:36:A0
          inet6 addr: fe80::20d:9dff:fe86:36a0/64 Scope:Link
          UP BROADCAST MULTICAST  MTU:1500  Metric:1
          RX packets:0 errors:0 dropped:0 overruns:0 frame:0
          TX packets:297 errors:0 dropped:0 overruns:0 carrier:0
          collisions:0 txqueuelen:1000
          RX bytes:0 (0.0 b)  TX bytes:99454 (97.1 KiB)
          Interrupt:10 Base address:0xe000
```

If you still don't see your network cards, you may have a physical problem with the card or connection; read ahead for more information. But assuming you're on an IPv4 network, there's still a problem. You need an IPv4 network address.

 An IPv6 address is shown in the settings associated with a network card. This is a manufacturer-assigned address, which is probably not suitable even if you're configuring an IPv6 network. If you use IPv6, you probably derive addresses from a hierarchy of authorities, as with IPv4.

If there's a DHCP server for your network, check it with your DHCP client command. Different distributions use client commands such as *dhcpcd*, *dhclient*, and *pump* to ask for an address from that server. If you have multiple interfaces, you should specify one; for instance, the following command asks for DHCP service for the Ethernet card on my computer:

```
dhclient eth0
```

Ideally, you'll now see something similar to the following IPv4 address information in the output to *ifconfig*:

```
inet addr:192.168.0.11  Bcast:192.168.0.255  Mask:255.255.255.0
```

Now you can test the connection between your computer and the network card. In this case, you can do so with the following command:

```
ping 192.168.0.11
```

You'll need to stop the output by pressing Ctrl-C. Alternatively, you could use the *-c 4* switch to limit the output to four pings, i.e.:

```
ping -c 4 192.168.0.11
```

Checking connectivity

Now you can check connectivity to the rest of the network. The first step is to check the connectivity to a neighboring computer. If you're a Linux administrator for the network, you should be able to find these addresses through */etc/hosts* or a local DNS computer IP address in */etc/resolv.conf*.

If you don't know how to determine what IP addresses are on your network, refer to the IP Sub-Networking mini-HOWTO at *http://www.tldp.org/HOWTO/IP-Subnetworking.html*.

For example, the following command verifies connectivity to my Internet gateway router:

```
ping 192.168.0.1
```

Next, you can check connectivity to your network's IP address on the Internet. It's available through the other network interface on your gateway computer or router. If the gateway is a Linux or Unix system, you can find the interface's address with an *ifconfig* command on that computer. If it's another operating system, consult appropriate documentation.

For example, if the Internet address on my network gateway is 11.12.13.14, I'd try:

```
ping 11.12.13.14
```

Now, unless you know a specific IP address on the Internet, that's as far as you can go with just IP addresses.

Checking names on your LAN

As we don't normally connect to the Internet with IP addresses in our browsers, we also need to check connectivity through computer names. If you've configured static IP addresses, you should be able to find the computer names on your network in */etc/hosts*. Alternatively, if you have a DNS server for your network, you should be able to find the list with the appropriate *host* command. For example, if you use *example.com* as your private network domain, you'd run:

```
host -l example.com
```

The *host -la* command may be required for later versions of DNS.

Popular domain names for private LANs include *example.com*, *example.net*, and *example.org*. Per the Internet society's RFC 2606, these domain names can't be used on the Internet and are reserved for testing and documentation.

I had previously configured *example.com* on my network; one of the results was *enterprise3d.example.com*, which I could then ping from another computer on my network.

```
ping -c 4 enterprise3d.example.com
```

Checking names on the Internet

If you're connected to the Internet, you can check name connectivity in a wider setting. Run the *ping* command to your favorite web site:

```
% ping -c 1 www.oreilly.com
PING www.oreilly.com (208.201.239.36) 56(84) bytes of data.
64 bytes from www.oreillynet.com (208.201.239.36): icmp_seq=1 ttl=45
time=40.1 ms
```

This response verifies that the DNS servers that you use for Internet addresses are working properly. If you have a problem here, you should check your connection to your ISP's DNS servers. If your gateway computer runs on Linux, you'll find it in that computer's */etc/resolv.conf*.

Alternatively, your computer gateway may not know where to route requests. The following shows that your system knows where to route request to two internal networks. But if the IP address is associated with a different network, your system doesn't know where to route the request:

```
% netstat -r
Kernel IP routing table
Destination Gateway      Genmask        Flags MSS Window  irtt Iface
192.168.0.0 *            255.255.255.0 U      0 0          0 eth1
192.168.1.0 *            255.255.255.0 U      0 0          0 eth0
```

What you need is a default route, which applies to IP addresses not otherwise specified. Assuming your network is connected to the Internet and the interface on the gateway that receives data from your system is 192.168.0.1, this command should solve your routing problem:

```
% route add default gw 192.168.0.1
```

And the next time you run *netstat -r*, you'll see the following output.

```
  default    192.168.0.1 0.0.0.0       UG     0 0          0 eth1
```

The 0.0.0.0 in the output refers to the network mask; it means that all addresses go through 192.168.0.1. Sometimes, the output also lists default as the destination address in place of 0.0.0.0; the two are synonymous when it comes to IPv4 addressing. In some cases, you may even see the fully qualified domain name (FQDN) of the gateway.

Firewalls

When you're able to connect to other computers on your LAN but not to an external network such as the Internet, you may have a firewall that is too restrictive. For example, the firewall could allow you to ping web sites on the Internet but not connect to those sites using TCP to get a web page.

In many cases, the only computer configured with a firewall is the gateway computer or router between your network and an external network, such as the Internet.

On the gateway computer, if you trust internal users (a big if), you may disable firewalls on the network card associated with the internal LAN. Unless you're working in a location such as an Internet café, crackers normally come from outside the network.

You might want to create defenses within your network as well. For example, you might configure outgoing email servers to stop internal users from sending out an excessive number of emails, which might qualify as spam. Or you might want to create firewalls within your network to further protect critical areas within your enterprise from external and internal users.

 If your company wants you to block access to certain sites on the Internet, one alternative is a proxy server. For more information on the Squid proxy server, see *Squid: The Definitive Guide* by Duane Wessels (O'Reilly).

If you need a firewall to regulate traffic within your LAN, you'll probably need a number of open ports to support services such as Samba, NFS, and SSH. All these open ports are difficult to configure, complex to maintain, and make internal firewalls less valuable.

Because many Linux distributions configure a firewall by default, that may prevent some types of network communication within your LAN. To check the operation of, and then disable, an *iptables* firewall, run the following commands:

```
iptables -L
iptables -F
```

The first command lists all rules currently being used to filter traffic, and the second flushes the rules so no filtering is done.

To make sure Linux doesn't reactivate the firewall the next time you reboot, you'll need to disable or delete the appropriate command file in the */etc/sysconfig* directory. The file varies by distribution. SUSE encourages users to disable firewalls using YaST.

A detailed discussion of firewalls is beyond the scope of this book. For more information on firewalls, see *Linux iptables Pocket Reference* by Gregor Purdy (O'Reilly).

Physical Network Troubleshooting

Loose cables, problematic network cards, and—given that so many of us now run wireless networks—the presence of too many walls between a wireless card and an access point are the most common reasons network connections fail. I assume that you already understand the basic functionality of network hardware; I summarize the components in Table 7-2.

Table 7-2. Network components

Component	Potential physical problem
Network Interface Card (NIC)	Not seated in the motherboard slot or PCMCIA socket. Check lights to confirm connectivity.
Wireless NIC	Too distant from access point; too many walls blocking signal; interference from devices in similar frequencies—e.g., handheld telephones.
Cable	Wrong cable type, such as the incorrect use of a crossover cable between a PC and a hub. Severe bends can affect performance.
Hub/Switch/Router	Lack of power. Check lights to confirm connectivity. Make sure lights are active for all connections.
Gateway/Router	Lack of power. Check lights to confirm connectivity. Requires at least two NICs on the computer gateway.

When there is a solid connection between a Network Interface Card (NIC) or Hub/Switch/Router and a cable, you should see lights on each component. Generally, a solid light means you have power or connectivity; a blinking light is a sign of network activity.

Troubleshooting Network Services

If you've verified your physical network connections and still have problems, check your network services. Because some of these services are associated with other annoyances, this discussion is limited to general principles.

- Make sure the service is active. You can test it by starting the associated script from */etc/init.d*. Once you find the service is operational, make sure the service starts in appropriate runlevels the next time you boot Linux.

- Unless you need to secure your systems from inside attack, deactivate firewalls on computers internal to your LAN.

- Check the appropriate configuration file for your service. You must list each directory in the configuration file (or use the generic terms homes and printers in Samba) in order for others to access it over the network.

- See if you can access the shared network directory on the local computer. If you can't get to a shared directory locally, you probably can't get to it from other computers on your LAN.

Wireless Network Issues

The advance of wireless networks led to additional annoyances. We've briefly addressed interference with other wireless devices. Worst of all, an unsecured wireless network makes it easy for outsiders to break in. In general, we assume that you're configuring a connection to an access point, such as a gateway router. However, it's also possible to connect wirelessly to a peer, such as a wireless card attached to a different computer.

 This section contains just a brief overview of what you can do to avoid wireless annoyances. An excellent option for more in-depth coverage is *Linux Unwired* by Roger Weeks et al. (O'Reilly).

As described in "My Wireless Card Works on Another Operating System, but Not Linux" in Chapter 5, a working wireless NIC will show up in the output to *ifconfig -a*.

To manage a wireless network on Linux, you need the commands associated with the *wireless-tools* package. (At least, that's the name of the package on Red Hat/Fedora, SUSE, and Debian.)

If your wireless card fits into a PCMCIA slot, you'll also need separate configuration files in the */etc/pcmcia* directory. The package that installs these files varies by distribution and by major kernel version. Table 7-3 lists some sample names under which you can find the package.

Table 7-3. Wireless package

Distribution	Major kernel version	Package
Debian	2.4/2.6	*pcmcia-cs*
SUSE (older versions)	2.4	*kernel-pcmcia-cs*
SUSE 9.X/10.x	2.6	*pcmcia*
Red Hat Enterprise Linux 3	2.4	*kernel-pcmcia-cs*
Fedora Core 3/4, Red Hat Enterprise Linux 4	2.6	*pcmcia-cs*

These configuration files may not work with special wireless tools or drivers installed from third-party sources such as Linuxant (*http://www.linuxant. com*) or SourceForge (*http://sf.net*), which we discussed in more detail in Chapter 5.

Once you have the right packages installed, you can configure your wireless card from the command-line interface. The key commands are *iwconfig*, *iwevent*, *iwgetid*, and *iwlist*. Once your wireless network operates to your satisfaction, you'll need to modify the appropriate configuration files with your desired settings. The commands are described in the following subsections.

iwevent

The *iwevent* command can help you monitor the wireless network. You can run this command in the background:

```
iwevent &
```

Once started, the command can help you monitor major changes to your wireless network, such as hardware, speeds, and more. Even while being run in the background, the output goes to the command console.

iwgetid

The *iwgetid* command identifies the name of the wireless network to which you're connected. For example, I might see the following output, which reflects the ESSID of my wireless network:

```
wlan0:     ESSID:"randynancy"
```

If this isn't the network you want, you can do something about it with the *iwlist* and *iwconfig* commands.

iwlist

The *iwlist* command is powerful. It can help you scan available networks, manage transmission power, check available communication channels, list access points, and more. You can run it in the following format:

```
iwlist [device] option
```

Generally, it's more efficient to specify the network device when you run this command. For example, if your wireless interface is wlan0, and you want to scan available wireless network ESSIDs, run the following command:

```
iwlist wlan0 scanning
```

Key information from this output includes the frequency (channel), ESSIDs, available bit rates, signal strengths, and access modes.

Other key *iwlist* command options are listed in Table 7-4. In several cases, there are two options, such as rate and bit rate, that produce the same result.

Table 7-4. iwlist command options

Option	Description
scanning	Scans for available access points, returning the ESSIDs, transmission frequencies, bit rates (from the access points), signal strengths, and access modes
frequency channel	Lists available channels and their corresponding reception frequencies available to your network card
bitrate rate	Lists available bit rates for your network card
encryption key	Lists encryption keys for your network card
power	Specifies the power-management modes for your network card
txpower	Reports the transmission power from your network card
ap accesspoints	Reports detected access points
peers	Lists detected access points and configured peers

iwconfig

In the same way you can configure a regular network card with the *ifconfig* command, you can configure a wireless network card with the *iwconfig* command: you can change access points, set bit rates, adjust transmission power, and more. Just remember that, once you've verified that your changes work, you'll need to revise the applicable configuration files or scripts for your wireless device so they take effect each time the system boots.

Running *iwconfig* without options returns the wireless characteristics of each wireless network device:

```
wlan0  IEEE 802.11-DS  ESSID:"randynancy"  Nickname:"unknown"
       Mode:Managed  Frequency:2.412 GHz  Access Point: 00:09:5B:FA:BB:76
       Bit Rate=5.5 Mb/s   Tx-Power=20 dBm
       RTS thr:off   Fragment thr:off
       Encryption key:off
       Power Management:off
       Link Quality=38/100  Signal level=-62 dBm  Noise level=-154 dBm
       Rx invalid nwid:0  Rx invalid crypt:0  Rx invalid frag:0
       Tx excessive retries:0  Invalid misc:0   Missed beacon:0
```

When you specify the wireless device, you can change its configuration. For example, you may be able to connect to more than one wireless network:

```
# iwlist wlan0 scanning | grep ESSID
ESSID:"randynancy"
ESSID:"default"
```

You might have trouble connecting to your preferred network. In my case, I want to make sure that I connect to my home network (instead of my neighbor's network). Thus, I specify the network to which I connect as follows:

```
# iwconfig wlan0 essid randynancy
```

There are a number of other wireless characteristics that you can configure with the *iwconfig* command. Using the format shown in the previous example, you can change the settings described in Table 7-5.

Table 7-5. iwconfig options

Option	Function
essid	Sets the wireless network to which your device connects.
channel	Specifies the channel where your wireless card communicates. It's best if it matches the transmission channel configured at your access point.
mode	Changes the operating mode to either centralized communication with an access point or ad hoc communication with other wireless peers; options include: • Ad-Hoc if there's no access point • Managed with access points • Master if this network card is the access point • Repeater for forwarding from access points • Secondary as a backup Repeater • Monitor if the card receives only data
ap	Defines a specific access point.
rate	Specifies a communication rate in bits per second.
key	Sets an encryption key.
txpower	Specifies the transmission power.

I Need to Work with Microsoft-Formatted Partitions

Users who continue to run Microsoft Windows on dual-boot systems with Linux need access to Windows filesystems from Linux. Even users in the process of converting to Linux may retain important files on Microsoft-formatted partitions and want to read or write them from Linux. Naturally, you'll want to encourage users to run Linux whenever possible. Therefore, you'll need to help your users access Microsoft partitions from Linux on a local computer. Samba is no help in this case because it offers access to filesystems on running operating systems, not on alternative operating systems that haven't been booted.

Linux has no problems with local partitions formatted as one of the various File Allocation Table (FAT) filesystems. You can read and write files to any partition with this format. If the FAT partition is available on a local hard drive, you can mount that partition like any Linux partition on that computer. Read and write access to such partitions are enabled by default in current Linux kernels.

Unfortunately, Linux does not work as well with the various Microsoft New Technology File Systems (NTFS). It's easy enough to mount an NTFS partition. Current Linux kernels allow you to read and copy files from such partitions. However, writing to an NTFS partition with current Linux distributions puts all the files on that partition at risk, due to corruption. But there is another option based on Jan Kratochvil's Captive NTFS system.

> Users with dual-boot systems can also access their Linux files while running Microsoft Windows. There are several ways to read Linux *ext2/ext3* formatted filesystems. For more information, see the SourceForge Ext2 package (*http://sourceforge.net/projects/winext2fsd/*) or Explore2fs (*http://uranus.it.swin.edu.au/~jn/linux/explore2fs.htm*).

Mounting Microsoft Partitions

The following is just a brief overview of how to configure access to Microsoft-formatted partitions on a local computer. If you need more information, refer to the SourceForge NTFS Project (*http://linux-ntfs.sourceforge.net/*).

Current distributions don't always include software to mount NTFS partitions, even in read-only mode. However, if you're running Red Hat/Fedora distributions, you may be able to get RPMs for this purpose from the NTFS Project.

If your first IDE hard drive partition is formatted as a VFAT file system, you can mount it locally with the following command (assuming the */mnt/vfat* directory exists):

```
# mount -t vfat /dev/hda1 /mnt/vfat
```

If you want to configure permanent access to this partition, configure the mount in your */etc/fstab*. The following command allows the *root* user to mount, read, and write to the noted partition.

```
/dev/hda1  /mnt/vfat  vfat  defaults  0 0
```

But *root*-only access to Microsoft data can be annoying. To configure regular user access to the partition, you'll need to specify user and/or group IDs. For example, because all regular users on a SUSE computer are members of the users group, the following command in */etc/fstab* enables read access for all regular SUSE users:

```
/dev/hda1  /mnt/vfat  vfat  defaults,users  0 0
```

By default, however, write and execute access may be forbidden. To permit these, you'll need to set an appropriate umask. The following */etc/fstab* entry allows complete access to all users:

```
/dev/hda1 /mnt/vfat   vfat   users,gid=users,umask=000   0 0
```

For an NTFS system, you'll probably want to limit access to read-only. Otherwise, users may try to use experimental writing tools that could corrupt the partition. Thus, if */dev/hda2* is formatted to NTFS, you might include the following line in */etc/fstab*:

```
/dev/hda2 /mnt/ntfs   ntfs   ro,users,gid=users,umask=000   0 0
```

If you're on a distribution without a group for all users, you can create one. Alternatively, you can substitute a specific user ID. This could be sufficient on a workstation dedicated to a single user.

Configuring Captive NTFS

The Captive NTFS system searches through and configures connections to partitions formatted to that filesystem. As of this writing, it uses NTFS drivers available on a local partition. If you have an NTFS partition, you should already have a licensed version of Microsoft Windows with the needed drivers.

The drawback of Captive NTFS is speed. A simple transfer of a 15 MB file to a Captive NTFS mounted filesystem took about six minutes in one test I ran. A similar transfer to a Microsoft VFAT partition took a couple of seconds.

While I've had good success with Captive NTFS, the slow speed of data transfer makes it difficult to test extensively for corruption. The speed also makes Captive NTFS impractical for many applications; network transfers to NTFS partitions are much faster.

The Captive NTFS package is available as a tarball and an RPM from the associated home page at *http://www.jankratochvil.net/project/captive/*. Once Captive NTFS is installed, check your */etc/fstab* configuration file. If there's a current NTFS partition on your hard disks, Captive NTFS should have detected it and configured an installation command in that file. For instance, it added the following to my Debian */etc/fstab*:

```
/dev/hda1 /mnt/captive-noname captive-ntfs defaults,noauto 0,0
```

Next, you'll need to find and copy the appropriate NTFS system files from your Microsoft Windows installation. Captive NTFS includes its own search tool for this purpose, which you can start with the *captive-install-acquire* command. It's a slow process; it took all of the resources on my laptop with 768 MB of RAM for nearly an hour. It searches and then copies critical NTFS files to the */var/lib/captive* directory, as shown in Figure 7-5.

```
┌─────────────────────────────────────────────────────────────────────┐
│  ▢  ▐    Captive Microsoft Windows Drivers Acquire    ▌    _ ▢ ✕      │
│ ┌──────────────────────────────────────────────────────────────────┐ │
│ │ Local Disks Drivers Scan                                          │ │
│ │ ┌─Currently found drivers──────────────────────────────────────┐  │ │
│ │ │ cdfs.sys      MS-Windows XP Service Pack 1/1a Free Build 5.1.2600.1106 CD-ROM/iso-9660 │  │ │
│ │ │ ext2fsd.sys   ext2 Filesystem v0.10a by http://sys.xiloo.com Checked Build English │  │ │
│ │ │ fastfat.sys   MS-Windows XP Service Pack 1/1a Free Build 5.1.2600.1106 FastFAT/vfat │  │ │
│ │ │ ntfs.sys      MS-Windows XP Service Pack 1/1a Free Build 5.1.2600.1106 NTFS │  │ │
│ │ │ ntoskrnl.exe  MS-Windows XP Service Pack 1/1a Free Build English 5.1.2600.1106 Kernel │  │ │
│ │ └──────────────────────────────────────────────────────────────┘  │ │
│ │ ┌──────────────────────────────────────────────────────────────┐  │ │
│ │ │           We will scan your local hard drives to find any       │  │ │
│ │ │           existing drivers usable for this project.             │  │ │
│ │ └──────────────────────────────────────────────────────────────┘  │ │
│ │ ┌─Scanned File...──────────────────────────────────────────────┐  │ │
│ │ │ /dev/hda1 #libntfs:/Documents%20and%20Settings/Administrator/Application%20Data/MACRON │  │ │
│ │ └──────────────────────────────────────────────────────────────┘  │ │
│ │                                                                    │ │
│ │  ✗ Cancel     ⬅ Back      ➡ Forward     ↻ Skip       ⬇ OK          │ │
│ └──────────────────────────────────────────────────────────────────┘ │
└─────────────────────────────────────────────────────────────────────┘
```

Figure 7-5. Searching for NTFS system files

 There's a way to shortcut this process. Mount your NTFS partition with Microsoft Windows. Copy the following critical files to the */var/lib/captive* directory: *cdfs.sys*, *fastfat.sys*, *ntfs.sys*, and *ntoskrnl.exe*. If you've installed a Microsoft XP service pack, you can find the latest version of these files in the *\WINNT\ServicePackFiles* directory.

Now you can mount NTFS partitions in read/write mode. Using the configuration line added to my */etc/fstab*, I can mount my NTFS partition with the following command:

```
mount /dev/hda1
```

Unmounting the NTFS partition is a critical part of the process. It may seem to take a long time on your computer. That's because it's syncing any changes that you've made to the NTFS partition with the data on the actual hard disk.

Because it may be annoying to have to remember to unmount a directory, you may wish to use the automounter for this purpose. We've addressed the basic configuration of this system earlier in this chapter.

## CHAPTER 8

System Maintenance

Whether you're just running your own system and want maximum flexibility and performance, or are responsible for delivering a wide variety of applications and capabilities to multiple users, you need a wide variety of skills to maintain a Linux system. One of the annoyances covered in this chapter can help you speed up your system; others prevent serious headaches down the line when users outgrow the disk space you've assigned them or when you have to upgrade software that contains dependencies on other software. Finally, there are solutions to annoyances included that people will remember and thank you for, as when you recover data they thought they'd lost forever from a failing disk.

In this chapter, I illustrate some of the annoyances related to maintaining a Linux system.

I Can't Boot Because the Partition Is Corrupt

There are a number of reasons why partitions become corrupt. You may have lost power. Minor electrical surges can affect what is written to a drive. As hard drives wear out, bad blocks can corrupt your data.

Yes, hard drive specifications suggest that the mean time between failures is several hundred thousand hours, which corresponds to several decades. But that's just an average, under ideal conditions. If all hard drives were that reliable, RAID would not be quite so popular.

If your hard drive is failing, you may not be able to fix the problem. The best that you can do is minimize the corruption until you can create a backup. We'll show you how to back up data from a failing hard drive in the next annoyance.

One reason for the popularity of the Reiser filesystem is its sensitivity to hard drive corruption. If you find corruption on your *reiserfs*-formatted filesystems, you'll probably have a bit more time to save your data.

Symptoms of Corruption

In this chapter, we'll describe two categories of filesystem corruption. The first, whose symptoms are described in the following annoyance, occurs when a hard drive wears out. The second is the occasional glitch that you can recover from while preserving the data on your disk. The temporary glitch is most commonly associated with a power failure. For example, once when I tripped over a cord, I lost power on my desktop computer. The next time I booted that computer, I saw the following message:

```
*** An error occurred during the filesystem check.
*** Dropping you to a shell; the system will reboot
*** when you leave the shell.
Give root password for maintenance
```

This problem is most commonly associated with filesystems that do not include a journal, such as *ext2*. Whenever there's corruption, there's a risk that Linux won't be able to find some of your files. Journaling filesystems keep a static database of file locations. But journaling is not a guarantee. I've had this error even on a journaled *ext3* filesystem.

Basic Checks with fsck

Whenever there is corruption, the first Linux command you should use is *fsck*. Ideally, you can apply this command alone to a specific, unmounted partition. For example, I managed to clean one partition with this simple *fsck* command:

```
# fsck /dev/hda6
fsck 1.35 (28-Feb-2004)
e2fsck 1.35 (28-Feb-2004)
/: recovering journal
Cleaning orphaned inode 16915 (uid=1000, gid=0, mode=0140600, size=0)
Cleaning orphaned inode 16914 (uid=1000, gid=0, mode=0140600, size=0)
Cleaning orphaned inode 16909 (uid=1000, gid=0, mode=0140600, size=0)
Cleaning orphaned inode 302828 (uid=0, gid=0, mode=020600, size=0)
/: clean, 165245/525888 files, 694569/1050241 blocks
```

 Do not run *fsck* on a mounted partition. If you can't unmount the desired partition, run *fsck* from a rescue CD such as Knoppix.

On most Linux systems, *fsck* works on a variety of filesystem formats. Try entering *ls /sbin/fsck**. You should find a variety of commands, such as:

```
/sbin/fsck        /sbin/fsck.ext3   /sbin/fsck.msdos   /sbin/fsck.xfs
/sbin/fsck.cramfs /sbin/fsck.jfs    /sbin/fsck.reiserfs
```

Thus, *fsck* is a frontend for all the filesystem-specific commands on your system. The proper utility is chosen automatically by *fsck* based on the type of the filesystem you run it on.

Finding Bad Blocks

If your system still has bad blocks, it may be the first sign of an impending failure. Hard drives can include hundreds of thousands of blocks. If one goes bad, that may not be the end of the world. But it may be a symptom of other problems. Many Linux gurus believe that is the time to get a new hard drive.

If you're still not sure, the *badblocks* command can help you determine if your hard drive is in trouble. For example, the following command writes the ID number associated with each bad block to the *blockbad* file:

```
# badblocks -v /dev/hda7 -o blockbad
Checking for bad blocks (read-only test):   697008/   1050241
```

 Make sure the target partition is unmounted before running the *badblocks* command.

The previous *fsck* command probably fixed any errors on that filesystem, and you can continue using Linux normally. The following output is evidence that the repair was completely successful:

```
0 bad blocks
```

When bad blocks remain, you should rerun *fsck* with more severe options, described in the next section.

If you need to keep the hard drive working until a new one arrives, back it up as soon as possible. We show you how to do this with a partially corrupt partition in the next annoyance. But until that new hard drive arrives, there are things you can do to keep your current hard drive going.

Fixing Bad Blocks

The *fsck* command can help you check, mark, and fix bad blocks, and can help preserve the health of your filesystems. For that reason, current distributions force a periodic *fsck* on each filesystem formatted in the popular *ext2* and *ext3* formats. You can do your own *fsck* maintenance with the switches shown in Table 8-1; some of these switches are not documented on the *fsck* manpage.

Table 8-1. fsck command switches

Switch	Description
-b	Specifies a different superblock, which you can find on ext2/ext3 systems with the *dumpe2fs* command
-c	Calls the *badblocks* command with the existing superblock size
-f	Salvages unused chains to files
-v	Sets verbose mode
-y	Specifies a default answer of "yes"; otherwise, *fsck* interactively asks if you want to mark bad blocks

 SUSE formats its partitions by default as ReiserFS filesystems. This filesystem is considered so reliable that SUSE doesn't force a periodic *fsck* on such partitions.

For example, the following command marks the bad blocks on your system. If you're fortunate, each *fsck* "pass" of your partition proceeds without incident. The following is sample output from a run on a good partition.

```
# fsck -cyfv /dev/hda5
fsck 1.35 (28-Feb-2004)
e2fsck 1.35 (28-Feb-2004)
Checking for bad blocks (read-only test): done
Pass 1: Checking inodes, blocks and sizes
Pass 2: Checking directory structure
Pass 3: Checking directory connectivity
Pass 4: Checking reference counts
Pass 5: Checking group summary information
 . . .
```

However, I had problems with a different partition. In the middle of this process, the test seemed to stop. I was tempted to interrupt the command by pressing Ctrl-C, but progress continued after a few minutes. As you can see here, the test turned up problems:

```
Duplicate blocks found.... invoking duplicate block passes
Pass 1B: Rescan for duplicate/bad blocks
Duplicate/bad block(s) in inode 1448: 13568
Pass 1C Scan directories for inodes with dup blocks.
Error reading block 697043 (Attempt to read block from filesystem resulted
in a short read). Ignore error? yes
Force rewrite? yes
....
Pass 1D: Reconciling duplicate blocks
```

```
(There are 4 inodes containing duplicate/bad blocks)

File <The journal inode> (inode #8, mod time Fri Nov 12 08:43:05 2005)
  has 10 duplicate block(s), shared with 1 file(s):
        <The bad blocks inode> (inode #1, mod time Fri Jan 7 12:11:24 2006)
Clone duplicate/bad blocks? yes

Error reading block 4049 (Attempt to read block from filesystem resulted
in short read). Ignore error? yes

Force rewrite? yes
```

The check continued, revealing hundreds of errors. But the most important
error is near the beginning of the file. As you can see, there is corruption
even in the journal. Any pointers from the journal to other files are thus
suspect.

After your bad blocks are marked, Linux knows to avoid reading data from
those locations. The time is right for a backup. If standard techniques
described in Chapter 2 don't work, see the next annoyance.

My Hard Drive Is Failing and I Need a Backup—Fast

It's best to configure a regular backup of your entire system. But hard drives
are large. Gigabytes of data take time to copy. So you can't be blamed for
avoiding backups as long as possible. (That is, until there is a hard drive failure.) While you might have configured backups for those workstations that
you administer, other people might not have been so farsighted and may
look to you as a Linux geek when they hit the inevitable disk problem. Thus,
you may be asked to recover the data of a less experienced Linux user who
forgot to back up his hard drive.

 The techniques listed in this annoyance may or may not
work for you, depending on the level of damage to your hard
drive. I can testify, though, that without these techniques, I
would have spent several days reloading programs onto my
laptop computer.

Symptoms

One symptom of an imminent hard drive failure is the following message,
which you might see during the Power On Self Test (POST) process:

```
1720 - S.M.A.R.T Hard Drive detects imminent failure(Failing Attr:05h)
Please back up the contents of the hard drive and run
HDD self test in F2 setup
```

While you could run the HDD self-test, chances are good that if you see this message, your hard drive is about to fail. So you should take steps right away to recover what you can.

The first thing you should do is mark the bad blocks; we've described this process in the previous annoyance.

At this point, you've applied the *fsck* command to your system. You've tried the regular backup techniques described in Chapter 2. You've marked the bad blocks with the techniques described in the previous annoyance. Commands such as *dd* or *tar* fail because they find errors when they hit bad blocks.

First and foremost, save the files that you can't live without. Next, proceed with an emergency backup of the entire hard drive, described in the next section.

Configuring an Emergency Backup

To explain what you should do to back up a failing drive in terms as concrete and easy to follow as possible, I'll revisit a recent frightening day when my laptop hard drive failed, and describe the steps I took. It should not be hard for you to apply the lesson to another disk failure. I start with a narrative, followed by a step-by-step description of what I did to recover and transfer my data to a new hard drive. While this may be repetitive, if your hard drive is failing, it's important to get these steps right the first time.

When the symptoms described in earlier sections showed me that my laptop hard drive was failing, my first step was to save the critical files that I absolutely needed. But that was not enough. I had spent several hours configuring Debian on this laptop computer and would have been really annoyed if I had to start over. I needed an emergency backup.

Fortunately, I had a large external IEEE 1394 (FireWire) hard drive, which had plenty of space for my Debian partitions. Generally, most distributions with Linux kernel 2.6 have no problems with IEEE 1394 hard drives.

I bought another hard drive to replace the one currently on my laptop. It turned out that I could get a significantly larger drive for just a little more money. This made things easier because I could specify slightly larger partitions than I had on my old disk, rather than spend a lot of effort trying to re-create each partition at exactly the same size. Once you realize that you need a new hard drive, you may want to order it as soon as possible, as shipping can take time.

Because my hard drive seemed ready to fail, I needed to minimize the stress on that drive. I also needed a magic tool that could ignore the errors associated with the bad blocks on my drive while copying the partitions or all the files within them.

What I needed was a Linux distribution that recognized my IEEE 1394 hard drive, included a magic backup tool, and could be loaded directly from a CD. From previous experience, I knew that when I boot Knoppix with kernel 2.6, it recognizes and allows me to partition, format, and mount my IEEE 1394 hard drive. If that didn't work, I knew Knoppix recognized my network card; I could have backed up my partitions over my network.

As for the magic tool, current versions of Knoppix include the *dd_rescue* command. As it's designed to ignore errors such as bad blocks on a partition, it was what I needed at that moment. For more information on *dd_rescue*, see *http://www.garloff.de/kurt/linux/ddrescue/*.

I booted my system with a Knoppix CD. Because it loaded Linux and the associated utilities onto a RAM disk, it minimized the stress on my hard drive. If you have a different magic tool, you may be able to use another CD-based distribution such as Ubuntu or SUSE Live CD.

Next, I loaded and mounted my backup media. I formatted my external hard drive to the *ext3* filesystem. Knoppix recognizes standard external drives and network connections, generally with little difficulty.

 As of this writing, the current version of Knoppix is 4.0, which supports booting with the Linux 2.6 kernel. If you're using modern backup devices such as external IEEE 1394 or USB 2.0 drives, use kernel version 2.6. It provides better support. If you're using an older Knoppix CD, the default may be associated with Linux kernel 2.4; you may be able to start with Linux kernel 2.6 by entering *knoppix26* at the boot: prompt.

After formatting partitions on my IEEE 1394 drive, I rebooted into Knoppix to make sure the new partitions were properly written. Most of these commands require superuser mode, but when you boot Knoppix from a CD, no *root* password is required. Finally, I could use *dd_rescue* to save the data I could, and then write that data to the new laptop hard drive.

Before you start, make sure you have the following available:

- Space on another hard drive to save your data. A remote or portable hard drive can work for this purpose.
- A reliable connection to the hard drive you're using for backup. Network and even IEEE1394 cables can come loose.

- A replacement hard drive, suitable for your system.
- A Linux installation that you can boot directly from a CD, such as Knoppix. Make sure it has tools such as *dd_rescue*.
- Appropriate tools to replace the physical hard drive.

Now that I had the basic story and the tools I needed, I took the following steps to rescue my laptop hard drive:

1. I saved the files that I absolutely needed to a different computer. These included personal, data, and perhaps configuration files. In case the backup didn't work, I would have preserved at least these files.

2. I used the tools described in the previous annoyance to mark bad blocks, including *badblocks* and *fsck*.

3. I booted my laptop with a Knoppix CD. Knoppix boots to a K desktop environment, with icons for the partitions on my laptop and IEEE1394 hard drives.

4. Based on the output from a *fdisk -l /dev/hda* command, I recorded the sizes of the partitions that I wanted to back up.

5. I used QTParted (*http://qtparted.sourceforge.net*) on Knoppix to make room on my IEEE1394 hard drive.

6. I ran the *fdisk* utility to create a partition (*/dev/sda1*) large enough for my failing laptop hard drive partitions. I then formatted this partition to the *ext3* filesystem:

   ```
   mkfs -t ext3 /dev/sda1
   ```

7. After rebooting to make sure the partition table reflected the new configuration, I mounted the new *ext3* partition on my IEEE1394 hard drive. Knoppix makes appropriate mount points available; the following command uses the Knoppix default for the noted partition:

   ```
   mount /dev/sda1 /mnt/sda1
   ```

8. I used the *dd_rescue* command to back up each partition on my hard drive. Most of the commands took less than an hour to copy each partition image to the specified image file (*.img*). As you might guess from the filenames I chose, my laptop had a dual boot of Windows XP and Debian Linux:

   ```
   dd_rescue /dev/hda1 /mnt/sda1/xppro.img
   dd_rescue /dev/hda5 /mnt/sda1/debboot.img
   dd_rescue /dev/hda6 /mnt/sda1/debhome.img
   ```

9. However, the initial results were less than perfect. The *dd_rescue* command got stuck when I tried to back up the partition with my top-level root (*/*) directory. Fortunately, *dd_rescue -r* was able to read my partition

backward, skipping over the errors on that drive. While it took hours, I was pleased to see that it saved all of my data:

```
dd_rescue -r /dev/hda7 /mnt/sda1/debroot.img
```

 If you aren't able to save all of your partitions with the *dd_rescue* command, there's one more option. The *dd_rhelp* project, based at *http://www.kalysto.org/utilities/dd_rhelp*, uses other techniques to move past bad sectors more quickly.

10. I then exited from Knoppix. Standard commands such as *poweroff* can be used because the Knoppix Live CD/DVD provides password-free access to superuser mode.

11. I disconnected power to my laptop computer.

12. Next, I installed the new hard drive. Be careful. If your computer is still under warranty, take care to follow your manufacturer instructions. In any case, take care to avoid static in handling any computer parts.

13. I navigated to my laptop's BIOS menu to make sure it correctly detected the new hard drive.

14. I restarted Knoppix once again.

15. I partitioned and formatted my new hard drive. Because it was larger, it was easy for me to make sure that each partition that I created was equal to or larger than the one on my previous hard drive. I partitioned the disk with the *fdisk* command and formatted with the *mkfs.ext3* command.

16. I was finally able to restore data from the disk images that I created. As no special handing was required, I was able to use the *dd* command:

```
dd if=/mnt/sda1/xppro.img of=/dev/hda1
dd if=/mnt/sda1/debboot.img of=/dev/hda5
dd if=/mnt/sda1/debhome.img of=/dev/hda6
dd if=/mnt/sda1/debroot.img of=/dev/hda7
```

Alternatively, I could have mounted these images and saved the individual files. This would take full advantage of any additional space I could spare on the new hard drive. For example, I could have used the following commands to restore the files from the *debboot.img* file (assuming */mnt/back* existed):

```
mount -o loop /mnt/sda1/debboot.img /mnt/back/
mount /dev/hda5 /mnt/hda5
cp -ar /mnt/back/* /mnt/hda5/
```

17. Before rebooting, I wrote my bootloader to the MBR. I'll show you how to do so in the next annoyance.

A Windows User Reinstalled Windows on a Dual-Boot System

Microsoft Windows power users may reinstall that operating system periodically. Reinstallation can provide fresh, unfragmented copies of key utilities, driver libraries, and more. Furthermore, Microsoft Windows power users work hard to deal with the fragmentation associated with Microsoft filesystems. While Microsoft provides defragmentation utilities, they are not completely reliable, in my opinion. Reinstallation is often the easiest solution. Unfortunately, if a user reinstalls Windows on a dual-boot computer, it overwrites any existing Linux bootloader such as GRUB or LILO, and possibly the Linux portion of the dual boot.

This annoyance assumes you know the basics of configuring and formatting hard drives and associated partitions with the *fdisk* utility. More information is available on any standard Linux book, including *Running Linux* by Matthias Kalle Dalheimer and Matt Welsh (O'Reilly).

Restoring the Bootloader

The first thing to check in this situation is whether Linux is still there. You won't be able to boot Linux from a Microsoft Windows bootloader, at least just after Windows is reinstalled. So you'll need a rescue disk of some sort to boot into Linux. There are three basic scenarios:

- You have a rescue disk customized for your configuration. In this case, it should include a bootloader, and you should be able to boot Linux and proceed directly to step 7 in the following list.

- You have the first installation CD associated with Red Hat/Fedora. If you boot from the CD, and type *linux rescue* at the *boot:* prompt, it searches through the existing partitions for your Linux installation. Once you reach the Rescue screen, click Continue. If it finds an existing system, you'll be taken to a prompt. At that point, the following command puts the system in a state where it treats the old Linux partition as the root of the filesystem, after which you can restore your bootloader. (If you need more information on this process, see the "My Server Is So Secure I Can't Log In as Root" annoyance in Chapter 6.)

      chroot /mnt/sysimage

  Afterward, you can proceed to step 7 in the following list.

- You need to boot from a different rescue CD, such as the Debian from Scratch CD, the first SUSE installation CD, or the Knoppix CD. I'll detail the procedure here, based on the Knoppix CD. The procedure with the other CDs is similar.

The steps for recovering Linux are as follows:

1. Set your system to boot from the CD/DVD drive, and start your computer.

2. If you're using a Knoppix CD, it should normally boot directly into the Knoppix KDE desktop environment, where you can start a command-line console.

3. At the command line, use the *su* command to log in as the *root* user. The rescue CDs do not require a password for *root* access.

4. Take stock and find the partitions on your hard drive with the *fdisk -l* command. If you use more than one partition for your Linux system, some trial and error may be required. Sometimes you can make intelligent guesses based on the output. For example, I can surmise from the system, the devices, and the sizes of the partitions that my */boot* directory is associated with partition */dev/hda6* and my top-level root (/) directory with */dev/hda7*:

```
   Device Boot      Start        End      Blocks   Id  System
/dev/hda1    *          1       2676    21494938+   7  HPFS/NTFS
/dev/hda2            2677       4136    11727450    c  W95 FAT32 (LBA)
/dev/hda3            4137       7296    25382700    5  Extended
/dev/hda5            4137       4259      987966   82  Linux swap
/dev/hda6            4260       4273      112423+  83  Linux
/dev/hda7            4274       5247     7823623+  83  Linux
```

5. Mount the partitions associated with the top-level root (/) directory. At this point, if you're uncertain about other partitions, you'll be able to find them in your normal *fstab* configuration file. If you mount your root (/) directory on */mnt/hda7*, for instance, you'll find that file in */mnt/hda7/etc/fstab*:

```
mount /dev/hda7 /mnt/hda7
```

If you can't find your *fstab*, you've probably mounted the wrong partition as the root (/) directory and need to try again.

6. Set up your filesystems. The following commands are based on the output from step 4, and assume that the contents of your */boot* directory are actually located on */dev/hda6*:

```
mount /dev/hda6 /mnt/hda7/boot
chroot /mnt/hda7
```

7. Now restore your original bootloader to the MBR with one of the following two commands; the command that you use depends on whether you use GRUB or LILO:

```
grub-install /dev/hda
lilo
```

8. Finally, reboot the computer. If the bootloader pointer is now on the MBR, you'll be able to boot into either operating system.

Recovering from Backup

If the steps in the previous section failed because you couldn't find your Linux partitions, it means the Windows installation might have wiped out the partitions in addition to the bootloader. In any case, at this point you need to restore Linux from a backup. What you need to do depends on the backup and the status of the partitions. Because Linux isn't available on the local computer, you'll need to boot with a CD-based distribution. We'll use a Knoppix CD for this purpose:

1. Set your system to boot from the CD/DVD drive, and start your computer. If you're restoring from an external drive connected via IEEE1394 or USB2, and are using an older Knoppix CD/DVD, use the *knoppix26* command at the boot: prompt.

2. If you're using a Knoppix CD, it should normally boot directly into the Knoppix KDE desktop environment, where you can start a command-line console.

3. At the command line, use the *su* command to log in as the *root* user. No password is required.

4. Check the current state of your partitions with the *fdisk -l* command. If you see partitions still configured for Linux, as shown in the previous section, skip to step 7.

5. If you no longer have Linux partitions, you'll need to back up the current Microsoft Windows operating system. Use the techniques described in "I'm Afraid of Losing Data" in Chapter 2.

If you have a single partition with Microsoft Windows, you may be able to save it using the *parted* utility without restoring it from backup. *parted* can even resize NTFS partitions. For more information, see *http://www.gnu.org/software/parted/parted.html*. Alternatively, Knoppix includes the *QTParted* utility, which is a GUI frontend to *parted*.

6. Now re-create the partitions that you need. For example, if the drive is */dev/hda*, use the *fdisk /dev/hda* command. Make sure that the partition types correspond to the required filesystems, such as Linux, W95 FAT32 (LBA), or HPFS/NTFS. The size depends on the amount of data in your backup.

7. Format each partition in the desired filesystem format. For example, if you're formatting partition */dev/hda7* for the ext3 filesystem, use the following command:

```
mkfs.ext3 /dev/hda7
```

8. Restore Linux from your backup. If possible, use the techniques described in Chapter 2. If you had to use the *dd_rescue* command to create an image, you can restore your system with the *dd* command, as described in the previous annoyance.

9. Don't forget to restore your bootloader; we described one technique for that in the previous section.

My /home Directory Is Too Small

As the data you store on computers grows—and as the number of users grows on your server—you'll eventually need more space for your */home* directory partition.

Before logical volumes were available for Linux, finding space was rather annoying. It meant that you would back up the */home* partition. Then you'd create a new partition, probably on one or more new physical drives. Finally, you'd restore the */home* partition. Then the number of users would grow again, and you'd have to repeat the process.

With logical volumes, you can "grow" your */home* partition fairly easily. Just add a few logical extents, and you have a partition as large as you need. The process is known as Logical Volume Management (LVM). Several Linux distributions, including Red Hat/Fedora, are starting to use LVM in their default installations.

To make sense of the instructions that follow, you need to understand some fundamental LVM concepts:

Physical volume (PV)
> A PV is created from a primary or logical volume on a hard drive.

Physical extent (PE)
> A PE is a chunk of disk space created out of one or more PVs. Normally, all your PEs have the same size.

Logical extent (LE)
> An LE is a chunk of disk space. Every LE has a corresponding PE. LEs are the building blocks of a logical volume.

Logical volume (LV)
> An LV is a designated collection of LEs. Once created, you can mount directories such as */home* on an LV.

Volume group (VG)
> The LVs on your system, taken together, are organized in a VG. LVM commands are usually applied to a VG, thereby affecting every LVM partition on your system.

In this annoyance, we'll use just a few of the commands associated with LVM. For more information, see the LVM HOWTO at *http://www.tldp.org/HOWTO/LVM-HOWTO/*. The latest version of LVM available as of this writing is the *lvm2* package, which overcomes the original 1 TB limit for mounted volumes. The package name is the same for Debian, Red Hat/Fedora, and SUSE.

Backing Up /home

Creating a backup is a straightforward process, which we described in more detail in Chapter 2. To summarize, there are a number of ways to back up a specific directory such as */home*.

The most straightforward backup is a copy of all files and directories to another partition. The standard backup process involves collecting all files and subdirectories from a high-level directory such as */home* to a single archive file, which is then saved to media such as a network drive, CD/DVD, or tape drive.

If you've already configured */home* on a separate partition, you can also use the *dd_rescue* tool described in "My Hard Drive Is Failing and I Need a Backup—Fast," earlier in this chapter.

If your current */home* directory is already mounted on an LV, you can skip to the end of this annoyance, where you'll add more LEs to your current LV.

Configuring a Logical Volume

Configuring an LV from existing hard drives is a detailed process. It starts with appropriately configured hard drives or partitions and ends with mounting the LV on an appropriate directory such as */home*. I suggest the following steps.

Preparing a partition

First, you need to decide if you want to allocate all or part of a hard drive. If you're allocating a partition as an LV, you'll need to assign the appropriate type using *fdisk* or *parted*. For example, if you're allocating the second partition on the second SCSI drive as an LV, you need to run the following commands on *fdisk*:

```
# fdisk /dev/sdb
Command (m for help): t
Partition number (1-15): 2
Hex code (type L to list codes): 8e
```

The *t* command allows you to modify the partition type—in this case, the second partition on this hard drive. If you've checked the Hex codes, you'll know that *8e* is associated with the Linux LVM partition type. Once you've written this configuration to the hard drive, you can proceed to the next section.

Creating a physical volume

You can create a PV from a properly prepared partition with the *pvcreate* command:

```
pvcreate /dev/sdb2
```

Alternatively, if you're allocating a complete hard drive as a PV, you don't need to create separate partitions. For example, if your second SCSI drive is new, you can create a PV from it as follows:

```
pvcreate /dev/sdb
```

If you have a older hard drive with data that you now want to dedicate as a PV, you'll first need to erase the partition table. This command destroys all data on that hard drive:

```
dd if=/dev/zero of=/dev/sdb bs=512 count=1
```

You can then proceed with the *pvcreate /dev/sdb* command.

Once you've configured two or more PVs, proceed to the next section.

Creating a volume group

It takes two or more PVs to create a VG. If you need more space for your LV partitions, you can add more PVs at a later date. The command is straightforward. For example, if you want to create a VG named *homevg* from */dev/sdb* and */dev/sdc1*, run the following command:

```
vgcreate homevg /dev/sdb /dev/sdc1
```

The default VG includes PEs in 4 MB chunks. As there is a current maximum of 64,000 PEs per LV, that limits the size of an LV to 256 GB. If that's not large enough, you can change the size of a PE with the *-s* option. For example, the following command configures 16 MB PE chunks:

```
vgcreate -s 16M homevg /dev/sdb /dev/sdc1
```

This supports a theoretical maximum LV size of 1,024 GB. You can review the defaults associated with the homevg VG with the following command:

```
vgdisplay homevg
```

Growing a VG

If you choose to dedicate an additional PV named */dev/sdd* to the VG, you can extend homevg with the following command:

```
vgextend homevg /dev/sdd
```

Creating a LV

Now you can create the LVs that you need, in units of PEs. For example, if you've accepted the default PE size of 4 MB and want an LV of 4 GB, you can create an LV named homevol with the following command:

```
lvcreate -l 1000 homevg -n homevol
```

This configures an LV that you can use as a partition. In this case, the LV is associated with the following device file:

```
/dev/homevg/homevol
```

Configuring an LV as a partition

Finally! Now you can work with the LV as if it were a partition on another hard drive. As with other partitions, you need to format it as the filesystem of your choice:

```
mkfs.reiserfs /dev/homevg/homevol
```

Once formatted, you can mount the partition:

```
mount -t reiserfs /dev/homevg/homevol /home
```

Test the result. Restore your backup of the */home* directory. If it works, you can document it in */etc/fstab*, so your system mounts it on the LV the next time you boot Linux. One possible line in */etc/fstab* might be:

```
/dev/homevg/homevol   /home    reiserfs  acl,user_xattr   1 1
```

Expanding a LV

Now if your users need more space than exists in your current */home* partition, you can expand it. Just extend the LV. Assuming you have the PEs available, the following command increases the size of */dev/homevg/homevol* to 1,000 MB:

```
lvextend -L1000M /dev/homevg/homevol
```

My Hard Drive Is Too Slow

The defaults associated with the latest Linux distributions do not take full advantage of the latest improvements in IDE/ATA (Integrated Drive

Electronics/Advanced Technology Attachment) hard drives. For example, Linux is normally set to communicate with IDE/ATA hard drives in 16-bit mode. While this may seem irrational in current 32- and 64-bit environments, it helps Linux retain its reputation for extending the life of older hardware. If you don't have an older hard drive, you can modify the Linux defaults to take full advantage of its data-transfer capabilities.

Before running any of the commands in this annoyance, I strongly suggest that you back up the data on your hard drive. The commands described in this annoyance may stress your hard drive beyond its capabilities. For best results during the backup, set your computer to single-user mode (*init 1*), which reduces the load from most services and network connections.

In this annoyance, we focus on the *hdparm* command, based on a Freshmeat project of the same name (*http://freshmeat.net/projects/hdparm*). If you can't find this command, install an *hdparm* package native to your distribution; it's available for at least Red Hat/Fedora, SUSE, and Debian.

> For SCSI hard drives, there is no command to adjust hard drive parameters the way *hdparm* does for IDE hard drives. But given the way SCSI hard drives communicate with controllers, it is less important for these drives.

Hard Drive Defaults

Before adjusting any device, you should establish a baseline by figuring out the default settings and checking its performance. To that end, the following command tests the speed at which Linux can read data from your hard drive, directly (*-t*) and through a buffer (*-T*):

```
# hdparm -Tt /dev/hda
/dev/hda:
 Timing buffer-cache reads:   384 MB in  2.01 seconds = 191.04 MB/sec
 Timing buffered disk reads:   66 MB in  3.06 seconds =  21.57 MB/sec
```

You may want to run this command more than once, to make sure that you have consistent baseline readings. I find small variations, under 20 percent, to be fairly common.

Next, find the baseline settings for communication between Linux and your hard drive:

```
# hdparm /dev/hda
/dev/hda:
 multicount   = 16 (on)
 IO_support   = 0 (default 16-bit)
 unmaskirq    = 0 (off)
 using_dma    = 1 (on)
```

```
keepsettings = 0 (off)
readonly     = 0 (off)
readahead    = 8 (on)
geometry     = 1940/240/63, sectors = 29336832, start = 0
```

Make a record of your *hdparm* parameters. If after making changes, you encounter problems, you can then return to your original parameters. Here is a description of the parameters:

multicount

Every time a process or program looks for data, it sends an I/O interrupt request. The multicount option is associated with IDE Block Mode, where several disk sectors are transferred per interrupt. Modern Linux distributions are generally set to a multicount of 16 or higher. While your system may be able to handle higher multicount settings, do so at your own risk. Failures can corrupt your filesystem and cause the loss of all data on that hard drive. Some Western Digital hard drives can only handle smaller multicount values (4 or 8), due to small (32KB) buffers. This parameter can be controlled by the *hdparm -m* command.

IO_support

This option determines how data is transferred between the PCI bus and the hard drive interface card. There are three possible values: 0 disables 32-bit transfers; 1 enables 32-bit data transfers; and 3 supports 32-bit synchronous data transfers. (There is no value 2.) An IO_support of 3 is supported by most hard drives. This parameter can be controlled by the *hdparm -c* command.

unmaskirq

If enabled, this allows other interrupts while data is read from a hard drive. This parameter can be controlled by the *hdparm -u* command.

using_dma

Modern hard drives almost always use a Direct Memory Access (DMA) channel to bypass the CPU. The ability to perform DMA is often detected and set on the latest versions of SUSE, Red Hat/Fedora, and Debian. However, this is not supported by all hard drives. This parameter can be controlled by the *hdparm -d* command.

keepsettings

Activate only if you want to retain drive settings after soft resets associated with errors. I don't recommend that you use this option except possibly when you're trying to diagnose a hard drive hardware problem. Otherwise, you could lose data.

readonly

Set for a read-only drive, such as a CD/DVD drive. This parameter can be controlled by the *hdparm -r* command.

readahead

> The number of sectors that are read when Linux accesses a hard drive. Most Linux distributions generally set a *readahead* of 8 sectors. This parameter can be controlled by the *hdparm -a* command.

geometry

> Documents what Linux sees about your hard drive. It should match your hard drive documentation, as well as what you see in your BIOS menu. If it does not match, *do not* use the *hdparm* command to alter any geometry settings, because it would cause Linux to misinterpret the drive and its use could cause you to lose all of the data on that drive.

There are a substantial number of additional *hdparm* options, listed on the associated manpage.

Adjusting Hard Drive Parameters

With the right *hdparm* command, you may be able to increase the effective speed of your hard drive. Given the number of settings, some trial and error is required. In other words, test the throughput of each change with the *hdparm -Tt* command.

I'll now detail some of the more common changes that you can make to IDE/ATA hard drive parameters. See the associated manpage for details.

Sometimes, *hdparm* will tell you if your hardware or distribution can't handle a setting associated with faster data transfer. For example, when I try to configure a multicount of 32 on three of my systems, I get the following result:

```
# hdparm -m32 /dev/hda

/dev/hda:
 setting multicount to 32
 HDIO_SET_MULTICOUNT: Invalid argument
 multicount    = 16 (on)
```

No problem, time to try something else. When I try to configure 32-bit I/O support on my computers, I see the following:

```
# hdparm -c3 /dev/hda

/dev/hda:
 setting 32-bit IO_support flag to 3
 IO_support   = 3 (32-bit w/sync)
```

Now that you've changed the setting, it's time to test the result. Run the *hdparm -Tt* command again. It's OK to run this command more than once, to see if the change is significant. If so, make a note of the change. You'll want to make sure Linux implements this change the next time you boot that computer.

You can set up commands such as *hdparm -c3* in the appropriate configuration file, which varies by distribution: Debian uses */etc/hdparm.conf*; SUSE uses settings in */etc/sysconfig/ide* based on variables in */etc/init.d/boot.idedma*; Red Hat Enterprise Linux uses */etc/sysconfig/harddisks*. Starting with Fedora Core 5, Red Hat has deprecated the use of such configuration files; these settings can be added to */etc/rc.local*.

Find the Right Update Repository

Default configurations can be annoying when you're trying to keep your system up-to-date. If you're located outside the U.S., default update repositories for U.S.-based distributions can doom you to long wait times, and sometimes even failures, when you try to update your systems to the latest features and security updates.

Some distributions such as Debian suggest that it is inappropriate to connect directly to Debian servers for all but security updates. It increases the costs for this distribution of volunteers and makes access more difficult for those who mirror the Debian repositories.

In general, repositories are organized into separate installation and update repositories. The installation repository includes all packages associated with the original release of a distribution; for example, the installation repositories for Fedora Linux include the packages that you would find on the Fedora Linux CDs. The corresponding update repository includes any packages built after the initial distribution release. One exception is Red Hat Enterprise Linux (RHEL), where update packages are incorporated into the main repository (which is known as a *channel* on the Red Hat Network).

In this annoyance, we'll examine default update servers, and how you can reconfigure your systems to point to mirrors more well suited to your system. As this book is limited to Red Hat/Fedora, SUSE, and Debian, I do not address mirrors available for other distributions. However, the techniques are similar.

In some cases, the best update channel is one that you configure yourself. In "Too Many Computers to Update over the Internet" in Chapter 11, I'll show you how to configure a mirror of your preferred update server. A local mirror can minimize update-related traffic on your Internet connection and often speeds updates if you have more than a few Linux computers on your network.

Be careful about repositories from different sources. For example, if you configure repositories from Fedora and from third parties on the same system, you may end up with incompatible packages and unresolvable dependencies.

Debian

Debian Linux uses the *apt* commands to keep its systems up-to-date. The *apt* commands rely on sources configured in the */etc/apt/sources.list* configuration file. Before you modify this file, you need to know how the directives that you can add to this file work. I've summarized some of the more important directives in Table 8-2. As you can install the *apt* commands on many RPM-based systems, I've included some directives you might see on RPM-based distributions.

Table 8-2. /etc/apt/sources.list directives

Directive	Description
deb	Uses the *deb* command to install packages
rpm	Uses the *rpm* command to install packages; assumes that *apt* packages are installed on an *rpm*-based system
deb-src	Applies to Debian-style source packages
rpm-src	Applies to RPM-style source packages
file:///	Connects to locally mounted directories
oldstable	Specifies the former stable distribution, which is Debian Woody as of this writing
stable	Specifies the current stable distribution, which is Debian Sarge as of this writing
testing	Specifies the current beta distribution, which is Debian Etch as of this writing
unstable	Specifies the current developmental distribution, which is Debian Sid as of this writing
main	Notes the primary Debian repository, which includes most freely licensed packages
contrib	Notes the Debian repository of free packages on which non-free packages depend
non-free	Notes the Debian repository with non–open source licenses

Now you'll want to configure your */etc/apt/sources.list* file to point to repositories closer to your network. Unless the mirror is slow, pick the mirror physically closest to you. The official list of Debian mirrors is available from *http://www.debian.org/mirror/list*.

For example, if I were closest to Berkeley, CA, I'd connect to the mirror at the University of California at Berkeley. As you can see, FTP and HTTP mirrors are available. If you have a special architecture, make sure it's listed in the righthand column. I prefer FTP servers for my system; I can link to the noted server at *ftp://linux.csua.berkeley.edu/debian/*.

In my *letc/apt/sources.list* file, I start with the deb directive, proceed with the URL of the repository, and add the label for the distribution, as well as the repositories to which I want access. As I use Debian Sarge, that is the stable distribution. As I want access to all three repositories, I end up with the following line in my configuration file:

```
deb ftp://linux.csua.berkeley.edu/debian/ stable main contrib non-free
```

If I want access to the source code for each of these repositories, I can add the following line:

```
deb-src ftp://linux.csua.berkeley.edu/debian/ testing main contrib non-free
```

Unfortunately, Debian does not support mirrors of its security updates; you'll need to keep the following entry in your *letc/apt/sources.list* file:

```
deb http://security.debian.org/ testing/updates main contrib non-free
```

 Courtesy of the developers behind Conectiva Linux (now a part of Mandriva), you can install and use the *apt* commands on a number of RPM-based distributions. In fact, there are *apt*-based repositories available for Fedora Core and SUSE Linux.

SUSE

While some have created *apt* repositories for SUSE Linux, the company encourages the use of official repositories and mirrors through YaST Online Update (YOU). While SUSE encourages the use of its GUI interface, you can also configure YaST updates from the command line. As the *root* user, run the *yast online_update* command to open the update menu shown in Figure 8-1.

Naturally, you'll want to configure updates from the mirror closest to you. The Installation Source drop-down text box includes several preconfigured locations. It also allows you to select a User-Defined Location, which you can select from one of the SUSE mirrors.

If you're running SUSE Linux Professional, you can select your mirror from the official list at *http://www.novell.com/products/suselinux/downloads/ftp/int_mirrors.html*. To configure your own location, take the following steps:

1. Select the mirror you prefer from the list described above. Make a note of the URL.

2. Press Alt-I, and select User-Defined Location.

3. Tab to and select New Server. When this opens the "Select Type of URL" window, select the type of server. If it's remote, it's an FTP or HTTP server. Make the selection and click OK.

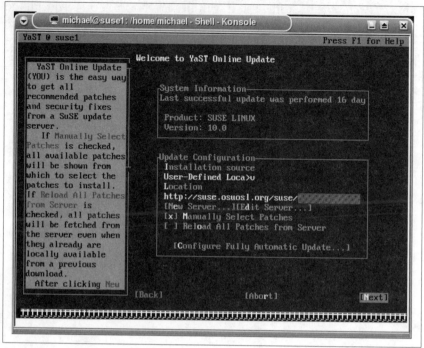

Figure 8-1. YaST Online Update

4. When the "Server and Directory" window opens, make sure the right protocol (FTP or HTTP) is marked, and then enter the URL for the server in the Server Name text box.

5. Enter the directory with the SUSE repository in the "Directory on Server" text box.

6. For most SUSE Linux Professional mirrors, the default anonymous authentication is sufficient. If you're configuring an update for SUSE Linux Enterprise Server, you'll need your Novell account information. Select OK.

7. Now you should be ready for your update.

While the list of official mirrors seems limited, you may want to search further. I've found SUSE repositories on servers listed in the Fedora mirror list. For example, I've been able to configure updates from the servers at the University of Mississippi. The URL for its server is *ftp://mirror.phy.olemiss.edu*, and the associated "Directory on Server" is *suse/suse/*.

In "Too Many Computers to Update over the Internet" in Chapter 11, I show you how to configure a local mirror. Once you share that mirror on your network, you can reconfigure YaST Online Update to point to that share.

Fedora

For much of this book, Red Hat Enterprise Linux (RHEL) and Fedora are essentially the same distribution. Both distributions use the same basic Red Hat tools. However, unlike RHEL, Fedora updates are freely available. Fedora's default version of */etc/yum.conf* points to files in the */etc/yum.repos.d* directory for updates.

Older versions of Fedora did not include an */etc/yum.repos.d* directory; all repositories were listed in */etc/yum.conf*.

By default, Fedora Core includes six files in that directory, described in Table 8-3, which you can use to link to the repositories.

Table 8-3. Fedora repository files in /etc/yum.repos.d

File	Description
fedora.repo	Connects to the repository with the original installation packages
fedora-updates.repo	Links to the repository with update packages
fedora-updates-testing.repo	Connects to proposed updates; don't use unless you're willing to risk installing beta software
fedora-devel.repo	Connects to developmental packages, which may change daily; formerly known as Rawhide
fedora-extras.repo	Connects to the Extras repository with packages beyond the standard installation
fedora-extras-devel.repo	Connects to proposed updates to the Extras repository; don't use unless you're willing to risk installing beta software

By default, there are no active directives in the *devel* and *testing* files. Unless you're willing to take the risks associated with software that is not ready for production, you should not activate directives in those files. In fact, you can delete *fedora-updates-testing.repo, fedora-extras-devel.repo,* and *fedora-devel. repo* without problems—and probably should on systems for regular users.

However, you will want to change the defaults in the first two files. The default version of *fedora.repo* includes:

```
[base]
name=Fedora Core $releasever - $basearch - Base
#baseurl=http://download.fedora.redhat.com/pub/fedora/linux/core/
$releasever/$basearch/os/
mirrorlist=http://fedora.redhat.com/download/mirrors/fedora-core-$releasever
enabled=1
gpgcheck=1
```

By default, $releasever is the released version number as defined in */etc/ redhat-release* and $basearch comes from the *uname -i* command, which specifies the hardware platform. If you want to disable a repository, set enabled=0.

As you can see, the repository depends on the mirrorlist directive, which points to a URL with a list of specified repositories. For Fedora Core 4, the default mirrorlist file is *fedora-core-4*, which includes a list of mirrors on several different continents. When *yum* looks for an update repository, it takes a random URL from this file, which is less than ideal.

Therefore, you'll either want to specify a repository closer to you or at least revise the mirrorlist file to one that makes more sense. There is a directory of mirrorlist files available at *http://fedora.redhat.com/download/mirrors/* with lists for a number of different countries. I use the *fedora-core-3.us.west* file, which includes a number of mirrors suitable for me.

Alternatives for Updating Packages

If you prefer the Red Hat Update Agent, also known as *up2date*, on Fedora Linux, apply the settings described in this annoyance to the */etc/sysconfig/rhn/ sources* configuration file.

As of Fedora Core 5, the Update Agent is not part of the default Fedora installation (but is still available for Fedora Core, and remains the default for Red Hat Enterprise Linux). Future Fedora Core releases will use tools such as the Package Updater, also known as Pup. As it serves as a frontend to *yum*, see the next annoyance, "Avoid Dependency Hell with yum" for more information.

If you prefer *apt* for Fedora Core, there are *apt*-related packages you can install from a third-party repository such as *atrpms.net* (*apt* and *synaptic*). These packages are preconfigured to help you select an appropriate mirror; just run the *apt-get mirror-select* command.

Red Hat Enterprise Linux

Updates for Red Hat Enterprise Linux (RHEL) are supported through the Red Hat Network. They are organized differently from most other Linux distributions, in that there is no separate update repository. When an update is released, you can install it from the same channel as the main installation repository. (RHEL repositories are known as *channels*.)

Each system requires a subscription, which provides access to several update channels. As shown in Figure 8-2, I can assign a number of different channels to one of my systems that is subscribed to RHEL 4.

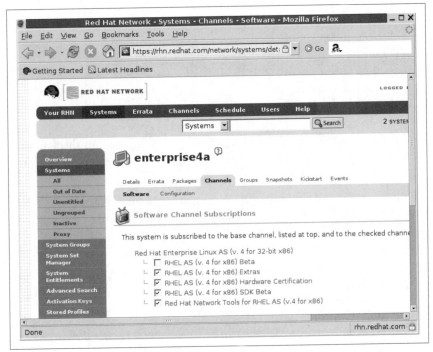

Figure 8-2. Red Hat Network channels

The channels shown in the figure are just those to which I subscribe. If you have a Red Hat Network subscription, you can click Channels on the top bar to review a full list of available channels. I describe some of the Red Hat Network channels in Table 8-4. For more information, navigate to *https://www.redhat.com/software/rhn/* or contact Red Hat sales at 866-273-3428.

Table 8-4. Red Hat Network channels

Channel	Description
Main	The channel associated with a distribution; includes the original binary packages
Beta	Packages planned for RHEL updates
Extras	Packages not available under open source licenses
Hardware certification	Packages to test hardware compatibility with RHEL
Software development kit	Red Hat's application build environment
Network tools	Network and kickstart configuration tools

If you want to verify the channels to which you've subscribed, run the following command:

```
# up2date --show-channel
rhel-i386-as-4
rhel-i386-as-4-extras
rhel-i386-as-4-hwcert
rhel-i386-as-4-sdk
rhn-tools-rhel-4-as-i386
```

As you can see from the output, this particular system is subscribed to five different channels, all of them based on RHEL 4. In order of display, they correspond to the following channels: main, extras, hardware certification, software development kit, and network tools.

If you want to cache content locally, you can set the Red Hat Update Agent to save downloaded RPMs in the */var/spool/up2date* directory. You can then use the *yum* tools described in the next annoyance to create headers from this repository. Downloaded RPMs are, by default, deleted after installation.

To make the Red Hat Update Agent save the RPMs after installation, take the following steps:

1. Run the *up2date-nox --config* command.
2. Select the number associated with the keepAfterInstall option (it varies).
3. When you're prompted for a New Value for keepAfterInstall, type Yes.
4. Press Return twice to save your new settings.

 You can also use the Red Hat GUI tool to configure updates. Start with the *up2date-config* command to open the Red Hat Network Configuration window. Under the Retrieval Installation tab, check the "After installation, keep binary packages on disk" option.

The Red Hat Network also offers specially configured Proxy and Satellite Servers, which can cache update content locally. For more information, read the associated manuals at *http://www.redhat.com/docs/manuals/RHNetwork/*.

Avoid Dependency Hell with yum

RPM packages include all the dependency information you need. Each RPM includes headers that list any other RPMs that are required to make it work. For example, when I tried to install the GNU C Compiler (*gcc*) on Fedora Core 3, I got the following message:

```
# rpm -i gcc-3.4.2-6.fc3.i386.rpm
error: Failed dependencies:
    glibc-devel >= 2.2.90-12 is needed by gcc-3.4.2-6.fc3.i386
```

Thanks to the information in the header of the *gcc* RPM package, I now know that I need a *glibc-devel* RPM of a certain version or greater. So I download the *glibc-devel* package from my favorite Fedora mirror, and try to install that:

```
# rpm -i glibc-devel-2.3.3-74.i386.rpm
error: Failed dependencies:
    glibc-headers is needed by glibc-devel-2.3.3-74.i386
    glibc-headers = 2.3.3 is needed by glibc-devel-2.3.3-74.i386
```

I'm a patient person, so I try again. I download the *glibc-headers* RPM and try installing that. I get the following result:

```
# rpm -i glibc-headers-2.3.3-74.i386.rpm
error: Failed dependencies:
    kernel-headers is needed by glibc-headers-2.3.3-74.i386
    kernel-headers >= 2.2.1 is needed by glibc-headers-2.3.3-74.i386
```

This process, which can go on for several levels, is also known as dependency hell.

With the *yum* command, you can take advantage of the headers to trace back through all dependencies automatically. Because *yum* repositories collect these headers in a database, you can install the GNU C Compiler and all dependent packages with the following command:

```
yum install gcc
```

This command searches through the repositories configured in your */etc/yum.repos.d* directory. As you can see from the following excerpt, the command searches through the headers for each dependency and lists the packages to be downloaded and installed with the GNU C Compiler:

```
--> Processing Conflict: glibc-common conflicts glibc > 2.3.3
--> Processing Dependency: kernel-headers >= 2.2.1 for package: glibc-headers
```

```
--> Processing Dependency Resolution with new changes.
--> Populating transaction set with selected packages. Please wait.
---> Package glibc-common.i386 0:2.3.5-0.fc3.1 set to be updated
---> Downloading header for glibc-kernheaders to pack into transaction set.
glibc-kernheaders-2.4-9.1 100% |===================| 71kB 00:00
---> Package glibc-kernheaders.i386 0:2.4-9.1.87 set to be updated
--> Running transaction check

Dependencies Resolved
Transaction Listing:
  Install: gcc.i386 0:3.4.3-22.fc3 - updates-released

Performing the following to resolve dependencies:
  Install: glibc-devel.i386 0:2.3.5-0.fc3.1 - updates-released
  Install: glibc-headers.i386 0:2.3.5-0.fc3.1 - updates-released
  Install: glibc-kernheaders.i386 0:2.4-9.1.87 - base
  Install: cpp.i386 0:3.4.3-22.fc3 - updates-released
  Install: glibc.i686 0:2.3.5-0.fc3.1 - updates-released
  Install: glibc-common.i386 0:2.3.5-0.fc3.1 - updates-released
  Install: libgcc.i386 0:3.4.3-22.fc3 - updates-released
Total download size: 28M
Is this ok [y/N]:
```

But to optimize how *yum* works on your system, you should customize the related configuration files, understand different *yum* subcommands, configure a nightly update, and create your own *yum* repository. To customize the related configuration files, read the previous annoyance.

The yum Subcommands

There are a substantial number of *yum* subcommands. Run the *yum* command by itself to see the variety of options available. I've illustrated my output in Fedora Core 5:

```
[michael@FedoraCore64 ~]$ yum
Loading "installonlyn" plugin
You need to give some command

usage: yum [options] < update | install | info | remove | list |
    clean | provides | search | check-update | groupinstall |
    groupupdate | grouplist | groupinfo | groupremove |
    makecache | localinstall | erase | upgrade | whatprovides |
    localupdate | resolvedep | shell | deplist >

options:
  -h, --help            show this help message and exit
  -t, --tolerant        be tolerant of errors
  -C                    run entirely from cache, don't update cache
  -c [config file]      config file location
  -R [minutes]          maximum command wait time
  -d [debug level]      debugging output level
```

```
    -e  [error level]     error output level
    -y                    answer yes for all questions
    --version             show Yum version and exit
    --installroot=[path]  set install root
    --enablerepo=[repo]   enable one or more repositories (wildcards allowed)
    --disablerepo=[repo]  disable one or more repositories (wildcards allowed)
    --exclude=[package]   exclude package(s) by name or glob
    --obsoletes           enable obsoletes processing during updates
    --noplugins           disable Yum plugins
[michael@FedoraCore64 ~]$
```

I'll explain some of the more important options here. For more information, see the *yum* HOWTO at *http://www.phy.duke.edu/~rgb/General/yum_HOWTO/*:

yum update

When run by itself, the *yum update* command checks all current packages against the listed repositories for later versions. If the packages are found (and you confirm you want installation), *yum* proceeds to upgrade them. If there is a new version of the kernel, this command proceeds to install the kernel. If you aren't ready to install a specific package, you can rerun the command with the *--exclude* option. For example, the following command excludes kernel-related packages from the update:

```
yum --exclude kernel* update
```

Alternatively, you could run the command with the package name of your choice. One common option is *yum update yum*, which ensures that you have the latest version of this utility before proceeding with updates. It may be best to first inspect all packages that can be updated with the *yum check-update* command.

yum install package

You can install one or more packages with this command. If the package is already installed, it is upgraded. You can use wildcards; for example, new versions of the X Server are often associated with several different packages, which you could install with the *yum install xorg** command.

yum info package

You can get more information about a package with this command. The output includes the version number and repository as specified in the appropriate */etc/yum.repos.d* directory.

yum remove packages

You can remove the packages you specify, along with dependencies, with this command.

yum list repository

You can list the packages available in the repositories of your choice with this command. If you do not specify a repository, this command lists all packages available from every repository configured in the */etc/yum.repos.d* directory.

yum clean sub-option

Repository data can become corrupt. If you're seeing unexpected errors from your *yum* commands, you may try refreshing downloaded repository data; it's similar to refreshing the cache on a browser. There are five sub-options:

packages

Cleans RPMs from the */var/cache/yum* subdirectory

headers

Cleans the downloaded header information related to each repository

cache

Cleans download information files with a *.pickle* extension that keeps *yum* start times to a minimum

metadata

Cleans the compressed XML files associated with some *yum* repositories

all

Cleans all of the preceding items

yum provides filename

If you're looking for the RPM that provides a specific file, this command can help. It's most useful when you don't already know the name of the RPM that you need.

yum search searchterm

If you're looking for a package associated with a specific topic, this command can help. For example, the *yum search madwifi* command can help you find all packages associated with the project of the same name.

yum check-update

This checks all repositories listed in */etc/yum.repos.d* for later versions of currently installed packages. If there are packages such as *kernel** or *firefox** that you're not ready to update, you can use the *--exclude packagename* switch the next time you run the *yum update* command.

There are several *yum* commands related to groups, which are listed in the *comps.xml* file in the */usr/share/comps/`uname -i`* directory. You can install or remove all of the mandatory and default packages in a group, along with dependencies. The details are beyond the scope of this annoyance.

Configuring a Nightly yum Update

The *yum* RPM includes its own cron job, which you can modify and activate to keep your system updated on a nightly basis. The job is located in the *yum.cron* file in the */etc/cron.daily* directory. As defined in */etc/crontab*, jobs in this directory are automatically run at 4:02 A.M. The default version of *yum.cron* includes some simple commands:

```
if [ -f /var/lock/subsys/yum ]; then
    /usr/bin/yum -R 120 -e 0 -d 0 -y update yum
    /usr/bin/yum -R 10 -e 0 -d 0 -y shell /etc/yum/yum-daily.yum
fi
```

In other words, as long as no other *yum* command is already running at the noted time, this job first checks for an update of the *yum* package within the preceding two hours (*-R 120*). The second command, within the first 10 minutes (*-R 10*), updates the repository, as directed in *yum-daily.yum*. It proceeds to show only critical errors (*-e 0*), disable debugging (*-d 0*), and answer all prompts (including those that download and install) with a yes (*-y*).

The default directives in */etc/yum/yum-daily.yum* (update, ts run, and exit) download all updates from your configured update repositories, use those updates to upgrade appropriate RPMs, and exit the *yum* shell.

If you want to exercise more control over certain updates, you may want to add an *--exclude* switch. For example, if you substitute the following for the first *yum* command, kernel-related packages are excluded from the update:

```
/usr/bin/yum -R 120 -e 0 -d 0 -y --exclude=kernel* update
```

Once you're satisfied with the cron job, you can let it run the next time your system is active at 4:02 A.M.; all you need to do is activate the *yum* daemon with the following command:

```
chkconfig yum on
```

Preparing Your Repository for Yum

In "Too Many Computers to Update over the Internet" in Chapter 11, I'll show how you can create your own Fedora repository from an available mirror. If you already have the packages you need, you can make it *yum*-aware; in other words, you can prepare your repository for *yum* with the right command.

Until recently, the standard for *yum*mifying a repository has been the *yum-arch* command. It's already a part of current *yum* RPMs. Starting with Fedora Core 3, Red Hat has adapted the *createrepo* command, which is part of an RPM of the same name.

The commands are simple; all you need to do is navigate to the directory with the RPMs that you want to configure as a *yum* repository and then run one of the following commands:

```
yum-arch .

createrepo .
```

The *yum-arch* command separates the headers from the RPMs and collects them in a *headers/* subdirectory. The *createrepo* command takes the headers, collects them in XML format, and then compresses them in the *repodata/* subdirectory.

Once complete, you can share this directory using NFS, HTTP, or FTP, and connect to it from the clients of your choice.

Avoid Dependency Hell with apt

RPM and DEB packages include all of the dependency information that you need. Each package includes headers that list any other RPMs that are required to make it work. I've illustrated one of the problems you might encounter at the start of the previous annoyance.

While the use of *yum* is limited to RPM-based distributions, *apt* can be used on distributions based on both the DEB and RPM package-management systems. There are even a number of *apt*-capable repositories available for Fedora Core and some of the RHEL rebuild distributions.

But to optimize how *apt* works on your system, you should customize the related */etc/apt/sources.list* configuration file, understand different *apt* commands, and configure a nightly update. For the best way to configure */etc/apt/sources.list*, read the "Find the Right Update Repository" annoyance earlier in this chapter. You can mirror your own *apt* repository based on the related annoyance in Chapter 11.

 I personally prefer *apt* in all situations because it is faster than *yum*, and there are *apt* repositories available for Fedora Core, some of the RHEL rebuilds, and SUSE Linux Professional. On the other hand, some believe that *yum* better fits Red Hat/Fedora Core, as it is written in python. And only *yum* supports the *--exclude* switch.

The apt Commands

This section provides the briefest of introductions to the *apt* commands. They vary somewhat for DEB- and RPM-based distributions. For more information, see the Debian version of this HOWTO at *http://www.debian.org/doc/manuals/apt-howto/index.en.html* and the apt+rpm HOWTO at *http://www.ccl.net/cca/software/UNIX/updating-redhat/apt-howto/.*

The *apt* commands, in my opinion, go into much more depth than *yum*. However, the Fedora and *yum* developers are working rapidly to close this gap.

apt-cache

With *apt-cache*, you can search through the repositories that you've configured. A few of the key versions of this command include:

apt-cache search term
> You can search through the *apt* repositories for the search term of your choice. For example, the following command searches through the information for all packages for those related to the MadWiFi project:

```
apt-cache search madwifi
```

apt-cache show packagename
> If you want more information on a specific package, this command can help. For example, if you want to learn more about the *madwifi-tools* package before installing it, run the following command:

```
apt-cache show madwifi-tools
```

apt-get

Perhaps the key command for handling *apt* repositories is *apt-get*. Once you've configured your repositories, the next thing you should do is run the following command, which synchronizes your cache:

```
apt-get update
```

If you see an error from this command, run it again. It may take a couple of cycles to synchronize the cache. You can then run the commands shown in this annoyance and more:

apt-get install package
> You can install the packages of your choice. You need to specify the right package name. If you're not sure, search with the *apt-cache search term* command described earlier.

apt-get check
> This command can help if you have trouble with dependencies. It updates the current cache of packages as well.

apt-get mirror-select
> If you've installed the *apt* commands on Fedora Core, this command can help you select an appropriate repository for your system.

Configuring a Nightly apt Update

You can configure your own cron job for *apt* updates. If you've read the previous annoyance, you know that there is a standard cron job for *yum* updates. You can adapt this job for *apt*.

First, you need to make sure no other script is running *dpkg* at the same time. That means you need to know the associated lock file that *apt* creates for your distribution when it is running. For example, when *apt* is trying to install a package on Debian Linux, it's actually trying to run the *dpkg* command. In this case, the */var/lib/dpkg/lock* file stops others from running *dpkg* (or *apt-get install package*, which invokes *dpkg*) at the same time.

Thus, when you create a cron job for *apt*, you'll want to make sure there is no current *dpkg* lock file. The following wrapper in *bash* makes sure none of the commands within it run unless nobody else is running *dpkg* on this computer:

```
if [ -f /var/lib/dpkg/lock ]; then
...
fi
```

Within this stanza, you can add the commands you need. As described earlier, it's important to make sure that the current package cache is up-to-date with the following command:

```
/usr/bin/apt-get update
```

You may want to repeat this command in the cron job, to make sure there are no problems with the update.

Now you can update your system. If you're satisfied with your update repositories and want to download and install all available updates, you could run the following command, which runs in "quiet" mode (-*q*) and responds to prompts with a yes (-*y*):

```
/usr/bin/apt-get -q -y dist-upgrade
```

Putting it all together, you'll have the following cron job:

```
#!/bin/sh
if [ -f /var/lib/dpkg/lock ]; then
    /usr/bin/apt-get update
    /usr/bin/apt-get update
    /usr/bin/apt-get -q -y dist-upgrade
fi
```

If you're concerned about specific packages such as the kernel, read about configuring the *preferences* file in the */etc/apt* directory in the following section.

Keeping packages in apt

Naturally, you may not want to accept all updates. To keep *apt* from upgrading everything, you can specify the packages you want to keep in the preferences file in the */etc/apt* directory.

The format of */etc/apt/preferences* is straightforward. For each package, you'll need three entries: Package, Pin, and Pin-Priority. For example, if you want to make sure that the *rsync* package is not upgraded, add the following to */etc/apt/preferences*:

```
Package: rsync
Pin: version 2.6.3-2
Pin-Priority: 1001
```

You can make sure *apt* is aware of your restriction in the policy associated with this package, specifically with the following command:

```
apt-cache policy rsync
```

You can do more with the preferences file; details are beyond the scope of this annoyance. For more information, see the *apt* HOWTO at *http://www. debian.org/doc/manuals/apt-howto/ch-apt-get.en.html*.

I Need Those Microsoft Applications on Linux

Most desktop applications today were originally designed for Microsoft Windows. If users who are accustomed to these applications can use them under Linux, it can help them make the transition from Windows to Linux. And the more people you get on Linux, the sooner vendors will create native Linux versions of their applications.

If your users need their Microsoft-based applications, there are five basic options:

- Look to the application vendor; they may have "ported" their application to Linux.
- Consider virtual machines, as they support Microsoft Windows inside Linux.
- Try to install the application in Linux with the help of the Wine libraries.
- Install the application directly within Linux using CrossOver Office.
- Configure TransGaming's Cedega, which supports Microsoft games within Linux.

Some of these options require proprietary software and may not be available for free. Cost and licenses vary.

Find a Linux Port

As the popularity of desktop Linux grows, more vendors will port their applications. What they develop for Microsoft and possibly Apple will be ported directly to Linux. If you're fortunate, the vendor has already created a Linux version (a.k.a. *port*) of the Microsoft-based application. Start your search at the vendor's web site. Proceed to the web page for downloads or operating systems. You may find Linux in the same list as other operating systems such as Mac OS, Sun Solaris, and Microsoft Windows.

There are many excellent Linux applications that are functionally equivalent to most Microsoft Windows–based programs. We've explored some of these applications in the first four chapters. While it's simpler for you if your users adapt these applications, forcing them to do so may lead some users to reject Linux.

Windows Inside a Virtual Machine

If you need an application that will work only within Microsoft Windows, you could configure a dual boot on your computer. But that can be awkward. A user who needs a Microsoft application several times a day might not want to reboot every time. If you're able to run Windows inside a virtual machine (VM), that may be more efficient. Your user may even be able to cut and paste between Linux and Windows applications. There are three major VM options. (As of this writing, you can't run a Microsoft operating system inside the fourth popular option, Xen. For more information on Xen, see *http://www.cl.cam.ac.uk/Research/SRG/netos/xen/*.)

Bochs

> The Bochs SourceForge project (*http://bochs.sourceforge.net*) supports a virtual machine emulator that can run at least Windows 95, MS-DOS, and Windows NT 4 inside Linux.

Win4Lin

> The Win4Lin system allows you to install Microsoft Windows 95/98/ME within current Linux distributions. As of this writing, it is available for $89.99 or $99.99 as a download or a CD from *http://www.netraverse.com*.

VMWare

> The most flexible of the virtual machines, VMWare allows you to install even the latest version of Microsoft Windows, as well as other versions of Linux, Sun Solaris, and more. VMWare offers a wide variety of workstation and server software that lets you install other operating systems on Linux (or even install Linux on Microsoft Windows). For more information, see *http://www.vmware.com*.

Two more popular VM options are Xen and Qemu. Xen is from the University of Cambridge. As of this writing, the developers are working on supporting Windows XP/2003 inside a Xen VM. For the latest information, see *http://www.cl. cam.ac.uk/Research/SRG/netos/xen/index.html*. Qemu includes features similar to Bochs and can run a wide variety of operating systems on several different architectures. For more information, see *http://fabrice.bellard.free.fr/qemu/*.

Wine

An open source project called Wine Is Not an Emulator (Wine) supports the installation of some Microsoft applications on a Linux computer. Its development has profited from the work of CodeWeavers and TransGaming, which I'll describe briefly in the following sections.

The Wine software itself is fairly slow. Work is far from complete; Wine allows you to "emulate the look and feel" of Windows 3.1, 95, or 98. Packages customized for different distributions (Red Hat/Fedora, SUSE, Mandrake, Slackware, Ubuntu, Debian) can be downloaded from the Wine web site, *http://www.winehq.org*. You can find the fairly short list of nearly fully compatible applications at *http://appdb.winehq.org*.

The steps you take to install Wine and compatible Microsoft applications vary slightly by distribution. When I installed Microsoft Word 2000 on my Debian Linux computer, I did the following:

1. I navigated to my home directory.
2. I installed the Wine software along with the TK language emulator for my GNOME desktop environment:

   ```
   apt-get install wine
   apt-get install winesetuptk
   ```

If Wine is not included with your distribution, you may be able to download a customized binary package from *http:// www.winehq.org/site/download*.

3. I mounted a Microsoft Office 2000 CD, and used *wine* to start the appropriate Microsoft Office installation utility:

   ```
   wine /media/cdrom/SETUP.EXE
   ```

4. The first time I started Wine, it looked for a configuration file. Not finding one, it displayed the options shown in Figure 8-3.

Figure 8-3. Ready to configure Wine

5. I clicked Configure Wine, which started the Wine Configuration Wizard. I accepted the default installation of a "fake" Microsoft partition in ~/.wine/fake_windows. Alternatively, I could have configured Wine on a mounted Microsoft partition.

6. Wine started the Microsoft Office installation process. I followed the associated steps and then restarted Linux.

7. I could now start Microsoft Word 2000 from my Linux home directory with the following command:

```
wine .wine/fake_windows/Program\ Files/Microsoft\ Office/Office/WINWORD.
EXE
```

As you can see, Wine works with some of the latest Microsoft applications. If you configure a *fake_windows* partition, you'll find a standard Microsoft Windows directory tree in the associated directory.

Configuring CrossOver Office

CodeWeavers has taken the work of the Wine project and built an application that can help you run a wide variety of Microsoft applications on Linux. (They've also shared their improvements with the Wine project.) While the company has focused on helping to make the Microsoft Office applications work on Linux, CrossOver Office can also help you with dozens of major applications from QuickBooks to FrameMaker.

CrossOver Office is faster and easier to use than plain Wine. Windows applications installed through CrossOver Office start and run more quickly. CodeWeavers has consistently responded to market demand; for example, they have recently added support for the Apple iPod. CrossOver Office uses a convenient GUI installer to guide you all the way through the process; it even adds an item on your GUI menu.

Different versions of CrossOver Office are available for workstations and servers, starting at $39.95. Downloaded trial copies work for 30 days.

Once downloaded, you can install Microsoft applications with the Cross-Over Office setup tool. It includes an installation wizard, which guides you to the applicable setup utility. Once the application is installed, CrossOver Office even simulates a Microsoft reboot cycle.

As you can see in Figure 8-4, the result includes GNOME menu icons for Microsoft Word and Internet Explorer.

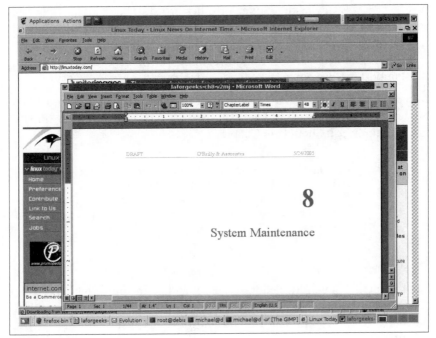

Figure 8-4. Debian with CrossOver Office

Working with Cedega

Lots of Microsoft users can't live without their games. If you expect them to convert to Linux, you need to find a way to help them run games on an open source operating system. TransGaming is in the forefront of this effort, with their Cedega system. Cedega includes Linux-compatible versions of the Microsoft Win32 APIs associated with the DirectX system. For more information, see *http://www.transgaming.com/products_linux.php*.

Keeping Up with Security

Linux distributions share their news relating to security issues in different ways. We'll examine how you can learn about security updates for the major distributions covered by this book: Fedora Core, Red Hat Enterprise Linux, SUSE, and Debian.

Linux security announcements are often publicized through major Linux news sites, such as *http://www.linuxtoday.com* and *http://www.linux.org/news*. However, they may not get all security announcements, and you may miss security issues in the clutter of other articles about Linux. The best option is to go to the source; normally, the group behind the distribution lists all updates related to the packages they've released somewhere on their web site. It can help you make a judgment about which security updates are most important for you.

In many cases, you can add a running list of security updates as a Rich Site Summary (RSS) feed to your Firefox browser, which is described in "Firefox Isn't Working as It Should" in Chapter 3.

 If, in fact, you're reluctant to upgrade specific packages for every last security update, you can exclude those packages from upgrades with the *yum --exclude* switch or the */etc/apt/preferences* file. I describe how these options work earlier in this chapter.

Fedora Core

Appropriately enough for Fedora's market and open source nature, Fedora Core updates—including those associated with security—are maintained in a Fedora News blog at *http://fedoranews.org/blog/*. Updates are added by its volunteer writers.

The Fedora News blog includes updates related to Fedora Legacy projects. As currently defined, that includes Fedora releases that are more than one year old, as well as some updates related to Red Hat Linux 9 and older releases.

As of this writing, security updates associated with Fedora Core 1 and 2, prior to November 8, 2004, are archived at *http://fedoranews.org/updates*. As Fedora Core releases advance, expect to see security updates for more releases here.

Security updates for Red Hat Linux 7.2–9 may be available from third parties. One option is the Progeny Transition Service, which may still offer support in 2006. For the latest information, see *http://transition.progeny.com*.

Alternatively, you may be able to find some updates through the Red Hat mailing lists (*http://www.redhat.com/mailman/listinfo*). Security announcements for Red Hat Linux 9 are available through May 2004.

Red Hat Enterprise Linux 3/4

If you have an official subscription to Red Hat Enterprise Linux 3/4, Red Hat will send security and bug fix announcements to the email address associated with your account. You should be able to update your systems using the *up2date* utility described earlier.

Red Hat copies many of its security announcements to the public Enterprise Watch mailing list, available at *https://www.redhat.com/mailman/listinfo/enterprise-watch-list*.

SUSE

SUSE maintains its security updates differently. Its security updates generally apply to all active SUSE distributions. Many of the security updates are listed in "Summary Reports" available at *http://www.novell.com/linux/security/securitysupport.html*.

There is also a SUSE security-related mailing list, *suse-security-announce*. More information is available at *http://www.novell.com/linux/security/securitysupport.html*. You should be able to update your systems using the YaST Online Update utility described in "Find the Right Update Repository," earlier in this chapter.

Debian Security Updates

The Debian security team has focused its efforts on the stable distribution. You can find more information on Debian security advisories and updates at *http://www.debian.org/security/*. You can get email updates by subscribing to the *debian-security* and *debian-security-announce* mailing lists at *http://lists.debian.org*.

You'll need to include the Debian security repositories in your */etc/apt/sources.list* file. As of this writing, the security repositories for Debian Sarge and Etch are available at:

```
deb http://security.debian.org/ sarge/updates main contrib non-free
deb http://security.debian.org/ testing/updates main
```

Once you're ready, you can access the latest security updates with the appropriate *apt-get update* command.

Debian does not support mirrors for security updates at this time and does not support security updates to the unstable (Sid) release. It addresses security issues to Sid with new packages in the regular repositories.

Other Packages

If you've installed packages from sources other than those maintained for your distribution, you'll need to go to the source for security updates. For example, SUSE can't provide security updates for CrossOver Office. Generally, you should subscribe to any security lists associated with any nondistribution-based package that you install.

My Firewall Blocks My Internet Access

Linux firewalls can be difficult to configure. The commands appear complex. While the *iptables* command is powerful, it cannot hide the complexity of risks that Internet-connected systems face. Therefore, customized firewalls that allow users on your network the access they desire can include dozens of commands.

This annoyance includes a basic overview of the current *iptables* firewall tool. There are many good sources for additional information, including Purdy's *Linux iptables Pocket Reference* (O'Reilly). One interesting iptables web site is Ziegler's Linux Firewall and Security Site at *http://www.linux-firewall-tools.com/linux*, which can help you customize a firewall.

In this annoyance, we'll review the basics of *iptables*, show you how to prevent the "ping of death," and, finally, review the firewall configuration tools from Red Hat/Fedora, SUSE, and Debian. If you use these tools to configure your firewall, you should have no problems accessing the Internet from within your network.

Basic iptables Commands

Before you're overwhelmed with *iptables* commands, it's time for a quick review. There is a basic format associated with *iptables*:

```
iptables -t table option pattern -j target
```

There are two basic alternatives for a table in the *-t* option: *nat* and *filter*. A *nat* table is associated with Network Address Translation. The default is *filter*.

I'll start by describing a basic masquerading command, which can help you configure a private network for your LAN. Then I'll illustrate one basic command that you can use to block traffic. Because you may not want to block all traffic from outside your network, I'll show you how you can let through one specific type of traffic. Finally, I'll show you the command that can help you fight the so-called "ping of death." Naturally, these commands are rich and complex; for more information, see the references described at the start of this annoyance.

Masquerading

A proper *iptables -t nat* command allows IP addresses on one side of a firewall, even private IP addresses, to masquerade as a different address. For example, the following command allows the computers on a private 192.168.0.0/24 network to masquerade as the IP address associated with *eth1*. In this case, *eth1* is configured as the NIC that represents your LAN on outside networks such as the Internet.

```
iptables -t nat -A POSTROUTING -s 192.168.0.0/24 -o eth1 -j MASQUERADE
```

The other computers on the 192.168.0.0/24 network should be connected to a different network device, such as *eth0*.

Blocking

In contrast, the following *iptables* command rejects all TCP-based connection requests from outside the network:

```
iptables -A INPUT -p tcp --syn -j REJECT
```

You can also affect traffic going to the outside network:

```
iptables -A OUTPUT -p tcp --syn -j REJECT
```

Or block traffic going through your computer as a gateway:

```
iptables -A FORWARD -p tcp --syn -j REJECT
```

These commands reject TCP connection requests that expect an acknowledgment, which are indicated here as a synchronous (*--syn*) reply. Such traffic is rejected with a message to the sender. You can also reject UDP traffic. If you're willing to let the message hang for the sender, you can replace *REJECT* with *DROP*.

Letting traffic through

Naturally, if you want to make any sort of connection, you'll want to let some traffic through your firewall. For example, the following command accepts (*-j ACCEPT*) DNS traffic (*--sport 53*) from a server on 192.168.0.1, to any destination address (*-d 0/0*):

```
iptables -A INPUT -p udp -m udp -s 192.168.0.1 --sport 53 \
         -d 0/0 -j ACCEPT
```

Stopping the "ping of death"

One older but still common attack on the Internet is the so-called "ping of death." It's a *ping* command configured in a "flood" so severe that it slows or even stops a web server from responding to legitimate requests. Thus, it's one of many possible DoS attacks. For more information, see *http://www. attrition.org/security/denial*. Stopping all DoS attacks is well beyond the scope of this book.

Generally, you do not want to stop others from using *ping* on your web site. The *ping* command is an important test of connectivity. If an administrator can't test connectivity to your site with a *ping*, she may assume, incorrectly, that your site and associated computers are down. She may then look for alternatives.

You can prevent *ping* floods by using your firewall to regulate the rate at which your computer accepts *ping* requests. The following command is one example, which limits *ping* commands to one per second.

```
iptables -A INPUT -p icmp --icmp-type echo-request -m limit 1/s -j ACCEPT
```

If you're having trouble and are willing to stop *ping* commands completely, you can delete the limit and change *-j ACCEPT* to *-j REJECT*. If you administer a web site on the Internet, it's important to test a *ping* flood on your system. You can do so with the *ping -f computername* command.

 Do not test the *ping -f* command on someone else's web site. You could flood that web site with packets. In some jurisdictions, there may be legal consequences.

Red Hat/Fedora

Starting with Red Hat Enterprise Linux 3 and Fedora Core 1, Red Hat helped users to configure a default firewall with the Security Level Configuration tool, which you can start from a GUI command line with the *system-config-securitylevel* command (*redhat-config-securitylevel* through Red Hat Enterprise Linux 3).

As you can see in Figure 8-5, Red Hat's tool allows you to configure:

Trusted devices

These are NICs on which the firewall does not block any traffic. It's common to designate an internal network device on a gateway computer as a trusted device. The firewall you create would then block trouble from an outside network such as the Internet.

Trusted services

A trusted service is one that you want to make available through the firewall. As shown in Figure 8-5, you can select some common services.

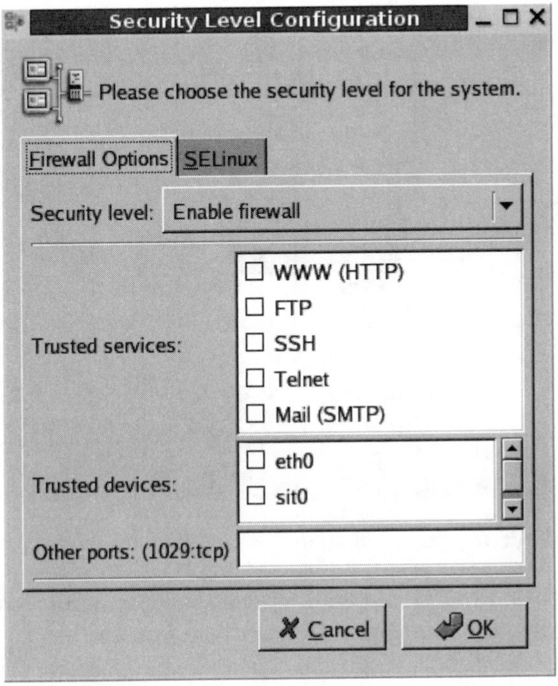

Figure 8-5. Red Hat Security Level Configuration tool

The result is saved in */etc/sysconfig/iptables*. If you want to enable additional services through the firewall, you can edit this file manually, despite the warning in the version of this file created with the Security Level Configuration tool.

If you want to allow other services through your firewall, you'll need the appropriate TCP/IP port numbers. They're available on most Linux distributions in */etc/services*.

SUSE

Naturally, SUSE includes its firewall configuration tool as part of YaST. Start YaST, and you can access this tool under the Security and Users → Firewall menu.

The SUSE firewall configuration tool starts by asking you to define your network devices as internal and external interfaces. SUSE assumes that you'll apply the firewall only to the external interface. Next, this tool displays the screen shown in Figure 8-6, where SUSE allows you to customize your firewall.

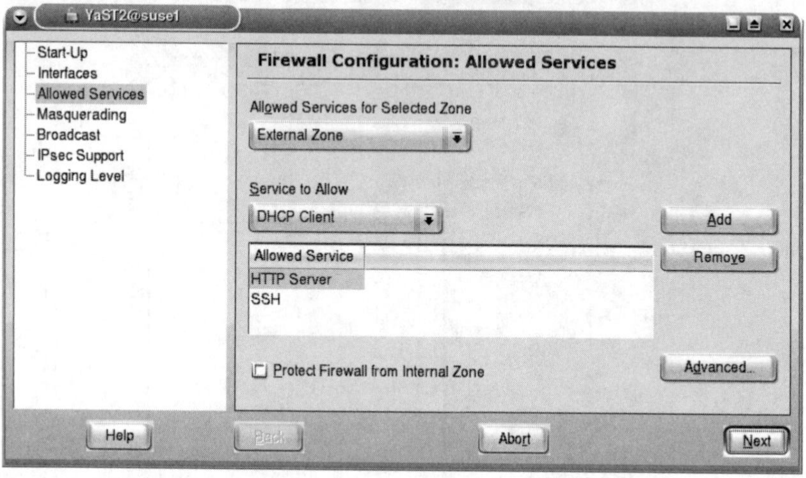

Figure 8-6. Customizing a firewall in SUSE YaST

YaST saves the firewall commands in */etc/sysconfig/SuSEfirewall2*. Read it carefully; it includes comments that can help you further customize your firewall.

Debian

While Debian uses the standard *iptables* command to configure firewalls, the distribution also supports a wide variety of tools. Try them out, but be careful to install only one on your system for production use. Otherwise, you may end up with a firewall that takes commands from several different configuration files. The effects may not be easy to predict.

If you're familiar with slightly older versions of Red Hat Linux, you can install a familiar tool, *lokkit*, with the following command:

```
apt-get install lokkit gnome-lokkit
```

Once it's installed, run *lokkit* in a command-line interface. Look at the labels. You'll see that Debian supports a tool originally developed by Red Hat. No shock here, as *lokkit* was released under an open source license. Alternatively, you can start the GNOME frontend with the *gnome-lokkit* command. The result is stored in */etc/default/lokkit*.

A simple search for Debian firewall tools reveals others, including:

FireHOL

You can start the FireHOL tool with the *firehol-wizard* command. If you've configured IP forwarding, it proceeds with a series of questions to help you secure your network. It saves its firewall configuration to */etc/firehol/firehol.conf*.

Guarddog

Guarddog is a KDE-based firewall configuration utility. It works well in GNOME. It's a fairly impressive tool that allows you to configure a firewall based on known applications, as shown in Figure 8-7. It saves its configuration in */etc/rc.firewall*.

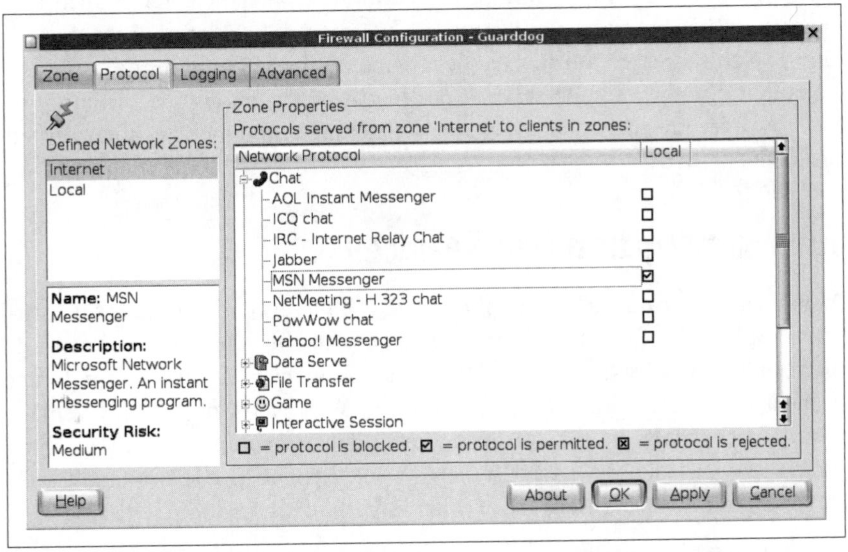

Figure 8-7. The Guarddog firewall tool

CHAPTER 9

Servicing Servers

This chapter solves annoyances related to specific services, such as web access, FTP, and email. A lot of these services, even though they have zillions of configuration options, can be enabled through the check of a box during Linux installation and often work satisfactorily without any tweaking. On the other hand, some of the common annoyances covered in this chapter are hard to puzzle out using the standard documentation for the services. So this chapter doesn't try to replace the basic configuration instructions that come with each service, but just provides enough information to get you over the hump of particularly common and poorly documented problems.

Too Many Options for Services

As you can tell from a glance at sites such as SourceForge that offer free software applications, the free-flowing creativity of the free software community has led to an explosion of choice. Developers have created for Linux users a broad selection of choices for the Web, FTP file sharing, email, remote access, and more. You may find a dozen or more options for running a service such as a web server. While Apache is the dominant web server on the Internet, there are excellent alternatives, including:

- AOLServer (*http://www.aolserver.com*)
- Boa (*http://www.boa.org*)
- Caudium (*http://www.caudium.net*)
- Jigsaw (*http://www.w3.org/Jigsaw*)
- Resin (*http://www.caucho.com*)
- Roxen (*http://www.roxen.com*)
- Zeus (*http://www.zeus.com/products/zws*).

Because it's hard to tell how the services differ and which ones are most reliable, this degree of choice can turn into an annoyance. For many, it feels like the first time someone from a poorer country shops in a modern supermarket (or the first time I visited Fry's Electronics, a U.S. high-tech superstore); the choice can be overwhelming. To keep things simple, you could stick with a "brand name," such as BIND for DNS or Apache for web services, but the results may not be best suited for your needs.

In the following sections, I'll describe some of the issues you should consider in selecting the right server:

- Servers vary in functionality.
- Some options are included with your preferred distribution, or integrated well with it, while others are not.
- Servers have different levels of support from their developers and user communities.
- Some servers are proprietary, while others are somewhat open but may be encumbered with license clauses that may not be acceptable to some users.

Distribution Support

The developers behind each Linux distribution may include one or many options for servers. For example, if you're looking for an FTP server, Red Hat Enterprise (RHEL) includes only the vsFTP package. To drive the point home, if you've purchased a RHEL subscription, you may get technical support if you install vsFTP but not for any other FTP server. Debian repositories allow you to install WU-FTPd, OFTPd, PureFTPd, and TwoFTPd, but Debian does not provide any official support. Generally, if a server is included with your distribution, you know it will work. However, watch carefully between releases, as the default servers may change when you least expect it.

If your distribution includes a binary package for your desired server, use it. The developers behind your distribution have configured it with customized locations for scripts, configuration files, logs, and more. While these file locations are supposed to conform to the Linux Standard Base (*http://www.linuxbase.org*), there are variations between distributions, so you should stick to services released for your distribution whenever possible.

If there isn't a package available for a server you've decided you need, check its associated web site. You may be able to find a binary package customized for your distribution. Otherwise, you may need to live with putting configuration files and other resources in directories that differ from other services.

Consider particularly whether distribution support makes it easier to handle security updates. This should be a high priority, because vulnerabilities are discovered in nearly every server from time to time, and patching the server on your system must be done quickly. When a distribution supports a service, the team is more likely to notify you directly when a vulnerability is found and to provide an easy-to-install fix. (In fact, you can generally get the fix through a routine update operation, if you feel comfortable automating system administration to such an extent.)

Your distribution should provide security updates for every service it supports. But for mission-critical services, that may not be enough. Go to the web site associated with the service. You may be able to sign up for security-related mailing lists or news updates for that service.

If your service isn't supported by your distribution, it may be more difficult to keep up with critical security updates. The developers at the distribution, or at the project developing the server, may or may not create a package promptly that you can download and install with the fix. You may or may not be notified. (Luckily, many independent services report security flaws and fixes, so you should subscribe to one of those.)

 A couple of options for security alert services include the SANS @RISK newsletter at *http://www.sans.org/newsletters/ risk/* and the Linux Weekly News security alert database at *http://lwn.net/Alerts/*.

Functionality

Check feature lists in server documentation to find out whether they can meet your specialized needs, and follow mailing lists or newsgroups associated with the servers to find out whether they truly support key features in a robust manner. For example, while both sendmail and Postfix perform the central task of transferring email to destination servers, they offer a wide range of extras that most sites need in modern mail environments and solve major problems such as spam in different ways. Trial and error may be required to find out whether a service is good enough for you. Some measures of functionality include:

- Does it do what you want?
- Will it still meet your needs as your network grows (scalability)?
- Are there problems interacting with other services?

These are just general measures. Functionality varies by your needs and the service you're assessing.

Developer and User Support

Many sites pay consultants for server support, and that may be the safest option even if you're a geek. But you should be aware of two community sources of support: the people behind a distribution and the developers behind a service.

Open source software generally gives rise to a range of support options of varying cost and responsiveness. If you have a problem with your sendmail server, for example, you may be able to get some level of support from the volunteers on the mailing lists at *http://www.sendmail.org*. Alternatively, you may be able to get dedicated support with the proprietary version of Sendmail through *http://www.sendmail.com*.

Users are generally delighted to help one other with the typical Linux service. You can find such volunteer support on at least two types of mailing lists: those associated with your distribution and those associated with the particular service. In addition, most distributions and many services maintain IRC (Internet Relay Chat) channels that Linux users monitor constantly. IRC may be the quickest way to an answer. One list of Linux IRC channels is available from *http://www.linux.org/docs/irc.html*.

Before you ask questions on a mailing list or IRC channel, do your homework. Read through applicable documents. Search the archives for the list and do generalized web searches with your error message or symptoms as search terms. Try various options and make careful notes of the output. Prepare your question with backup information, citing the research that you've done. If you've helped others on these mailing lists before, others will be more willing to help you. For more information on this process, see the last annoyance in Chapter 5.

Licensing

For many in the Linux community, licensing is critical. People associated with Richard Stallman's Free Software Foundation (FSF) at *http://www.fsf.org* are loath to use any software that does not meet their standard for freedom. And now the difference between free and proprietary software is embedded in Linux technology. For example, I find a number of messages similar to the following in my SUSE */var/log/messages*:

```
Jan 24 11:45:33 suse1 kernel: bluetooth: unsupported module, tainting
kernel.
```

This message refers to a Bluetooth module, not licensed to the GPL, installed in the default version of SUSE 9.2.

Tainting in the Kernel

What does "tainting" mean in this context? Every developer of a module (such as a driver) must decide whether the module meets the GPL requirements for free distribution. Many modules do not meet these requirements—for example, because the vendor wants to hide information about the functioning of the device, or because government agencies such as the FCC require hiding information that could be used to make a wireless device dangerous—so the developers do not release their source code.

Linux developers, and many distribution developers, prefer all code to be freely viewable and distributable. They point out, with some logic, that any problem reported with a proprietary part of a kernel may be due to binary code whose source they can't examine. The practical ideal of seeing all source code in order to debug a problem reinforces the idea that non-free code is bad. And this is why Linux developers insist that a single piece of non-free code taints the kernel. Many developers refuse to help someone with a kernel problem if the kernel is thus tainted.

The dividing line between free and proprietary can be bridged in many ways. For example, there are two versions of the email server, one free and one proprietary, available from the Sendmail organization. The commercial version is known as Sendmail, available from *http://www.sendmail.com.* The open source version is known as sendmail (lowercase), available from *http://www.sendmail.org.*

On the other hand, a substantial number of self-described "open source" services do not conform to GPL license specifications. For example, the djbdns service for DNS described later in this chapter includes a license that does not allow others to modify and redistribute the associated source code. Many open source licenses do allow modification and redistribution; for a full list, see *http://www.opensource.org.*

Users Need to Download Files

Many people depend on exchanging files for collaboration and information sharing. If you're working with just a few people, it may be sufficient for you to send the files directly to those people in an email attachment. This is not a problem as long as the associated files and number of users are relatively small. But as demand grows, you'll need a different method to distribute downloads.

One efficient method for distributing downloads in a TCP/IP network is the File Transfer Protocol (FTP). The most secure (for FTP) configuration provides anonymous-only access and is run in a *chroot jail*, which keeps users on your FTP server and away from any non-FTP related directories on your system. One advantage of vsFTP is that it configures a chroot jail and anonymous access by default.

There are other excellent FTP servers. Those listed earlier in this chapter may meet your needs more closely than vsFTP. However, note that Red Hat, SUSE, and the Berkeley Standard Distribution (BSD—a cousin of the Linux operating system) use it to share their operating system distributions quickly and securely.

Configuring vsFTP

You can download the vsFTP server from an installation CD or network source on Red Hat/Fedora, SUSE, and Debian distributions. In each case, the package name is *vsftpd*, and there are slight variations between distributions. The vsFTP configuration file, *vsftpd.conf*, can be found in your */etc* or */etc/vsftpd* directory, depending on your distribution.

Red Hat/Fedora

Red Hat/Fedora installs the basic vsFTP configuration files in a dedicated directory, */etc/vsftpd*. It configures an individual *vsftpd* start script in the */etc/init.d* directory. However, if you want to limit this vsFTP server to anonymous access, you'll need to disable this setting:

```
local_enable=YES
```

Otherwise, users can log in to their individual home directories through that FTP server. If you've provided FTP server access to outside networks, that can be a security breach. The breach can be worse unless you disable this setting, which allows users to write over files on your FTP directory:

```
write_enable=YES
```

If you want to provide reliable downloads for your users, you don't want to allow a cracker to overwrite downloads on your FTP server with the viruses of her choice.

A few advantages of the standard Red Hat/Fedora vsFTP configuration include support for limiting logins by username, for TCP Wrapper security in *etc/hosts.allow* and *etc/hosts.deny*, and for PAM modules. To enable these forms of security, include the following directives:

```
userlist_enable=YES
tcp_wrappers=YES
pam_service_name=vsftpd
```

Red Hat/Fedora configures a default *ftp* user in */etc/passwd*. That user has a home directory in */var/ftp* and a login shell that prevents logins, */sbin/nologin*. (Other distributions may use a */bin/false* login shell.) To activate and make sure vsFTP starts in the appropriate runlevels, use the following commands:

```
/etc/init.d/vsftpd start
chkconfig vsftpd on
```

Now you can copy the files that you want others to download to the */var/ftp* directory. I've even created a Red Hat/Fedora installation server by copying the files from the installation CDs to that directory.

Log in to this server yourself. Try to log in as a regular user, and check out the result. If you've disabled the *local_enable* directive, vsFTP will allow only anonymous access.

Once logged in, try the *pwd* command. While it looks as though you're in the top-level root (/) directory, you're actually in */var/ftp*; vsFTP's native chroot jail prevents users from going up to your root (/) directory, limiting any potential damage.

SUSE

SUSE configures vsFTP as an *xinetd* Super Server. Its operation and security is governed by the *xinted* daemon, using settings in */etc/xinetd.d/vsftpd*.

If you want your SUSE vsFTP server to run as a typical standalone daemon, associated with a script in the */etc/init.d* directory, set the following variable in */etc/vsftpd.conf*:

```
listen=YES
```

If you set this variable, remember to configure an appropriate script in */etc/init.d*, as well as consistent links from individual runlevel directories such as */etc/rc.d/rc3.d*.

You can also configure TCP Wrappers security support in */etc/hosts.allow* and */etc/hosts.deny* with the following command in the vsFTP configuration file:

```
tcp_wrappers=YES
```

In the *letclxinetd.d/vsftpd* startup file, you'll need to activate the service and designate an appropriate account. The default version of the startup file includes:

```
user=root
```

which would lead to problems if a cracker could find a way to force the vsFTP server to let him log in. To support anonymous access, you'll need a dedicated account. For this purpose, the vsFTP service adds the following entry in */etc/passwd*:

```
ftp:x:40:49:FTP account:/srv/ftp:/bin/nologin
```

In other words, to configure vsFTP on SUSE, you need to do three things: change the user directive in *letclxinetd.d/vsftpd* from root to ftp, change the disable directive from no to yes, and restart the *xinetd* daemon with the *letcl init.d/xinetd restart* command. To minimize the risk associated with this account, you should also make sure the login shell for this account in */etcl passwd* is one that prevents logins (*/sbin/nologin* or */bin/false*), as described earlier.

Debian

As with Red Hat/Fedora, Debian configures an individual *vsftpd* script in the */etc/init.d* directory. It includes an */etc/vsftpd.conf* configuration file that's already configured for secure, anonymous-only access. However, you'll need to create an *ftp* user and appropriate directory before your users can log in to Debian's vsFTP server.

The following commands create a Filesystem Hierarchy Standard (FHS)–compliant vsFTP directory with permissions that prevent all but the *root* user from writing to that directory.

```
mkdir /srv/ftp
chown root.root /srv/ftp
chmod 755 /srv/ftp
```

Next, you'll need to create an appropriate user, *ftp*, with */srv/ftp* as its home directory. A standard shell (*/bin/bash*) enables users who log in to your vsFTP server to navigate through its directories:

```
useradd -d /srv/ftp -s /bin/bash ftp
```

Now you can fill */srv/ftp* with the files that others need to download.

Activate vsFTP to start in the appropriate runlevels with the following commands:

```
/etc/init.d/vsftpd start
update-rc.d -f vsftpd start 20 2 3 4 5 .
```

Now you can copy the files that you want others to download to the */srv/ftp* directory. Log in to this server yourself, and try the *pwd* command. While it looks like you're in the top-level root (/) directory, you're actually in */srv/ftp*, courtesy of vsFTP's native chroot jail.

Users Are Still Demanding Telnet

Telnet is an old protocol that allows users to log in to remote systems in almost the same way as they log in to local text terminals. Security experts have been warning users about Telnet for decades and telling people to use a more modern protocol, such as the Secure Shell (SSH).

The main problem with Telnet is that it sends messages in clear text. In other words, anyone with a protocol analyzer (more popularly known as a "sniffer") and a connection to your network can read all network traffic that uses the Telnet protocol. They can even capture the username and password that are sent when someone logs in and then impersonate that user. Naturally, you don't want users making their passwords so easily accessible to crackers—or even the curious.

But many users are familiar and comfortable with Telnet, and want to use it despite its security problems. Many administrators like the way Telnet is configured as an Internet Super Server (*inetd.conf* or *xinetd.conf*) service. Fortunately, there are secure ways to configure Telnet. These methods use the Kerberos protocol, developed at MIT, to encrypt communications. There are two stages to this process: first, you'll need to install Kerberos clients and servers, with appropriate keys; then you can install the Kerberos-enabled Telnet clients and servers. I assume you'll want to install both clients and servers on your Kerberos/Telnet server computer, so you can test the results locally.

 Treat the solution in this section as a transitional measure. Prepare your users to migrate to SSH, which I cover in "My Other Computer Has No Monitor" in Chapter 11.

Finally, the last section under this annoyance shows how to limit access to particular remote hosts or networks, using TCP Wrappers.

Preparing Kerberos for Telnet

If you want to secure Telnet, you'll need a Kerberos server, as well as Kerberos clients, for the systems where Telnet users are located. Kerberos is a well-established security system that allows identities and access rights to be shared by multiple systems. For a basic overview, see the Kerberos Infrastructure HOWTO, available from *http://www.tldp.org/HOWTO/Kerberos-Infrastructure-HOWTO/*.

The packages you need depend on the distribution; for more information, see Table 9-1. Naturally, the components in each package vary by distribution; for example, SUSE's Kerberos server components are divided into three RPMs.

Table 9-1. Kerberos client/server packages

Package name	Distribution	Functionality
krb5-admin-server	Debian	Kerberos Master Server
krb5-kdc	Debian	Kerberos MIT Key Server
krb5	SUSE	Kerberos configuration files and libraries
krb5-client	SUSE	Kerberos management commands
krb5-server	SUSE/Red Hat/Fedora	Kerberos Master Server

 If you're using a Microsoft Windows 2000/2003 server, it may already have a Kerberos server.

To prepare a Kerberos server, take the following steps:

1. Download and install the appropriate packages from those noted in Table 9-1, including dependencies. If you're using Debian and are installing the *krb5-admin-server* package, ignore the configuration options also available with the *dpkg-reconfigure krb5-admin-server* command.

2. Edit the default Kerberos server configuration files: */etc/krb5.conf*, *kdc.conf*, and *kadm5.acl*. The locations of the last two files vary by distribution; they may be in the */etc/krb5kdc*, */etc/krb5*, or */var/kerberos/krb5kdc* directories.

   Replace each instance of EXAMPLE.COM with the name of your realm and domain. They may be the same. In fact, for the purpose of this annoyance, I use EXAMPLE.COM as the name of my domain and my Kerberos realm.

 The IETF has decreed that *example.com* can't be assigned, and should be used for documentation; while I use *example.com* in this book, you should not do so on your networks.

3. Start the Kerberos Key Distribution Center (KDC) database with the following command:

```
/usr/sbin/kdb5_util create
```

You're prompted for a Kerberos database master password. Don't store it online, but put it on paper or a removable disk and store it somewhere safe. If you forget this password, you may have to reinstall and reconfigure your Kerberos server.

4. Start the KDC, and confirm the master password you've just created:

```
/usr/sbin/krb5kdc -m
```

5. Now you can use the */usr/sbin/kadmin.local* administrative database to start adding users and hosts. The *kadmin.local* command opens a sub-shell with the name of the command as a prompt. At the prompt, a *?* displays a list of available Kerberos administrative commands.

Kerberos works with policies. You'll want to add policies for hosts, users, and an administrator with the following commands:

```
kadmin.local: addpol hosts
kadmin.local: addpol users
kadmin.local: addpol admin
```

6. Now create the users you need, including those who will log in to the local Kerberos Telnet server. Repeat as needed.

```
kadmin.local: add_principal -policy users michael
Enter password for principal "michael@EXAMPLE.COM":
Re-enter password for principal "michael@EXAMPLE.COM":
principal "michael@EXAMPLE.COM" created.
```

7. Create an administrator; as you can see from the command list, you can substitute *ank* or *addprinc* for *add_principal*:

```
kadmin.local: ank -policy admin michael/admin
```

Enter the same Kerberos database master password for this user when prompted.

8. Create host computer accounts. The *-randkey* option creates a random encrypted key for communication. In the following example, *debian. example.com* is one of the hosts on my network.

```
kadmin.local: ank -randkey -policy hosts host/debian.example.com
```

Repeat this command for the other hosts that will be using Kerberos Telnet to connect to this system.

9. Create a KDC keytab file, with the generic administrator account (kadmin) for your Kerberos server. The keytab file is as defined in the *kdc. conf* file—normally *kadm5.keytab*, in the same directory as the *kdc.conf* file:

```
kadmin.local: ktadd -k /etc/krb5kdc/kadm5.keytab kadmin/admin \
kadmin/changepw
```

10. Exit from the *kadmin.local* interface with the *quit* command.

11. Start the Kerberos Administration service:

    ```
    /usr/sbin/kadmind -m
    ```

12. Test and then list your Kerberos user credentials. I've tested mine as user *michael*:

    ```
    kinit michael
    klist
    ```

13. Now make sure the Kerberos Administrative system works in regular (nonlocal) mode with the */usr/sbin/kadmin* command. If you see the kadmin: prompt, it worked.

14. Start the Kerberos key server. If it works, you'll see messages indicating the server is listening on certain IP addresses, commencing operation in the */var/log/krb5kdc.log* file, and so on.

    ```
    /usr/sbin/krb5kdc
    ```

15. Make sure the Kerberos administrative (*kadmind*) and key servers (*krb5kdc*) are active the next time you start Linux. Depending on your distribution, that may require specific *chkconfig* or *update-rc.d* commands.

Now you can configure the Kerberos version of Telnet. Users who are enabled on your Kerberos server will be able to log in from hosts, as long as the hosts are also enabled on your Kerberos server.

 If you don't configure a Kerberos server, you can still use the Kerberos Telnet packages. However, without a Kerberos server, passwords will still be transmitted in clear text.

Secure Telnet

Kerberos versions of Telnet are available for most Linux distributions, including those covered in this book. However, the package names vary widely, as shown in Table 9-2. While many of these packages include Kerberos-enabled clients and servers for other services, the focus in this annoyance is on Telnet.

 Kerberos is itself a rich and complex topic. This annoyance covers only those skills required to start Kerberos sufficiently to configure a secure Telnet system. For more information on Kerberos on Linux, read the associated HOWTO at *http://www.tldp.org/HOWTO/Kerberos-Infrastructure-HOWTO*.

Table 9-2. Kerberos Telnet packages

Package name	Distribution	Functionality
krb5-telnetd	Debian	Kerberos-enabled Telnet server
krb5-clients	Debian	Kerberos-enabled clients for Telnet, FTP, and the remote shell
krb5-workstation	Fedora/Red Hat	Kerberos-enabled clients and servers for Telnet, FTP, and the remote shell
krb5-apps-servers	SUSE	Kerberos-enabled servers for Telnet, FTP, and the remote shell
krb5-apps-clients	SUSE	Kerberos-enabled clients for Telnet, FTP, and the remote shell

Before you continue, make sure you've installed the packages customized for your distribution. If you've properly configured your update systems, the installation command should be straightforward.

If you're running Debian, the following command should install the noted packages:

```
apt-get install krb5-telnetd krb5-clients
```

To make sure your users don't use the insecure version of Telnet, you'll also want to uninstall the associated package with a command such as:

```
apt-get remove telnet
```

If you're running Red Hat Enterprise Linux, assuming your system is subscribed to the right channels, you can install (or check for upgrades to) the *krb5-workstation* package with the following command:

```
up2date -u krb5-workstation
```

Alternatively, with Fedora Linux, you can use *yum* commands to make sure your systems are up-to-date and can install or upgrade your systems with the following command:

```
yum install krb5-workstation
```

Or with SUSE Linux, you can use YaST to install the *krb5-apps-servers* and *krb5-apps-clients* packages (or you can just use the appropriate *rpm* command to install these packages directly from the installation source).

For any RPM-based distributions, you should make sure that the regular insecure Telnet package is uninstalled with a command such as:

```
rpm -e telnet
```

If you're running SUSE Linux, you can keep your YaST system, and install the aforementioned packages with the following command:

```
yast2 -i krb5-apps-servers krb5-apps-clients
```

If you have problems, see the related annoyances on *apt*, *yum*, the Red Hat Update Agent, and YaST described in Chapter 8.

Secure Telnet Client

Now that you've configured the secure Kerberos Telnet server of your choice, you need Telnet clients. I'll show you what you need to do to make a Telnet client work for workstations based on the three major distributions I cover in this book.

This section assumes you've already configured your Telnet users and hosts under the Kerberos server, using the instructions described earlier in this annoyance. Otherwise, even the Kerberos version of the Telnet client defaults to sending all data in clear text, including passwords.

Debian Telnet client

On Debian, if you want to run the Kerberos-secured version of the Telnet client, you need both to install this client and to uninstall the regular Telnet package, as described earlier.

When the Kerberos Telnet client is installed, it includes a series of links from the standard *telnet* command well known to many regular users:

    telnet hostname

This */usr/bin/telnet* command is symbolically linked indirectly to the Kerberos-secured version of this client at */usr/bin/telnet.krb5*.

SUSE Telnet client

When you install the SUSE RPM with the Kerberos Telnet client (*krb5-apps-clients*), you'll need to make it easier for users to start the client. The location is not in a standard user's PATH. Therefore, you'll want to take one of the following steps to make it more accessible:

- Add */usr/lib/mit/bin* to each user's PATH. The easiest way to do so for all SUSE users is by editing */etc/profile*. SUSE suggests that changes by local administrators should be incorporated into */etc/profile.local*.

  Open */etc/profile.local* in a text editor, and add the following line to add the noted directory to each user's PATH:

      PATH=$PATH:/usr/lib/mit/bin

- Create a link from a standard directory already in every user's path. For example, the following command creates a link from */usr/bin/telnet* to the Kerberos Telnet client:

      ln -s /usr/lib/mit/bin/telnet /usr/bin/telnet

- Create a menu item in the GUI. For more information on how to do so on the GNOME or KDE desktop, see Chapter 1.

Red Hat/Fedora Telnet client

When you install the Red Hat RPM with the Kerberos Telnet client (*krb5-workstation*), you've presumably already installed the Kerberos server, which adds the Telnet client directory (*/usr/kerberos/bin*) to users' paths. You should also make sure to uninstall the regular Telnet package, as described earlier.

When the Kerberos Telnet client is installed, it includes a series of links from the standard *telnet* command well known to many regular users:

```
telnet hostname
```

Limiting Access to Particular Hosts

As with any service, you can specify which hosts can log in with Telnet and which hosts cannot through the TCP Wrappers package. Thus, if your Telnet daemon is */usr/sbin/telnetd*, you can limit access to the 192.168.0.0 class C network by adding the following line to */etc/hosts.allow*:

```
/usr/sbin/telnetd: 192.168.0.
```

Naturally, you should also prohibit access to others, so deny access to Telnet with the following command in */etc/hosts.deny*:

```
/usr/sbin/telnetd: ALL
```

TCP Wrappers reads the *hosts.allow* file before the *hosts.deny* file, so your class C network is still allowed to connect.

While */usr/sbin/telnetd* regulates the Kerberos Telnet service on Debian Linux, the daemon locations, and therefore what you specify in */etc/hosts.allow* and */etc/hosts.deny*, vary by distribution. On SUSE Linux, the Kerberos Telnet service is in a slightly different directory: */usr/lib/mit/sbin/telnetd*. On Red Hat/Fedora, it's */usr/kerberos/sbin/telnetd*.

I Can't Send out Email Because the ISP's Server Is Down

Despite the reliability of Linux, everyone experiences downtime, even your ISP. Power failures can outlast available battery backups. Surges and kernel upgrades can force reboots. And many ISPs rely on Microsoft Windows. Your network may still be working, but your ISP's email servers might go down.

If you work from an Internet café, you may not be able to send email through your ISP's mail server. Many of those servers aren't accessible from outside their networks. While you can use a web-based email interface, that interface can't download directly to an email manager such as Novell Evolution or KMail.

In this situation, there are two basic options:

- Route your email through a different ISP.
- Create your own email server.

This annoyance explores each of those solutions.

Route Email Through a Different ISP

If you don't want to configure an email server on your network, the simplest option is to route your email through a different ISP, such as one associated with your personal web site. In fact, this is what I do because large-scale MTA programs such as sendmail and Postfix make little sense for my home network.

If your alternate ISP supports outgoing email, they'll have an email server with a URL such as *mail.otherisp.net*, which you can use in the account information for your email manager.

You may have a backup ISP for emails and not even realize it. If you run your own web site, the ISP with the web server usually provides free email addresses. They'll have incoming and outgoing mail servers for those accounts. While regulations vary by ISP, yours may allow you to use their outgoing email servers for any email account.

If you have an email address on a different domain from your ISP, with POP3/IMAP4 support, you may have another option. POP3/IMAP4 support requires incoming and outgoing email servers. Once you find the third-party domain URL for the outgoing email server, you can substitute that account information in your email manager.

As I've configured my primary emails through my personal domain name, I can send and receive emails even when my primary ISP goes down. All I need to do is connect at a nearby Internet cafe, or use my neighbor's wireless network (with permission). It doesn't matter what domain is associated with my email address.

Create Your Own Email Server

If your ISP's outgoing email server goes down, you have another option: you can set up your own email server. Because the default settings associated with the sendmail, Exim, and Postfix services are acceptable for small-scale uses, the process is simple.

Despite their popularity, I do not cover any of these services in detail. One excellent book on sendmail is *sendmail* by Bryan Costales and Eric Allman (O'Reilly). (It's over 1,200 pages long.) For more information on Exim, see *http://www.exim.org*, and for more information on Postfix, see *http://www.postfix.org*.

 There are two basic versions of the sendmail email server. More information on the open source version of sendmail is available from *http://www.sendmail.org*. There is also a closely related commercial version, known as Sendmail; more information is available from *http://www.sendmail.com*.

For the purpose of this annoyance, I'll show you how to configure sendmail on Red Hat Enterprise Linux 4, Postfix on SUSE 9.3, and Exim on Debian Sarge. Naturally, the steps you take to configure one server on one distribution generally apply to the other distributions as well, with small changes such as directory locations.

 If you have a dial-up connection to the Internet, it's generally best to use the mail server provided by your ISP. Otherwise, when a user sends email, she may believe that it's sent, when in fact it is stuck waiting for your modem to make a connection.

Once you configure an outgoing email server, you'll want to make sure that the email clients on your network point to that server. That process varies by client and is an elementary part of the configuration process for a client such as Evolution, Thunderbird, or Kmail.

Configuring outgoing sendmail on Red Hat

When you configure sendmail from a Red Hat or Fedora package, you're configuring the open source version of sendmail, as opposed to the commercial version of Sendmail.

When you install the sendmail RPM package, you'll find a series of configuration files in the */etc/mail* directory. Some are macro files with an *.mc* extension, which are generally all you need to edit. Once editing is complete, you can then process the *.mc* macro files into the actual sendmail configuration files.

When editing a sendmail macro file, you need to be aware of two conventions:

- The way directives are set is unusual; the quotes you see start with a backtick or back quote (`), which is above the Tab key on most U.S. keyboards, and end with a standard single quote (').

- The comment code associated with a sendmail macro file is dnl. Any line that starts with this code is ignored by the m4 processor, which creates the sendmail configuration file from the macro file.

 The sendmail configuration file, *sendmail.cf*, includes a couple of thousand lines. It's easier to configure the sendmail macro file, *sendmail.mc*, which is then processed by the m4 macro processor. See the comments in *sendmail.mc* or *sendmail* by Bryan Costales and Eric Allman (O'Reilly) for more information.

In the default versions of the sendmail configuration files from the Red Hat/ Fedora package, you need to change one line in *sendmail.mc*. The following directive in the default version of the file limits access to the local computer:

```
DAEMON_OPTIONS(`Port=smtp,Addr=127.0.0.1, Name=MTA')
```

Naturally, this won't help you if you're configuring sendmail for other computers on your network. The easiest solution is to disable this directive by adding a *dnl* in front.

Now you can enable sendmail with the following commands, and then point the email clients such as Evolution, Thunderbird, pine, and KMail to the sendmail server host:

```
chkconfig sendmail on
service sendmail restart
```

Configuring outgoing Postfix on SUSE

The default mail server on SUSE Linux is Postfix, which you can configure either through YaST or directly through the */etc/postfix/main.cf* configuration file. The key directives are:

myhostname
> Set this to the FQDN of the local system that you're using as a Postfix server—for instance:
>
> ```
> myhostname = suse.example.com
> ```

mydomain
> This is the domain of the local network, such as *example.com*. If this is not set, it is by default set to myhostname minus the actual hostname of the local computer.

inet_interfaces

This is set to localhost by default. If you want to use your server as an outgoing email server for your network, you'll need to change this to all, as follows:

```
inet_interfaces = all
```

mynetworks

This limits access to a desired network, such as your LAN. For example, you can limit email users to the local computer and network with the following directive:

```
mynetworks = 192.168.2.0/24, 127.0.0.0/8
```

You can also configure Postfix using YaST. If you do, inspect the results in the */etc/postfix/main.cf* file. Despite the quality of YaST, no GUI tool is infallible. If it doesn't include the directives as shown here, you'll have problems and will want to try again.

Configuring outgoing Exim on Debian

When you install many Debian packages with the *apt-get* command, you'll get an opportunity to configure it right away. For example, to install the packages required for the Exim email server, you can run the following command:

```
apt-get install exim4-config
```

This installs the required packages, including *exim4*, *exim4-config*, *exim4-base*, *exim4-daemon-light*, *mailx*, and *qpopper*. When you run the command shown above, you're prompted to configure the mail server. Once the process starts, follow these steps:

1. When you're prompted for the domain for which *exim4* should administer email, enter the domain for your LAN, such as *example.com*.

   If you ever need to restart the configuration process, you don't need to reinstall Exim; just run the following command:

   ```
   dpkg-reconfigure exim4-config
   ```

2. The first choice you make is whether to split the configuration into small files in the */etc/exim4/conf.d* directory. Unless you know what you're doing, select No. The process continues, and you can configure */etc/exim4/exim4.conf*.

3. Select one of the following six ways to configure Exim:

   Internet site; mail is sent and received directly using SMTP
   Suitable for receiving mail from other hosts on a LAN, as well as sending mail to outside networks. Requires a static IP address. The actual server used still depends on the email client.

Mail sent by smarthost; received via SMTP or fetchmail
> Allows sending and receipt of email via Exim; suitable if your IP address is dynamically assigned by your ISP.

Mail sent by smarthost; no local mail
> While you might think this prohibits email on the LAN, that's not quite true; for more information, see Debian bug report 297841.

Local delivery only; not on a network
> Mail is delivered by Exim only to users on the LAN.

Manually convert from handcrafted Exim v3 configuration
> If you have an existing Exim 3 server and have upgraded to Exim 4, this option suggests that you use the *exim_convert4r4* tool to convert your configuration files.

No configuration at this time
> No further configuration is done, and the utility stops.

4. Now you can set the "System mail name," which corresponds to the hostname of the email server. The default is the current hostname.

5. Set the IP addresses governed by this Exim server. Unless you're running an ISP, you'll want to limit it to your LAN; for example, if your LAN uses the 192.168.0.0 class C network address, enter:

   ```
   127.0.0.1 : 192.168.0.0/24
   ```

6. If you're using Exim for incoming email, select the domain for which your network is the final destination, such as *example.com*.

7. Now if you're configuring Exim for other domains, you can relay mail for them. You can enter their domain names, separated by colons, in the "Domains to relay mail for" field.

8. If you've configured Exim for other domains, you'll get a chance to enter their IP network addresses in the same CIDR format as in step 5; multiple networks can also be separated by colons.

9. If your system connects to the Internet through a dial-up connection, you'll want to keep DNS queries to a minimum by answering Yes at a prompt. Otherwise, select No.

10. This tool now writes your configuration file to */etc/exim4/update-exim4. conf.conf* and restarts the *exim4* service.

11. Run the *update-exim4.conf* tool. This processes the configuration file created in the previous step with Exim defaults, and writes the result to */var/lib/exim4/config.autogenerated*.

12. Restart the Exim4 daemon with the following command:

   ```
   /etc/init.d/exim4 restart
   ```

I Need Multiple Web Sites but Have Only One IP Address

Even though there are over four billion IPv4 addresses, they're scarce in some areas. IPv4 addresses today are rationed through ISPs. Quite often, a site needs to offer many instances of a server—each with a different domain name—but has only one public IP address that they all have to share. For instance, you might be offering web sites to many users at low cost, or merging organizations but allowing each to keep its own web site with its original domain name. Apache lets you accomplish this through a feature called *virtual hosting*.

Until Apache 2.0, it was difficult to configure more than one web site per IPv4 address. Now, you can configure as many web sites as you need using a single IP address. While virtual hosting has now been backported to the latest versions of Apache 1.x, I'll show you how to configure virtual hosts based on the default versions of Apache 2.x available for Debian Sarge, SUSE Linux Professional, and Red Hat Enterprise Linux/Fedora Linux.

 As the Apache web server is a complex system, I can cover only a few associated directives in detail here. For more information, start with *http://httpd.apache.org* and O'Reilly's *Apache Cookbook* by Ken Coar and Rich Bowen.

Variations Among Distributions

Each of our major distributions varies in its default Apache configurations, as well as how it accommodates virtual hosts:

- Red Hat/Fedora encourages configuration of virtual hosts as a part of the main Apache configuration file, */etc/httpd/conf/httpd.conf*; sample commands are included near the end of the default version of this file.

- Debian's default Apache configuration file has an Include directive that allows you to configure virtual hosts in the */etc/apache2/sites-enabled* directory.

- SUSE's default Apache configuration file has an Include directive that allows you to configure virtual hosts in the */etc/apache2/vhosts.d* directory, in a *.conf* file.

In theory, you could take configuration files and directory structures from one distribution and copy them to another. However, every distribution may use different methods and defaults when it builds its Apache package. Related systems may process Apache directives differently. Even though each distribution starts with the same Apache source code, the results vary.

Configuring a Virtual Host

In this section, I'll show you how to configure multiple virtual hosts on each of our major Linux distributions, using their default configuration files. First, I'll show you the more commonly configured directives. Then, in separate subsections, I'll show you how to modify the default configuration files for each of the covered distributions to create the virtual hosts you need.

Assuming you're satisfied with the defaults in the configuration files, you'll want to focus on the following directives:

NameVirtualHost

Set this directive to the IP address of your web server, e.g.:

    NameVirtualHost 192.168.0.11

Once you set the shared IP address for your web server, you can define each virtual host in stanzas, delineated by a <VirtualHost> container. In other words, every virtual host container on this web server will start with <VirtualHost 192.168.0.11> and end with </VirtualHost>.

UseCanonicalName Off

Keep this Off; otherwise, this web server assumes the default ServerName is the URL for all virtual hosts.

ServerAdmin

Set this directive to the email address of the administrator. Error messages normally include a link to this address. Include this directive within <VirtualHost> containers if each of your web sites has a different webmaster.

ServerName

Within a <VirtualHost> container, set this directive to the FQDN for the web site.

DocumentRoot

Assign the directory containing your web pages to this directive. Make sure to configure a different DocumentRoot directory for each virtual host. Create these directories if they don't already exist.

ErrorLog / CustomLog

Assign these directives to the name and location you want for these logs. Once they are configured, you can measure access attempts (CustomLog) and errors (ErrorLog) for each web site. In my opinion, it's best if you use the same directory as DocumentRoot. However, you may also want to assign a subdirectory of *var/log* so they're managed by the standard cron job, as defined in */etc/cron.daily/logrotate*.

Now I'll show you how these directives (and others) can be used to create virtual hosts, based on the default Apache configuration files associated with Debian, SUSE, and Red Hat/Fedora Linux.

Debian virtual hosts

On a Debian Sarge system, the first step is to make sure you have the right packages installed. Apache 1.x and 2.x packages are available from the standard repositories. Don't install both, unless you're prepared to run them on different ports or, better yet, on different virtual machines such as Xen. For the purpose of this annoyance, install the *apache2* packages. Taking advantage of dependencies, the easiest way to do so is with the following command:

```
apt-get install apache2-utils
```

Before you start configuring a virtual host, take a look at the base Apache configuration file, */etc/apache2/apache2.conf*. You'll see the following lines near the end of the file:

```
# Include the virtual host configurations:
Include /etc/apache2/sites-enabled/[^.#]*
```

This particular Include directive incorporates the code within all files from the specified */etc/apache2/sites-enabled/* directory.

Now make a copy of the *default* file from the noted directory. Store the copy in that same directory. Once configured, you can use the *a2ensite* command as described in the following list of instructions to create a symbolic link in the */etc/apache2/sites-enabled/* directory.

My copy of the *default* file starts with the NameVirtualHost directive, which suggests that this file should contain all VirtualHost web site containers for this web server. To create your first virtual host, take the following steps:

1. If you haven't already done so, make a copy of the *default* file in the */etc/apache2/sites-available* directory and open the copy in a text editor.

2. Change the NameVirtualHost directive to point to the IP address that you're sharing for your web servers—for example:

   ```
   NameVirtualHost 192.168.0.11:80
   ```

   You don't need the :80 at the end of the directive if you include the following directive in the main */etc/apache2/apache2.conf* file:

   ```
   Listen 80
   ```

3. Copy the <VirtualHost> container, with default contents. Make a copy for each web site that you want to configure on this server.

4. Configure your first web site. Start with the first `<VirtualHost>` container. Set the `ServerAdmin` directive to the email address of the webmaster of this web site.

```
ServerAdmin webmaster@example.com
```

5. Set the `DocumentRoot` to the directory that will contain the files for this web site.

```
DocumentRoot /var/www/yum
```

6. Generally, you don't need to change the defaults for the `<Directory />` container; they support symbolically linked files, which are often necessary for links to images, as well as to prevent crackers from changing access permissions on this web server.

```
<Directory />
      Options FollowSymLinks
      AllowOverride None
</Directory>
```

7. Configure access to the directory for this web site. At minimum, change the `<Directory /var/www>` directive to match the `DocumentRoot`. The default `Options` directive supports showing an index of files if there's no `DirectoryIndex` file in the `DocumentRoot` directory, following symbolic links outside the directory and content negotiation based on the default language of the browser. The other directives forbid overrides, allow access from all users, and allow redirection to a different directory (*/etc/apache2-default/*):

```
<Directory /var/www/>
      Options Indexes FollowSymLinks MultiViews
      AllowOverride None
      Order allow,deny
      allow from all
      # This directive allows us to have apache2's default start page
      # in /apache2-default/, but still have / go to the right place
      RedirectMatch ^/$ /apache2-default/
</Directory>
```

8. Generally, you won't need to change the next stanza either. CGI programs are commonly used on web sites; the default `ScriptAlias` directive links such programs in the *cgi-bin/* subdirectory of `DocumentRoot` with the */usr/lib/cgi-bin* directory. The `Options` directive supports execution of CGI scripts, prevents content negotiation, and follows symbolic links only if they are owned by the same user:

```
ScriptAlias /cgi-bin/ /usr/lib/cgi-bin/
<Directory "/usr/lib/cgi-bin">
      AllowOverride None
      Options ExecCGI -MultiViews +SymLinksIfOwnerMatch
      Order allow,deny
      Allow from all
</Directory>
```

9. Configure the logfiles for your virtual host so they're segregated from others. You can configure them in a subdirectory of the DocumentRoot or a subdirectory of */var/log/apache2*. You can segregate logfiles with the following directives in your virtual host container:

```
ErrorLog /var/log/apache2/yum/error.log
CustomLog /var/log/apache2/yum/access.log combined
ServerSignature On
```

10. Generally, you won't need to change the next Alias directive and stanza; they specify a link to a documents directory accessible only on the web server computer.

```
Alias /doc/ "/usr/share/doc/"
        <Directory "/usr/share/doc/">
        Options Indexes MultiViews FollowSymLinks
        AllowOverride None
        Order deny,allow
        Deny from all
        Allow from 127.0.0.0/255.0.0.0 ::1/128
</Directory>
```

11. Now return to step 3 and repeat the process for the other web sites you want to configure on this system.

12. Make sure to add appropriate entries to your DNS server. Most DNS servers allow a CNAME record to specify more than one hostname for each IP address, so you can simply list all your virtual hosts' URLs in your DNS database.

13. Make sure you have directories and appropriate web site files for each of the directives shown.

14. Run the *a2ensite* command, which creates a link from the configuration you created to the */etc/apache2/sites-enabled* directory.

15. Restart the Apache server.

16. Add appropriate HTML files to the DocumentRoot directory for each web site.

17. Test your new virtual host-based web sites.

SUSE virtual hosts

SUSE strongly encourages the use of YaST for most configuration tasks; however, I've found this to be problematic for virtual hosts. I will therefore show you how to configure a SUSE virtual host from the configuration files. On SUSE Linux 9.3, they are organized similarly to Debian's. The Apache 2.x packages have names beginning with apache2. The configuration files are stored in the */etc/apache2* directory.

The main Apache configuration file for SUSE is *httpd.conf*. Look near the bottom of the default version of this file; it includes a section entitled Virtual Server Configuration, with one directive:

```
Include /etc/apache2/vhosts.d/*.conf
```

This directive includes the code from any *.conf* files in the *vhosts.d/* subdirectory. To make this work with one IP address, you'll also need to include a NameVirtualHost directive in the main *httpd.conf* configuration file, with the shared IP address. For example, the following directive shares 192.168.0.11:

```
NameVirtualHost 192.168.0.11:80
```

You may not need the :80 at the end of the directive, if you include the following Listen directive:

```
Listen 80
```

With the following steps, I show you how you can use the *vhosts.template* file. While you can include almost any Apache directive, these steps are limited to the *active* default directives, which I've modified slightly, assuming a web site URL of *yum.example.com*:

1. Make a copy of *vhosts.template*. The following commands match the aforementioned Include directive. You can make additional copies if you're configuring more than one virtual host:

   ```
   cd /etc/apache2/vhosts.d
   cp vhosts.template vhost1.conf
   ```

2. Open the copy that you've created of *vhosts.template* in a text editor. Add the IP address that you're using to the VirtualHost container directive:

   ```
   <VirtualHost 192.168.0.12:80>
   ```

3. Set the ServerAdmin to the email address of the webmaster for this site, the ServerName to the URL that you want used for the site, and the DocumentRoot to an exclusive directory:

   ```
   ServerAdmin michael@example.com
   ServerName yum.example.com
   DocumentRoot /srv/www/vhosts/yum.example.com
   ```

4. Configure the logfiles. The following directives identify them with the name of the web site, in the standard directory where they're stored with other logfiles:

   ```
   ErrorLog /var/log/apache2/yum.example.com-error_log
   CustomLog /var/log/apache2/yum.example.com-access_log combined
   ```

5. The following default directives, in order, eliminate lookups of the URL of the requesting browser; allow the use of different URLs for each

individual virtual host; and add a footer, normally with a link to the webmaster's email address, to error messages:

```
HostNameLookups Off
UseCanonicalName Off
ServerSignature On
```

6. If you have CGI scripts, the following directive and Directory stanza allow you to store those scripts in the noted directory. The options in the Options directive support execution of CGI scripts and prevent the use of server-side includes:

```
ScriptAlias /cgi-bin/ "/srv/www/vhosts/yum.example.com/cgi-bin/"
<Directory "/srv/www/vhosts/dummy-host.example.com/cgi-bin">
    AllowOverride None
    Options +ExecCGI -Includes
    Order allow,deny
    Allow from all
</Directory>
```

7. You can allow users to browse their home directories with the following stanza, but I do not recommend it. This stanza may allow others to browse individual home directories. I therefore recommend that you comment out the following directives:

```
<IfModule mod_userdir.c>
    UserDir public_html
    Include /etc/apache2/mod_userdir.conf
</IfModule>
```

8. You should also configure settings for the directory with web site files for this virtual host. The example shown here supports directory listings if there is no *index.html* page, as well as symbolic links:

```
<Directory "/srv/www/vhosts/yum.example.com">
    Options Indexes FollowSymLinks
    AllowOverride None
    Order allow,deny
    Allow from all
</Directory>
```

9. Now return to step 1 and repeat the process for the other web sites you want to configure on this system.

10. Make sure to add appropriate entries to your DNS server. For example, on a regular DNS server, a CNAME record can support more than one hostname for each IP address.

11. Make sure you have directories and appropriate web site files for each of the directives shown.

12. Restart the Apache server.

13. Test your new virtual host-based web sites.

Red Hat/Fedora virtual hosts

On a Red Hat Enterprise Linux or a Fedora Linux system, the first step is to make sure you have the right Apache packages installed. For these distributions, they have names such as *httpd*. Taking advantage of dependencies, the easiest way to install the packages is with the following command:

```
up2date -u httpd
```

 If you want a secure web site using the HTTPS protocol on RHEL or Fedora, you'll also need to install the *mod_ssl* RPM, which installs a sample virtual host configuration in */etc/httpd/conf.d/ssl.conf*.

On Red Hat–based distributions, virtual hosts are most easily configured as part of the main */etc/httpd/conf/httpd.conf* configuration file. Sample code is already available in the default version of this file. I'll show you how you can configure virtual hosts using these suggested directives:

```
#NameVirtualHost *:80
#<VirtualHost *:80>
#    ServerAdmin webmaster@dummy-host.example.com
#    DocumentRoot /www/docs/dummy-host.example.com
#    ServerName dummy-host.example.com
#    ErrorLog logs/dummy-host.example.com-error_log
#    CustomLog logs/dummy-host.example.com-access_log common
#</VirtualHost>
```

If you prefer to configure virtual hosts in separate files, you can add an appropriate Include directive. As SUSE and Debian both configure virtual hosts in separate files, you can find guidance on how to configure the Include directive in those sections listed earlier.

Now, for Red Hat–based guidance on creating virtual hosts, start by making a backup of the default *httpd.conf* file. Copy the commented code shown above and place it at the end of the file. Make as many copies as you need virtual hosts. Then take the following steps:

1. Uncomment the code that you're planning to use.
2. Specify the IP address that you're using for the web server by uncommenting the following directive and adding the IP address that you're using for your virtual hosts (in this case, 192.168.0.11):

   ```
   NameVirtualHost 192.168.0.11:80
   ```

   If you've installed the *mod_ssl* RPM, you need to specify the port (80 for standard web sites) to distinguish this virtual host from a secure virtual host.

3. Add the IP address to the `VirtualHost` container for your first web site:

```
<VirtualHost 192.168.0.11:80>
```

4. Specify an email address for the administrator for the web site:

```
ServerAdmin michael@example.com
```

5. Set a `DocumentRoot` and `ServerName` for the web site; Red Hat encourages the use of the web site URL in the directory. I use *yum.example.com* here:

```
DocumentRoot /www/docs/yum.example.com
ServerName yum.example.com
```

6. Configure appropriate logfiles. Based on the `ServerRoot` directive earlier in the file, these logs are stored in a subdirectory of */etc/httpd*; the *logs* subdirectory is linked to */var/log/httpd*.

```
ErrorLog logs/yum.example.com-error_log
CustomLog logs/yum.example.com-access_log common
```

7. Now return to step 1 and repeat the process for the other web sites you want to configure on this system.

8. Make sure to add appropriate entries to your DNS server. For example, on a regular DNS server, a `CNAME` record can support more than one hostname for each IP address.

9. Make sure you have directories and appropriate web site files for each of the directives shown.

10. Restart the Apache server.

11. Test your new virtual host-based web sites.

I Can't Remember Which Printer to Use

Administrators of large networks commonly have to work with a substantial number of printers. Busy offices may have several printers in a dedicated location. As an administrator, you could randomly assign one of the printers as a default for different workstations in the area. In this section, I'll present a more robust solution.

Fortunately, most Linux distributions now use CUPS to administer printers. Developed by Easy Software Products, the standard version of CUPS (*http://www.cups.org*) is open source and works well with the Foomatic printer driver database available from *http://www.linuxprinting.org*.

 If you want commercial support for CUPS, support and software with additional drivers and administrative tools are available from Easy Software Products at *http://www.easysw.com*.

When you install CUPS on your system, you get access to a web-browser-based tool that can help you administer the printers on your network. If you're administering multiple printers, CUPS allows you to organize them into groups. When you print to one group, CUPS directs the print job to the first available printer in the group.

Many Linux distributions include their own printer configuration tools that work with CUPS. However, if you want to configure printers in groups, you'll want to use the CUPS command-line tools or web-based interface.

Installing CUPS

Installing the CUPS service and associated printer driver database is a straightforward process. It may already be installed on your system. There are a number of different CUPS packages. As different distributions configure each package differently, all I can provide are general guidelines:

Package names starting with cups
> The main CUPS services have RPM and DEB package names that start with *cups*. The names may vary. Debian's CUPS server package is *cupsys*; SUSE and Red Hat use *cups*. Other packages in this category may include drivers, clients, and configuration tools.

Package names starting with foomatic*
> Open source printer databases are available as the Foomatic database from *http://www.linuxprinting.org*.

Package names starting with libcups*
> Driver libraries are often configured in *libcups** packages.

These are general descriptions. For more information on packages associated with a specific distribution, use the search feature available for that distribution, such as:

- The Red Hat Network for RHEL packages
- SUSE's YaST Online Update
- The *yum search cups | less* command on Fedora Linux and other systems that use *yum* for updates
- The *apt-cache search cups | less* command for Debian Linux and other systems that use *apt* for updates

Configuring CUPS Printers

As the process of installing a printer on CUPS is straightforward, I won't describe it in detail here. While setting up */etc/cups/cupsd.conf* is a complex process, the associated configuration tools available on Red Hat/Fedora (*system-config-printer*), SUSE (YaST), and Debian Linux (*foomatic-gui*) make the procedure elementary for the Linux geek. In most cases, you can also use the web-based tool for CUPS to configure printers.

> The CUPS administration tool native to Red Hat/Fedora distributions does not include most of the printer drivers from *linuxprinting.org*. If you want to configure a printer via CUPS on these distributions, use their Printer Configuration tool, which you can start with the *system-config-printer* command. You can still organize these printers into groups as described in this section.

To set up a printer on CUPS, you need to know its manufacturer, model, and connection (USB, Serial, Parallel port, or network location). CUPS print tools can often detect printers shared from remote systems; otherwise, you can enter a Universal Resource Identifier (URI), which can be a URL or one of the other locations specified in Table 9-3.

Table 9-3. Universal Resource Identifiers for CUPS printers

URI example	Explanation
file:/home/print/new.prn	Processes the print job and send the output to the *new.prn* file
http://hostname:631/printers/printername	Processes the print job to the computer named *hostname*, on the printer named *printername*.
ipp://hostname:631/printers/printername	From another CUPS print server, processes the print job to the computer named *hostname*, on the printer named *printername*.
lpd://hostname/printername	From another CUPS print server, processes the print job on an LPD server on the computer named *hostname*, on the printer named *printername*.
socket://hostname	From a CUPS print server, prints to a network print server such as an HP Direct Jet. Some print servers require the use of port number 9100.

Sharing CUPS Printers

Not all distributions support sharing of CUPS printers. If you see a *cupsd-browsing.conf* file in your */etc/cups* directory, edit it and change the Browsing directive from off to on. Alternatively, you may need to configure sharing in the *cupsd.conf* <Location /> stanza. For example, if you're running CUPS on

Debian Linux, the following is the default version of that stanza, which supports printing from the local computer only:

```
<Location />
    Order Deny,Allow
    Deny from All
    Allow from 127.0.0.1
</Location>
```

You can expand this to the local network by specifying the associated IP addresses with a directive such as:

```
Allow from 192.168.0.0/255.255.255.0
```

Alternatively, you can support sharing via the local network cards by adding the following directive to the stanza:

```
Allow from @LOCAL
```

Configuring CUPS Administrators

In this section, I'll show you how to configure administrative privileges for more than just the *root* user. You've read about CUPS, and you know about the web-based interface. So you navigate in your browser to what you've read is the TCP/IP port associated with CUPS, 631:

```
http://127.0.0.1:631
```

You're taken to the main CUPS menu, as shown in Figure 9-1.

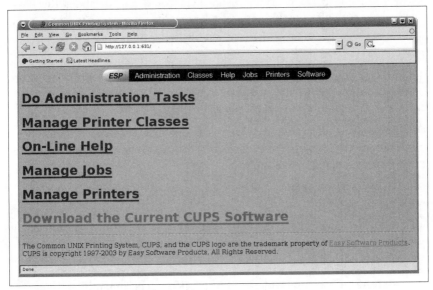

Figure 9-1. CUPS administrative menu

If you select the Do Administration Tasks link, you'll see a pop-up window that asks for your username and password. Some distributions preconfigure the *root* account to configure CUPS. If the *root* account does not work, or if you want to assign another user as a CUPS administrator, you need to know how to configure the main CUPS configuration file and use the *lppasswd* command (see "Adding CUPS administrators," later in this annoyance).

Configuring CUPS for multiple administrators

The <Location /admin> stanza defines the users and systems allowed access to CUPS administrative functions. Most distributions, including Red Hat/Fedora, SUSE, and Debian, limit access to the local computer with the following directives:

```
Order Deny,Allow
Deny from All
Allow from 127.0.0.1
```

If you want to configure different users as CUPS administrators, you'll need the following directives within the <Location /admin> stanza:

```
AuthType BasicDigest
AuthClass Group
```

Without an AuthType directive, all users would be able to administer CUPS printers. The BasicDigest option supports basic authentication using */etc/cups/passwd.md5* as a password-verification file. While this file encrypts passwords using MD5 encryption, crackers could still decipher the password, given enough time. As with */etc/shadow*, it's important to limit access to this file to the file owner (by assigning the permission 600).

The AuthClass directive defines the level of authentication. If set to User, a valid username and password are required. It's best to set it to Group, where a valid username and password are required, and the user must belong to the group defined by the AuthGroupName directive.

You'll also need an appropriate entry for the AuthGroupName directive; one commonly used group name is *lpadmin*. You can even make up your own group name with a directive such as:

```
AuthGroupName printadmin
```

Once you're satisfied with your <Location /admin> stanza, save your changes and restart the CUPS daemon. The name varies between distributions. You can restart CUPS with the following command on Red Hat or SUSE:

```
/etc/init.d/cups restart
```

You can restart CUPS on Debian with the following command:

```
/etc/init.d/cupsys restart
```

Adding CUPS administrators

Now you can add the users you want as CUPS administrators. The usernames and passwords don't even have to correspond to any on your system. In fact, it's an excellent idea to configure a special CUPS account so ordinary users don't play around administering your printers.

To add a CUPS administrator, use the *lppasswd* command. For example, if I wanted to add user *nancy* as an administrator, and I included the AddGroupName printadmin directive in the <Location /admin> stanza in my *cupsd.conf* configuration file, I'd run the following command:

```
lppasswd -g printadmin -a nancy
```

I can delete this user from the administrative database with another straightforward command:

```
lppasswd -g printadmin -x nancy
```

Organizing Printers by Classes

Now that you've set up administrators, you can work on the strength of CUPS, which can organize printers by groups. Presumably, you've already installed more than one printer via CUPS, which you can verify via the */etc/cups/printers.conf* file.

Adding a printer class is a straightforward process. If you use the web-based tool, take the following steps:

1. Open the web-based tool. On the system with the CUPS server, navigate to *http://127.0.0.1:631*. Log in using one of the administrative accounts.

2. From the top menu bar, click Classes. Near the bottom of the page, click the Add Class link.

3. In the Add New Class page, designate a Name, Location, and Description for the group. The Name is what users will call from other clients. The Location is the hostname or network domain. And the Description is what users see when searching for a printer, and therefore can be whatever you want to show them.

4. Now select the printers that you want as part of a class. You can select from printers already configured through this CUPS server. If you've configured CUPS printers using Red Hat's *system-config-printer*, SUSE's YaST, or Debian's *foomatic-gui* tool, you'll see those printers in the list.

   In most cases, you'll want to configure a group of printers from the same physical location as a class.

5. Now the printer class name that you selected should be immediately available to other computers on the network.

BIND Is Too Complex for My Growing Network

There was a time where every node on the worldwide network could easily be stored in one file. When the Advanced Research Projects Agency started its network (ARPANET), there were four nodes.

As this network grew, there was a need for a distributed database; out of this grew the Domain Name Service (DNS). The most common version of DNS is known as the Berkeley Internet Name Daemon (BIND). Unfortunately, the BIND configuration process is complex and is a common target of cracker attacks.

An alternative DNS server is D.J. Bernstein's djbdns. As noted on his web site, *http://cr.yp.to/djbdns/install.html*, he has offered to pay anyone for a verifiable security hole. For more information on djbdns, see *http://www. lifewithdjbdns.com* and Michael Bauer's *Linux Server Security* (O'Reilly).

 If you're a stickler for open source licenses, djbdns may not be for you. For Bernstein's view on licenses, see *http://cr.yp. to/distributors.html*.

djbdns Components

There are several components associated with djbdns. djbdns contains a caching nameserver, acquiring data from other authoritative nameservers on other networks. It also includes an authoritative nameserver component, which you can use for your growing local network. The components of djbdns are:

dnscache
> The key to djbdns is dnscache, which is a caching nameserver. As long as you keep it separate from other nameservers, it is secure.

tinydns
> While dnscache can take data from other authoritative nameservers, tinydns can serve as the authoritative nameserver for your local network. Make sure to install it on a computer other than the one hosting dnscache.

axfrdns
> Whenever you run an authoritative DNS server, even tinydns, you need to be able to transfer information. The axfrdns software allows tinydns to exchange data with authoritative and caching DNS servers.

Installing djbdns

To install djbdns, navigate to *http://cr.yp.to/djbdns/install.html* and follow these steps:

1. Install the *daemontools* package. Navigate to *http://cr.yp.to/daemontools/install.html* and download the latest version of this package from the associated link.

2. Unzip and unpack the associated package with the following command:

   ```
   tar xzvf daemontools-*.tar.gz
   ```

3. Navigate to the directory with the unpacked files:

   ```
   cd admin/daemontools-*
   ```

4. Start the installation program to compile and configure this package, which is available in the *package/* subdirectory (which requires *root* permissions):

   ```
   package/install
   ```

5. Install the *ucspi-tcp* package. Navigate to *http://cr.yp.to/ucspi-tcp/install.html* and download the latest version of this package from the associated link.

6. Unzip and unpack the associated package with the following command:

   ```
   tar xzvf ucspi-tcp-*.tar.gz
   ```

7. Navigate to the directory with the unpacked files:

   ```
   cd ucspi-tcp-*
   ```

8. Compile the associated programs:

   ```
   make
   ```

9. Install the associated programs; by default, they're installed in */usr/local/bin*:

   ```
   make setup check
   ```

10. Download the latest version of the *djbdns* package from the URL listed at the beginning of this section.

11. Unzip and unpack the associated package with the following command:

    ```
    tar xzvf djbdns-*.tar.gz
    ```

12. Navigate to the directory with the unpacked files:

    ```
    cd djbdns-*
    ```

13. Compile the unpacked files:

    ```
    make
    ```

14. Install the associated programs; by default, they're installed in */usr/local/bin*:

    ```
    make setup check
    ```

15. Repeat the previous steps on another computer. You can then configure the dnscache caching server on one system and the tinydns authoritative server on another system.

 If you see an error during one of the *make* commands, you may need to run the following command (or something similar) to add the noted code. Depending on the package, the *conf-cc* file may be in the directory where you've unpacked files, or in the *src/* subdirectory:

```
echo gcc -02 -include /usr/include/errno.h > conf-cc
```

If everything works, you can confirm it with the */usr/local/bin/dnsip* command, which works like the *nslookup* command. I've done so on my computer as follows:

```
# /usr/local/bin/dnsip www.linuxexam.com
64.202.167.192
```

The *daemontools* package includes special service configuration tools in the */usr/local/bin* directory. Specifically, the *svscan* and *svstat* scripts check the */service* directory for linked services, which you'll configure in the next section.

Configuring djbdns

Now you can configure djbdns on your systems. Remember, you'll want to configure the dnscache and tinydns components on different computers, as described in the following two sections.

Configuring dnscache on one computer

To configure dnscache on one computer, use the *dnscache-conf* script in the */usr/local/bin* directory. You'll also want to reconfigure the directory with the associated logfile. Take the following steps:

1. Create appropriate users for the dnscache service. As suggested by *http://www.lifewithdjbdns.com*, the users are *dnscache* and *dnslog*.

   The *-s* option specifies the default shell; for these users, it should never point to a regular shell. It's best to keep it consistent with other users, as defined in your */etc/passwd* file. For example, on SUSE Linux, enter:

   ```
   useradd -d /dev/null -s /sbin/nologin dnscache
   useradd -d /dev/null -s /sbin/nologin dnslog
   ```

In many cases, you may be able to use */dev/null* as a home directory for each user. That would be safest. But that's not allowed on all distributions. You can specify instead a directory that does not exist.

2. Now use the *dnscache-conf* command to configure the account, the log account, the configuration directory, and the local IP address.

   The following command assumes the account is *dnscache*, the log account is *dnslog*, the configuration directory is */etc/dnscache*, and the local IP address is 192.168.0.12:

   ```
   /usr/local/bin/dnscache-conf dnscache dnslog /etc/dnscache 192.168.0.12
   ```

3. Add your subnet to the directory of allowed hosts, */etc/dnscache/root/ip*. Based on the previous step, you can add your subnet with the following command:

   ```
   touch /etc/dnscache/root/ip/192.168.0
   ```

4. Tell the *svscan* script about the djbdns service. You can do so by making a link to the */service* directory:

   ```
   ln -s /etc/dnscache /service
   ```

5. Verify that the dnscache service is running:

   ```
   /usr/local/bin/svstat /service/dnscache
   ```

   You may see a message to the effect that the service has been up for 0 seconds. That is not necessarily a problem. It may simply mean that no computer on your network has used this DNS service yet.

6. Use the DNS Query command, */usr/local/bin/dnsqr*, with a DNS record type and the URL of your choice. Standard name records include an *a*; mail server records are associated with *mx*. One example is:

   ```
   # /usr/local/bin/dnsqr a www.oreilly.com
   1 www.oreilly.com:
   65 bytes, 1+2+0+0 records, response, noerror
   query: 1 www.oreilly.com
   answer: www.oreilly.com 20441 A 208.201.239.36
   answer: www.oreilly.com 20441 A 208.201.239.37
   ```

7. Now you can configure clients on this and other computers on your network to use this DNS server, typically through */etc/resolv.conf*.

8. Finally, it's best to store all logfiles in the */var/log* directory. In that way, the *logrotate* script that is normally configured as a daily cron job can maintain and manage the size of your dnscache logs. To do so, open the */etc/dnscache/log/run* file in a text editor and make sure it includes the following two lines:

   ```
   #!/bin/sh
   exec /usr/local/bin/setuidgid dnslog multilog t /var/log/dnscache
   ```

9. Naturally, this means you'll also need to create the new log directory, and make sure the ownership matches the user you've created for this service. Once complete, you can then restart the dnscache service with the following commands:

```
mkdir /var/log/dnscache
chown tinydns /var/log/dnscache
/usr/local/bin/svcstat -h /service/dnscache
```

Configuring tinydns on a second computer

To configure tinydns on a second computer, you can use the *tinydns-conf* script in the */usr/local/bin* directory. You'll also want to reconfigure the directory with the associated logfile. To configure tinydns, take the following steps:

1. Create appropriate users for the tinydns service. As suggested by *http://www.lifewithdjbdns.com*, appropriate users are *tinydns* and *dnslog*. But remember, you're on a different computer, so you'll need to create both users:

```
useradd -d /dev/null -s /sbin/nologin tinydns
useradd -d /dev/null -s /sbin/nologin dnslog
```

2. Configure the tinydns service. The *tinydns-conf* command can configure the account, the log account, the configuration directory, and the local IP address.

   The following command assumes the account is *tinydns*, the log account is *dnslog*, the configuration directory is */etc/tinydns*, and the local IP address is *192.168.0.15*:

```
/usr/local/bin/tinydns-conf tinydns dnslog /etc/tinydns 192.168.0.15
```

3. Now start the *tinydns* service. As described in the previous section, you can do so with a link to the */service* directory:

```
ln -s /etc/tinydns /service
```

4. Make sure the service is running with the following command:

```
/usr/local/bin/svstat /service/tinydns
```

5. Next, add the names and IP addresses for the computers on your network. The file with the data you need is */etc/tinydns/root/data*. You can use the scripts in the */etc/tinydns/root* directory to add IP addresses to that file. For example, the following commands point your tinydns server to authoritative nameservers on external networks:

```
/etc/tinydns/root/add-ns had1.or.comcast.net 204.127.205.8
/etc/tinydns/root/add-host debian.example.com 192.168.0.15
/etc/tinydns/root/add-host suse1.example.com 192.168.0.12
/etc/tinydns/root/add-host enterprise4a.example.com 192.168.0.11
```

Other commands are available in the */etc/tinydns/root* directory, including:

- *add-alias* for aliases, such as web or FTP servers
- *add-mx* for mail servers
- *add-childns* for other DNS servers

Run the commands you need to identify all of the hosts and servers on your network.

6. Navigate to the */etc/tinydns/root* directory and then run the *make* command. This processes the information from the datafile into *data.cdb*, which is read by the tinydns server.

7. Now configure clients on this and other computers on your network to use this DNS server, typically through */etc/resolv.conf*.

8. Finally, do the following to store all logfiles in the */var/log* directory. Open the */etc/tinydns/log/run* file in a text editor and make sure it includes the following two lines:

```
#!/bin/sh
exec /usr/local/bin/setuidgid tinydns multilog t /var/log/tinydns
```

Now, the *logrotate* script, which is normally executed as a daily cron job, can maintain and manage the size of your dnscache logs.

9. Naturally, this means you'll also need to create the new log directory, and make sure the ownership matches the user you've created for this service. Once complete, you can then restart the tinydns service with the following commands:

```
mkdir /var/log/tinydns
chown tinydns /var/log/tinydns
/usr/local/bin/svcstat -h /service/tinydns
```

The Windows Computers on My Network Don't Show Up

When you make Linux and Microsoft Windows work together through Samba, you're configuring a Linux system on a Microsoft network. If you're having trouble finding Windows computers on a network, you may need to use Microsoft tools. And that can be supremely annoying to a Linux administrator.

This annoyance is essentially a skeletal troubleshooting primer on Samba. For more information on Samba, see *Using Samba* by Jay Ts et al. (O'Reilly).

 When diagnosing a problem on a Microsoft/Samba network, the first thing to check is the network, which may lead to a different set of annoyances, described in "I'm Having Trouble Connecting to an Existing Network" in Chapter 7.

When you're responsible for a network of Linux and Microsoft Windows computers, you're at the mercy of the vagaries of NetBIOS broadcasts. For example, Microsoft computers may not show up on a Samba network until they have a chance to broadcast their presence on the network. So after you bring up a system, wait about 15 minutes before you worry about hosts that fail to show up when you browse the network (or worry that your new host fails to show up in the browse lists of other hosts).

> One key point about Microsoft networks is that they can be organized into *workgroups* or *domains*. Workgroups are peer-to-peer networks, where sharing can be authorized by passwords alone or by usernames and passwords from the sharing server. Domains are hierarchical networks, where sharing can be authorized from the Domain Controller.

Samba does not fulfill all of the functions of the latest Microsoft servers. The developers do their best to clone Microsoft features after they are brought to market. For example, Samba does not yet support Linux as a Windows 2003 Active Directory Domain Controller.

As of this writing, you can configure a Linux computer with the Samba service as:

- A member of a Microsoft workgroup
- A member server of a Microsoft domain, with or without an Active Directory server
- A Primary Domain Controller (PDC)
- A Backup Domain Controller (BDC)
- A browse master, which maintains the list of computers on the workgroup or domain

If you have problems, read the following sections. If you're running Samba 3.x, you may be able to use the *net* commands described at the end of this annoyance to help troubleshoot your systems.

Sharing from a Microsoft Computer

Naturally, before you can connect to a Microsoft computer, you need to authorize sharing from that computer. While details vary, sharing from a Microsoft computer requires that you authorize "File and Print Sharing" in the properties associated with the network device, and then actually share a directory or a printer from that computer.

The authorized username and password database depends on whether you're in a peer-to-peer workgroup or a domain. For more information on these topics, see the *Windows Annoyances* series by David A. Karp (O'Reilly) (consult the edition appropriate to the Windows OS version you're running).

If you don't see a computer on a Samba network, you may not have authorized sharing. On a Linux computer, other than network connections, there are several things you should check, as described in the following subsections.

Is the Samba service running?

To share printers or directories on a Windows network, you need a running Samba server on the computer that you want to share. The following command checks to see whether the Samba service is running:

```
ps aux | grep smbd
```

Another way to check on some distributions is with the service script (the Debian Linux version of this script does not have this capability; some distributions may have a slightly different name for this script, such as *samba*):

```
/etc/init.d/smb status
```

Does the Samba configuration make sense?

Samba includes a configuration checker in the *testparm* command. Try it out for yourself. It will identify syntax errors in your Samba configuration file, which is generally *smb.conf* in the */etc/samba* directory.

However, the problem is often in the details. For example, does the workgroup directive specified in the Linux configuration file match the workgroup or domain on each of the Windows systems? Do the shared directories have appropriate permissions? The details are as extensive as the directives available to the Samba configuration file; see the *smb.conf* file or the *Windows Annoyances* series by David A. Karp (O'Reilly) for more information.

Do you have an account on a domain?

Most larger Windows networks are configured in domains, with dedicated servers acting as controllers. You need to make sure each computer in a Windows network has an account on that domain. You can use the *net join* or *net ads join* commands described later in this annoyance to join an available domain.

Have you consolidated account databases?

Joining a Microsoft domain implies a single database of usernames and passwords. However, joining a domain is not enough. You need the *winbind* service to associate the Samba database with the Windows database. Once it's installed, you'll need to add appropriate mapping commands to your Samba configuration file.

One example of this from Debian Linux includes the following directives:

```
idmap uid = 10000-20000
idmap gid = 10000-20000
template shell = /bin/bash
```

These directives assign user and group ID numbers to those mapped from a domain authentication database. The `template shell` directive assigns a shell to users who log in to this system.

Is there a problem with the browse master?

Lists of computers on a Windows network, whether they be on a workgroup or a domain, are maintained by a computer known on the network as the browse master. In a Microsoft network, the browse master is chosen by "election," based on browse master values, which can range from 1–255. By default, Domain Controllers have a value of 32; you can configure your system as a master browser by setting the `os level` directive to a higher value.

Generally, you'll want to set up at least one Samba workstation as a browse master. There are three key directives associated with this system:

`local master`
> Specifies whether the system will participate in browse master elections; this directive can be `local master` = yes or `local master` = no.

`os level`
> Specifies the value associated with this system in a browser election; it may range from 1 to 255. Unless defaults have been changed on other systems, a value of 33 or higher is sufficient to establish the current system as the master browser.

`preferred master`
> You should set no more than one computer with the `preferred master` = yes directive; otherwise, browser elections may take some time, and browse lists may be delayed.

If you administer more than one network, you may have more than one browse list. You can synchronize browse lists with the `remote browse sync` directive. For example, when I ran the following command on the computers on my networks:

```
nmblookup -M workgroup
```

I found two different master browsers, 192.168.0.15 and 192.168.1.2. To make sure their browse lists were synchronized, I added the following directive to each computer's */etc/samba/smb.conf* configuration file:

```
remote browse sync 192.168.0.15 192.168.1.2
```

Finding Microsoft-Networked Computers

As I just noted, Microsoft networks work on the concept of a *browse list*. If you can find a computer on a browse list, you can find the resources that it's sharing. Once you find a shared resource, you can connect to it from a remote computer.

The command-line method for finding a browse list uses the following command:

```
smbclient -L computername
```

This produces the browse list, which comprises the directories and printers shared from the given computer. For example, I see the following, with Net-BIOS names of each computer, in the output:

```
Server          Comment
--------        -------
DEBIAN          debian server (Samba 3.0.14a-Debian)
ENTERPRISE4A    Samba Server
SUSE1           Samba 3.0.13-1.1-SUSE
WINXP           Other PC
```

If you don't see the computer NetBIOS names that you expect, you may or may not have a connection problem. There is often a delay of several minutes between a change in connection status and its appearance on (or disappearance from) the browse list. If the browse list does not reflect the status of actual connections in a few minutes, you may have other problems, such as different master browsers.

You might notice that the output is identical to what you might see on a Microsoft computer, in the output to the *net view* command.

If you're browsing computers across networks, check your firewall. If it's blocking access to ports 137, 138, 139, and 445, you won't be able to access Samba across the network. Naturally, a firewall on a computer within a LAN can also prevent access to a computer via Samba.

Authorized Sharing

If you have trouble connecting to a shared directory with Samba, you may be having trouble with authentication. To isolate the problem, you need to know the five basic ways you can share directories and printers on a Microsoft network. (Much of this discussion is focused on networks with Microsoft Windows NT, 2000, and XP systems.) These methods are expressed as the directives that you'd see in the appropriate Samba configuration file:

security = share

> Share-level security requires only a password for access to a shared directory. This is typical for workgroups of Windows 95/98/ME computers.

security = user

> User-level security is the standard and is what you'll see on a Linux computer configured as a Domain Controller. This directive performs lookups in the local authentication database.

security = server

> This directive passes authentication requests to another server. Requires that you include the Authentication Server directive to identify the computer with the authentication database.

security = domain

> Domain-level security, contrary to expectation, is what you would see on a Samba server configured as a member server on a Microsoft domain. Requires that you include the Authentication Server directive to identify the PDC, BDC, or DC for the authentication database.

> An account is also required on the PDC, BDC, or DC. If you're using Samba 2.x and are connecting to a PDC or BDC, use the *smbpasswd -j domainname -r computername* command. This should automatically create an account on the PDC or BDC. If you're connecting with a Samba 3.x system, use the *net rpc join* command described in the next section.

security = ads

> Similar to security = domain, this directive allows a Samba 2.x or 3.x server to become a member server on an active directory network. You'll also need a directive to identify the password and Kerberos servers for this domain. For example, if the password and Kerberos server are the same as *delilah.example.com*, you'd include the following directives in your Samba configuration file:

```
realm = kerberos.example.REALM
password server = delilah.example.com
```

The net Commands

Samba 3.x has introduced a set of *net* commands, which can help you troubleshoot and manage the Samba service for your network. They are somewhat different from the *net* commands that you might use on a Microsoft system.

If you're having trouble with connections on your network, you might check how Samba translates NetBIOS names to IP addresses with a command such as:

```
net lookup debian
```

If you need to join the local member server to a Microsoft domain named patio, you could use a command such as:

```
net join -S patio -U administrator
```

If you want to join an Active Directory domain, the command is slightly different:

```
net ads join -U administrator realm
```

In either case, you're prompted for the administrator's password on the applicable PDC or DC.

If you need to know who is connected to your shared directories, the following commands can help. The first identifies the user and client IP address; the second identifies the shared directory and connection time:

```
net status sessions
net status shares
```

If you're working with an Active Directory (AD) service, you'll be interested in the *net ads* series of commands. For example, if you want to recheck your status on an AD domain, the following command can check:

```
net ads testjoin
```

If you're working with regular PDC or BDC, you may be interested in the *net rpc* series of commands. Many of the commands described for AD domains work in a similar fashion for PDCs and BDCs. For example, you may be able to join a domain administered by a PDC with the following command:

```
net rpc testjoin
```

If you want authentication information, the following command performs a raw search of the PDC database, creating a "dump" of users and groups from the domain controller:

```
net rpc samdump
```

One interesting option that can help you maintain a BDC is the following command, which synchronizes a PDC's users and groups into the local database:

```
net rpc vampire
```

CHAPTER 10
User Management

One of the critical tasks of the Linux geek is user administration. It's easy enough to add new users. But not all users are equal. You may need to set up space limits on home directories, security by service, and special groups for projects. And users leave the company all the time. What you do with such accounts depends on if and when they're coming back, as well as any security policies that may apply.

Whatever you do, it is best to keep a set of standard written operating procedures, consistent with corporate policies and any applicable legal restrictions. It will help you explain your actions to supervisors, lawyers, and newer administrators.

Keeping users satisfied is often more than a full-time job. Your site may need multiple administrators, and not all Linux administrators are as skilled as you are. To limit your risks, you may want to limit the access of newer administrators. With the tools I describe in this chapter, you can manage access to the tools of your choice.

The Boss Wants to Set Up a Special Group of Users

When the boss wants to set up a group for a special set of users, such as *managers* or *accountants*, you need to know how to create the group, along with a directory accessible only to the user members of that group.

To understand what you need to do, it helps to know the baseline user and group settings on various Linux distributions. Then you'll know exactly what you need to do to create a special group on your systems.

Linux distributions classify users in different ways. Most distributions configure regular users as members of a single "Users" group. In contrast, Red Hat/ Fedora configures users in their own exclusive groups, in the so-called "User

Private Group" scheme. The permissions on each user's Red Hat/Fedora home directory keep users from reading files in other users' home directories.

What's best? It depends. In some organizations, it can be helpful to allow users to read one another's files. If you're running an ISP, you don't want that. The Red Hat/Fedora scheme can help you keep user files private.

 It's not difficult to convert between the Red Hat/Fedora User Private Group scheme and the standard Linux scheme. All you need to do to convert to the Red Hat scheme is change the file creation mask so that each user's private group has read (and perhaps even write) access, modify user membership in groups, and change permissions on user home directories.

This annoyance assumes you have a single database of users and groups on your network. That database might be on a Network Information System (NIS) server, as defined in *http://www.tldp.org/HOWTO/NIS-HOWTO*; it could be a part of a Lightweight Directory Access Protocol (LDAP) server, as defined in the book *LDAP System Administration* by Gerald Carter (O'Reilly); it could even be a part of a Microsoft user database and accessed through Samba (see *Using Samba* by Jay Ts et al., also published by O'Reilly).

For the purpose of this annoyance, I'm assuming that the database works through standard authentication schemes on one Linux computer, as configured in files such as */etc/passwd* and */etc/group*, and with defaults in */etc/default/useradd* and */etc/login.defs*.

Now I'll define how user schemes work on standard and Red Hat/Fedora Linux distributions. Then I can show you how to create a special group on any Linux distribution.

The Standard User Scheme

Linux distributions normally configure all users in the same group. In other words, all users are assigned the same Group ID (GID), which happens to be 100.

You can confirm group memberships, also known as GIDs, in */etc/passwd* and */etc/group*. They are defined in the fourth column in */etc/passwd*. As an example, I've taken the following excerpt from one of my */etc/passwd* files. Users *michael* and *editor* both belong to the same group, with a GID of 100:

```
michael:x:1000:100:author,,,:/home/michael:/bin/bash
editor:x:1001:100:editor,,,:/home/editor:/bin/bash
```

You may recall that permissions for files and directories are classified by owner, group, and others. While this provides the opportunity to help users share their files, that is not enough. By default on our distributions, users have only read access on the files of other users in the same group. For example, when I create *laforgeeks-ch10.sxw* on my home directory, it has the following permissions, as defined by an *ls -l* command:

```
-rw-r--r--  1 michael users   40800 2005-09-28 18:07 laforgeeks-ch10.sxw
```

In other words, even if user *editor* is also a member of the *users* group, she can only read the noted file. To allow the editor to make changes to that file, the owner would have to change the permissions.

A user who wants to allow others to write to his files has to modify the associated permissions. Fortunately, the owner has the right to change the permissions on his own files with a command such as:

```
chmod 664 laforgeeks-ch10.sxw
```

Few regular users understand the *chmod* command. But users can change permissions in GUI file browsers such as Nautilus and Konqueror. All they need to do is right-click on the desired file, select Properties from the pop-up menu, and change group permissions so the group can write to the file.

Unfortunately, this method makes the file writable to everybody in the general-users group—everyone with a regular account on that system. You may not want to let everyone write to your files. To address these issues, I'll describe a special group scheme and procedures later in this annoyance.

You may also want to configure limits on how much disk space can be occupied by a particular group. You can do this with group-based quotas, as defined in the "Some User Is Taking Too Much Disk Space" annoyance later in this chapter.

The Red Hat User Private Group Scheme

Red Hat/Fedora configures users differently from most Linux distributions. Every time a new user is created on a Red Hat system, he's assigned as the only member of his own private group. For example, on my Red Hat Enterprise Linux 4 computer, I have the following entries:

```
donna:x:501:501::/home/donna:/bin/bash
nancy:x:502:502::/home/nancy:/bin/bash
```

The third and fourth columns specify the user and group IDs. As you can see, the user and group IDs are the same for each user. In other words, both *donna* and *nancy* are members of their own special groups.

In addition, you'll find that the permissions are limited on home directories on Red Hat/Fedora distributions; for example, when I run the *ls -l /home* command, I get the following output:

```
drwx------   3 donna    donna    4096 Jul  5 16:41 donna
drwx------  38 michael  michael  4096 Sep 29 10:38 michael
drwx------   2 nancy    nancy    4096 Jul 22 18:18 nancy
drwx------   4 randy    randy    4096 Jul 22 17:57 randy
```

In other words, read, write, and execute permissions on user home directories are limited to that user. As a consequence, when I log in as user *michael* and try to list the contents of user *nancy*'s home directory, I get the following message:

```
ls: /home/nancy: Permission denied
```

In contrast, if you examine the permissions on SUSE or Debian-based home directories, you'll find that permissions aren't so limited, and users can read the contents of other users' home directories.

While the Red Hat User Private Group scheme does help keep user files secure, it does not encourage collaboration. When there's a need for any shared work, you'll have to take some special steps, but these are different from the steps necessary on other Linux distributions.

Configuring a Special Group

There are many reasons why you might configure a special group. Accountants may want to share their files with one another but keep their files secure from regular users. Supervisors may want to keep employee evaluations confidential. Team members on a special project may need to share information without interference from other employees. Whatever the reason, configuring a special group requires:

- Creating the new group, specifying the desired list of users
- Creating a special directory for the members of the group, with appropriate ownership and the Group ID bit
- Making sure the files that are copied to the special directory are writable by members of the group—and only by them

As an example, I'll illustrate how you can set up a special group for users who want to share their secrets in wine making. I'll call the group *winos* and make users *napa*, *sonoma*, *willamette*, and *columbia* part of this group. To do so, I take the following steps:

1. Add the specified users, if they don't already exist. While each of our distributions includes GUI tools, the command-line method employs

the *useradd -m* command, which makes sure to create the appropriate home directory, with default files as specified in the */etc/skel* directory.

```
useradd -m napa
```

Assign passwords if these are new accounts, with commands such as *passwd napa*.

2. Create the *winos* group, and specify an appropriate GID. The second task is tricky because automated tools that create accounts assign IDs of their own, and it's important not to let the IDs overlap with yours. In addition to the *useradd* and *adduser* commands, IDs are generated when a Linux system, through the `idmap uid` and `idmap gid` directives in a Samba configuration file, takes accounts from a Microsoft-style Domain Controller database, which by default takes user and group ID numbers of 10000–20000. If you choose a high GID, such as 30000, you can be confident it will lie outside the range of these automatically generated IDs. (With Linux kernel 2.6, the maximum number of users has been increased from 65,000 to over 4 billion.)

```
groupadd -g 30000 winos
```

3. Now add the desired users to the group you just created. You can do so by opening up */etc/group* in a text editor and adding the desired users to the end of the *winos* group directive (don't include any spaces in the directive):

```
winos:x:30000:napa,sonoma,willamette,columbia
```

4. For distributions that support shadow groups, make sure the new group memberships are reflected in */etc/gshadow* with the following command:

```
grpconv
```

Red Hat/Fedora and Debian Linux support shadow groups and have an */etc/gshadow* file; as SUSE Linux does not, the *grpconv* command leads to an error message.

5. Create the shared directory for these special users:

```
mkdir /home/winos
```

6. Assign appropriate ownership to this directory; the owner should be either the administrative user (*root*) or another user no cracker can log in as, such as *nobody*. Assign group ownership to the group you created:

```
chown nobody /home/winos
chgrp winos /home/winos
```

You can also combine these commands:

```
chown nobody.winos /home/winos
```

7. Assign appropriate permissions to this directory; most of the time you want to limit permissions to members of the *winos* group, which you can do by running the following command:

```
chmod 070 /home/winos
```

8. Set the SGID bit on this directory. This is critical. It allows all members of the *winos* group to read, write, and execute all files copied to */home/winos* by other users in the special group:

   ```
   chmod g+s /home/winos
   ```

   Naturally, you can combine steps 7 and 8 with the *chmod 2070 /home/winos* command.

9. On distributions other than Red Hat/Fedora, your users will have to change permissions to the files that they want to share. They can do so by right-clicking the file in Nautilus or Konqueror and clicking Properties from the pop-up menu. This opens a Properties window for the file, where they can enable read and write permissions on the file for the group under the Permissions tab.

   Alternatively, you could configure other distributions with a Red Hat–style User Private Group scheme, with the same value for *umask* (0002) and the same configurations in */etc/default/useradd* and */etc/login.defs* before creating the users associated with the special group.

10. Now test the result. Log in as one of the users in the special group.

11. Create a file. In this case, I've started OpenOffice.org Writer and saved some instructions to the *winemaking.sxw* file.

12. Copy the file that you want to share to the common directory:

    ```
    cp winemaking.sxw /home/winos
    ```

13. On distributions other than Red Hat/Fedora, make sure the permissions support group writing by modifying the aforementioned properties in Nautilus or Konqueror (see step 9), or with a command such as:

    ```
    chmod g+w /home/winos/winemaking.sxw
    ```

    On Red Hat/Fedora distributions, this is not necessary, as the default *umask* is 0002, which supports group write permissions.

14. Log in as a different user in the special group. Open the file in OpenOffice.org Writer. Make changes and save the file, making sure you save it to the shared directory.

Now you can provide instructions to users in your special group on how they can share and access files in the directory that you've created.

If multiple users are adding information to a shared file simultaneously, it's important that they open the file from the shared directory, using the same application. When one user has opened this file, Linux applications create a temporary, hidden "lock file" that prevents other users from writing to the file. Other users can still open the file with *read-only* settings. You'll need to inform your users that a read-only message means someone else has opened that file, and that they should wait until the other person closes the file.

But before you let your users open shared files, test them with the applications that they'll use. Make sure the lock mechanism works. Log in as two different users in your special group. Open a file in the shared directory. If the lock mechanism works, the second user that opens the file gets read-only access.

Unfortunately, file locking is disabled in the OpenOffice.org 1.x suite. As of this writing, it doesn't work for the OpenOffice.org 2.0.x suite. A fix is scheduled for OpenOffice.org 2.0.3, which is scheduled to be released about the time this book reaches the shelves. For more information, see Open-Office.org bug 57712.

There Are Too Many Users Accessing the Internet from the Office

High-speed, business-quality Internet connections can be expensive. While some companies try to regulate personal use of the corporate Internet connection, that can be difficult. Many use the Internet in their work. For those who allow employees to access the Internet during their free time (e.g., during the lunch hour), they may find employees overloading the connection. Some may abuse the connection for their own purposes, such as by downloading music or movies.

Whatever the cause, anything that can reduce the overall demand on a high-speed Internet connection can save significant amounts of money. A proxy server can help you reduce the load on your Internet connection, caching data commonly accessed from the Internet, and regulating access to unwanted sites, such as those with "sex" in the URL.

The standard open source method for regulating Internet connections in this way is the Squid Web Proxy Cache, documented at *http://www.squid-cache.org*. Commercial support for Squid is available through ViSolve, at *http://squid.visolve.com/squid/*. If you want the full capabilities of Squid, with content filtering, you'll also want to install SquidGuard, which is a combined filter, redirector, and access controller plug-in (*http://www.squidguard.org*).

Squid supports the use of multiple computers; load from one client can be sent to a *cache_peer* parent or sibling computer, also configured as a Squid proxy server.

Squid System Requirements

Any web proxy places heavy demands on a computer. When you're caching pages for a group of users who browse the Internet, you're going to need a lot of disk space, and you're going to need to get to that locally cached data fast. If the cached data is already in your RAM, so much the better. As described in the Squid documentation available from *http://squid-docs.sourceforge.net/*, caching stresses certain hardware systems more than others, focusing on the following hardware characteristics (in order of decreasing importance):

- Disk random seek time
- System memory (RAM)
- Sustained disk throughput
- CPU power

Installing Squid

As of this writing, the latest stable version of Squid is version 2.5. It is available as a standard package on our selected distributions; version 3.0 is in beta and is available in RPM format on the SUSE Linux installation CDs. The installation process is straightforward; I recommend that you use the most appropriate repository-management system to make sure to take care of dependencies (SUSE's YaST, Fedora's *yum*, or Debian's *apt*).

Squid packages use a slightly different format for names; stable packages are often named as such. For example, the Squid package on my Fedora Core 4 system is named *squid-2.5.STABLE11-2.FC4.i386.rpm*.

The companion *squidguard* package (version 1.2 as of this writing) is available from the Debian repositories as well as the SUSE installation CDs; if you want *squidguard* for Fedora/Red Hat, you'll have to install it from a third-party repository, such as *http://dag.wieers.com/packages/squidguard/*.

Debian organizes Squid packages somewhat differently; files that are included in the standard Squid package on other distributions are divided up into separate packages on Debian:

Squid CGI
> Debian splits out support for web-based administration of this service into a separate *squid-cgi* package.

Squid Client
> Debian includes the *squidclient* utility in a separate package of the same name.

Squid PreFetch
> Debian includes the *squid-prefetch* service, which loads web pages linked to those currently being read. When the user clicks on those pages, they are loaded from cache. You can configure prefetching with the regular Squid package with the range_offset_limit directive. For more information, see *http://squid.visolve.com/squid/squid24s1/tuning. htm*.

Squidview
> Debian includes the *squidview* package to monitor Squid access logs. For more information (and a tarball download for other distributions), see *http://www.rillion.net/squidview/*.

Configuring Squid

Once the Squid proxy server is installed, it's fairly easy to configure. For a minimal setup, all you need to do is change three settings in the basic configuration file, *squid.conf*, in the */etc/squid* directory:

visible_hostname *hostname*
> You'll want to specify the name of the local computer; you can use an FQDN such as *squid1.example.com*. If you have multiple Squid proxy servers, the hostname you use can help you identify the problem server.

http_access allow *local_net*
> Naturally, you'll want to allow access to the Squid proxy to workstations on your LAN. This http_access directive supports access from the specified *local_net*. When you browse the *squid.conf* file, you'll see similar directives; this one supports access by the Squid service to manage the cache on the local computer:
>
>   http_access allow manager localhost

acl *local_net* src 192.168.0.0/255.255.255.0
> This acl directive specifies an access control list and defines the *local_net* for the http_access directive shown above. Here I've assumed a typical address and netmask for a local area network.

If you're using a SquidGuard database, you'll want to make sure that *squid.conf* points to the associated configuration file. Normally, it's */etc/squid/squidguard.conf*; if you've installed the SUSE Linux version of this package, it's */etc/squidguard.conf*. To make the redirection work, add the following directive to */etc/squid/squid.conf*:

```
redirect_program /usr/bin/squidguard /etc/squid/squidguard.conf
```

or if you're working on SUSE Linux:

```
redirect_program /usr/sbin/squidguard /etc/squidguard.conf
```

Once you've configured Squid, you'll want to create the basic cache directory structure in */var/spool/squid* (*/var/cache/squid* on SUSE Linux). You can create the Squid cache directory structure with the following command:

```
/usr/sbin/squid -z
```

This command also serves as a configuration check; for example, if you haven't set the `visible_hostname` directive, this command exits with an error message. The directory structure may look a little weird; the following is the output from an *ls /var/spool/squid* command:

```
00  01  02  03  04  05  06  07  08  09  0A  0B  0C  0D  0E  0F
```

If you look further in these directories, you'll find a large number of additional directories, ready for caching. To see this for yourself, run the following command:

```
ls /var/spool/squid/00
```

Once Squid starts caching files, you'll actually begin to see stuff in directories such as */var/spool/squid/00/00*.

Starting Squid

As with any service, you'll want to start it once configured, and make sure it starts the next time you reboot your system. In our selected distributions, you can start the Squid Web Proxy daemon with the following command:

```
/etc/init.d/squid start
```

The actions you take to make sure this service starts upon every system boot depend on whether you're on Red Hat/Fedora/SUSE or Debian. On the first set of distributions, you need to run the following command, which starts the Squid daemon in the standard multiuser and multiuser-with-GUI runlevels:

```
/sbin/chkconfig --level 35 squid on
```

Naturally, the runlevel in question should conform to the default associated with the `id` directive in */etc/inittab*. If, for some reason, you want to keep

Squid from starting in any runlevel (e.g., if you're not ready to implement Squid on your network) or want to keep it from starting when you next reboot your system, run the following command (which deactivates the Squid service on all runlevels):

```
/sbin/chkconfig squid off
```

Alternatively, on Debian distributions, new services are configured to start by default on the next reboot. To confirm, I find the following file in the */etc/ rc2.d* directory, which lists services that are killed and started in runlevel 2 (which corresponds to the default runlevel as defined in my Debian */etc/ inittab*):

```
S30squid
```

Scripts that are started in a runlevel start with an *S*; scripts that are killed in a runlevel start with a *K*. If you want to keep Squid from starting in any run-level, run the following command:

```
update-rc.d -f squid remove
```

When you're ready to restore Squid, run the following command, which makes sure it starts in runlevels 2 through 5 (don't forget the dot at the end of the command):

```
update-rc.d -f squid start 20 2 3 4 5 .
```

In Debian distributions, there may be additional Squid-related daemons. Based on the packages described earlier, they include the Squid PreFetch and Squidtail services.

Connecting Clients

Naturally, Squid is only one part of the equation. For Squid to do its work, you need to make sure that clients, specifically web browsers, are config-ured to use the Squid proxy server.

If you're testing Squid, you can configure a client web browser on one of your systems to point to the proxy server. For example, Figure 10-1 depicts where to configure a connection from a Firefox web browser through a proxy server configured on a LAN on IP address 192.168.0.1.

One way to implement this configuration for all Firefox clients on your net-work is to copy the appropriate configuration file, which is *prefs.js* in the *~/. mozilla/firefox/*.default* directory. If you want to make the change perma-nent, you can disable write permissions for the user.

 The actual Firefox configuration directory varies randomly by user, but is always in the format shown and always includes a *prefs.js* configuration file.

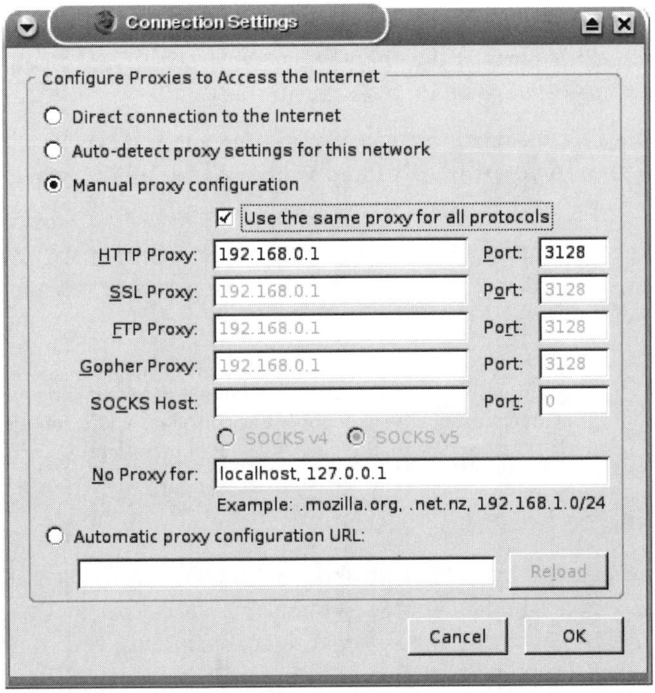

Figure 10-1. Configuring a manual proxy on Firefox

Some User Is Taking Too Much Disk Space

Disk space is relatively inexpensive. However, it's finite. No matter how much disk space you add, users can find ways to occupy it with their files. For example, users who download big files such as movies or ISO files with Linux distributions (hint, hint) may consume several gigabytes of space for each file.

Space Management

As an administrator, you need to know whether users need more space. You need to know how to regulate the space allowed to different users. As the Linux administrator, you could periodically peruse the files in your users' home directories, and you technically have permissions to edit and even delete users' files. But your users and management might not appreciate that kind of administration; it may even violate corporate policies.

There are a number of things you can do. For example, you can regulate the space associated with user-accessible directories, specifically the */home* and

/tmp directories. You can configure these directories in dedicated partitions; if one or more users then overload these partitions, the data does not spill over to other parts of the operating system. Conceivably, you can even configure a dedicated partition for a specific user.

The standard Linux method for regulating the space taken by a user uses *quotas*. Without quotas, users can go wild and load all the space available on your servers.

When you configure a quota, you're regulating either the space or the number of files, as defined by their inodes, in each partition mounted in */etc/fstab*.

 If you're implementing user-based limits for the first time, be prepared for negative reactions. Explain what you're doing. Help your users with alternatives for all of their data.

Quotas in the Kernel

Quotas are enabled by default on modern stock Linux kernels. However, many Linux geeks build their own kernels, as discussed in Chapter 7. If you've built your own kernel and forgot to enable quotas, you won't be able to get them to work, no matter how you configure quotas. That could be supremely annoying.

To make sure your kernel supports quotas, check the associated kernel configuration file. For example, on my Debian computer, I can see if quotas are allowed with the following command:

```
grep QUOTA /boot/config-2.6.8-mj1
```

The output is:

```
CONFIG_XFS_QUOTA=y
CONFIG_QUOTA=y
CONFIG_QUOTACTL=y
```

Kernel settings are configured directly into the kernel (*y*), configured as modules (*m*), or disabled (*n*).

Installing Quota Packages

The quota packages are installed by default on our selected distributions. However, you'll want to make sure they're up-to-date. On Debian Linux, I can do so with the following command:

```
apt-get install quota quotatool
```

Alternatively, once you've confirmed installation (*rpm -q quota*), you can use the *yast2 online_update* command to start SUSE's update tool. Normally, all current packages (except the kernel) should be updated automatically if a newer version is available. If necessary, you can use the search function to see whether the quota package requires an update.

For Red Hat Enterprise Linux, assuming you have a subscription to the Red Hat Network, the update command is simple:

```
up2date -u quota
```

For Fedora Linux, you can use the same command as Red Hat Enterprise Linux, or use the following *yum* command to check your current repositories for available quota package updates:

```
yum update quota
```

Quotas in Start Scripts

The common theme on our selected Linux distributions is that they run the *quotacheck* and *quotaon* commands. The first ensures that disk consumption records are up-to-date, and the second starts enforcement of the quotas.

Red Hat/Fedora handles quota start scripts somewhat differently from Debian and SUSE. The Red Hat/Fedora script that activates quotas is */etc/rc. sysinit*. This script is run by */etc/inittab* as the "System Initialization" script, and checks and activates scripts during each boot with the *quotacheck* and *quotaon* commands.

Debian and SUSE Linux start quotas in fairly standard scripts in the */etc/init.d* directory. SUSE uses the script *boot.quota*, and Debian uses *quota*. In either case, the responsible script runs the *quotacheck* and *quotaon* commands to manage quotas.

Quotas When Mounting

To configure quotas in Linux, you'll need to configure appropriate options in */etc/fstab*. Typically, quotas are configured on the partition mounted on the */home* directory. Fortunately, the process is the same for all our selected distributions.

For the purpose of this annoyance, I'm assuming that you've configured a separate partition for the */home* directory and want to regulate the space taken by users and groups on that partition. If */home* is not mounted on a separate partition, you can certainly configure quotas on the partition with the parent directory, such as the top-level root directory (*/*).

Typical Red Hat/Fedora directives in */etc/fstab* are slightly different from other distributions, in that standard mount directories are associated with the partition devices with a label. For example, the following line from a Red Hat Enterprise Linux 4 */etc/fstab* file associates the */home* directory with a partition so labeled.

```
LABEL=/home          /home          ext3          defaults          1 2
```

You can find the partition associated with a specific directory in */etc/mtab*.

Alternatively, many Red Hat/Fedora systems are configured with Logical Volumes. Unless specifically labeled, the associated devices are listed in */etc/fstab*, with a line similar to:

```
/dev/VolGroup00/LogVol00     /home          ext3          defaults          1 2
```

Normally, on Debian and SUSE Linux, each mounted partition is specifically defined by device, with a line similar to:

```
/dev/hda2      /home          ext3          defaults,errors=remount-ro      1 2
```

The errors=remount-ro directive supports remounting the partition in read-only mode if errors are detected.

Whatever the distribution, user and group quotas are configured as a mount option in */etc/fstab*. To understand how this works, you need to know the available mount options. Some of the more important options are shown in Table 10-1.

Table 10-1. Mount options in /etc/fstab

Option	Definition
async	Reads and writes data at different times (asynchronously)
auto	Searches through */etc/filesystems* for a compatible filesystem; contrast with noauto
defaults	Includes async, auto, dev, exec, nouser, suid, and rw
dev	Supports access to character devices such as terminals; supports block access to drives
errors	Specifies what is done if there is an error; a common setting is errors=remount-ro for remounting a partition as read-only
exec	Allows binaries; contrast with noexec
grpquota	Supports group-based quotas
remount	Remounts a currently mounted filesystem; often done with the *mount* command with different mount options
ro	Mounts read-only
rw	Mounts with read/write permissions
suid	Allows SUID or SGID permissions
sync	Supports reads and writes to disk at the same time
user	Allows regular users to mount this filesystem; common on filesystems such as CD/DVD drives
usrquota	Supports user-based quotas

To support quotas, you'll need to add the appropriate mount option. For example, if you want to add user and group quotas to the above mounts of the */home* directory, you'd modify those lines as shown here. For */home* partitions with a label, use:

```
LABEL=/home          /home          ext3     defaults,usrquota,grpquota    1 2
```

For */home* partitions mounted on a logical volume, use:

```
/dev/VolGroup00/LogVol00   /home   ext3     defaults,usrquota,grpquota    1 2
```

For */home* partitions mounted on a specific partition, use:

```
/dev/hda2  /home  ext3  defaults,errors=remount-ro,usrquota,grpquota    1 2
```

Once you've configured quotas (as I'll describe shortly) and modified the appropriate */etc/fstab* lines, you can force your system to reread the line with the following command:

```
mount -o remount /home
```

If you've implemented quotas on a different partition, substitute for */home* accordingly.

Quota Management Files

Before you can start configuring quotas, you'll need to create quota-management files in the associated directory. One method of doing so is with the *quotacheck* command. One command that I run is the following:

```
quotacheck -ugm /home
```

Note the use of the *-u*, *-g*, and *-m* switches:

- With the *-u* switch, *quotacheck* scans for user quotas. If quotas don't already exist, it adds the appropriate user quota file (*aquota.user* on Fedora/Red Hat and SUSE; *quota.user* on Debian).
- With the *-g* switch, *quotacheck* scans for group quotas. If quotas don't already exist, it adds the appropriate group quota file (*aquota.group* on Fedora/Red Hat and SUSE; *quota.group* on Debian).
- With the *-m* switch, *quotacheck* remounts the scanned filesystem.

User quotas are saved in the *aquota.user* or *quota.user* configuration file (depending on distribution and version), which is in binary format.

Quota Configuration Commands

Once you've installed the appropriate packages and configured quotas in */etc/fstab*, you can start configuring quotas for individuals and groups.

The standard method is with the *edquota* command: *edquota -u username* for users, and *edquota -g groupname* for groups.

 You can also use *setquota* to configure quotas for one or more users or groups. In my opinion, *edquota* does a better job helping someone visualize quota settings.

When I run the *eduquota -u columbia* command, I get some data that may look a bit strange, similar to what you see here:

```
Disk quotas for user columbia (uid 1014):
  Filesystem         blocks    soft    hard    inodes    soft    hard
  /dev/hda7           10920       0       0       401       0       0
```

What you actually see in a default 80×25 terminal reflects line wrapping. (If you're running a terminal in the GUI, you can remove the wrapping by increasing the width of the terminal.)

This data illustrates quotas for user *columbia* on a filesystem mounted on */dev/hda7*. You can make changes, as *edquota* opens the desired quota file in the vi editor. Quotas are based on hard and soft limits. If you expand the console, you'll be able to see the seven columns, as defined in Table 10-2.

Table 10-2. Quotas defined

Column	Description
Filesystem	Specifies the partition associated with this filesystem.
Blocks	Notes the number of blocks (1k) taken by the user/group.
Soft	The first Soft column specifies the space limit for the user/group.
Hard	The first Hard column specifies the absolute space limit for the user/group, during a grace period.
Inodes	Notes the number of inodes taken by the user/group; corresponds to the number of files.
Soft	The second Soft column specifies the maximum number of inodes for the user/group.
Hard	The second Hard column specifies the maximum number of inodes for the user/group, during a grace period.

Soft limits specify the space or inodes allocated on a permanent basis by user or group. If there's a grace period, hard limits can be set a bit higher. After the grace period expires, the user or group has to delete enough files to get back within the soft limits as configured. If the user does not take the responsibility to remove the extra space or inodes during the grace period, the account does not allow writes until the user has done so.

You can edit the quotas associated with a group. For example, for the special group created in the first annoyance in this chapter, you can edit its quotas with the following command:

```
edquota -g winos
```

You're taken to a configuration file similar to that shown earlier.

Quota Grace Periods

If you've set soft and hard limits for users and/or groups, you'll want to set a grace period. The standard is seven days, as you can see when you run the following command:

```
edquota -t
```

You can specify a different grace period for the amount of space (Block Grace Period) and number of files (Inode Grace Period).

On older Linux systems, there is one idiosyncrasy: the quota system doesn't work if you have a space in the grace period—e.g., a standard one-week grace period is 7days, not 7 days.

Applying Quotas to Others

Naturally, as a geek, you may need to apply quotas to multiple users. You could edit each user's quota individually, but that would be time-consuming. Alternatively, you can apply quotas to several users with the *edquota -up* command, which takes one user quota and applies it to the others in the list. For example, the following command takes the quota configured for user *columbia* and applies it to the users *napa*, *sonoma*, and *willamette*:

```
edquota -up columbia napa sonoma willamette
```

Quota Reports

Naturally, once you've configured quotas, you may want to check their status periodically, to make sure they are meeting the needs of you and your users. If you see lots of users nearing their quota limits, you may need more space. If you have a few users near their limits, you may wonder if they're storing appropriate information in their home directories and if they have legitimate needs.

Anyone can get a quota report for his own account. For example, as user *michael*, I can get my own quota report with the following command:

```
quota -v
```

Try this command on your own system. It should look familiar. It is a read-out of the quota, similar to what you edited earlier with the *edquota* command.

Naturally, you may want to get quota reports for multiple users; this can be done with *repquota -a*.

For more information on administering quotas, see *http://www.tldp.org/ HOWTO/Quota.html*.

Too Many Tasks, Too Few Qualified Administrators

Sometimes, as a Linux geek, there is too much to do. While you may have several folks who are helping you, they may not have all the skills you expect. They may be fresh out of school, may have qualified with some paper computer certification, or may be in transition from administering operating systems other than Linux.

Newer geeks often learn one service at a time. Once you trust their skills on a service, you set up administrative privileges on a per-command basis.

 In "Securing by User," at the end of this chapter, I'll show you how you can use Pluggable Authentication Modules (PAM) to support access to individual administrative tools.

You don't always have to log in as the *root* user to administer your systems. In this annoyance, I'll also show you how you can configure access to the *sudo* command from your regular account. Any command preceded by the word *sudo* causes the command to run with *root* privileges, just as if you had issued *su* first.

Even the best Linux geeks make mistakes. To minimize the effect of mistakes, many geeks disable logins to the *root* account. Even if *root* is not disabled, administrators are encouraged to run Linux as a regular user and to use the *sudo* command when running administrative commands.

Another advantage of *sudo* is that its use is automatically monitored by Linux. The actual logfile varies by distribution: Red Hat/Fedora uses */var/ log/secure*, SUSE uses */var/log/messages*, and Debian uses */var/log/auth.log*. By checking the appropriate file, you can monitor activity by your newer administrators, as well as anyone who might be trying to crack into your system.

A big advantage of *sudo* is that you don't have to distribute the *root* password as widely. When another administrator uses *sudo* to run an administrative command, she is prompted for her regular account password. She does not need to know the *root* administrative password for that server.

An annoyance associated with *sudo* is that the shell continues to interpret commands according to the regular user's PATH, not the PATH of the *root* account. This means that when you issue common system administration commands, such as *sudo ifconfig*, the shell complains with command not found messages. Either add the directories containing such commands (*/sbin* and */usr/sbin*) to the PATH of each administrator, or get used to issuing commands with full pathnames.

Some of the material in this annoyance is covered in more depth in *Linux Security Cookbook* by Daniel J. Barrett et al. (O'Reilly).

The Ubuntu Method

Ubuntu is one distribution quickly gaining popularity as a version of Linux that's great for the desktop. Part of its appeal is the way it controls access to the administrative account. The *root* account is disabled in */etc/shadow*, with the use of an asterisk in the second (password) column. Nobody can log in as *root*, or *su* to the *root* account (except with the *sudo su* command).

The proper way to run administrative commands in Ubuntu is with the *sudo* command. The defaults are unique in Ubuntu's */etc/sudoers* and are something you should consider on other distributions:

```
Defaults    !lecture,tty_tickets,!fqdn
```

As you should know, the "bang," represented by the exclamation point (!), reverses the intent of a function. The first directive (!lecture) disables the lecture function that warns regular users about administrative commands. tty_tickets requires separate password entries when *sudo* is run on different terminals. Finally, !fqdn disables any requirement for Fully Qualified Domain Names.

Full sudo Privileges

By default, regular users aren't allowed to use *sudo*. You need to specify the accounts of your administrators directly in */etc/sudoers*, or add them as a group. The *wheel* group is often available for this purpose. If security is not a big concern, you can even configure *sudo* to work from your regular account without passwords.

Adding a user to /etc/sudoers

The simplest approach to allow a trusted user to run administrative commands is to specify privileges for that user in the *etc/sudoers* file. The best way to edit this file is with the *visudo* command. It creates a lock file, which prevents multiple administrators from saving different changes to this file, even with other editors.

 It's possible to edit */etc/sudoers* from the regular administrative account with the editor of your choice. But there is no lock, and others can edit this file simultaneously. Only *visudo* creates a lock that prevents others from editing this file with any regular text editor in Linux. *visudo* doesn't require you to use the *vi* editor; as with many interactive commands, it checks your EDITOR environment variable, which you can set to emacs, nedit, or any other editor you prefer.

In our selected distributions, */etc/sudoers* includes the following subsection, which provides access to the *root* account:

```
#User privilege specification
root    ALL=(ALL) ALL
```

If you have a fully trusted user, (such as your regular account), you can add that user with the same privileges. To do so for myself, I add the following line:

```
michael    ALL=(ALL) ALL
```

With this line, as user *michael*, I no longer have to log in as *root* to run administrative commands. For example, I can run the following command to view the basic error log in */var/log/messages*:

```
sudo less /var/log/messages
```

The first time I run the *sudo* command from my regular account, I have to enter my account password. I also get a message, the "lecture" described in the sidebar, "The Ubuntu Method":

```
We trust you have received the usual lecture from the local System
Administrator. It usually boils down to two things:

    #1) Respect the privacy of others
    #2) Think before you type
```

If I run the *sudo* command again within the next five minutes, I don't have to re-enter the password.

If I'm a bit more paranoid about security, I might want users to enter their password *every time* they use *sudo* to run an administrative command. To do so, I include the Defaults timestamp_timeout = 0 directive in */etc/sudoers*.

If you want to limit user *michael*'s access a bit, you might substitute the following line in your */etc/sudoers*:

```
michael    rhel4=(printop) ALL
```

This directive limits user *michael*'s access to the computer named *rhel4*, as the user *printop*, but supports the use of *ALL* commands, subject to those limits. In other words, directives in */etc/sudoers* are in the following format:

```
localuser   host=(target_user) command
```

Securing with the wheel

If you have several users who need administrative privileges, you can configure them as part of the *wheel* group. *wheel* is a default group available in Red Hat/Fedora and SUSE Linux, and you can add the group yourself in Debian Linux. I've added a couple of users to my *wheel* group with the following steps:

1. I opened the */etc/group* file and navigated to the preconfigured *wheel* group, which is associated with GID 10 in Red Hat/Fedora and SUSE Linux; it looks similar to:

   ```
   wheel:x:10:
   ```

   If you're in Debian Linux, you'll need to create the *wheel* group yourself. As Debian's GID 10 is already assigned to the *uucp* user, you'll have to associate *wheel* with a different GID. (Remember, GIDs below 100 are reserved for services, and those above 100 are associated with regular users and groups.) Some judgment is required. You might want to select a high GID. In my case, GID 11 was available, and I added the following line:

   ```
   wheel:x:11:
   ```

2. I added the desired users to the *wheel* group. By definition, users in a group are defined in the fourth column of that group. The result will look similar to:

   ```
   wheel:x:11:nancy,randy
   ```

 You can also use GUI tools that assign users to groups, such as Fedora's *system-config-users*.

3. I saved the result. For distributions associated with the shadow password suite (where passwords are encrypted in the *root*-only */etc/shadow* file), you'll want to make sure your changes are reflected in the group shadow file, */etc/gshadow*. You can do so with the following command:

    ```
    grpconv
    ```

4. I opened the */etc/sudoers* file with the *visudo* command. If, as a regular user, you already have privileges in */etc/sudoers*, you can do so with the following command (otherwise, you'll have to log in as *root*):

    ```
    sudo /usr/sbin/visudo
    ```

5. I then configured the *wheel* group with appropriate privileges. In this case, I allowed the users in the *wheel* group to configure printers with the *lpc* command, by adding the following line to */etc/sudoers*.

    ```
    %wheel localhost=/usr/sbin/lpc
    ```

6. Once saved, I told my administrators that they can start using *lpc* to administer printers on this system, using *sudo*.

Let us analyze the last command line in */etc/sudoers* a bit. The example specified that members of the *wheel* group can run any switch or option associated with the *lpc* command. You can further limit access in */etc/sudoers* to particular options of particular commands. For example, if you wanted to let user *nancy* reboot her own computer, you could substitute the following line:

```
nancy ALL = (ALL) shutdown -r now
```

When you're so specific, the target user is prohibited from running the command with other switches. For example, while user *nancy* can now run the following command:

```
sudo /sbin/shutdown -r now
```

user *nancy* can't run variations on that command. For example, if she ran the following command to halt the computer:

```
sudo /sbin/shutdown -h now
```

she would get an error message to the effect that she's not allowed to run that command as *root* on the target computer.

You can just as easily substitute a different group for %wheel. Naturally, any group you specify, such as the *winos* group described earlier in this chapter, has to include the % in front of the group name—i.e., %winos.

With the localhost directive, members of the *wheel* group can run the *lpc* command only from a local command-line interface. For those members of the *wheel* group who want to administer printers from a remote workstation, they can log in remotely via *ssh*.

Configuring sudo without passwords

If you run administrative commands frequently, it's annoying to enter your password again and again, even though it's good on some distributions for several minutes after each *sudo* command you enter. If you're the main administrator, you should already know the *root* password. Alternatively, you could enter your regular account in the */etc/sudoers* configuration file and use your regular password.

However, if entering passwords becomes an annoyance, you can modify the privileges in */etc/sudoers* with a line such as the following:

```
michael    ALL=(ALL) NOPASSWD: ALL
```

In most cases, this is bad for security. With these settings, if someone ever gets access to your regular account, she'll have password-free access to all administrative commands.

If you leave your workstation and are still logged in to your regular account, anyone who sits down at your system has that same password-free access.

Aliases in sudoers

You may want to configure multiple users to administer using multiple commands. The directives can get complex. One way to keep things simple is to use aliases when you configure */etc/sudoers*. As with aliases in electronic mail, aliases in */etc/sudoers* let you cover an arbitrary collection of users by specifying one name.

As noted in the manpage for *sudoers*, aliases must start with an uppercase letter. If you want to define more than one alias on a line, you can do so by separating the lists with a colon.

Four types of aliases are available:

User_Alias
> If you don't want to bother with another group, you can use the User_ Alias directive to define a group of users, such as:
>
> ```
> User_Alias    Managers = cindy,linda,wendy : Teachers = mike,rick,cliff
> ```

Runas_Alias
> The Runas_Alias directive defines users with desired permissions. For example, if you've configured a Printer Administrator (*printadm*) and a Database Manager (*dbmgr*) with special permissions, you could config- ure a Runas_Alias to represent multiple users with a directive such as:
>
> ```
> Runas_Alias    PA = root,printadm
> Runas_Alias    DA = root,dbmgr
> ```

Host_Alias

When you configure a Host_Alias, you configure multiple computers with a single alias. For example, the following directive configures MAILERS as the Host_Alias for the hosts named *mail1*, *mail2*, and *mail3*.

```
Host_Alias   MAILERS = mail1,mail2,mail3
You could also configure a Host_Alias as a subnet, substituting 192.168.
0.0/24 for mail1,mail2,mail3.
```

Cmnd_Alias

If you want to configure multiple commands for a specific user, you can use the Cmnd_Alias to represent them. For example, the following directive configures PRTCMDS as representative of the *lpc* and *lprm* commands.

```
Cmnd_Alias   PRTCMDS = /usr/sbin/lpc,/usr/sbin/lprm
```

Managing sudoers

You can provide partial administrative privileges to the users of your choice. The standard Linux method is with appropriate settings in the */etc/sudoers* configuration file. Here I show you a couple more things that you can do with this file.

Authorizing password changes

One simple task for newer administrators is password management. People forget their passwords all the time. Resetting passwords is an annoyance that you can avoid if you have help.

Sometimes, you'll want to give supervisors or teachers access to the *passwd* command for their employees or students. As an example, assume that the employees in your group have the following user IDs: *drafter1* through *drafter9*, *engineer1* through *engineer9*, and *office1* through *office9*. First, you can configure the following User_Alias for your supervisors and employees:

```
User_Alias   Supers = cecile,michelle,erin,donna : Employees = drafter[1-
9],engineer[1-9],office[1-9]
```

Now you can add this directive to authorize password privileges for your *Supers* on all of your systems:

```
Supers   ALL = NOPASSWD: /usr/bin/passwd Employees
```

Now you can tell your supervisors that they can change employee passwords with the following command:

```
sudo passwd username
```

This assumes the username is one of those listed previously.

Disabling Root Logins

When you're working with a number of administrators, discipline is important. You need to discourage administrators from logging in as the *root* user. Less experienced administrators can accidentally erase whole systems when logged in as *root*.

Yes, administrators can make mistakes when using *sudo*. However, anyone who uses *sudo* should remember that she is administering a system and must take care with any associated commands.

The easiest way to disable direct access to the *root* account is to modify the login shell in the password configuration file, */etc/passwd*. On our selected distributions, the first line in the password configuration file is:

```
root:x:0:0:root:/root:/bin/bash
```

When I change this to:

```
root:*:0:0:root:/root:/bin/false
```

logins as *root* are now disabled. If you try logging in directly from the console, you're taken back to the login prompt. If you try logging in to the X Window as the *root* user, you're given a message to the effect that the account has been disabled. If you try logging in as a regular user and then try accessing the *root* account via the *su* command, you're taken back to your regular user prompt.

Then, the only way you can access *root* administrative commands is via *sudo*, and only if your account has appropriate privileges in the */etc/sudoers* configuration file.

 The one time where it may be best to log in as the *root* user is during the Red Hat certification exams. The tasks associated with these exams are all administrative and generally require *root* user permissions. When logged in as *root*, your PATH supports easier access to administrative commands. (For example, as *root*, you can run the *ifconfig* command without typing in the full path to the command.) The time you save by not having to enter a password or a full directory path can give you the extra few minutes that you need to pass the Red Hat exams.

Former Employees Keep Accessing the Server

As an administrator, you'll have to deal with employee turnover. You know how to add accounts for new employees. But when current employees leave the organization, there's more to do. You have to make sure important emails don't get lost, files are transferred to people who know what to do with them, and the account is deleted.

Naturally, employee situations can get more complex, such as when someone goes on medical leave or is transferred internally. What you do depends in part on your corporate policies, and may be affected by factors such as security clearances. Things can get more sensitive with employees who are leaving, voluntarily or otherwise.

Therefore, you want to be able to explain what you do clearly to nontechnical users. If there are other interested parties, such as the U.S. Department of Defense, you may have to demonstrate how your actions comply with their policies.

In addition, what you share from a user may be subject to privacy laws of your state, province, or country. For example, you may not be allowed to copy stored emails from one user to another. If there are conflicts, consult with your management.

When an Employee Leaves

When an employee leaves a company or organization for good, you'll have to take care of the following things:

- Delete or transfer the account.
- If the account is deleted, transfer the files to an appropriate user.
- If the account is transferred, change the account identity to make sure the former user can't access his old account.
- Make sure email is transferred and forwarded to an appropriate successor.

Whatever you do, you'll need to make sure that it's consistent with the policies of your company or organization.

It's best for your organization if you have advance notice of any pending layoffs or terminations. If you do, you can back up the files from the accounts of targeted users and disable access at appropriate times. Needless to say, this is a serious responsibility that assumes trust from your supervisors.

You need to know how to keep this kind of information confidential and secure. If you do not, your position may be at risk.

The steps I describe in this annoyance are just suggestions, which you may want to change depending on your corporate policies.

Transfer files and delete an account

Before you delete the account of any employee, you'll need to save that user's files. You need to make sure any files related to work are transferred to appropriate users. In other words, take the following steps:

1. Ask your managers to inform you of any pending employee moves.

2. Back up the files of any user who will soon leave the organization.

3. Deactivate the account of any user when she leaves, unless other arrangements have been made.

   One secure way to deactivate an account is to modify */etc/passwd* or, if you use shadow passwords, */etc/shadow*. Specifically, I change the password column for departing users to an asterisk (*) and the default shell to one where logins are not allowed, such as */bin/false*.

4. Scan the files of the user for viruses and worms. If they are using Microsoft Windows workstations, you'll have to use Microsoft tools. If they are using Linux or Unix workstations, there are open source alternatives, such as Clam AntiVirus (*http://www.clamav.net*).

5. Normally, management assigns the responsibilities of those who are leaving to others. Be prepared to transfer the datafiles from the home directories of the users who are leaving to those others.

   Do not just copy users' home directories to others, as that may overwrite settings associated with key applications such as the Firefox web browser. While such settings are normally stored in hidden directories (which start with a dot, such as *.mozilla*), defaults can be overridden. A more robust way to transfer files is to make copies to appropriate subdirectories.

6. Document what you do. When employees leave, people need to know what was done with their work. It's best if you can show what you've done in writing.

   Make sure your documentation complies with any company policies on the subject. Be aware of any requirements from third parties, such as the U.S. Department of Defense.

7. There are also files that the user may have left in other directories. For example, if you want a full list of files owned by user *columbia*, run the following command:

   ```
   find / -user columbia -print > columbiafiles.txt
   ```

8. If there are files that you've missed, you can transfer ownership to others with the following command. These users can then make a judgment on what files to save or delete:

   ```
   find / -user columbia -exec chown napa.napa "{}" \;
   ```

If you're working with a distribution where all users belong to the *users* group, change napa.napa to napa.users.

9. After all of these changes are made, you're ready to delete the departing user's account. For example, you can delete user *columbia*'s account and home directory with the following command:

```
userdel -r columbia
```

Transferring an account

Unless you want to dedicate a specific account to a job position, it's generally best to delete old accounts after appropriate files have been saved. I describe what you can do to transfer an account later in this annoyance.

Managing email

If an employee is leaving, you need to make sure that any business email is transferred to appropriate contacts. There are a couple of basic ways to arrange email forwarding. As they go beyond Linux, I'll describe them in general terms.

Use Email Managers

Domain-management tools may include the ability to forward emails from one address to another.

Use Email Services

If you're using sendmail or Postfix as your email service, you can configure */etc/aliases* to redirect email from one user to another. The process is straightforward; when you configure the system with the Email server, just add the email address of the old employee and the forwarding address to */etc/aliases*.

You may see options for domain forwarding in your email server, which forwards all emails associated with your domain to a different domain. This is generally not appropriate, unless your corporate identity is changing in some way.

When an Employee Leaves Temporarily

Employees may leave temporarily for many reasons. Some may leave to care for children or infirm relatives. Others may leave to go to school full-time. Still others may leave temporarily for medical reasons. If the leave is not too long, it makes sense to retain that user's account. You could disable it, and provide access to that user's home directory to others.

However, longer leaves suggest that user may be placed in a different job after his or her return. Others will have to take responsibilities for the person on leave. When the employee returns, it may make more sense to treat the person as a new employee, at least with respect to his user account.

The definition of a "temporary" leave is a matter of policy for your organization. If that policy is not already defined, you may use the guidelines described in this annoyance to help.

In this section, I assume that the leave is temporary and the user will return to his or her previous position. In that case, you should:

- Disable that user's account
- Provide temporary access to appropriate users
- Forward that user's email (see the previous subsection "Managing email")

Disabling an account

When you disable an account, you're disabling logins to that account. You do not change or delete any files or directories associated with that user's account, especially her home directory. As described earlier, the most straightforward way to disable access is to modify the password column in the */etc/passwd* or */etc/shadow* configuration files. I described this process earlier in this annoyance.

Provide access to appropriate users

While the user is on leave, others will need access to her files. Where possible, consult with that user and her management.

Linux certainly makes it easy for administrators to copy files from one user's home directory to another. But you don't want to transfer all files, unless you want to overwrite the defaults, bookmarks, and other defaults of the user who is taking the responsibilities of the user on leave.

When an Employee Is Transferred

Sometimes, all you need to do is transfer an account. Perhaps a supervisor has been promoted. Perhaps a materials buyer in the company has been replaced. If you've configured special groups for that user, it may be easier to transfer the account, rather than creating a new account and adding it as a member of the special group.

With these factors in mind, transferring an account involves different challenges. You're setting up the original user's files for a new job and configuring that account for her successor. I assume the employees who are moving have accounts on different servers, run by different administrators. To make the transfer, I suggest the following steps:

1. Back up the account owner's home directory.

2. Before the original account owner leaves, help her identify and move any files that she will need in her new position. She'll want to keep at least her emails and quite possibly default settings associated with her account, such as those in the ~/.mozilla directory, which govern the Firefox web browser.

   Naturally, this assumes that your company policies, or those who might monitor user accounts, such as suppliers or the U.S. Department of Defense, approve your procedures.

3. Identify any files that should stay in the current account. Naturally, you should keep at least those files associated with the current job. Depending on company and security policies, it may be acceptable to make copies for the user who is moving, as she may be helping her successor during any transition period.

4. Talk to the administrator associated with the employee's new location. Make arrangements to transfer at least those files identified in step 2 from the account owner's home directory.

5. Make arrangements to forward email. While filters can help, you'll have to rely at least in part on the transferred user to forward important messages back to the new owner of the account. Alternatively, you can create a filter on many email servers that forwards a copy of all messages to the new account owner.

6. Change the password and inform the new user of the account. Make sure the new user changes her password the first time she logs on to your system.

Securing by User

There are a number of services and tools that you can secure on a per-user basis. I divide them into two categories. Some services, such as FTP servers, are customizable on a per-user basis. Others may be secured based on user accounts.

Securing by Service

As there are a substantial number of Linux network services, I can only describe securing by service in general terms. I provide an example of securing by user on an Apache and an FTP server.

If you want to secure by user on a shared NFS directory, explore an earlier annoyance in this chapter, "The Boss Wants to Set Up a Special Group of Users." Once you set up a special group and directory, you can share the associated directory with other Linux/Unix systems on your network using NFS. Assuming you have a single database of users and groups, such as the LDAP or Microsoft database mentioned near the beginning of this chapter, the way you configure your special group applies to all systems.

Allowing user access on FTP

There are a variety of FTP services available. Many allow you to configure various forms of access, including:

- Anonymous-only, which limits access to the default FTP data directory
- Local user access, which allows users to log in to their accounts via FTP

Whatever FTP server you choose, be aware that FTP has a variety of security issues. Choose your FTP server carefully.

However, one reasonably secure solution is vsFTP. It is the default FTP server on Red Hat and Fedora distributions, and it is available for all major Linux distributions. For detailed information on vsFTP, see *http://vsftpd. beasts.org/*.

The vsFTP service is most commonly used for anonymous access. To see what you can do, open the associated configuration file (*/etc/vsftpd.conf* on SUSE and Debian; */etc/vsftpd/vsftpd.conf* on Red Hat/Fedora). Anonymous access is supported with the following directive; naturally, you can also disable anonymous access with this directive:

```
anonymous_enable=YES
```

The vsFTP service also supports access by local users. The key directive is:

```
local_enable=yes
```

If you want to prevent writes via FTP, you can reverse the following directive:

```
write_enable=yes
```

You can limit access to specific users. Naturally, you'll want to deny access to nonstandard users, including *root*, *bin*, *adm*, and *operator*. To do so, you'll want to make sure the following directive is set, which denies users in the list defined in */etc/vsftpd.user_list*:

```
userlist_deny=YES
```

With Pluggable Authentication Modules, the vsFTP server can also help you deny access to users as defined in */etc/pam.d/vsftpd*. This file points the system to another file that lists users to be denied access to the vsFTP server. Depending on the distribution, the default version of the file may be either */etc/vsftpd.ftpusers* or */etc/ftpusers*. (It changes from time to time; Fedora Core 5 will apparently use */etc/vsftpd/users_list*.)

Allowing user access on Apache

You can configure password-protected username access to the Apache web server to support file sharing for operating systems where more secure remote access services are not available.

 Any remote access is a security risk. Allowing remote access via Apache creates additional risks, as any cracker with a web browser and knowledge of a username and password can get onto your system. For more information, see Recipe 6.1 from *Apache Cookbook* by Ken Coar and Rich Bowen (O'Reilly).

If this level of risk is acceptable, you can cite your */etc/passwd* authentication file for usernames and passwords. As noted in the aforementioned *Apache Cookbook*, you could include */etc/passwd* as the authentication file, using the `AuthUserFile` directive:

```
<Directory "/home">
    AuthType Basic
    AuthName HomeDir
    AuthUserFile /etc/passwd
    Require valid-user
    Satisfy All
</Directory>
```

But that might be a bit too insecure. You could further limit access to computers on the local network; the following directives limit access to computers on the 192.168.0.0/24 private local network:

```
Order deny,allow
Deny from all
Allow from 192.168.0.
```

Yes, a cracker could spoof an IP address on a local network, but perhaps the information on your systems does not require such a high level of security.

Instead of referring to the *passwd* file, you can create your own authentication data for your web server. (Alternatively, you can configure a separate secure web site using the HTTPS protocol, but that's more work.) For example, if you include the following directives on a virtual host, you can limit access to the users of your choice:

```
<Directory "/www/docs/testwebsite.example.com>
    AuthType Basic
```

```
        AuthName "Members Only"
        AuthUserFile /www/docs/users
        Require user michael,donna
    </Directory>
```

Before this works, you'll have to use the *htpasswd* command to create a username and password database in the AuthUserFile. The first time you create a
web password, you'll have to run the *htpasswd -c* command. The following
example is consistent with the stanza for the *testwebsite.example.com* web
site:

```
    htpasswd -c /www/docs/users michael
```

You can add another user, to the same configuration file, without the *-c*
switch:

```
    htpasswd /www/docs/users donna
```

In either case, *htpasswd* prompts you for a password, which is encrypted in
the AuthUserFile you select.

Securing by Pluggable Authentication

Pluggable Authentication Modules (PAM) allow you to change how you
secure key administrative commands. PAM modules are stored in the */etc/
pam.d* directory. One interesting module is *su*, which regulates access to
other accounts. When used alone, it allows a regular user to log in to the
root account.

The *root* user is given full access to the *su* command with the following
directive:

```
    auth      sufficient     pam_rootok.so
```

In that way, the *root* user can log in as the user of his choice, without knowing that user's password. For example, as *root*, I can log in to user *michael*'s
account with the following command:

```
    su - michael
```

With other modules, you may want to limit access to regular users. For
example, you may want to limit access to Red Hat/Fedora configuration
tools. One method was already described earlier; you can limit by user via a
configuration file. The following directive in the */etc/pam.d/vsftpd* file points
to */etc/ftpusers* for a list of users to deny access to the vsFTP service.

```
    auth      required     pam_listfile.so item=user  sense=deny file=/etc/
    ftpusers
```

You can use the same type of directive to regulate access within other PAM
modules. For example, take the */usr/sbin/setup* utility in Red Hat/Fedora

Linux, which serves as a frontend to other text-based configuration modules. The associated PAM configuration file is straightforward:

```
auth       sufficient    pam_rootok.so
auth       required      pam_stack.so service=system-auth
account    required      pam_permit.so
session    required      pam_permit.so
```

These are straightforward modules, which provide unlimited access to the *root* user and require authentication through the *system-auth* module for other users, who must have a valid account and be logged in to a valid session.

Now assume you set up a */etc/ssh/sshallow* configuration file, with a list of users not allowed to log in to your Secure Shell server. If you add the following directive to */etc/pam.d/ssh*, the users listed in the */etc/ssh/sshallow* file are the only ones allowed to log in to the local server from a remote location:

```
auth required pam_listfile.so item=user sense=allow file=/etc/ssh/sshallow
onerr=fail
```

This is just one way you can regulate remote access by your administrators. Similar commands work well for other PAM-aware administrative commands and tools.

## CHAPTER 11

Administration Tips

For the final chapter, I'll describe some annoyances associated with computer administration. This chapter includes a number of topics (gateways, remote logins, logfile management, automated scripts) that don't quite fit with annoyances in other chapters. Perhaps the most important annoyance is the first, which deals with how every computer on a network downloads identical copies of the same updates, overloading your Internet connection.

Too Many Computers to Update over the Internet

If all you administer is one or two Linux computers, updates are a straightforward process. All you need to do is configure updates from the most appropriate mirror on the Internet. If desired, you can automate downloads and installations of updates using a cron job. For more information on how to configure updates from *yum* and *apt*-based mirrors, see Chapter 8.

However, when you administer a large number of Linux computers, the updates can easily overload standard high-speed Internet connections. For example, if you're downloading updates to the OpenOffice.org suite, you could be downloading hundreds of megabytes of packages. If you're downloading these packages on 100 computers simultaneously, that may be too much for your Internet connection, especially when other jobs are pending.

In this annoyance, I'll show you how you can create a local mirror of your favorite update server. You can then share the appropriate directory and configure your updates locally.

Where possible, I'll show you how you can limit what you mirror to updates. For example, Fedora Linux includes dedicated update directories. Most downloads are associated with updates, so it's appropriate to limit what you mirror to such packages.

One other approach is to download just the packages and create the repository systems yourself. For example, the *createrepo* command strips the headers from each RPM and configures a database that helps the *yum* command find the dependencies associated with every package.

I assume you have the hard disk space you need on your mirror server. Repositories can be very demanding with respect to disk space; be aware, if you're synchronizing repositories for multiple architectures and distributions, that downloaded mirrors can easily take up hundreds of gigabytes of space.

Available Mirror Tools

There are a number of ways to download the files associated with a mirror. The most common standard is based on the *rsync* command. With *rsync*, you can synchronize your mirrors as needed, downloading only those parts of those packages that are new or have otherwise changed. I'll show you how you can use *rsync* in this annoyance.

There are a number of other tools available. Naturally, you can use any FTP client to download mirrors to local directories. Commands such as *wget* and *curl* do an excellent job with large downloads. If you're working with an *apt* repository, the *apt-mirror* project provides another excellent alternative (*http://freshmeat.net/projects/apt-mirror/*).

Basic Steps

To create your mirror, you can take these steps, which I'll detail in the following subsections:

1. Find an appropriate update mirror, specifically the one that gives you the best performance for individual updates. Some trial and error may be required. While the best update mirror is usually geographically close to you, that may not always be the case.

2. Make room for the updates. Several gigabytes may be required, especially if you're making room for updates for multiple distributions and/or versions. You may even consider using a dedicated partition or drive.

3. Synchronize the mirror locally. The first time you download a mirror, you may be downloading gigabytes of data.

4. If required, make your local mirror usable through your preferred update system.

5. Test a local update after you've downloaded a mirror to make sure it works.

6. Automate the synchronization process.

7. Point your clients to the local mirror.

Find the Best Update Mirror

The best update mirror may not be the one that is physically closest to your network. Some mirrors have faster connections to the Internet. Others have less traffic. Some mirror administrators may discourage full mirror downloads or even limit the number of simultaneous connections. And many public mirrors don't support *rsync* connections.

Red Hat Enterprise Linux Updates

As updates for Red Hat Enterprise Linux (RHEL) are closely controlled, there are no authorized public mirrors available. However, if you've paid for RHEL subscriptions for enough workstations or desktops, Red Hat may allow you to configure a *proxy server* or a *satellite server* to distribute updates from your local network. These servers ensure that updates are applied only to subscribed systems.

Alternatively, you could use the *yum* package to create your own update repositories. The so-called "rebuild" distributions, such as CentOS (*http://www.caosity.org*) and WhiteBox Linux (*http://www.whiteboxlinux.org*), use *yum* to power their updates. You can use their *yum* package and associated configurations on your *subscribed* RHEL systems, and update your other RHEL systems from that repository, which saves you the trouble of learning how to configure the RHEL Proxy Server or Satellite Servers. (Naturally, non-RHEL packages such as *yum* and *createrepo* are not supported by Red Hat.)

Our selected distributions have "official" lists of update mirrors. More may be available. If a mirror includes a Fedora repository, it may also include a SUSE repository. For example, while the University of Mississippi is not (currently) on the official list of mirrors for SUSE Linux, updates are available from its server at *http://mirror.phy.olemiss.edu/mirror/suse/suse/*. Here's where to find the "official" list of mirrors for our selected distributions:

Fedora Core Linux
   http://fedora.redhat.com/download/mirrors.html includes a list of mirrors accessible through the *rsync* protocol; don't limit yourself to those specified, as others may also work with *rsync*.

SUSE Linux

Official mirrors of the open source SUSE distribution can be found at *http://en.opensuse.org/Mirrors_Released_Version*. Trial and error is required to find *rsync*-capable mirrors.

Debian Linux

Official Debian mirrors can be found at *http://www.debian.org/mirror/list*. Many support a limited number of architectures. Trial and error is required to find *rsync*-capable mirrors.

To see if a mirror works with the *rsync* protocol, run the *rsync* command with the URL in question. For example, if you want to check the mirror specified in the Debian Mirror List from the University of Southern California, run the following command (and don't forget the double colon at the end):

```
rsync mirrors.usc.edu::
```

When I ran this command, I saw a long list of directories, clearly associated with various Linux distributions, including SUSE, Fedora, and others. If there is no *rsync* server at your desired site, the *rsync* command will time out, or you'll have to press Ctrl-C to return to the command line.

Finding the best update mirror is somewhat subjective. Yes, you could go by objective measures, such as the time required for the download. But conditions change. Internet traffic can slow down in certain geographic areas. Servers do go down. Some trial and error may be required.

 Fedora had implemented an *"apt-get mirror select"* for *apt*-based repositories. But Fedora is moving away from the *apt* commands, and Red Hat developers are working on plug-ins for *yum* that function in the same way.

Make Room for the Updates

Updates can consume gigabytes of space. The choices you make can make a significant difference in the space you need. Key factors include:

Architectures

Every architecture that you maintain locally can multiply the space you need. For example, if you're rolling out both 64-bit and 32-bit workstations, you'll need at least double the space.

Distributions

If you're maintaining mirrors for more than one distribution, your space requirements increase accordingly.

Distribution Versions

If you're maintaining mirrors for more than one version of a distribution (such as for Fedora Core 4 and 5), your space requirements can multiply.

Installation Files

Many administrators find it convenient to include a copy of the installation trees in the update repository partition. This increases the space required by the size of the installation CDs/DVDs.

You may want to create a dedicated partition for your update repositories. That way, you can be sure that the space required by the repository does not crowd out the rest of your system.

 If you're configuring mirrors for 64-bit Linux RPM-based distributions, focus on *yum*. The *apt* tools currently have trouble with repositories that mix 32-bit and 64-bit packages, as is currently required for a number of applications. I know of no similar problems for Debian distributions.

Synchronize the Mirror

Along with perhaps most of the world of Linux, I like the *rsync* command. With appropriate switches, it's easy to use this command to copy the files and directories that you want. Once you've set up a mirror, you can use the *rsync* command as needed to keep your local mirror up-to-date.

The *rsync* command is straightforward; I use it to back up the home directory from my laptop computer with the following command:

```
rsync -a -e ssh michael@laptop.example.com:/home/michael/* /backup
```

 If you've set the environment variable ENV_RSYNC=ssh, you don't need the *-e ssh* option. For more information on *rsync*, see the "I'm Afraid of Losing Data" annoyance in Chapter 2.

In the following subsections, I illustrate some simple examples of how you can create your own *rsync* mirror on our selected distributions. This assumes you're using an appropriate directory, possibly configured on a separate disk or partition.

Synchronizing a Fedora mirror

For this exercise, assume you want to synchronize your local update mirror with the one available from *kernel.org*. The entry in the list of Fedora mirrors is a little deceiving. When you see the following:

rsync://mirrors.kernel.org/fedora/core/

You'll need to run the following command to confirm that *rsync* works on that server, as well as to view the available directories (don't forget the trailing forward slash):

```
rsync mirrors.kernel.org::fedora/core/
```

When I ran this command, I saw the result shown here:

```
MOTD:    Welcome to the Linux Kernel Archive.
MOTD:
MOTD:    Due to U.S. Exports Regulations, all cryptographic software on this
MOTD:    site is subject to the following legal notice:
MOTD:
MOTD:    This site includes publicly available encryption source code
MOTD:    which, together with object code resulting from the compiling of
MOTD:    publicly available source code, may be exported from the United
MOTD:    States under License Exception "TSU" pursuant to 15 C.F.R. Section
MOTD:    740.13(e).
MOTD:
MOTD:    This legal notice applies to cryptographic software only.
MOTD:    Please see the Bureau of Industry and Security,
MOTD:    http://www.bis.doc.gov/ for more information about current
MOTD:    U.S. regulations.
MOTD:

drwxr-xr-x        4096 2005/06/09 09:40:43 .
drwxr-xr-x        4096 2004/03/01 08:39:30 1
drwxr-xr-x        4096 2004/05/14 04:18:24 2
drwxr-xr-x        4096 2004/11/03 15:00:14 3
drwxr-xr-x        4096 2005/06/09 09:41:47 4
drwxrwsr-x        4096 2005/12/16 23:49:44 development
drwxr-xr-x        4096 2005/11/22 06:14:23 test
drwxrwsr-x        4096 2005/06/07 08:29:19 updates
[michael@FedoraCore4 rhn]$
```

Naturally, Fedora Core production releases (which should also be available on the installation CDs/DVDs) are associated with the numbered directories. But the focus in this annoyance is on updates, which is the last directory listed on the server. Hopefully, this directory includes updates divided by Fedora Core releases.

To make sure this server includes the updates I need, I ran the following command:

```
rsync mirrors.kernel.org::fedora/core/updates/
```

I continued the process until I confirmed that this server included the update RPMs that I wanted to mirror. I wanted to create an Apache-based repository, so I mirrored the RPMs to the */var/www/html/yum/Fedora/Core/ updates/4/i386* directory.

By default, the DocumentRoot associated with the default Fedora Apache configuration points to the */var/www/html* directory; if I configure a local Apache server, I can use the *Fedora/Core/updates/4/* subdirectory.

Then, to synchronize the local and remote update directories, I ran the following command:

```
rsync -a mirrors.kernel.org::fedora/core/updates/4/i386/. \
/var/www/html/yum/Fedora/Core/updates/4/i386
```

Synchronizing a SUSE mirror

Because the SUSE list of mirrors doesn't specify which are *rsync* servers, some trial and error is required. For this exercise, I attempted to synchronize my local update mirror with that available from the University of Utah. The listing that I saw in the SUSE mirror list as of this writing was:

suse.cs.utah.edu/pub/

I tried the following command, which led to an error message:

```
rsync suse.cs.utah.edu::pub/
@ERROR: Unknown module 'pub'
rsync: connection unexpectedly closed (0 bytes received so far) [receiver]
rsync error: error in rsync protocol data stream (code 12) at io.c(359)
```

So I tried the top-level directory and found the SUSE repositories at the top of the list:

```
rsync suse.cs.utah.edu::
suse            The full /pub/suse directory from ftp.suse.com.
people          The full /pub/people directory from ftp.suse.com.
projects        The full /pub/projects directory from ftp.suse.com.
```

And, with a little browsing, as described in the previous section, I found the SUSE update directories with the following command:

```
rsync suse.cs.utah.edu::suse/i386/update/10.0/
```

I wanted to download updates associated with SUSE 10.0 to the following directory:

```
/var/lib/YaST2/you/mnt/i386/update/10.0/
```

I could run the following command to synchronize all updates from the update directory at the University of Utah (the *-v* uses verbose mode, and the *-z* compresses the transferred data):

```
rsync -avz suse.cs.utah.edu::suse/i386/update/10.0/. \
/var/lib/YaST2/you/mnt/i386/update/10.0/
```

But that might transfer more than you need. If you explore a bit further, you'll find source packages as well as packages built for 64-bit and PPC CPU systems. If you have only 32-bit workstations, you don't need all this extra data. You can use the *--exclude* switch to avoid transferring these packages:

```
rsync -avz --exclude=*.src.rpm --exclude=*.ppc --exclude=*x86_64* \ suse.cs.
utah.edu::suse/i386/update/10.0/. \
/var/lib/YaST2/you/mnt/i386/update/10.0/
```

Synchronizing a Debian mirror

Debian mirrors are somewhat different. Besides the different package format, Debian mirrors do not include any separate update servers. Therefore, if you want to mirror a Debian update server, you'll have to install all the packages in the server (except any that you specifically exclude).

Because the Debian list of mirrors does not specify *rsync* servers, some trial and error may be required. For this exercise, I wanted to synchronize my local update mirror with that available from the University of California at Berkeley. The listing that I saw from this mirror was:

```
rsync linux.csua.berkeley.edu::
debian
debian-non-US
debian-cd
```

In other words, this revealed the directories associated with Debian CDs as well as non-U.S. packages. For now, I assume that you want to mirror the regular Debian repositories. I found them with the following command:

```
rsync linux.csua.berkeley.edu::debian/dists/Debian3.1r0/main/
```

But as you can see from the output shown below, there are a number of directories full of packages that you may not need, unless you want to include the installers, as well as the binary packages associated with the full Debian range of architectures:

```
drwxr-sr-x       4096 2005/06/04 10:20:54 .
drwxr-sr-x       4096 2005/12/17 00:33:29 binary-alpha
drwxr-sr-x       4096 2005/12/17 00:39:50 binary-arm
drwxr-sr-x       4096 2005/12/17 00:48:56 binary-hppa
drwxr-sr-x       4096 2005/12/17 00:55:50 binary-i386
drwxr-sr-x       4096 2005/12/17 01:01:22 binary-ia64
drwxr-sr-x       4096 2005/12/17 01:07:29 binary-m68k
drwxr-sr-x       4096 2005/12/17 01:15:06 binary-mips
drwxr-sr-x       4096 2005/12/17 01:23:07 binary-mipsel
drwxr-sr-x       4096 2005/12/17 01:29:11 binary-powerpc
drwxr-sr-x       4096 2005/12/17 01:35:33 binary-s390
drwxr-sr-x       4096 2005/12/17 01:41:44 binary-sparc
drwxr-sr-x       4096 2004/01/04 11:47:29 debian-installer
drwxr-sr-x       4096 2005/03/24 00:22:16 installer-alpha
```

```
drwxr-sr-x      4096 2005/03/24 00:22:16 installer-arm
drwxr-sr-x      4096 2005/03/24 00:22:17 installer-hppa
drwxr-sr-x      4096 2005/03/24 00:22:17 installer-i386
drwxr-sr-x      4096 2005/03/24 00:22:17 installer-ia64
drwxr-sr-x      4096 2005/03/24 00:22:17 installer-m68k
drwxr-sr-x      4096 2005/03/24 00:22:17 installer-mips
drwxr-sr-x      4096 2005/03/24 00:22:17 installer-mipsel
drwxr-sr-x      4096 2005/03/24 00:22:17 installer-powerpc
drwxr-sr-x      4096 2005/03/24 00:22:17 installer-s390
drwxr-sr-x      4096 2005/03/24 00:22:17 installer-sparc
drwxr-sr-x      4096 2005/12/17 01:45:08 source
drwxr-sr-x      4096 2005/06/04 11:40:37 upgrade-kernel
```

To download just the directories that you need, you can go into the appropriate subdirectory, or you can make extensive use of the *--exclude* switch. Debian recommends the latter. For example, if all of your workstations include Intel Itanium CPUs, you can run a command that excludes all files and directories not associated with the IA64 architecture. Debian recommends that you include the *--recursive*, *--times*, *--links*, *--hard-links*, and *--delete* switches, too. The basic steps to creating your mirror are:

- Recursively download and synchronize files from all subdirectories
- Preserve the date and time associated with each file
- Re-create any existing symlinks
- Include any hard-linked files
- Delete any files that no longer exist on the mirror

If I wanted to limit the downloads to the *ia64* directory, I would include the following switches:

```
rsync -avz --recursive --times --links --hard-links --delete
--exclude binary-alpha/ --exclude *_alpha.deb
--exclude binary-arm/ --exclude *_arm.deb
--exclude binary-hppa/ --exclude *_hppa.deb
--exclude binary-i386/ --exclude *_i386.deb
--exclude binary-m68k/ --exclude *_m68k.deb
--exclude binary-mips/ --exclude *_mips.deb
--exclude binary-mipsel/ --exclude *_mipsel.deb
--exclude binary-powerpc/ --exclude *_powerpc.deb
--exclude binary-s390/ --exclude *_s390.deb
--exclude binary-sparc/ --exclude *_sparc.deb
```

But things are beginning to get complicated. Debian provides a script that can help. All you'll need to do before running the script is to specify a few directives, including the *rsync* server, directory, and architectures to exclude. To see the script, navigate to *http://www.debian.org/mirror/anonftpsync*. For additional discussion of this *rsync* script, see *http://www.debian.org/mirror/ftpmirror*.

Making Your Mirror Work with Your Update System

Now that you have a local mirror of Linux updates, you'll need to make sure it's usable through your update system. For our selected distributions, I'm assuming that you're using *yum* for Fedora, *apt* for Debian, or YaST for SUSE Linux. This step involves creating the database that your packaging system consults on each host to know what it's already updated and to stay in sync.

I also assume that you've shared the update directory using a standard sharing service, such as FTP, HTTP, or NFS. I've described the basic methods associated with *yum* and *apt* updates in Chapter 8. If you're connecting to a shared NFS directory, substitute *file:///* (with three forward slashes) for *http://* or *ftp://*.

Generally, when you use *rsync* to copy and synchronize to local mirrors, you've also downloaded the directories that support the *apt* or *yum* databases.

Creating apt repository database files

If you're using *apt* for updates, such as for Debian Linux, you may already have the key database files: *Packages.gz* for regular binary packages and *Sources.gz* for source packages. Based on the Debian mirror described earlier, you can find these files in the following directories:

```
linux.csua.berkeley.edu/debian/dists/Debian3.1r0/main/binary-i386/
linux.csua.berkeley.edu/debian/dists/Debian3.1r0/main/source/
```

If you need to create your own versions of these database files, navigate to the directory with the binary packages and run the following command:

```
dpkg-scanpackages . /dev/null | gzip -9c > Packages.gz
```

And for the database of source packages, navigate to the directory with those packages and run the following command:

```
dpkg-scansources . /dev/null | gzip -9c > Sources.gz
```

For more information on this process, see *http://www.interq.or.jp/libra/oohara/apt-gettable/*.

Creating yum repository database files

There are two ways to create a *yum* repository database. Through Fedora Core 3, the standard was the *yum-arch* command, which is included in the *yum* RPM. Since that time, the standard has become the *createrepo* command, based on a package of the same name. For the older Fedora distributions (as well as the rebuild distributions of Red Hat Enterprise Linux 3 and

4, which use *yum* for updates), you can create your own *yum* repository database by navigating to the package directory and running the following command:

```
yum-arch .
```

As *yum* "digests" the package headers, it collects them in a *headers/* subdirectory.

For later Fedora distributions, assuming the packages are in the directory described earlier for Fedora updates, you'd run the following command:

```
createrepo /var/www/html/yum/Fedora/Core/updates/4/i386
```

This command creates an XML database in the *repodata/* subdirectory. If your mirror process already copied either of these directories, you don't need to create it.

Test a Local Update

Now you'll want to test a local update. I described some of the update systems in Chapter 8. To summarize, for any of our three distributions, you'll need to make some configuration changes to point the package manager to the update server you created on your local network:

Updating yum for Fedora
 If you're updating *yum* for Fedora, you'll want to update the appropriate configuration files in the */etc/yum.repos.d* directory. If your local mirror consists of Fedora updates, the file is *fedora-updates.repo*. For example, if you've shared the directory described in the previous section via NFS and have mounted the appropriate directory, you would substitute the following for the default *baseurl* directive:

```
baseurl=file:/var/www/html/yum/Fedora/Core/updates/4/i386/
```

Updating YaST for SUSE
 If you're updating YaST for SUSE Linux, you'll need to point the update server to the shared local directory. In the appropriate YaST menu, you can configure a connection to any of several servers, including FTP, HTTP, or NFS servers from the local network. For example, if I've created an FTP server that points to the SUSE repository directory created earlier, I'd select FTP, cite the name of the server, and point to the following directory on that server: */var/lib/YaST2/you/mnt/i386/update/10.0/*

Updating apt for Debian
 If you're updating apt for Debian Linux, you'll want to update the appropriate URLs configured in */etc/apt/sources.list*. For example, if you've mirrored a repository for Debian Sarge and created an HTTP

server on your local network, on a computer named *debianrep*, in the web server's */repo* subdirectory, you'd add the following line to each clients' *sources.list* file:

```
deb http://debianrep/repo sarge main
```

Once you change the appropriate configuration file, you can test updates from the local server that you created.

Automate the Synchronization Process

When you're satisfied that the local update server meets your needs, you'll want to automate the synchronization process. To do so, insert the *rsync* command(s) that you used in a cron job file. If you had to create *yum* or *apt* database files, you'll want to add those commands described earlier to the cron job.

Even after the first time you create a mirror, the downloads for updates can be extensive. For example, updates to the OpenOffice.org suite alone can occupy several hundred megabytes.

Therefore, you'll want to schedule the cron job for a time when few or no other jobs are running. And that depends on the schedule of other cron jobs, as well as any other jobs (such as database processing) that may happen during off-hours.

Connecting Local Workstations

Once you've tested your local mirror, and then configured regular updates to that mirror, you're ready to connect your local workstations to it. You'll need to modify the same files as described earlier in the "Test a Local Update" section.

If you want to configure automatic updates on your workstations from your local repositories, you'll need to configure cron jobs on each host.

 Remember, updates always carry some degree of risk. But when you update the system with the local repository, you're testing at least some of the updates. You have to decide if you want to do more testing or allow automatic updates to the production systems on your network. You can always create a script to log in to and update each of the production systems when you're ready.

Some distributions support GUI configuration of automated updates; SUSE supports it directly via YaST (which is saved to */etc/cron.d/yast2-online-update*).

If you've installed the latest version of *yum* on Fedora Core, there's a cron job already configured in */etc/cron.daily/yum.cron*. To let it run, you'll need to activate the *yum* service in the */etc/init.d* directory.

Creating an update script is a straightforward process, with the following general steps:

1. Create a cron job in the appropriate directory. If you want a weekly update, add it to */etc/cron.weekly*.

2. Make sure the script checks for the latest version of the update-management command. For example, if you're updating with *apt*, make sure it's up-to-date with the following command:

       apt-get install apt

   I use *apt-get install* and not *apt-get upgrade*, so I don't have to worry about pending updates to other packages. If the package is already installed, it is automatically upgraded.

3. If you're running *apt*, you'll need to make sure the local cache of packages is up-to-date:

       apt-get update

4. Finally, apply the update command that you need, such as the following:

       apt-get dist-upgrade

My Favorite Service Is Not Included with My Distribution

As distributions evolve, developers make changes. Sometimes, the developers behind a distribution choose to drop services. Sometimes the service that you're most comfortable with was never built for your distribution. Sometimes people convert from distributions or allied systems, such as HP-UX or Sun Solaris, where different services are available. In any of these situations, you'll have to look beyond the distribution repositories to install the service you want.

For example, while the WU-FTP server is the default on Sun Solaris 10, it has been dropped from Red Hat and Fedora distributions. It isn't even available in the Fedora Extras repository. Nevertheless, if a company is converting from Solaris to Red Hat Linux, the administrators would naturally look to install WU-FTP on Red Hat Enterprise Linux. (In my opinion, that would be a mistake, but we'll explore that issue in more detail in this annoyance.)

Check the Home Page for the Service

The developers behind your favorite service may have built what you want for your distribution. If they have, that is your best option, as it ensures that:

- Configuration files are installed in appropriate locations.
- The package becomes part of your database.
- The developers are motivated to help you if there are distribution-specific problems.

If the developers behind a service have built their software, and have customized a package for a specific distribution, they have an interest in making sure that it works on that distribution.

However, if the service is not built for your distribution, don't immediately try building or compiling the service from its source code. While that might be your best option (especially if you're customizing the service), I believe there are alternatives that should be explored first.

Explore Alternative Services

One of the joys associated with open source software is choice. Rarely is there only one option for a service. For example, there are a wide variety of FTP servers that you can install on Linux systems. They include ProFTP, vsFTP, Muddleftp, glFTP, Pure-FTP, and WU-FTP. I've left out a few, including those built on Java.

But if it's a major service, your distribution should have at least one natively configured option for that service. For example, Red Hat Enterprise Linux includes vsFTP as the only FTP server. That's quite an expression of faith from the leading Linux distribution, enough to make many geeks take a closer look at vsFTP.

You can also explore alternative software for your service. You may be able to find alternatives in the Linux application libraries, described in "So Many Options for Applications" in Chapter 4. You may be able to find other options in third party repositories described in the next section. You may also be able to find alternatives online, perhaps with a search through Wikipedia (*http://www.wikipedia.org*) or Google.

In other words, if you find that your preferred server software is not available for your distribution, you should look for alternatives. That means:

- Trying the software provided by your distribution for the service
- Looking for alternatives from third parties who may have built similar software for the desired service
- Examining other alternatives that can be installed on your system

Look for a Third Party Who Has Built the Package for Your Distribution

If you can't find the software you want included with your distribution, you can look to third parties to help. These developers generally take the source code from original developers and build appropriate RPM or DEB packages suitable for the distribution of your choice.

There are a number of third-party repositories available for Linux distributions. They generally include software not available from the main repositories. For example, in the "I Need a Movie Viewer" annoyance in Chapter 4, I described some third-party repositories that included the *libdvdcss* package needed to view commercial DVDs.

The drawback of a third-party repository is that its packages may not be fully tested, especially with respect to the libraries that you might install on your distribution. In fact, there are reports of geeks who have run into incompatible libraries when they use more than one third-party repository.

You can get direct access to a third-party repository through your update software. Specifically, you can point *yum*, *apt*, and YaST systems directly to the appropriate URLs for the third-party repositories of your choice.

Generally, third-party repositories include instructions on how to include them in your update software and/or configuration files. For our preferred distributions, you can find a list of third-party repositories in the following locations.

Red Hat/Fedora
> Individuals within the Fedora project help integrate connections with a number of third-party repositories. While the focus is on Fedora Core, most of these repositories include separate URLs you can use for Red Hat Enterprise Linux (as well as rebuild distributions based on Red Hat Enterprise Linux source code). Instructions are usually available on the web page for each third-party repository. As of this writing, the status for the major Fedora repositories can be found online at *http:// fedoranews.org*.

SUSE Linux Professional
> SUSE has traditionally included a lot of extra software with its DVDs. And more is available from third parties. Several are listed for your information at *http://en.opensuse.org/YaST_package_repository*. You can include them as an installation source in YaST. However, SUSE warns that "YaST fully trusts installation sources and does not perform any kind of authenticity verification on the contained packages." In other words, SUSE's third-party repositories might not include a GPG key, as you see with Fedora's repositories.

Many third-party repositories for SUSE distributions do have GPG keys. One central location for many of these repositories can be found at *ftp://ftp.gwdg.de/pub/linux/misc/apt4rpm/rpmkeys*.

Debian Linux

The repositories associated with Debian Linux are extensive, which is natural for a community-based distribution. Be careful with the list at *http://www.apt-get.org/main/*; many of the repositories are dedicated to specific versions of Debian such as Potato, which has been obsolete since 2002.

By their very nature, these lists of third-party repositories may not be complete. And as the developers behind these repositories may not coordinate their efforts, including more than one third-party repository on your Linux system may lead to unpredictable results.

Try Installing the Older Package

If a package used to be built for your distribution, it may still work for the newer version. For example, if you absolutely need the WU-FTP server on Red Hat Enterprise Linux (RHEL) 4, there are ways to get old versions.

For the purpose of this annoyance, I installed the latest available version of WU-FTP built for Red Hat. It's available from the Fedora Legacy project, at *http://fedoralegacy.org*, from the updates repository associated with Red Hat Linux 7.3. When I tried to install it on RHEL 4, I got a message suggesting that I install the Open SSL toolkit, which addresses the security vulnerabilities associated with WU-FTP, at least as of its release in 2004.

Because of the security issues associated with it, I do not recommend WU-FTP. However, it may be helpful in a transition from a different operating system where WU-FTP is the default, such as Solaris. The security issues can be managed behind firewalls until your transition is complete.

Once the appropriate packages were installed, I was able to get WU-FTP running on RHEL 4. While using old versions is not recommended as a general solution, the installation of familiar software and services can ease transitions, even for organizations moving just from one version of Linux (or Unix) to another.

Install from Source Package, if Available in the Appropriate Format

In some cases, the appropriate service is available as a source code package, customized for the desired distribution. This option is most common for the "rebuild" distributions associated with RHEL.

For RHEL, Red Hat complies with the GNU General Public License by releasing its source code. As Red Hat has released the source code in Source RPM packages, you can try to install those packages on any RPM-based distribution. These packages are publicly available from Red Hat at *ftp.redhat.com*, in the *pub/redhat/linux/enterprise/4/en/os/i386/SRPMS/* subdirectory.

If you're running RHEL Workstation, you don't have the server packages included with the RHEL Server distributions. One example is the vsFTP server. It goes almost without saying that if you install a package available only on RHEL Server on a RHEL Workstation, you should not expect support for that package from Red Hat. I've downloaded the RHEL 4 Source RPM for the vsFTP server on my RHEL Workstation. Once downloaded, I can install it using the following steps:

1. Run the following command to unpack the source code from the vsFTP server to the */usr/src/redhat* directory:

   ```
   rpm -ivh vsftpd-2.0.1-5.src.rpm
   ```

   The source code is unpacked to a *.spec* file in the */usr/src/redhat/SPECS* directory, as well as various source and patch files in the */usr/src/redhat/SOURCES* directory.

2. Navigate to the directory containing the *.spec* file.

3. Build the binary RPM (as well as source information) with the following command:

   ```
   rpmbuild -bb vsftpd.spec
   ```

   In this particular case, the *.spec* file creates two binary RPMs and stores them in the */usr/src/redhat/RPMS/i386* directory.

4. Install the binary RPMs just like any other Red Hat RPMs.

This process doesn't always work. As different tools are used by the rebuild distributions, you generally can't use the kernel source code released by Red Hat on a RHEL rebuild distribution, as they have been built by different teams of developers, using different tools.

Install from a Tarball

You can always install a Linux service (or any other Linux software) from the original source code. Generally, it's available only as a compressed *tar* archive. Once you download the archive, you'll want to decompress it. The command you use depends on the compression format, which is normally associated with the archive extension. For example, if the archive has a *.tar. gz* or *.tgz* extension, such as *archive.tar.gz*, you can decompress it with the following command:

```
tar xzvf archive.tar.gz
```

Alternatively, archives with a *.tar.bz* or *.tar.bz2* extension can be decompressed with the *tar xjvf* command. Normally, archived files packaged for a service are decompressed to a separate subdirectory, with the name of the archive.

The methods for installing from source code vary widely. Detailed instructions are normally made available in a text file in the decompressed archive.

Configuring a Linux Gateway

One popular use for Linux is as a gateway between networks. The software associated with the gateway is fairly simple. In fact, it can be loaded from permanent media, such as a CD. That technique prevents crackers from breaking into the gateway and thus breaking the security barrier, or firewall, commonly configured between networks.

Configuring a Linux gateway normally requires three basic administrative steps:

- Configuring your system to forward IP traffic.
- Setting up masquerading.
- Creating a firewall between networks.

The only thing you absolutely need to do is configure IP forwarding. It is disabled by default. For this annoyance, I assume you're configuring a computer with two network cards, and each card is connected to a different network.

There are many excellent firewall configuration tools, but this annoyance shows you how to configure the system by hand. If you use the tools, you'll overwrite the configuration files that you may create as you review this annoyance.

IP Forwarding

Linux normally disables IP forwarding between network cards, and it is disabled in the default configurations of our preferred distributions. The way you activate IP forwarding depends on whether you've configured an IPv4 or IPv6 network.

Here, I assume that your system supports the */proc* filesystem with kernel settings, along with the *sysctl* program to access kernel switches. Your system meets these requirements if you have a */proc* directory and an */etc/sysctl. conf* file.

If there are problems, you'll want to make sure the appropriate settings are active in your kernel. Specifically, you should see the following settings in the active *config-** file in the */boot* directory:

```
CONFIG_PROC_FS=y
CONFIG_SYSCTL=y
```

If these settings don't reflect what you need, you can't just edit this configuration file. In that case, you'll need to recompile the kernel, as described in the "Recompiling the Kernel" annoyance in Chapter 7.

Forwarding on an IPv4 network

To activate forwarding on an IPv4 network, you'll need to toggle the ip_ forward setting in the appropriate kernel configuration directory. The simplest way to do so is with the following command:

```
echo "1" > /proc/sys/net/ipv4/ip_forward
```

To make sure forwarding is turned on the next time you boot your computer, open */etc/sysctl.conf* and add the following directive:

```
net.ipv4.ip_forward = 1
```

Forwarding on an IPv6 network

To activate forwarding on an IPv6 network, you'll need to toggle the forwarding setting in the appropriate kernel configuration directory. The simplest way to do so is with the following command:

```
echo "1" > /proc/sys/net/ipv6/conf/all/forwarding
```

To make sure forwarding is turned on the next time you boot your computer, open */etc/sysctl.conf* and add the following directive:

```
net.ipv6.conf.all.forwarding = 1
```

This assumes you've installed all other components required to configure an IPv6 network. For more information, see the related HOWTO written by Peter Bieringer at *http://www.tldp.org/HOWTO/Linux+IPv6-HOWTO/*.

IP Masquerading

When you have one IP address on the Internet for your network, you need to find a way to share it with all the computers on your network. The standard is with IP masquerading. Once configured, your gateway substitutes the IP address of the network interface card it uses to reach the Internet for the address of any computer on your network that requests data from the Internet.

Naturally, IP masquerading assumes you've activated IP forwarding, as I described in the previous section.

The current standard for configuring IP address translation on a gateway is *iptables*, the same command used to erect firewalls. Here you use it to alter network packets with Network Address Translation, specifically with the *iptables -t nat* command.

As an example, if your Internet connection uses a device named *wlan0* and your LAN uses IP addresses on the 10.11.12.0/16 private network, the command you need is:

```
iptables -t nat -A POSTROUTING -s 10.11.12.0/16 -o wlan0 -j MASQUERADE
```

As described earlier, this command uses Network Address Translation. It adds (-A) the rule to the end of the *iptables* chain. It modifies network packets as they leave the network (*POSTROUTING*). It specifies (-s) source IP addresses to be those from your LAN (*10.11.12.0/16*). It points to *wlan0* as the output interface (-o). For all data that meets these standards, computers on your LAN *MASQUERADE* on the external network with the IP address assigned to *wlan0*.

To save this command, you'll need to run *iptables-save* and send the result to a file with a command such as:

```
iptables-save >> firewall
```

You could save the *iptables* commands to the standard configuration file for the distribution, but that would risk conflicts with settings written by tools such as Red Hat's Firewall Configuration tool. If you want to make these commands part of your firewall, you'll have to modify those files manually.

Firewalls

Detailed instructions on creating a firewall are beyond the scope of this book. However, the gateway between networks is the best place to create a firewall, so I'll mention some of the considerations for doing so.

Both Red Hat/Fedora and SUSE Linux have their own firewall configuration tools. These tools are excellent and can be used to create a fairly simple firewall. You can build upon the firewall created by these tools as needed.

You can start the standard Red Hat/Fedora Firewall Configuration tool with the *system-config-securitylevel* command. Results are saved to */etc/sysconfig/iptables*.

You can open the SUSE firewall tool in YaST. Results are saved to */etc/sysconfig/SUSEfirewall2*.

There is no standard firewall tool available for Debian. However, there are a substantial number of available options, including several excellent GUI tools.

In addition, a number of third-party firewall generators are available online. As is standard with open source software, neither I nor O'Reilly endorses any of these systems (or anything else in the book).

For more information, see the related annoyance "My Firewall Blocks My Internet Access," in Chapter 8.

My Other Computer Has No Monitor

There are two reasons why you may want remote access. First, the computer you want to use may be too far away. Second, the computer, as with many servers, may not even have a monitor.

There are several ways to configure remote access to a Linux server. As described in Chapter 9, in the "Users Are Still Demanding Telnet" annoyance, Telnet is one method. While Telnet is insecure, I described methods you can use to encrypt and further secure Telnet communications in that chapter.

Perhaps the best way to configure secure access to a remote Linux system is through the Secure Shell (SSH). Connections through SSH are encrypted. You can even set up encryption keys and password phrases that are not transferred during logins. As described in the next annoyance, you can even use SSH to access GUI applications remotely.

What I describe in this annoyance just covers the basics associated with creating an SSH server and connection. For more information, see *SSH, The Secure Shell: The Definitive Guide* by Daniel J. Barrett et al. (O'Reilly).

Configure SSH

Security is provided through the Secure Shell, and access can be configured through the appropriate SSH configuration file. You'll find two configuration files in the */etc/ssh* directory, *sshd_config* and *ssh_config*. You can configure both files: *sshd_config* on the server, and *ssh_config* on each client. You can also use some of the switches available with the *ssh* command or customize a client for an individual user with a file in the appropriate home directory.

One possible security issue with SSH is related to user keys, which are stored in *~/.ssh/* under their home directories. If your workstations use NFS to mount home directories from a central server, your encrypted keys will be transmitted over the network in clear text. Anyone who intercepts this transmission can eventually decrypt those keys. If this describes your configuration, consult *SSH, The Secure Shell: The Definitive Guide* by Daniel J. Barrett et al. (O'Reilly) for an alternative configuration.

 Generally, when you configure SSH, it's mostly done on the server. Any configuration you do on the client, through */etc/ssh/ssh_config*, is secondary.

After you make any changes to the configuration files, remember that you'll have to restart the SSH server. On Debian Linux, you can do so with the following command:

    /etc/init.d/ssh restart

On SUSE and Red Hat/Fedora Linux, the command is slightly different:

    /etc/init.d/sshd restart

Limiting Access on the SSH Server

The SSH server configuration file, */etc/ssh/sshd_config*, supports direct access by default. You can limit access by user, by group, and by network. If you're supporting access through a firewall, you'll need to provide appropriate access through that barrier.

Limiting access by user

You can limit access by user with the `AllowUsers` directive. If there is no such directive in the */etc/ssh/sshd_config* configuration file, all users are allowed on the SSH server (unless otherwise prohibited via Pluggable Authentication Modules, as described in Chapter 10).

For example, if I want to allow only *donna* to access this server via SSH, I can add the following directive:

```
AllowUsers donna
```

You can add `AllowUsers` directives for all users for whom you want to authorize access via SSH. For example, I could add the following directives to limit access to three users:

```
AllowUsers donna
AllowUsers nancy
AllowUsers randy
```

Alternatively, you can use the `DenyUsers` directive to prohibit access to certain accounts.

You may want to deny access to the most privileged user. This requires a different directive:

```
PermitRootLogin no
```

SSH allows *root* logins by default. So if you want to minimize the risk to the administrative account, this directive is important.

Specific network

You can further refine the `AllowUsers` directive. For example, you can limit access from users on the remote computer named *enterprise4a* to *donna*'s account:

```
AllowUsers donna@enterprise4a
```

Don't let the @ confuse you. This directive does not specify an email address. It specifies a local account and a remote computer from where users are allowed to log in to that account. You can substitute an FQDN for *enterprise4a*.

Some wildcards are supported. For instance, if you want to support access from the 192.168.0.0/24 network to all local accounts, use the following directive:

```
AllowUsers *@192.168.0.*
```

Specific group

Just as the AllowUsers and DenyUsers directives can help you regulate access via SSH to accounts on the local server, the AllowGroups and DenyGroups directives can do the same, based on group accounts as defined in */etc/group*.

External access via firewall

If you have a firewall between desired SSH clients and servers, you'll need to make sure that the firewall allows SSH connections. For your convenience, allowing SSH connections is a standard option with the Red Hat/Fedora and SUSE firewall configuration tools. If you're configuring your firewall manually, you'll have to make sure to allow TCP and UPD connections through port 22.

Create Encryption Keys

Sending passwords over a network can be a problem. While SSH communications are encrypted, if a cracker can determine when you send your password and intercept it over your network, he can eventually decrypt it.

The SSH system supports the use of passphrases, which can be more complex than regular passwords (you can even use complete sentences such as "I live 40 feet from the North Pole."). Commands such as *ssh-keygen* allow you to create a private and public key based on the passphrase. The standard is 1024-bit encryption, which makes the passphrase (or the associated keys) much more difficult to crack.

Once the public key is transferred to the remote system, you'll be able to use SSH to log in to the remote system. The passphrase activates the private key. If matched to the public key on the remote system, an SSH login is allowed.

Create and transfer the private and public keys as follows:

1. Choose an encryption algorithm (I've arbitrarily selected DSA) and generate a private and public key in your home directory (I use */home/michael/.ssh* here) with a command like:

    ```
    ssh-keygen -t dsa -b 1024 -f /home/michael/.ssh/enterprise-key
    ```

    When prompted, enter a passphrase. Passphrases are different from standard passwords. They can include whole sentences, such as:

    ```
    I like O'Reilly's ice cream
    ```

    This particular *ssh-keygen* command generates two keys, putting them in the *enterprise-key* and *enterprise-key.pub* files in the */home/michael/.ssh/* directory. You can (and probably should) choose a different passphrase for the encryption key.

---

2. Next, transmit the public key that you've created to the remote computer. The following command uses the Secure Copy command (*scp*) to copy the file to *donna*'s home directory on the computer named *debian*:

```
scp .ssh/enterprise-key.pub donna@debian:/home/donna/
```

3. Now log in to *donna*'s account on the remote computer. Assuming the Secure Shell service is enabled on *debian*, you can do so with the following command:

```
ssh donna@debian
```

You'll have to specify *donna*'s password because you have not yet set up passphrase protection. You should now be in *donna*'s home directory, */home/donna*, on the *debian* computer.

4. If it doesn't already exist, you'll need to create an *.ssh/* subdirectory. You'll also want to make sure it has appropriate permissions with the following commands:

```
mkdir /home/donna/.ssh
chmod 700 /home/donna/.ssh
```

5. Create the *authorized_keys* file in the *.ssh/* subdirectory:

```
touch .ssh/authorized_keys
```

6. Now take the contents of the public SSH key that you created and put it in the *authorized_keys* file:

```
cat enterprise-key.pub >> .ssh/authorized_keys
```

Note that I used the the append sign (>>) because I want to keep all previous keys that might be in the file; it can contain all the keys referring to all the remote hosts from which you want to log in.

7. Log out of *donna*'s account. The next time you log in, you'll be prompted for the passphrase as follows.

```
Enter passphrase key for '/home/michael/.ssh/enterprise-key':
```

Now you can connect securely, using SSH, without having to enter your password or a password on the remote system. With the other measures described earlier in this annoyance, you can also protect your SSH server by user, protect it by group, make sure SSH communications come from a permitted network, and allow SSH through firewalls.

SSH on the Client

The first time you use SSH to log in to a remote system, you may see the following message, which means you haven't configured passphrases:

```
The authenticity of host 'debian (10.168.0.15)' can't be established.
RSA key fingerprint is 18:d2:73:ec:53:ce:52:4f:2d:43:55:fb:0c:14:49:1e.
Are you sure you want to continue connecting (yes/no)?
```

Once you enter yes, you'll see the following message:

```
Warning: Permanently added 'debian,10.168.0.15' (RSA) to the list of known
hosts.
```

Then you're prompted for the password on the remote system.

If you've configured passphrases, you'll see only the second message, followed by a request for the passphrase.

In either case, the remote system sends your client a public key, which is added to the user's *~/.ssh/known_hosts* file. If the name or IP address of the remote system changes, you'll see an error, which you can address only by editing or deleting the *known_hosts* file.

I Need to Run an X Application Remotely

Sometimes you need to run a GUI application but can't get to your computer. You may want to support users who need remote access to their applications.

I'll assume that you've already set up Secure Shell (SSH) or VNC clients for these users. In this annoyance, I'll show you how you can configure secure remote access to your GUI applications. While you can use VNC, SSH is preferred, as it provides strong encryption, making it more difficult for a cracker to track your keystrokes. An SSH configuration means that you're networking only the GUI application that you happen to be running remotely, as opposed to a whole GUI desktop environment.

 There are relatively secure versions of VNC available; you can even tunnel VNC through an SSH connection. For more information on the wide variety of VNC servers and clients, Wikipedia provides an excellent starting point at *http://en. wikipedia.org/wiki/VNC*. If you don't like VNC, explore the increasingly popular FreeNX (which uses SSH) at *http:// freenx.berlios.de/*.

If you absolutely need remote access for GUI applications, keep it behind a firewall. If at all possible, don't open the firewall to external clients on the SSH ports. If you do, use the directives described in the following sections (and the previous annoyance) to minimize your risks.

Configuring the SSH Server for X Access

The configuration file for the SSH server is */etc/ssh/sshd_config*. While it offers a substantial number of directives, most of the defaults configured on our target distributions don't need to be changed for SSH to work. However, these defaults may not be secure. Depending on your distribution, you may need to make a few changes. I suggest you pay particular attention to the following directives:

X11Forwarding yes

As the object of this annoyance is how to safely configure remote access of GUI applications, I assume you'll use this directive to enable remote access.

Protocol 2

Specifies the use of the SSH2 protocol, which is currently being maintained and updated for any security problems. Without this directive, the SSH server can also take logins from SSH1 clients, which are less secure.

ListenAddress

Allows you to specify the IP address of the network card to take SSH connections, such as ListenAddress 192.168.0.12. Assumes you have more than one network card on this computer.

LoginGraceTime

Helps thwart crackers who try to break into an account with different passwords. The default is 120 seconds, after which no additional password entries are allowed. I would set a shorter period, such as LoginGraceTime 30.

PermitRootLogin no

The default is yes. In my opinion, you should never permit logins by the *root* user. Even if encrypted, *root* logins are a risk. If the login is intercepted, the *root* password may be eventually decrypted. In contrast, if you use the *su* or *sudo* commands after logging in via SSH, it's much more difficult for a cracker to determine which bits contain the *root* password.

Alternatively, you can create encryption keys as described in the previous annoyance. Once configured, SSH login passwords don't get sent over the network.

AllowUsers

By default, all users are allowed to log in via SSH. It's best to limit this as much as possible. You can limit logins by users, or even by users on specific systems. For example, if you wanted to limit SSH access to two users, you might use one of the following directives:

```
AllowUsers michael donna
AllowUsers michael@debian.example.com donna@suse.example.com
```

In the second directive, SSH logins to the local accounts for *michael* and *donna* are allowed from the remote *debian.example.com* system.

After saving changes to the SSH server configuration file, you'll need to restart the associated daemon. The name of the daemon may vary slightly by distribution; you can use the following command for Red Hat/Fedora and SUSE Linux:

```
/etc/init.d/sshd restart
```

The appropriate command on Debian Linux is slightly different:

```
/etc/init.d/ssh restart
```

Configuring the SSH Client for X Access

There are three ways to configure the SSH client to support networking of GUI tools and applications:

- Directly, via switches and options to the *ssh* connection command
- For all users on a client, via the */etc/ssh/ssh_config* file
- For a single user on a client, via the *~/.ssh/config* file

By default, any authorized user can log in to an SSH server, specifying access to GUI applications with the -*X* switch, e.g.:

```
ssh -X michael@debian.example.com
```

But GUI access may not be secure. The most secure approach is to limit X access for all users on a client and then enable it for only the desired users. To do so, open */etc/ssh/ssh_config* and set the following directives:

ForwardX11Trusted no
> The default for this directive varies by distribution. This setting minimizes risks to other clients.

ForwardX11 no
> Although this should be disabled by default on all Linux distributions, it doesn't hurt to make sure.

Next, on the *~/.ssh/config* file for the user that you want to authorize, include:

ForwardX11 yes
> This directive supersedes any default settings in the */etc/ssh/ssh_config* file, and allows remote GUI access to the applications of that user's choice.

Remote SSH Access to GUI Applications

Once configured, you can access remote GUI applications through the command line. To this end, you'll need to know the text commands that start

GUI applications, such as */usr/bin/oowriter*. Unless you're running a network with gigabit-level speeds, expect a bit of a delay as the application opens (and as it runs remotely on your workstation).

So Many Server Logs

I believe it's helpful for any Linux user to review her own logs on a regular basis. Familiarity can help any geek learn the value of logs. For one thing, log entries will be associated with failed logins, which suggest that a cracker is trying to break into your system. But logs can do much more. For example, web logs can give you a feel for where your customers are coming from, in terms of geography; clicked links associated with web ads; how long they stay on your web site; and more.

As a Linux administrator, chances are good that you're administering a substantial number of Linux computers. It may be useful to consolidate the logs on a single system. If a server goes down, you'll have the logs from that server available on the central log server. When there are problems, such as "critical" error messages, you may want an email sent to your address. You may need tools to help you go through all of these logs.

Central Log Servers

Logs on our selected distributions are governed by the system and kernel log daemons. While Red Hat/Fedora and Debian combine these daemons into a single package (*sysklogd*), SUSE includes them in separate packages (*syslogd* and *klogd*). While there are minor variations in how they're configured, they're all governed by a logfile in the same location, */etc/syslog.conf*.

If you want to dedicate a specific system as your central log server, first make sure you have enough space on that system. It may help to configure logs, such as those in the */var/log* directory, on a separate partition so that they can't fill up critical system partitions if they get too big. For more information, see the next annoyance.

On the system that you're configuring as a central log server, you'll have to configure the system log daemon (*syslogd*) to accept remote connections. The simplest way to do so is to stop the daemon, and then start it again with the *-rm 0* switch. The way you implement this varies slightly by distribution:

Red Hat/Fedora
> The Red Hat/Fedora distributions let you configure switches for the system log daemon in */etc/sysconfig/syslog*. The key directive is SYSLOGD_OPTIONS. To support remote log reception, change this directive to:
>
> ```
> SYSLOGD_OPTIONS="-rm 0"
> ```

SUSE

SUSE Linux handles standard options for the system log daemon in a similar fashion. The daemon log options are listed in */etc/sysconfig/ syslog*. To support remote log reception, change the SYSLOGD_PARAMS directive to:

```
SYSLOGD_PARAMS="-rm 0"
```

Debian

Debian Linux does not provide any */etc/sysconfig* files for daemon configuration. However, you can configure the system log daemon directly in the associated start script, */etc/init.d/sysklogd*. To support remote log reception, change the SYSLOGD directive to:

```
SYSLOGD="-rm 0"
```

Once you've made the configuration changes, you can implement them by restarting the system log daemon on each computer with the following command:

```
/etc/init.d/syslog restart
```

On Debian Linux, the script's location is slightly different:

```
/etc/init.d/sysklogd restart
```

Naturally, if there's a firewall between the log server and log clients, you'll need to make provisions in that firewall to allow traffic through port 514. As you can see in */etc/services*, that's the standard port for system log communications. To make sure your system log service now receives from remote computers, check your */var/log/syslog* (or, if that file doesn't exist, */var/log/ messages*) for the following entry (the version number may vary):

```
syslogd 1.4.1: restart (remote reception).
```

Forwarding Server Logs to a Central Server

Now that the central server is ready, you can configure your other Linux systems to send copies of their logs to that computer. The log configuration file on each of our preferred distributions is */etc/syslog.conf*, and the key directive is straightforward. If you want a copy of all logs sent to the *logmaster. example.com* computer, all you need in that file is:

```
*.* @logmaster
```

Unfortunately, the system log service can't handle fully qualified domain names. Logs on the central server from your remote systems will have only the regular hostnames.

If you're just concerned with kernel-based issues, to help diagnose shutdowns, you can send just the kernel messages to the remote log server:

```
kern.* @logmaster
```

Logwatch Monitoring

There are many excellent tools for monitoring logfiles. Many geeks even create their own scripts for this purpose. One excellent source for different monitoring tools and scripts is *Automating Unix and Linux Administration* by Kirk Bauer (Apress).

One of the major standards for log monitoring is known as Logwatch. It's available from both the Debian and Red Hat/Fedora Linux repositories. A logwatch RPM that works on SUSE is available from the Logwatch home page at *http://www.logwatch.org*.

Logwatch is organized into three groups of files. The overall configuration file is *logwatch.conf*. Other logfiles for many individual services are organized in a *services/* subdirectory. The logfiles are placed in groups based on configuration files in a *logfiles/* subdirectory. The actual directory varies by distribution, or by the release that you may have installed from *http://www.logwatch.org*.

As the directories associated with Logwatch vary so widely by distribution, I generally do not use full directory paths in this annoyance. If you're uncertain about the location of a file, you'll have to do your own searching with commands such as *locate*, and *rpm -ql logwatch* or *dpkg -L logwatch*.

Basic Logwatch configuration

Before I show you how to configure the basic Logwatch configuration file, I need to review its location on your system. If you've downloaded the latest version from *http://www.logwatch.org*, you'll need to make sure key settings are compatible with the scripts and configuration directories for your distribution.

The standard Logwatch configuration file is *logwatch.conf*. You can find it in the */etc/log.d/conf* or */etc/logwatch/conf* directories. As described earlier, there is no standard SUSE Logwatch package.

If you've downloaded the latest version from the Logwatch home page, you'll find key configuration files in different locations. The *logwatch.conf* configuration file (as well as default services and configuration logfiles) is stored in */usr/share/logwatch/default.conf*; detailed configuration changes can be added to files in the */etc/logwatch/conf* directory.

Administrators are now encouraged to add changes to Logwatch settings to *override.conf* and patterns that Logwatch should drop to *ignore.conf*. But those are advanced settings beyond what I can cover in this annoyance. Refer to the Logwatch web site for the latest information.

Logwatch's standard directives include:

LogDir
> The standard for logging directories on our preferred distributions is
> */var/log*.

MailTo
> While the default is MailTo = root, you're free to change this to the email
> address of your choice, assuming you have a working outgoing email
> server on this system.

Print
> The Print directive is unrelated to printers; it determines whether
> reports are sent to standard output, which is normally the screen. The
> usual default is Print = no. Change this directive to view output in real
> time on your console.

TmpDir
UseMkTemp
MkTemp
> These three directives all configure the use of temporary files. By default,
> the TmpDir directive points to the */tmp* directory. In the latest version of
> Logwatch, this directive points to the */var/cache/logwatch* directory.
>
> If your TmpDir is */tmp*, make sure the UseMkTemp directive is active. This
> uses the MkTemp directive to point to the *mktemp* utility for changing the
> name and permissions of temporary logfiles to keep them secure while
> they're stored in the */tmp* directory.
>
> If you've activated UseMkTemp, you need to point the MkTemp directive to
> the full path of the *mktemp* utility, normally */bin/mktemp*.

Range
> The Range directive specifies the timeline for the report. The standard is
> Range = yesterday; it's consistent with a log report, processed by the
> cron daemon, sometime after midnight.

Detail
> The Detail directive associated with a report specifies the amount of
> information you get. Detail = Low limits information to security and other
> critical service issues. A High level of Detail creates very verbose reports,
> especially if you're collecting information from multiple computers.

Service
> The Service directive gives you an opportunity to limit the services on
> which Logwatch prepares reports. While the default is Service = All, you
> can specify individual services with a directive such as Service = pam—or
> specify all except an individual service with two directives, such as:
>
> ```
> Service = All
> Service = -ftpd-messages
> ```

Mailer
>   The Mailer directive specifies the command-line utility associated with
>   text emails. Depending on your distribution, it should be set either to
>   */usr/bin/mail* or */bin/mail*.

Logwatch service configuration files

The service configuration files associated with Logwatch are stored in a
service/ subdirectory. While the list of files may seem extensive, don't worry
about configuring each file. The defaults are generally fine, unless you want
to specify a special file group. One example where you may want to specify a
special group is with the Clam AntiVirus software (*www.clamav.net*). The
following is based on the package downloaded from the Clam AV web site.

> These configuration files differ from those installed with
> specific services. For example, the *clamav.conf* file cited in
> this section, on a Debian system, is in the */etc/logwatch/
> conf/services* directory. It configures Clam AntiVirus soft-
> ware interactions with the logwatch system. It is not a sub-
> stitute for the main Clam AntiVirus configuration file,
> normally */etc/clamav/clamd.conf*.

By default, the following directive in the *clamav.conf* file (along with the
LogDir=/var/log directive in *logwatch.conf*) sends logs from this service to
the standard */var/log/messages*:

```
LogFile = messages
```

As it may be inconvenient to have so much traffic in */var/log/messages*, you
could send logs to a different file, such as */var/log/clam-update,* with the following directive:

```
LogFile = clam-update
```

Logwatch log groups

The Logwatch service can help you organize a wide variety of logfiles, as
configured in the *logfiles/* subdirectory. It includes a number of configuration files (with *.conf* extensions).

Logwatch scripts

Logwatch includes a wide variety of scripts in the *shared/* subdirectory.
They're generally configured to help you search through logs collected by
this service.

The Logs Are Overloading My Hard Drive

Logs can grow quickly, especially for services with a lot of activity. Logs for commercial web sites can easily add several hundred megabytes of files every day.

Unmanaged, this kind of growth can overwhelm your system, taking space needed by your users, occupying the empty space required to run a GUI, and making it impossible to boot your system.

If your logs grow quickly, you should consider creating dedicated partitions. Even with dedicated partitions and search scripts of dazzling sophistication, it can take quite a while to search through large logfiles for the data you may need. Therefore, you may consider configuring your system to start new logfiles more often, perhaps daily or even hourly.

Even large, dedicated partitions may not be good enough. The demands of logfiles can grow so large that you may need to move logfiles to different systems.

The associated cron jobs are run in alphabetical order; files starting with numbers come first. For example, the *00logwatch* script in */etc/cron.daily* is run before others.

 If you have more than one log-management service installed, such as *logrotate* or *logwatch*, the associated jobs may not be fully compatible.

Logfile Partitions

Logs can become quite large, and can easily grow by hundreds of megabytes of space (or more) every day. There are two basic options in this regard:

A dedicated log partition
> With a dedicated log partition, the space taken by a service or kernel log doesn't overwhelm the space required to run a Linux system. If you use a standard Linux distribution, the way to set this up is to mount the */var/log* directory on a dedicated partition.

A dedicated log server
> Even if you configure a dedicated server to collect logs from other Linux systems, I still recommend a dedicated log partition.

For most organizations, the data associated with logs isn't nearly as critical as, say, that associated with user home directories. Because logs grow quickly, one method to manage this growth is a RAID 0 volume with daily backups.

RAID 0 is the fastest possible media for large files and may be suitable for a log server. With appropriate controllers, it allows you to add more disks as logs grow.

Your management may have different feelings about the importance of logfiles. Perhaps you'll want to protect them as evidence, to help you track the activity of certain users, to establish patterns of visits to your web sites, or possibly even as evidence usable in a court of law. If logfiles are that important, you may want to use a more robust data storage system, such as RAID 5, or even back them up to stable archives such as DVDs.

Log Rotation Frequency

Log rotation means starting new files to contain incoming log messages, so that old logs can easily be backed up. Rotation also involves removing old messages to return needed disk space to the system. In Linux, log rotation is configured through the *logrotate* configuration files. In our preferred distributions, these files are stored in */etc/logrotate.conf*. To understand how this process works, it's useful to analyze it in detail.

Every day, on a schedule defined by your */etc/crontab* configuration file, Linux runs the */etc/cron.daily/logrotate* script. It includes the following command, which runs the *logrotate* service, based on the settings in */etc/logrotate.conf*:

```
/usr/sbin/logrotate /etc/logrotate.conf
```

To see how rotation works, we can analyze */etc/logrotate.conf*. The first four default commands in this file are identical in our preferred distributions:

weekly
> Logfiles are rotated by default on a weekly basis. You can set this to daily or monthly, or specify a maximum log size after which rotation occurs with a command such as:
>
> ```
> size=100k
> ```

rotate 4
> Linux distributions normally store four weeks of backlogs for each service.

create
> A new, empty file is created in place of the logfile that is now rotated.

include /etc/logrotate.d
> Configuration files in the */etc/logrotate.d* directory are included in the rotation process.

In some cases, the distribution developers have configured rotation of the *wtmp* and *btmp* access logs in */var/log*, as they are not associated with any specific package, nor are they maintained by any of the *letc/logrotate.d* configuration files.

If you add the following directive, you can enable compression of your logfiles, saving even more room:

```
compress
```

Compression still allows access by some dedicated logfile viewers and editors, including *vi*. There are a substantial number of options available; *Sourceforge.net* includes several hundred log-management suites, many of which can even search through directories of compressed logfiles.

Deleting Old Logs

Logs should normally be deleted automatically. However, if you see logs more than five weeks old, that suggests a problem with your *logrotate* script, or perhaps that your cron jobs aren't being run as scheduled.

For example, on my newer laptop computer, I haven't configured my winmodem to allow external logins by modem. I have no modem getty (*mgetty*) logs in my *lvar/log* directory. When I run the daily cron *logrotate* script, I get a related error:

```
# /etc/cron.daily/logrotate
error: error accessing /var/log/mgetty: No such file or directory
error: mgetty:1 glob failed for /var/log/mgetty/*.log
```

There are several ways to address this issue. I could configure *mgetty*, but that would be a waste of time. I could delete the *mgetty* configuration file in *letc/logrotate.d*, but that would cause more problems if I choose to configure it in the future. The option I chose was to create the */var/log/mgetty* directory, as the *root* user. After creating that directory, I ran the *logrotate* script again, without errors.

I also ran *touch .placeholder* in that directory, to make sure the directory wouldn't get deleted at the next update.

Create Jobs to Move Logs

If you've made some of the changes suggested in "So Many Server Logs," earlier in this chapter, you may have already sent your logs to remote systems. In short, you'll need to configure the System Log daemon on the log server to receive remote logs, and configure the other computers to send their logs to that log server. See the previous annoyance for details.

Administration Is So Repetitive

The first time you run a job, it's helpful to do it manually. The more you do a job yourself, the more you learn about that job.

However, once you've run a job a few times, there's little more that you can learn about that job, as least in your current environment. At that point, it's best to automate the process. Linux already has a service that runs automated jobs on a regular basis, whether it be hourly, daily, weekly, or monthly.

Another reason why you want to automate tasks is so you can go home. With appropriate logs, you can make sure the job was properly executed when you return to work. Thus, you can configure a database job to run once per year, so you don't have to be at work on New Year's Eve.

Finally, when you administer a group of systems, the number of things you have to do can be overwhelming. Automation is often the only way to keep up with what you need to do. This is why you need to learn to manage the cron service.

Basic cron Jobs

It's easy to learn the workings of the cron service. Every Linux system includes numerous examples of cron jobs. The cron daemon wakes up every minute Linux is running, to see if there's a script scheduled to be run at that time.

Standard administrative jobs are run as scheduled in */etc/crontab*. Red Hat and Debian configure this file in straightforward ways, with different command scripts for hourly, daily, weekly, and monthly jobs. The format starts with five time-based columns, followed by the user and the command:

```
minute / hour / day of month / month / day of week / user / command
```

Take a look at your own version of this file. While it varies by distribution, all use a variation of the same first two directives, SHELL and PATH.

```
SHELL=/bin/sh
SHELL=/bin/bash

PATH=/usr/local/sbin:/usr/local/bin:/sbin:/bin:/usr/sbin:/usr/bin
PATH=/sbin:/bin:/usr/sbin:/usr/bin
PATH=/usr/bin:/usr/sbin:/sbin:/bin:/usr/lib/news/bin
```

Both SHELL directives point to different names for the default bash shell. The PATH directives provide the baseline for other scripts executed from the embedded directories by the cron daemon. The simplest version of this script is associated with Red Hat/Fedora distributions:

```
01 * * * * root run-parts /etc/cron.hourly
02 4 * * * root run-parts /etc/cron.daily
22 4 * * 0 root run-parts /etc/cron.weekly
42 4 1 * * root run-parts /etc/cron.monthly
```

These directives point to the *run-parts* command, which runs the scripts in the noted directories, as the *root* user. While you could use the full path to the command (*/usr/bin/runparts*), that's not necessary because */usr/bin* is in the PATH, as cited at the beginning of this file.

In this case, hourly scripts are run at one minute past every hour, daily scripts are run at 4:02 A.M. every day, weekly scripts are run at 4:22 A.M. every Sunday, and monthly scripts are run on the first day of each month, at 4:42 A.M.

While Debian and SUSE run more complex versions of this script, the effect is essentially the same. On our preferred Linux distributions, the cron daemon runs the scripts in the */etc/cron.hourly*, */etc/cron.daily*, */etc/cron.weekly*, and */etc/cron.monthly* directories. Many scripts in these directories use the full path to all commands, despite the PATH directive in */etc/crontab*.

Creating a cron Job

You can create a cron job in any of the aforementioned directories, and it will be run at the intervals established in */etc/crontab*. To help you understand how all this works, I'll create a yearly cron job, with the following steps:

 As SUSE's */etc/crontab* calls the */usr/lib/cron/run-crons* script, the following steps (at least after step 6) won't work in that distribution.

1. Log in as the *root* user. (Alternatively, if your regular account is in the */etc/sudoers* file, you can log in as a regular user and use the *sudo* command to invoke the commands in this section.)

2. Create a */etc/cron.yearly* directory, with the same ownership and permissions as the other related directories. As those directories are owned by *root* and have 755 permissions, they happen to be compatible with standard *root* permissions for new directories. So all that is required is:

   ```
   sudo mkdir /etc/cron.yearly
   ```

3. Create a new script in the */etc/cron.yearly* directory. I'd call it *happynewyear*. Include the following commands in that script (which

saves the files from user *donna*'s home directory in user *randy*'s home directory):

```
#!/bin/sh
/usr/bin/rsync -aHvz /home/donna /home/randy/
```

4. Save the file. Make sure the script is executable with the following command:

```
chmod 755 /etc/cron.yearly/happynewyear
```

5. Test the script. Run it using the full path to the script:

```
/etc/cron.yearly/happynewyear
```

6. Now make sure it runs at the next new year. Open your */etc/crontab* and make a copy of the directive that runs the monthly cron scripts in */etc/cron.monthly*. Change the directory to */etc/cron.yearly*, and modify the time the script is run to something appropriate. For example, I use the following line in my Red Hat Enterprise Linux 4 system:

```
2 0 1 1 *  root run-parts /etc/cron.yearly
```

This directive runs the script at two minutes past midnight on January 1. As the day of the week associated with New Year's Day varies, the last time entry has to be a wildcard. I chose two minutes past midnight because the directive associated with the */etc/cron.hourly* directory is run at one minute past midnight.

7. Save your */etc/crontab* configuration file.

Any output from a cron job is sent to the user as an email. Most standard cron jobs you'll find in the directories discussed here are carefully designed not to create any output, so you won't see email from them. cron jobs suppress such output by redirecting both standard output and standard error to files (or to */dev/null*).

User-specific cron jobs

Users can create and schedule their own cron jobs. As a regular user, you can open a cron file for your account with the following command:

```
crontab -e
```

Use the steps described in the previous section to create your own cron job. With the appropriate SHELL, PATH, and commands, you can run the scripts of your choice at the regular times of your choosing. To review your account's crontab configuration, run the following command:

```
crontab -l
```

Naturally, most regular users won't understand how to create their own cron jobs. As the administrator, you'll have to create the jobs for them. For example, if you want to create a job for user *nancy* and have administrative privileges, run the following command:

```
crontab -u nancy -e
```

However, for any user to access individual cron jobs, he needs permission. There are several ways to configure permissions to use cron:

- If there's an empty */etc/cron.deny* file (and no */etc/cron.allow* file), all users are allowed to have individual cron jobs.

- If there is no */etc/cron.deny* or */etc/cron.allow* files, only the *root* user is allowed to have cron jobs.

- If there are specific users in */etc/cron.deny*, they're not allowed to use cron jobs, and the *root* user isn't allowed to create a cron job for them; all others are allowed to use cron jobs.

- If */etc/cron.deny* includes ALL (representing all users), and specific users are listed in */etc/cron.allow*, only those users listed in the latter file are allowed to have cron jobs.

What you do depends on whether some of your users need to create cron jobs, and whether they are capable and trusted to do their own cron jobs (or whether you're willing to create cron jobs for your users).

 Depending on how much work a cron job performs, it can noticeably increase the load on the system. If you create a user-specific cron job, try to schedule it for times when other cron jobs aren't also running. If you've authorized users to create their own cron jobs, give them times where they're authorized to run them. Audit their jobs. You can review a user's cron jobs with the *crontab -u username -l* command.

If you want to see how cron jobs are configured, check them out for all users in your spool directory. The actual directory varies slightly by distribution. Red Hat/Fedora uses */var/spool/cron/username*, SUSE uses */var/spool/cron/tabs/username*, and Debian uses */var/spool/cron/crontabs/username*.

I Don't Want to Work Late to Do That Special Job

Not all jobs have to be run on a regular basis. People who crunch statistical data may need to run scripts at different times. Weathermen who are trying to model future trends may want to try some scripts just once or maybe twice. What they run often takes all of the resources on your systems. The only time they can run their jobs is in the middle of the night. They have families and like to sleep at night, so they may ask you to run that job. Well, perhaps you also have a family and like to sleep at night. But you don't want to create a cron job for this purpose because it's a one-time task.

For this purpose, Linux has the batch-job system, governed by the *at* daemon. To schedule a batch job at a given time, you can use the *at* command.

Creating an at Job

When you run the *at* command to create a batch job, you have to specify a time when the job is to be run. You're then taken to an at> prompt, where you can specify the commands or scripts to be executed.

 Users who configure their own scripts can place them in their own *~/bin* directory. Scripts in these directories (with executable permission), such as *~/bin/fatdata*, can be run without specifying the full path. Debian Linux doesn't add *~/bin* to the PATH unless the directory exists.

For example, if you're about to leave for the day and have already configured the *fatdata* script in your home directory's command bin (*~/bin*), take the following steps to run the script in one hour:

1. Run the following command:

   ```
   at now + 1 hour
   ```

   The at> prompt is open. If you're in SUSE or Debian Linux, you'll see a note that reflects the default bash shell. (After these steps, I'll describe some alternative ways to specify the time you need.)

2. At the at> prompt, enter the commands that you want to run at the specified time. In my case, that would be the single command:

   ```
   /home/michael/fatdata
   ```

3. When you're done with the commands that you want run, press Ctrl-D.

4. If you want to review pending *at* jobs, use the *atq* command.

5. If you want to cancel a job, you can use the *atrm* command, based on the queue number shown in the output from *atq*. For example, if you know that your job will be run at 10:30 P.M. tonight, you'll see something similar to the following output from *atq*, which notes that this is job 7:

   ```
   7 2006-01-22 22:30 a michael
   ```

   You can then cancel the job with the *atrm 7* command.

As with cron jobs, any output from *at* jobs is sent via email to the user for whom the job ran.

The *at* command offers a rich syntax for configuring the job at the time of your choice. While you can specify a certain amount of time in the future, such as:

```
at now + 12 hour
```

you can also set a specific time, such as 1:00 A.M. tomorrow morning:

```
at 1 AM tomorrow
```

Alternatively, you can specify a date:

```
at 2 AM March 15
```

You'll need to make sure the *at* daemon is running. The following command shows whether it's running:

```
ps aux | grep atd
```

If it isn't running, make sure it's installed (it's the *at* RPM or DEB package on our preferred distributions) and configured to run at your default runlevel.

If you want to see how *at* jobs will be run, you can check them out in your spool. The actual directory varies slightly by distribution: Red Hat/Fedora and Debian use */var/spool/cron/atjobs*; SUSE uses */var/spool/atjobs*. If you also have batch jobs that use the *batch* command (see the next section), you'll note that the spool files associated with regular *at* jobs start with an a, while spool files associated with *batch* jobs start with a b.

Managing the Load of Your at Jobs

A *batch* job, in contrast to an *at* job, runs as soon as the CPU has time for it. All you need to do to create a batch job is to use the *batch* command. With the *batch* command, Linux won't run the job unless the load average on the CPU is less than a certain threshold, which depends on the distribution. If you're running Red Hat/Fedora or SUSE Linux, the threshold is .8, or 80 percent of the capacity of a single CPU. If you're running Debian Linux, the threshold is 1.5, or 150 percent of the capacity of a single CPU. Naturally, you'll want to vary this threshold depending on the CPUs on your system.

Except for the aforementioned CPU limits, the *batch* command works in the same way as the *at* command; both set you up with an at> prompt. If you want to change the parameters associated with batch jobs, you can do so with the help of the *atd* command. For example, if your system includes four CPUs, you may find it useful to run batch jobs unless more than three CPUs are loaded:

```
atd -l 3
```

If your batch jobs are intense, you may want to increase the time between such jobs. By default, they're run in 60-second intervals. The following command increases the interval to one hour:

```
atd -b 3600
```

Batch Job Security

For any user to access individual batch or *at* jobs, she needs permission. There are several ways to configure these permissions:

- If there's an empty */etc/at.deny* file (and no */etc/at.allow* file), all users are allowed to have individual batch or *at* jobs.

- If there are no */etc/at.deny* or */etc/at.allow* files, only the *root* user is allowed to have batch or *at* jobs.

- If there are specific users in */etc/at.deny*, they're not allowed to use batch or *at* jobs.

- If */etc/at.deny* includes ALL (representing all users) and individual users are listed in */etc/at.allow*, only those users listed in the latter file are allowed to have batch or *at* jobs.

What you do depends on whether some of your users need to create *at* jobs, and whether they are capable and trusted to do them on their own (or whether you're willing to create them for your users).

Index

Numbers

4G/4G kernel issue, 218

Symbols

\ (backslashes), 95
! (bang), 89
#!/bin/sh (bash shell directive), 61
/ (forward slash), 60
` (back quotes), 95
" (double quotes), 95
' (single quotes), 94

A

A+ certification, 175
AbiWord, 142
Absolute Value Systems, 190
Accessibility modules, 12
ACPI (Advanced Configuration and
    Power Interface), laptops, 188
Adobe Acrobat
   alternatives to, 151
   for Firefox, 106
alacarte RPM, 3
alien command, 216
Alps GlidePoint touchpad, 34
ALSA configuration tool (alsaconf), 54
anaconda-ks.cfg, 202
AOL (America Online), 135
Apache servers, virtual hosting (see
    virtual hosts)

application libraries, 136
   Freshmeat Project, 137
   Linux Online library, 136
   SourceForge, 137
application selection, 138
applications
   database managers, 148
   file managers, 162–167
     Konqueror, 162–166
     Nautilus, 166–167
   graphics applications, 157
   Microsoft Word on Linux, 144
   movie viewers, 167–173
   office applications, 139
   OpenOffice.org, 147
   personal finance, 153
   PostScript-compatible
     applications, 151
   presentations applications, 149
   spreadsheets, 147
   tax applications, 156
   web developer applications, 150
   word processors, 141, 142
   X Window System applications,
     remote access of, 452–455
applications-kmenuedit.menu, 7
apt, 330–333
   apt commands, 330
   nightly update configuration, 332
apt-mirror project, 428
Archive Manager, 96

We'd like to hear your suggestions for improving our indexes. Send email to *index@oreilly.com*.

N

name service (see djbdns)
NAT (Network Address
       Translation), 446
Nautilus File Browser, 166–167
   DVD burning, 76
   files, archiving and zipping with, 99
ncurses-devel library, 261
net commands (Samba 3.x), 390
Netscape web browser, 125
network mounts, 219
networks
   connecting to, 284–289
   Internet access, controlling, 398
   troubleshooting, 290–294
   Windows computers, making
      visible, 385
newsgroups, 207
   posting guidelines, 210
NFS directories, 219
NFS (Network File System), 278
   automounter share, 282
nonstandard services,
      installing, 439–444
   alternative services, 440
   installation from source, 443
   installation from tarball, 444
   older packages, 442
   service homepages, checking, 440
   third-party packages, 441
NTFS partitions, 296
NTLDR, 228
Nvu, 150

O

office applications, 139
OFX format, 154
online help (see help)
open source licensing, 349
OpenOffice.org, 139, 143, 147
   Base, 148
   Calc, 148
   Impress, 149
   Writer, 143
      on Microsoft systems, 144
      PDF creation using, 152
   Writer/Web tool, 150
Opera web browser, 126

os level, 388
Outlook, conversion to
      Evolution, 118–119

P

package databases, 216
PAM (Pluggable Authentication
      Modules), 237
   login management, 253
   options for strong passwords, 239
   restriction of services with, 425
Partition Commander, 228
Partition Magic, 228
partitioning
   Microsoft-formatted
      partitions, 294–297
     mounting, 295
     NTFS, 296
partitions
   corrupt partitions (see corrupt
      partitions)
   logfile partitions, 460
password management, 416
passwords
   BIOS, 241
   password-protecting LILO, 242
   root password
     lost password, 240
     single-user mode, protecting
      in, 241
   security of, 236
     PAM administration, 237
     password directives, 238
PATH, 91–93
   Linux distributions and, 92
   security and, 92
   sudo command and, 411
PCI cards, detecting, 181
PCMCIA cards, packages for, 190
PDF compatible applications, 151
PDFs, creating, 152
personal finance applications, 153
physical extent (PE), 310
physical volume (PV), 310
PID (Process Identifier), 19
pnpdump command, 180, 181
POST (Power On Self Test)
      process, 302
PostScript-compatible applications, 151

About the Author

Michael Jang, RHCE, Linux+, LCP, specializes in books on Linux and Linux certification. His experience with computers goes back to the days of jumbled punch cards. He's written or contributed to more than a dozen books on Linux, Linux certification, and Red Hat Linux, including *RHCE Red Hat Certified Engineer Linux Study Guide* (McGraw-Hill), *Linux Patch Management* (Prentice Hall), and *Mastering Red Hat Fedora Linux 5* (Sybex).

Colophon

The image on the cover of *Linux Annoyances for Geeks* is a man pulling a donkey. In 19th-century frontier America, the donkey was the pack animal of choice, owing to the species' longevity, endurance, agility, and low maintenance cost. During the Gold Rush, prospectors traversed the Old West terrain using burros to transport their supplies. Miners harnessed donkeys to haul water, wood, and rock, as well as to transport and grind ore.

By the turn of the century, the ascendance of the railroad had begun to render donkey labor obsolete, and prospecters and miners released their burros to the wild. To this day, a substantial population of donkeys roams free in the deserts of the American West.

The cover image and chapter opening images are from the Dover Pictorial Archive. The cover font is Adobe ITC Garamond. The text font is Linotype Birka; the heading font is Adobe Myriad Condensed; and the code font is LucasFont's TheSans Mono Condensed.

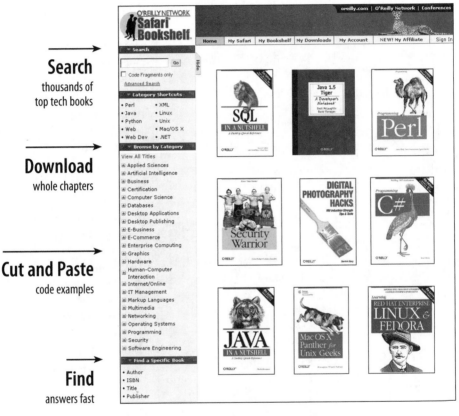

Related Titles from O'Reilly

O'REILLY®

Our books are available at most retail and online bookstores.

To order direct: 1-800-998-9938 • *order@oreilly.com* • *www.oreilly.com*

Online editions of most O'Reilly titles are available by subscription at *safari.oreilly.com*